There was a Green Hill

The History of Stillington

from its beginnings

until c. 1950

❖

Researched
and compiled by
John Donald Tuffs

Published by J. D. Tuffs, 202 Low Grange Avenue, Billingham, Cleveland TS23 3LY

Copyright © John Donald Tuffs 1999
All rights reserved.

Design and typesetting by D R Bungay Associates
Printed by Garden House Press Ltd
Bound by B&P Print Finishing Ltd

ISBN   0 9536655 0 X   *paperback*

There was a Green Hill

Contents

	Preface	vi
	Acknowledgments	vii
	Introduction	ix
1	The Early Landowners	1
2	Why was this site chosen for the manufacture of Iron	3
3	The development of the Village of the Carlton Ironworks/Stillington	8
4	Maps showing the development of the Village between 1833–1951	185
5	Influx and expansion of the Village population	202
6	Hardships endured by the families of the Village	206
7	Development of Village amenities and services	212
8	The governing of the Village	234
9	Community spirit and activities	236
10	Description of the men who influenced the formation of the Village	248
11	Summary of changes to the Village since 1950	262

Appendices

1	Brief History of the Clarence Railway	282
2	Details of doctors who practised in the Village	288
3	Examples of Carlton Iron Company Balance Sheets and Directors' Reports	291
4	Report on Dilapidation of Morrison Terrace 1891	305
5	Wages for Carlton Iron Company Workers and Teachers' salaries	307
6	The Royal Hotel	314
7	Persons contracted to do the Village 'scavenging'	316
8	St. John's Church – Stillington	318
9	Origin of the name Stillington	321
10	Local Entrepreneurs	322
11	Summary of Local Government Development	326
12	Photographs of groups and events relating to Stillington	332

Preface

Having retired from work because of ill health in 1987, I decided to initiate one of my hopefully achievable projects, the writing of the history of Stillington. Although totally lacking experience in historical writing I felt reasonably qualified to undertake this task by having been associated with the village, in one form or another, for the major part of my life and I was enthusiastic about the challenge.

The difficulty in writing about history is trying to decide where to start, where to finish and what to include in the chosen period. During the first years of research the information gleaned from the differing sources made it virtually impossible to decide what to leave out. I therefore resolved to make this work as definitive as possible, so that it can be treated as an archival/historical reference document as well as an interesting read.

Every attempt has been made to accurately convey the events detailed in the book by carrying out a finite study of all available documents and spending many hours eliminating minor ambiguities.

Although I have not lived in Stillington for many years I still have a great affinity towards it and the people with whom I grew up. I feel privileged to have been born and raised in a village that once supported a lively community, whose camaraderie made light of the desperately hard times suffered during two horrific world wars and many years of almost total unemployment and depression.

Stillington and its people have afforded me many happy memories and I hope this book gives many of them a little pleasure in return.

Don Tuffs

Note:

It was intended to include the 'History of Stillington Football and other Sports' within this volume but, although this is underway, the research is taking longer than anticipated. I therefore decided to present the sports history as a separate book enabling the main history to be finalised more quickly.

The unavailability of past editions of the Saturday Evening Sports Gazette, which carried news of all local sport, has caused difficulty in obtaining relevant information for the Football Section, but other sources are being sought and this should follow the main publication within about six months.

Acknowledgments

General research and information sources

I extend my thanks to the staff of the following 'places of research' where, in all instances, help was given courteously and unreservedly.

British Steel Records Services; Cleveland County Records Office; Durham County Record Office; Kew Gardens Record Office, London; Stockton Reference Library; Middlesbrough Reference Library.

Thanks also to:

Dr Stephen Gunn, College Archivist, Merton College, Oxford; Mr Stephen Black, Administrator, Christ's Hospital, Sherburn Hospital, Sherburn; Mrs J Carroll, retired Headmistress of the William Cassidi Church of England School; Mr Paul Moynihan, Archivist for the Scout's Association; Barbara Gent, Librarian, Giggleswick School, Settle, North Yorkshire; Simon Raine, Trustee, The Fitzhugh Library, Barnard Castle; L Hartshorne, Librarian, Castleford Library; Mrs L M Norris, Archives Dept., Courage Breweries.

A special thank you to Mr Geoffrey Kirk for vital information, and his memories regarding all aspects of Stillington industry, shared with me during our frequent discussions.

Finally, grateful thanks to my many friends in and around Stillington for their willingness to share their recollections of the 'Good Old Days' and the warmness of their welcome when I called upon them.

Maps

My thanks to Mrs Sheila Franklyn of the Ordnance Survey Organisation, Romsey Road, Southampton, for her help in my gaining permission to use their maps as a basis for those produced for inclusion in the book.

Maps based on Ordnance Surveys of 1947 or earlier, 'Reproduced from the 1853, 1897 and 1918 Ordnance Survey Maps.'

Maps based on Ordnance Survey after 1947, 'Reproduced from 1965 Ordnance Survey (Scale 1:1250, Plan NZ3623 and Plan NZ3723), with permission of the Controller of her Majesty's Stationery Office © Crown Copyright MC/98-257.

Thanks also to Durham Records Office for use of their Parish Chapelry Boundaries, c. 1800. Full acknowledgement under Ecclesiastical Maps of Stillington Parish.

Photographs

Many of the photographs reproduced and used in the book were loaned to me for that purpose from the private collections of friends. I thank them for allowing me that courtesy and list their names below.

Mr & Mrs Alan Argyle	Miss Betty Fox	Mr & Mrs John Swales
Mr Victor Argyle	Mr Jim Glass	Mr Peter Swales
Mr Jack Atkinson	Mrs Maureen Harrison	Mrs Maisie Taylor
Mrs V Bracknell	Mr & Mrs Edwin Hopps	Mrs Monica Tingle
Mr Cyril Butler	Mr John McPhee	Ms Judith Turner
Mrs Ann Calvert	Mrs Doris McWilliams	Mr & Mrs Norman Trotter
Mr Pat Carroll	Mr Geoff Peekman	Mrs Olive Wells
Mr Steve Connor	Mrs Eva Pernie	Mr Jim Whitwell
Miss Nellie Daniels	Mr Robert Robinson	Mr Brian Wills
Mr George Dilks	Mrs Sheila Sayers	Mr Ken Wilkinson
Mrs Eva Ditchburn	Mr Brian Simpson	Mr & Mrs Keith Wilkinson
Mr & Mrs Alan Farley	Ms Irene Storey	

I also thank the *Evening Gazette*; the *Darlington and Stockton Times*; Rydale Folk Museum (the Hayes collection); the J W Armstrong Trust; Dr C W Bilby, Durham Record Office; Mrs Henderson (Billingham); Mrs J Carroll, retired Headmistress of Stillington School; Mr K C Appleby (author of the railway book 'Shildon to Newport in Retrospect'); Mr Geoffrey Kirk; Mr W Norman (author of 'Luftwaffe over the North'); Giggleswick School and Darchem Engineering for granting me permission to use some of their photographs.

Specific acknowledgment has been placed alongside relevant photographs where requested.

Every attempt has been made to discover the origin of all photographs included in the book, but if there are any omissions or errors, then I apologise for this.

Financial contributions

Financial contributions towards the printing of this book were given by Mr and Mrs Hopps (Edwin and Lily) and Mr Cyril Butler. I thank them most sincerely for their extremely generous support which was not only given to help towards the cost of printing but because they, like me, felt that the history of the village was something to be remembered and cherished.

I also thank my wife Maureen for her patience and support during the many hours of research and compilation I spent preparing this book.

Introduction

Stillington is situated approximately five miles north west of Stockton on Tees and although it was for many years included within the boundaries of Durham in 1968 the village became part of the newly formed Teesside. This authority only lasted until 1974 when Stillington became an integral part of the newly formed county of Cleveland. In 1996 a Local Government Commission proposed the abolition of the Cleveland County Council and deemed that responsibility for all local services should be split amongst four 'unitary' district councils, namely Hartlepool Borough Council, Middlesborough Borough Council, Stockton on Tees Borough Council and Redcar and Cleveland Borough Council.

Stillington has, since that date, been under the jurisdiction of Stockton on Tees Borough Council.

At the beginning of the nineteenth century the area was one of peaceful countryside with gently undulating hills sweeping down to a beck which, after rising at Shotton, almost encircled the site of the village by taking a course that skirted the hamlets of Foxton, Old Stillington and Whitton. The beck played an important role in the region by suppling the water necessary to power the corn mills of Whitton

Bishopton Mill situated at bottom of Mill Bank, Whitton. The hay barn has now been converted into a luxury home. *Photograph 1988.*

(Bishopton Mill), Thorpe, Blakeston, Wynyard, Wolviston, Norton and Billingham as it meandered its way to the River Tees.

A series of hills created a gully that drained into the beck at a point equidistant between Old Stillington and Whitton, with one of the hills rising north westerly from this juncture to a height of 150 feet before levelling out to form a plateau. This hill and plateau comprised five fields, collectively known as Moor Closes, and it was here that the village of Stillington was developed to house workers who came to erect and operate the ironworks started in 1865 when Mr Samuel Bastow, a businessman from West Hartlepool, built two blast furnaces.

The ironworks brought habitation and some prosperity to the area, but they also brought all the pollution associated with the ironmaking industry. Smoke, fumes and grime were spewed from the furnaces for over fifty years, whilst molten slag was tipped and allowed to cool and harden until the gully and 30 acres of the adjacent countryside were engulfed by a massive heap of slag. During these fifty years the character of the hillside changed totally from a pleasant, peaceful country scene to a dirty industrial environment thus engendering the title of this book, 'There was a Green Hill'.

Note: Before proceeding further it is important to note that the original Stillington was the hamlet now named Old Stillington, situated ¾ of a mile south west of the village now known as Stillington. The new Stillington was developed by and around the ironworks and was originally named the Village of the Carlton Iron Works.

In order to avoid confusion we will henceforth refer to these places by their original names. ie. Stillington (the hamlet), and the Village of the Carlton Iron Works, until the date of their official name changing, which was around 1932.

Whitton Duck Pond c. 1900

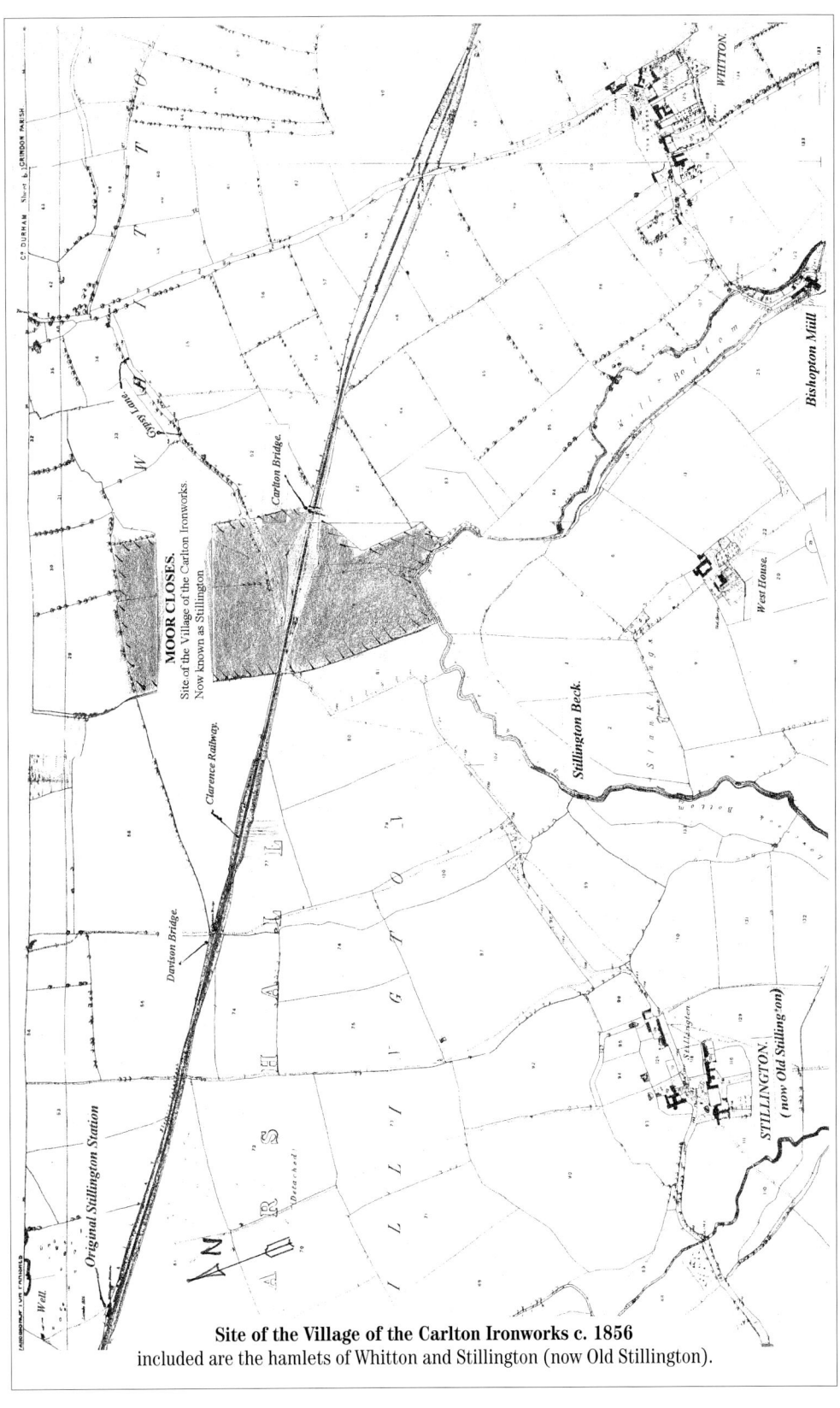

Site of the Village of the Carlton Ironworks c. 1856
included are the hamlets of Whitton and Stillington (now Old Stillington).

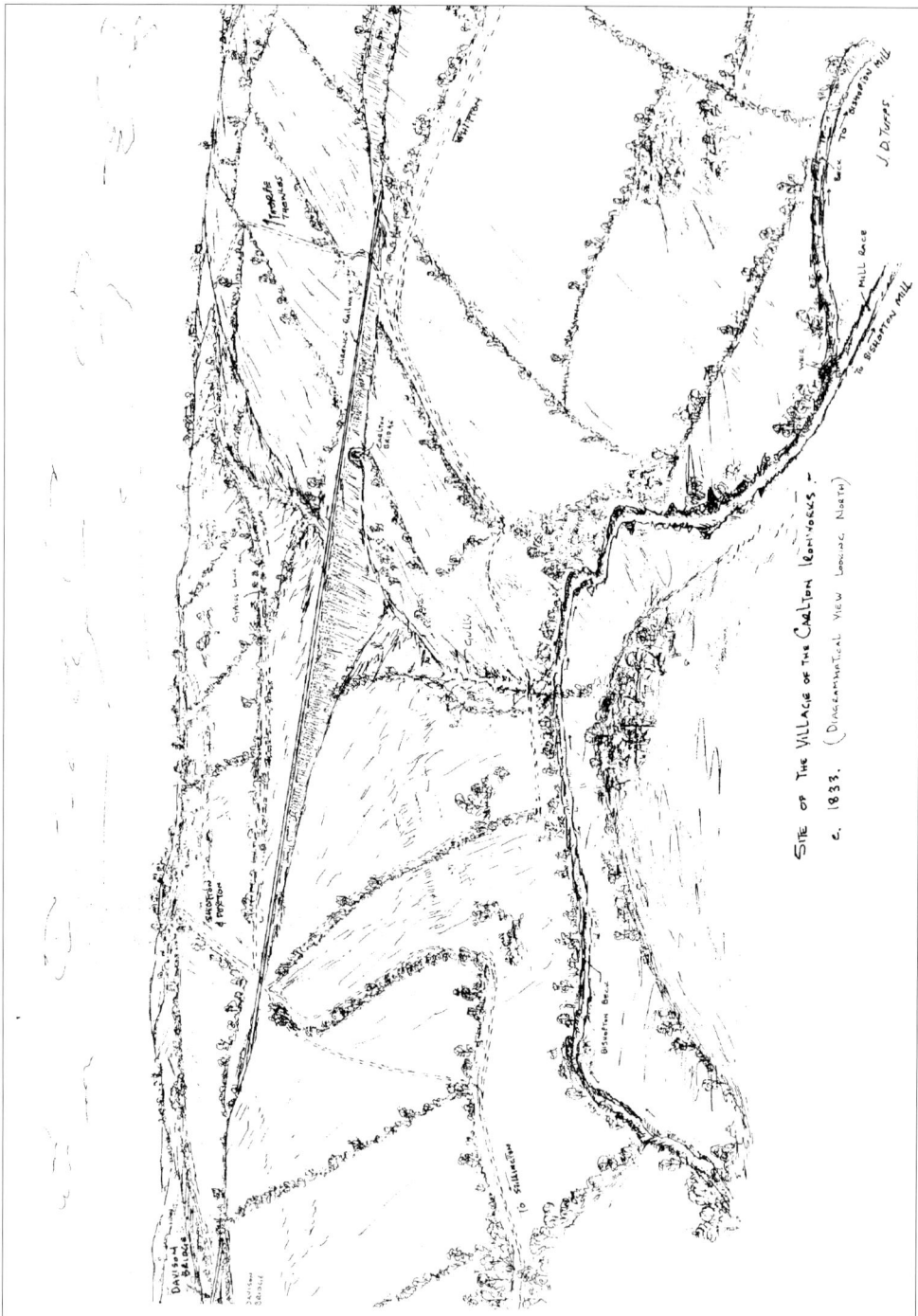

Site of the Village of the Carlton Ironworks

Pictorial sketch of area after completion of the Clarence Railway in 1833 and before the commencement of the Ironworks in 1865. Carlton Bridge, built at the nearest possible position to the existing path in order that horse drawn vehicles did not have to cross over the railway, became a central feature of the village. Davison Bridge is on the far left of the sketch.

The proximity of the beck to the eventual site of the ironworks was a major factor in the selection of the site. The Mill Race at the bottom right fed the water to Bishopton Mill.

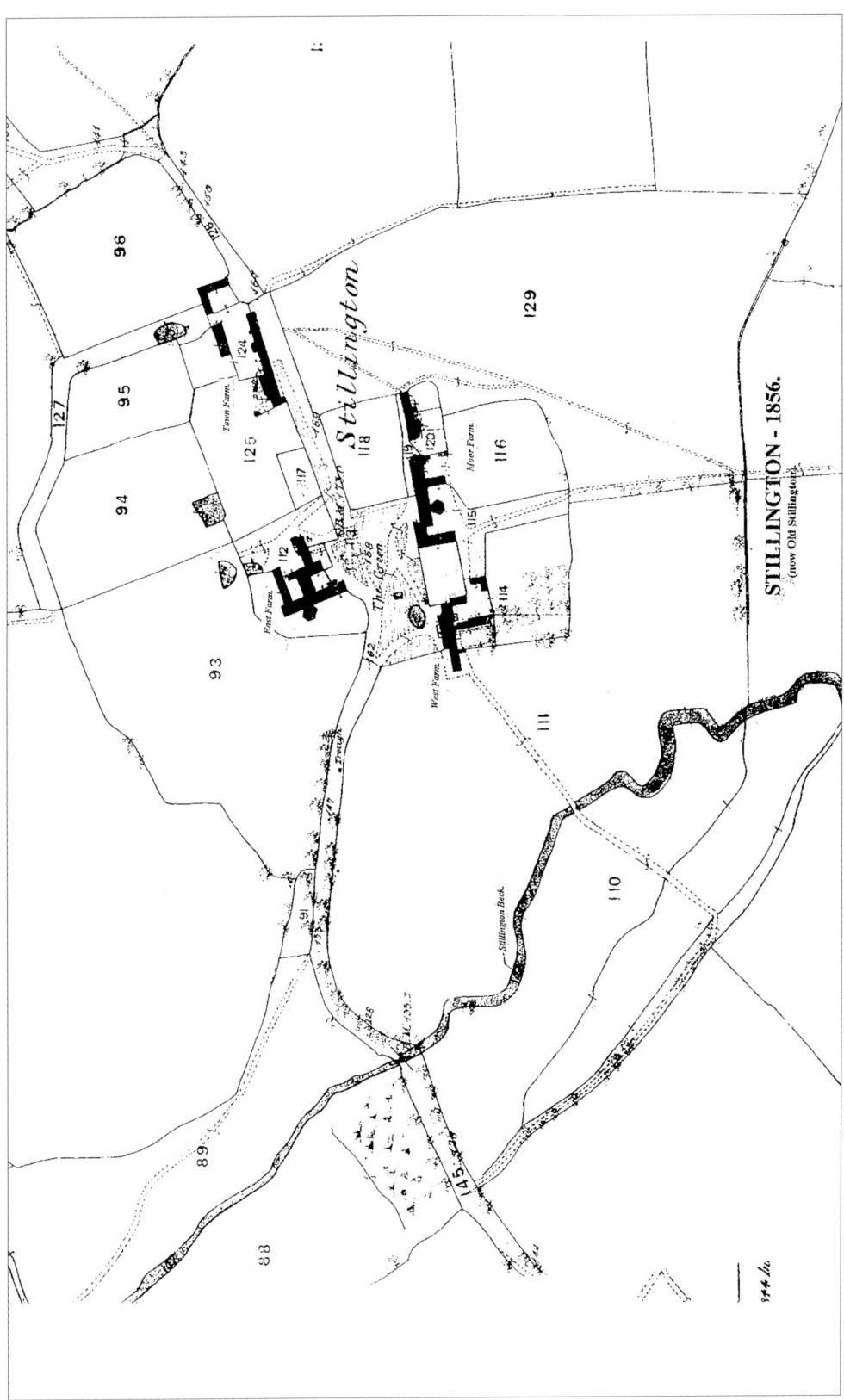

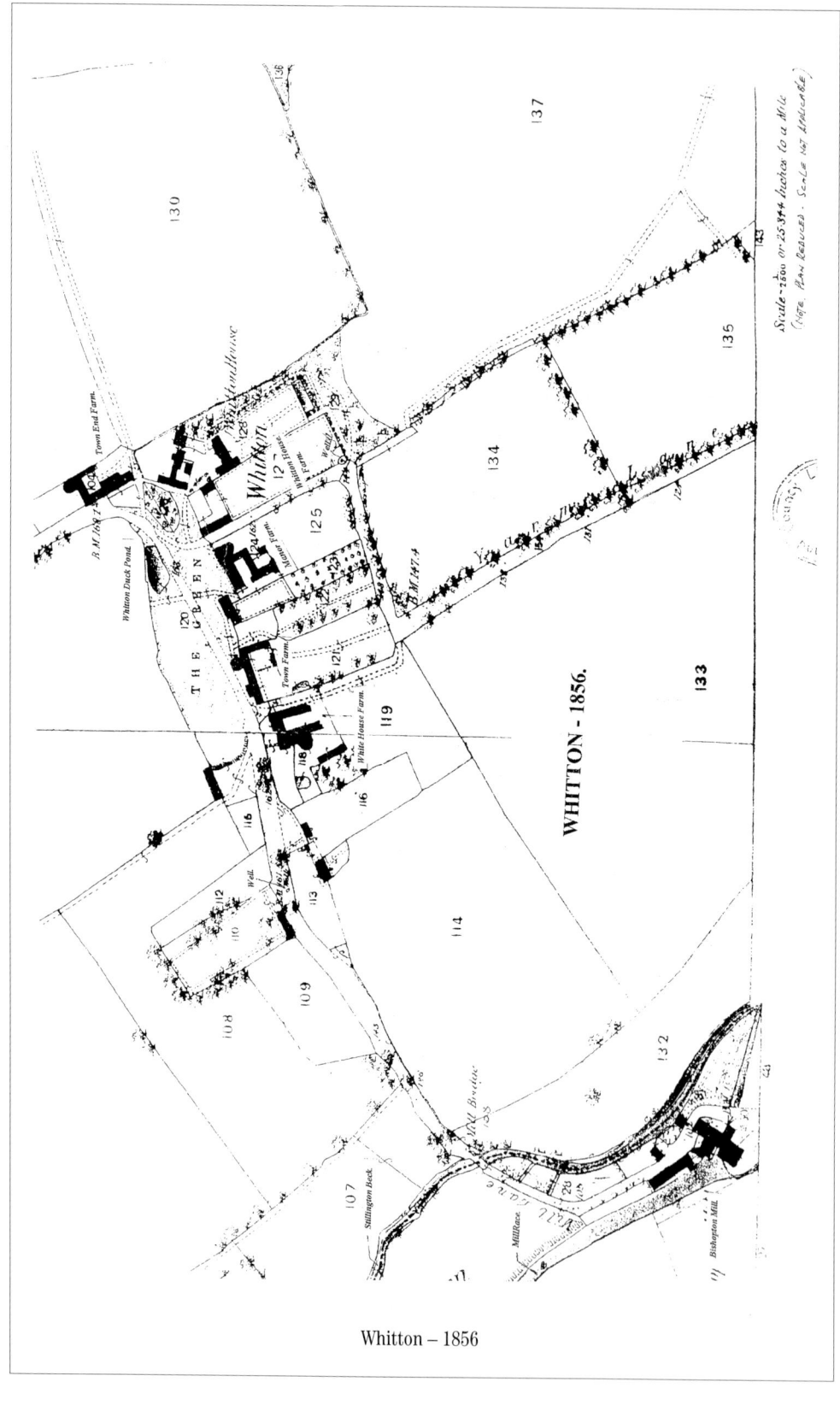

Whitton – 1856

1
The Early Landowners

Prior to the advent of the blast furnaces and the Village of the Carlton Iron Works, the land surrounding the village was in the possession of prominent land owners, a few of whom are listed in the following text. Although not greatly detailed, it does provide some interesting background information regarding the history of the area.

Merton College

In the 13th century the hamlet of Stillington was part of extensive estates held by the Amurdiville family, whose head was one of the powerful barons controlling the country throughout this period.

Around the year 1250, the Amurdiville's gave the manor of Stillington to Walter de Merton who, in 1274, founded Merton College, Oxford (the first university college). Merton transferred the ownership of the manor to the college in order to provide it with finance from the rents and leases, etc.

The Manor of Stillington comprised four farmhouses situated in the hamlet of Stillington together with all their associated land. The farms were East Farm, West Farm, Town Farm and Moor Farm and they remained the property of Merton College until the 1920s, when they were sold to the tenant farmers, who were Messrs Gibbin (East Farm), P B Hopps (West Farm), G R Hopps (Town Farm) and Wood (Moor Farm).

The Carlton Iron Company bought land from Merton College upon which to expand their ironworks, and also build the houses that eventually formed the Village of the Carlton Ironworks.

The Glykoline Lubricant Company also bought land from Merton College upon which they built a factory and Glykoline Terrace.

Sherburn Hospital

Sherburn Hospital owned extensive land and properties in and around Whitton which they gradually relinquished. In 1992 they sold Whitehouse Farm, the last of their properties in Whitton, whilst retaining a small parcel of land upon which to rehouse the tenant of the farm, Mrs D Atkinson.

Sherburn Hospital was founded in 1181 by Hugh Pudsey, the then Bishop of Durham, as a reception place for people suffering from leprosy. The Bishop endowed the hospital with considerable property and lands that included farms at Whitton and also the church at Bishopton, with all the tithes due to it.

The total extent of the lands and property that were given to the hospital is not known although, in one historical document, they were described as considerable. The Bishop's endowments were added to by local landowners who were constantly harassed by appeals from the Bishop to give support to the hospital.

The Hutchinson Family

The properties and land owned by Merton College and Sherburn Hospital accounted for a major proportion of the area that lay to the west and south of the Village of the Carlton Iron Works. The remainder of the encircling land belonged to wealthy individuals such as the Hutchinson's who lived in Whitton House (the Manor House of Whitton), from c. 1700 until the 1850s.

In 1851 George Hutchinson lived in the house with a general servant, a housekeeper and a cook/housemaid, but no other member of the family. He was the fifth generation of the Hutchinson's to own Whitton House and its estates, and he was also one of Her Majesty's Deputy Lieutenants of County Durham.

A link between the poet laureate, William Wordsworth, and the Hutchinson family was forged through John (brother of George's grandfather), who moved to Penrith from Whitton and whose granddaughter, Mary Hutchinson, married the famous poet in 1802.

Other Landowners

The remainder of the land in the area changed hands many times but individual landowners who appear most prominently in the last 200 years were the Reverend E Davison, Mr Anthony Wilkinson and Mr Spearman.

2

Why was this site chosen for the manufacture of iron?

Having set the scene encompassing the site upon which the Village of the Carlton Iron Works was developed, it is now important that we try to understand why Mr Samuel Bastow should envisage building blast furnaces amidst this peaceful countryside. We may never fully understand the reasons, but the following text explains various factors and events that will certainly have influenced the decision.

Apart from a satisfactory area of land upon which to build, the other basic essentials needed when the erection of blast furnaces was being considered were:

Raw Materials   The main raw materials required in the production of pig iron were coal, coke, iron ore, and limestone.
Good supplies of these commodities must be available locally and within easy access of a good transport system.

Transport   An efficient and reasonably inexpensive means of transportation was essential to bring raw materials to the site and enable easy delivery of pig iron to the ports and other industries.

Water   A plentiful and continual supply of water was required to:
(a) convert into steam with which to power the blast engines
(b) act as an industrial coolant
(c) for drinking and personal hygiene.

We must now consider the availability of these essentials and any other considerations affecting the choice of this site for ironmaking.

The Transport System

During the early years of the 1800s coal was being mined in abundance throughout the Durham coalfields, and coal owners were continually searching for improved methods of transporting their coal to the ports for nationwide distribution and export.

The original system of transport was a pack horse train that would, on average, take 6 tons of coal a distance of 20 miles in one day. This was not only slow but expensive and the coal owners decided that a new mode of transport was a priority if their profits were to be enhanced.

One consideration was the building of a Canal from the Durham Coalfields to the River Tees.

Waterways and canals were being used as a means of transport in other parts of the country and, in 1818, it was proposed to investigate the building of a canal that would link the River Tees to the West Auckland coalfields.

For many years previous, in fact since the days of the Roman occupation, corn and cattle had been carried in flat bottomed boats between Billingham and Thorpe using the Bishopton/Billingham Beck, which was tidal as far upstream as Thorpe. With the water reputed to be over ten feet deep at Billingham Bottoms, it was decided that this stretch of the beck would give an ideal start to the proposed canal.

An eminent engineer, George Leather, was chosen to select the route of the canal and then carry out a comprehensive survey. This was at the expense and under the personal direction of Mr Christopher Tennent, an inhabitant of Stockton, who instructed Leather to find the lowest, least expensive and shortest practical route for a canal from the River Tees into the working coalfields of West Auckland.

The route chosen commenced at the River Tees and followed the beck through Billingham Bottoms, past Norton, Blakeston, Thorpe, Whitton and on to Stillington, where it deviated from the beck and went towards Elstob and Mordon Carrs. After crossing the River Skerne near Bradbury, the canal route then ran south-westerly past Rushyford, Windlestone, Eldon, Shildon, Thickley and Brusselton, until it reached the River Gaunless near Evenwood Bridge.

The total course measured approximately 30 miles and the canal generally would have been about 24ft wide by 6ft deep, with the terminal at West Auckland being 48ft wide by 6ft deep.

The water in the canal would need to be raised a total of 442ft using over 50 locks and the cost of the project was estimated at £205,283.

By December 1818 the whole canal route had been surveyed and costed, but at this late stage the financial backers, mostly based at Darlington, withdrew from the scheme.

The reason for their change of heart was the advent of an even greater advance in the transportation field being proposed by George Stephenson. His idea was to transport coal by rail and the investors decided to back this system and abandon the proposed canal.

Consequently, instead of a canal with coal barges being towed towards the River Tees, probably stopping at Stillington to manoeuvre through one of the 50 locks, with the lock keeper's cottage close by, we now had one of the most significant features in the ultimate development of the Village of the Carlton Iron Works, the Clarence Railway.

The Clarence Railway

The Stockton and Darlington Railway Company built a line to carry coal from Whitton Park Colliery near Bishop Auckland, via Heighington to Darlington, then on through Preston Park before terminating at the quayside in Stockton. This line originally came into service in 1825 to carry freight between Shildon and Stockton. The success of this venture prompted Mr Christopher Tennent to form the Clarence Railway Company in 1828, in order to build a shorter more direct rail route from the coalfields to the River Tees, than that chosen by the Stockton and Darlington Railway Company.

The line he built was completed in 1833 and named The Clarence Railway. It ran from the existing Stockton and Darlington Company line at Simpasture junction (near Heighington) to Samphire Batts (now Port Clarence), with a branch line from Harrowgate House (between Blakeston Lane and Norton) down to the River Tees at North Shore.

At one point, the Clarence Railway came within 250 yards of Bishopton Beck, but the distance between line and beck quickly increased either side of this point, which coincidentally was where the gully, mentioned in the introduction, drained into the beck. The area adjacent to this position and stretching to the plateau, also mentioned in the introduction, was named Moor Closes and comprised five fields that were divided almost equally by the Clarence Railway.

Review of Moor Closes as a site for the Ironworks

When reviewing the foregoing features it can be concluded that, at the area named Moor Closes, we had three essential components complimentary to building the ironworks:

(a) the plateau (part of Moor Closes), afforded a relatively flat and extensive area of land that could be ideally utilised for building
(b) Bishopton beck would provide a sufficient and reliable source of water
(c) the Clarence Railway running directly through Moor Closes gave the site an excellent mode of transport.

The remaining requirements to make Moor Closes a totally viable site for the erection of the ironworks was an adequate and easily available supply of coal, coke, ironstone and limestone.

The Clarence Railway gave the site a direct route to:

(a) a plentiful supply of coal and coke from the Durham coalfields
(b) an abundance of iron ore from the ironstone mines in the Cleveland Hills
(c) a rail link to Weardale where a sufficient supply of limestone was available.

Thus, all essential raw materials were available in the required quantities and were easily accessible via the Clarence Railway and other rail networks, that were being extended continually throughout the region and the country.

Final Considerations

Although it is now easier to understand why the Moor Closes site was selected by Samuel Bastow for the erection of his blast furnaces in 1865 the same, if not better, facilities were available along the banks of the River Tees and these, at first glance, would seem to have been the more sensible choice. However, other considerations swayed Bastow in his decision to build at Moor Closes.

Firstly, he had been involved with the ownership of Moor Closes since around 1858 and had bought them outright in 1860, five years before he built his blast furnaces.

Secondly, since commercial quantities of ironstone had been found in the Cleveland Hills in 1850, many blast furnaces had been built along the banks of the Tees. By the year 1858 there were eleven blast furnaces in the Stockton area of the Tees, fourteen in the Middlesbrough area and fourteen at South Bank. This statistic suggests that the banks of the River Tees were already overcrowded and room for the expansion of a new company would be limited.

Thirdly, the area of Moor Closes on the south of the Clarence Railway was, from around 1858, being used as a clay quarry with a brickmaking plant installed. Bricks were required in great quantities when building an ironworks for the construction of chimneys, pig beds, blast engine houses and workshops. The quarry and the brickmaking plant were inclusive in the purchase of Moor Closes which Bastow had made in 1860 and so afforded him a plentiful and easily available supply of bricks.

When these and earlier mentioned factors are taken into consideration, it is not difficult to understand why Bastow chose to build his blast furnaces on the Moor Closes site and thus sow the seeds for the ultimate formation of the Village of the Carlton Ironworks.

Davison Bridge

Built in 1831 to allow horse drawn vehicles access under the railway on route between Foxton and Stillington. The bridge was extended in 1884 to accommodate the widening of the Clarence Railway. Photograph shows the original side of the bridge built from dry stone, the joint of the extension can be clearly seen from inside the tunnel. The bridge was named after the Reverend E Davison who owned land locally.

3

The Development of the Village of the Carlton Ironworks

The scene was now set with all components in place for this peaceful area to become the site of intense industrial activity, the consequence of which was the Village of the Carlton Ironworks.

To make each step in the development of the village as clear as possible, the following section been has set out in chronological order, with additional comments where they are considered helpful.

During the early years, the progress and expansion of the ironworks have been catalogued in detail, because of the major influence they had upon the village and the livelihood of its inhabitants.

1833 Opening of the Clarence Railway

The Clarence Railway was opened to provide a shorter and more direct rail system from the coalfields of West Auckland to the River Tees, via a route which took it past the eventual site of the ironworks around which the Village of the Carlton Ironworks was built.

Two dry-stone archways, adjacent to the site, allowed access through the railway for horse drawn vehicles travelling between Stillington and Foxton and Stillington and Thorpe. These arches were named Davison Bridge and Carlton Bridge respectively, with Carlton Bridge eventually becoming one of the centre points of the Village of the Carlton Ironworks.

> Mr Christopher Tennent, who championed the erection of the Clarence, had previously served in the Royal Navy and, in consequence, named the railway after the Lord High Admiral of the Fleet who, at that time, was the Duke of Clarence, later to become King William 1V.
>
> The Clarence was originally a mineral line with trucks being drawn by horses until 1836 when locomotives were introduced and, by 1841, had completely replaced the horses. Passenger services began in July 1835 and freight and goods services commenced in July 1877.
>
> In 1915 the Clarence was electrified between Shildon and Newport, using a 1500 volts DC overhead system, and 10 electric locomotives which were especially

constructed at Darlington North Road Works for use on the busy mineral line which passed through the Village of the Carlton Ironworks.

Electrification was discontinued in 1935 and all trace of cables and supports had disappeared by 1939.

1838 The original Stillington Station erected

This station was a single wooden platform built to serve the farms situated in the hamlets of Stillington and Foxton. It was sited at the closest practical point to where a line drawn between the two hamlets intersected the railway, about three quarters of a mile west of where the Village of the Carlton Ironworks was eventually built.

The station was manned by a station master and a mineral clerk and was equipped with a weighbridge and sidings. Mineral trucks using the line were weighed and their tonnage recorded by the mineral clerk, who also fastened a ticket stating all relevant details of the load onto the side of the truck for reference at their destination.

1838 Two cottages built adjacent to the original Stillington Station

These cottages were built by the railway company to accommodate the station master and the mineral clerk manning the station. When the station eventually closed, the cottages were then occupied by any railwaymen, such as platelayers or signalmen, who were working in the area.

The cottages were named the Weigh Cottages, due to the presence of the weighbridge, and because of their remote situation had only very basic amenities.

Wedding photograph taken outside Weigh Cottages c. 1930

The domestic water supply was obtained from a well, which was situated about 100 yards from the cottages, at a point close to where the beck ran under the railway.

The cottages were eventually given a mains supply of water but neither electric lights or flush toilets were ever provided.

1858 Sale of Moor Closes (eventual site of the ironworks)

An Agreement of Sale was reached between Mr R W Jackson (the owner) and Mr Samuel Bastow regarding five pieces of land, comprising 38 acres, adjacent to and divided by the Clarence Railway at a point close to Carlton Bridge.

These five pieces of land were known as Moor Closes.

> An Agreement of Sale usually meant that the land involved was automatically sold to the person making the agreement, in this case Mr Samuel Bastow. However, later in the year, a conveyance was drawn up and the land was sold to Mr T Hoyle. It would seem from other evidence that Mr T Hoyle was an associate of Samuel Bastow and was probably acting upon his behalf.

1858 The first industry at the Moor Closes site

Mr T Hoyle commenced quarrying clay on the part of Moor Closes sited on the southern side of the Clarence Railway. Within the confines of the quarry, Hoyle erected a brickmaking plant and used the clay he quarried to manufacture bricks, which were much in demand because of the industrial expansion taking place in the area. The ironmaking business in particular needed a vast quantity of bricks for the building of chimneys, blast engine houses, pig beds, winch houses and workshops.

> Samuel Bastow was at this time building ironworks at Cliff House, West Hartlepool and his close association with Hoyle would guarantee him an ample supply of bricks. The proximity of the brickworks to the Clarence Railway also ensured a convenient method of transport was available to take the bricks to the Cliff House site.

1860 Hoyle transfers Moor Closes to Samuel Bastow

This transfer gave Samuel Bastow the land upon which he would build his blast furnaces and so transform this peaceful rural environment into a bustling industrial area.

Samuel Bastow was therefore the instigator of circumstances that would eventually lead to the creation of the Village of the Carlton Ironworks.

> Bastow was already well established as a businessman and owned an iron foundry at New Stanton, West Hartlepool, where he had produced steam engines since 1846 and later manufactured locomotive boilers, railway trucks and cranes. In 1858 Bastow built the Cliff House ironworks, which were situated at the end of Mainsforth Terrace in New Stanton (West Hartlepool), overlooking the North Sea. At this time

he was also negotiating the purchase of Moor Closes from Mr Jackson and, having reached agreement on the sale, he allowed Hoyle to purchase the land on his behalf until 1860, when ownership was officially transferred to Bastow. Although continuing the operations of the quarry and the brickworks, Bastow delayed any further development of the site until 1865.

1865 Ownership of Moor Closes transferred to Bastow & Company Ltd

A conveyance passing the ownership of Moor Closes from Samuel Bastow to his company, Bastow & Company, was drawn up and the Deeds of Confirmation followed almost immediately.

Samuel Bastow was now ready to proceed with the development of the Moor Closes site.

1865 The start of the Ironworks

Workmen employed by Bastow & Company commenced building a blast furnace with the necessary ancillary plant on the Moor Closes site, at a position 250 yards north of the Clarence Railway.

1866 Blast Furnace brought into operation

The blast furnace was brought into operation and pig iron produced in June 1866, an event reported in the local newspapers and hailed as a great success by all concerned.

1866 Finance for the expansion of the Ironworks

Bastow & Company were keen to expand their ironmaking plant but were overstretched financially and mortgaged the works and land in order to raise extra capital. Mortgages were provided by the Earl of Minto; Admiral Drummond; Mr R G Clarke; Mr Shortridge; Sydney Gedge and Trustee and William Merrick. The company also sold some property to Mr Shortridge.

1867 Second blast furnace completed

With the added capital obtained from the mortgagees, Bastow & Company expanded the ironmaking plant and built a second blast furnace adjacent to the first. This also was successfully brought into operation.

1867 Furnaces closed down

Within six months of the second furnace being brought into operation, both furnaces were 'blown out' and with Bastow & Company in severe financial difficulties, all operations were halted.

> Bastow had been unfortunate since, when his blast furnaces were coming on stream and producing pig iron, the industry as a whole was undergoing one of its many recessions. This recession lasted from 1865 until the end of 1867, which meant that

Bastow was having to lay out considerable sums of money for raw materials, labour and development without being able to sell his pig iron at a realistic price.

1869 Samuel Bastow declared a bankrupt

Samuel Bastow's brave venture into the ironmaking industry ended when he was declared a bankrupt, with the consequence that the ironworks, quarry and brickworks on the Moor Closes site were officially closed down.

1870 Ironworks for sale

The ironworks were auctioned, under court order, at the Black Lion Hotel, Stockton on Tees with a reserve price of £13,300. The reserve price was not reached during auction but, after some private negotiation, the Moor Closes site including the ironworks, quarry and brickworks, were purchased for that price by Briggs Brothers, who were Yorkshire colliery owners.

1870 Re-opening of ironworks planned

Briggs Brothers formed the North of England Industrial Iron and Coal Company, with the intention of re-opening the ironworks under this name.

The company was officially registered on April 13th 1870.

The initial directors of the company were Henry Currer Briggs (Chairman), Archibald Briggs and William Lowson, a merchant from Dundee. They were joined a short time later by D Ramsay from Saltburn and Walter Morrison, a wealthy and influencial man from Malham Tarn, who was also the Member of Parliament for Skipton.

1870 Financing of the new company

In order to finance the necessary modernisation and expansion of the ironworks, the directors of The North of England Industrial Iron and Coal Company decided to issue a number of shares in the company.

In October a total of 10,000 shares were issued costing £10 each, thus creating £100,000 worth of capital with which to develop the ironworks and other projects such as the leasing or buying of coal mines, ironstone mines and the building of houses for the company's workers.

1870 Modernisation of the ironworks

Modernisation of the existing plant was essential to enable pig iron to be produced at a competitive price and, with sufficient money now available, The North of England Industrial Iron and Coal Company carried out the following improvements and additions to the existing plant:

(a) Raised the height of the two blast furnaces 20ft, making them a final 80ft high by 13ft diameter

(b) Erected one new blast furnace, 80ft high by 23ft diameter

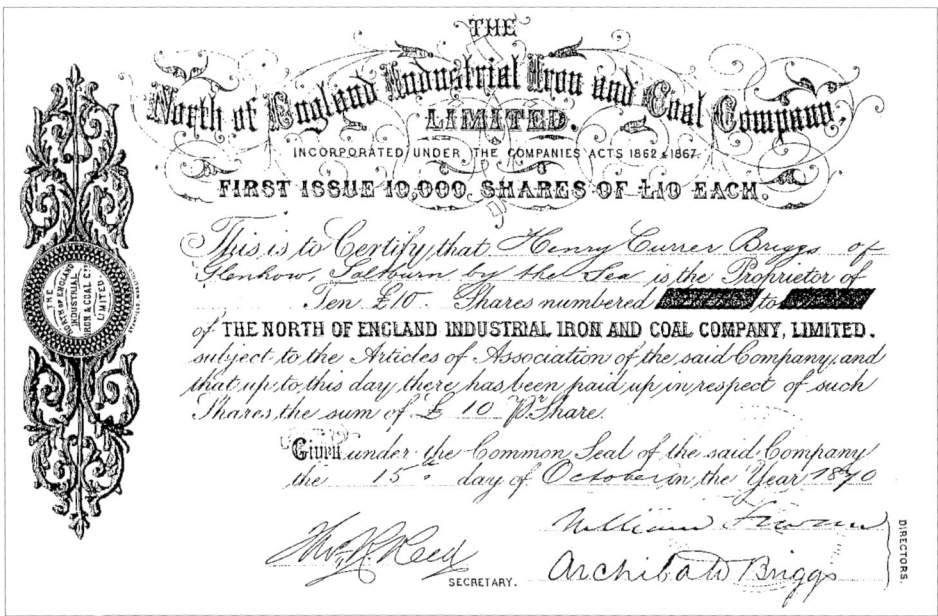

The First Share Certificates

This is a copy of one of the first shares to be issued by the North of England Industrial Iron and Coal Company. In 1870 they issued 10,000 shares costing £10 each with the issue being fully subscribed thus raising £100,000 capital to modify and extend the ironworks.

Modernisation of the two existing Blast Furnaces and erection of a third. 1870

The two original furnaces were built by Samuel Bastow & Company and brought into operation in 1866 and 1867. Lack of finance caused their closure. In 1870 the site and furnaces were bought by Briggs Bros of Leeds, who formed a new company named the North of England Industrial Iron and Coal Company, and immediately commenced the upgrading of the existing two furnaces and the erection of a third incorporating all known methods of improvement. The above shows the old furnaces have been heightened by around 20ft with a new lift shaft and gantry fitted. The Lodging House is shown centre left.

(c) Erected regenerator stoves around the blast furnaces which were designed to use the hot waste gases from the furnaces to preheat the blast. This system enabled the blast furnace to reach higher temperatures more quickly than when a cold blast was used.

Changes like these had resulted in a massive reduction in the amount of coke required to produce a ton of pig iron within the industry. In the 1850s, approximately forty two hundredweight of coke was required to produce one ton of pig iron whereas, in the 1870s, this had been reduced to just over twenty hundredweight.

1870 The Pump House

A good water supply was essential to the efficient working of the blast furnaces and also to the livelihood of the workers. With this in mind, The North of England Industrial Iron and Coal Company built a pump house and control valve adjacent to the beck and pumped the water through a water main directly to the ironworks. Some of the water was stored in tanks at a height suitable to create sufficient

Pump House and Valve
The pump house was situated adjacent to the beck and, from 1870 until 1888, pumped sufficient water from the beck to supply the ironworks and the village. After this date the domestic water and some of the industrial supply was piped to the village from Sadberge reservoir, but the pump house continued to take water from the beck for industrial purposes until the late 1930s.

pressure to ensure further distribution. Cooling water was recycled by the use of cooling ponds, and some of the water was channelled through filter beds, positioned just north of North Street, before being piped to the various standpipe positions for domestic use.

The exact date of the erection of the pump house and valve is not known, but there is no record of a well being sunk to supply water to the works or the village, which would indicate that any water used had always come from the beck with some form of pumping and piping being installed at an early stage of the works development. The filter beds, used for the purification of the domestic water supply, were provided much later, possibly around 1895.

> Note. In June 1872 the directors purchased, from Anthony Wilkinson, a further 37 acres of land adjoining the ironworks and told the shareholders that they had every reason to believe that workable seams of coal may be found under this land. They proposed to enter into a contract with the Diamond Rock Boring Company to prove the strata by boring a hole 600 to 800ft in depth, which would also secure an ample supply of water much needed for all purposes. There is no record that this proposal was ever carried out.

1870 Planning of Village begins

Having organised the modernisation and expansion of the works, it was necessary for the company to recruit and stabilise an experienced workforce. With so few suitable inhabitants in the immediate vicinity, the company planned to encourage the movement of workers to the area by:

(a) building a 'Model Lodging House' to accommodate the construction workers and the early production workers
(b) building two houses for supervisors sited within very close proximity to the works
(c) providing permanent housing as quickly as possible within the vicinity of the works
(d) introducing a Profit Sharing Scheme for the workers, as an inducement for higher productivity and a means of allowing workmen to benefit from greater effort. This scheme did not prove to be popular with the unions and did little to enhance the earnings of the workers.

On May 3rd, the need for housing was confirmed at a directors' meeting of the North of England Industrial Iron and Coal Company when the chairman, Mr Henry Briggs, reported a great want of suitable accommodation for the company's workmen at the Village of the Carlton Ironworks and also for those at South Belmont, Guisborough, where the company was mining ironstone under lease. It was resolved that 20 to 30 houses would be built at each location, and thereby started a housing programme governed by the needs of the company, to recruit sufficient workers to fulfill the work available.

The houses were initially used to accommodate works personnel only, with the added proviso that anyone allotted the tenancy of a house would have to agree to take in other workers as lodgers, to enable greater flexibility in the absorption rate.

1870 The Lodging House

A lodging house, quoted as being a model lodging house, was built by the North of England Industrial Iron and Coal Company to provide temporary accommodation for the construction workers or production workers awaiting permanent residence. Despite intensive research, the location of the lodging house cannot be defined exactly, but the most probable site is the building which, from around 1900, was used as a weigh house and store, ie. when it was no longer required to house workers.

1870 The first houses

Two houses were built close to the ironworks for the specific use of foremen working on the site. There are no details of the size or type of these houses for they were demolished at an early stage of the ironwork's expansion, but rateable value evidence puts them in a bracket superior to the houses in North Street. These houses can be seen on early photographs at a position midway between the works and North Street.

The Lodging House
Often referred to as the Model Lodging House it was built as a priority when the North of England Industrial Iron and Coal Company began the modernisation of the blast furnaces in 1870. Sketch shows original building that was later modified to accommodate more workmen.

1870 The first street – North Street (Slag Row)

The first street to be built at the Village of the Carlton Ironworks by the North of England Industrial Iron and Coal Company was North Street, which comprised 18 dwellings built in a terrace close to the ironworks. This street was built progressively between 1870 and 1872 and was first named Slag Row because of its proximity to the developing slag heap.

The houses in North Street had generous backyards with coal house and privy. Space was available for allotments at the rear of the houses. With no electricity or gas available, the only source of heat was the coal fires and artificial light was provided by oil lamps which were still in use when the houses were demolished in 1950. Water points were shared until c. 1910 when each house was given its own cold water supply.

North Street initially accommodated the construction workers who were employed to build the blast furnaces and ancillary plant but the tenancies changed hands almost completely when the production workers took over.

1870 December – Brickworks in full production

The half yearly Report of the North of England Industrial Iron and Coal Company stated: 'The brickworks have been in full operation and have produced a large number of bricks which have been used in the construction of workmen's houses and the building of a new fitting shop at the ironworks'.

These brickworks were those owned by the company and sited in the quarry on the south side of the Clarence Railway.

1870 Passenger Halt opened

In order to encourage workers to travel from local towns to the ironworks, the directors arranged with the railway company for a Passenger Halt to be erected as close as possible to the works. The railway company agreed and people were therefore able to use the passenger trains which operated a shuttle service between Ferryhill and Stockton.

This did not affect the core business and local administration of the railway which was still retained at the original Stillington station three quarters of a mile up the line.

1871 April – Census

The 1871 census showed that there were 10 houses completed and occupied in North Street, and also two houses occupied by work's foremen.

Of the families recorded at this time, only one remained when the 1881 census was taken. This was the Scurr family, although the Bell's, who lived in Weigh Cottages at the time of the 1871 census, had moved into North Street immediately a new house was available. They, like the Scurr's, were among the truly first residents of the village and both families remained for two or three subsequent generations.

The total population recorded in 1871 for the Village of the Carlton Ironworks was 79.

This comprised: 28 working males (10 of whom were boarders); 12 adult females (all wives of the heads of the household) and 39 children (16 boys and 23 girls).

The average age of the working men was 30, the oldest being 45 and the youngest 13. The average age of the adult women was 33, the oldest being 42 and the youngest 27.

One young girl, aged 12, was listed as being a general servant to the Scurr's household. From the details given, it would seem that she had come with the family when they had moved from the Barnard Castle area. The Scurr's had seven children at the time, the two eldest boys, aged 17 and 14, were employed at the ironworks.

The average number of residents per household was over six with the greatest number occupying one house being 12. The two foremen's houses were occupied by a foreman boilersmith and a foreman engine fitter, both of whom had previously worked in and around Middlesbrough. The first house in North Street was tenanted by the brickyard foreman, who hailed from Staffordshire.

The occupations of the workmen resident in the village included, ironwork labourers, brickyard workers, locomotive drivers and firemen, engine fitters, furnace keepers, boilersmiths, joiners and one shoemaker.

The main areas of origin of these workers was Staffordshire, Yorkshire and Durham.

Modernisation of Blast Furnaces almost complete. 1871
Regeneration stoves now fitted around furnaces, new chimney complete and pig beds nearing completion. One of the furnaces may have been in operation when this photograph was taken, judging by the fumes coming from the chimney.

THE DEVELOPMENT OF THE VILLAGE OF THE CARLTON IRONWORKS

North Street

North Street, comprising 18 houses, was built progressively from 1870 to 1872. Named Slag Row in the 1871 census, it was later officially named North Street but retained the nickname Slag Row, because of its close proximity to the slag heap, until the street was demolished in 1950. *photo approx 1900.*

A few of the North Street residents c. 1935
The houses featured are numbers fifteen and sixteen.
Adults l to r: Mrs Storey: Mrs Bell: Mr George Storey: Mrs Wilks: Mrs Anne Scott, (nee Jackson): Bob Scott: *children l to r:* Muriel, Harold and Violet Wilks.

1871 Blast furnaces brought into operation again

In 1871 the modernisation of No.1 blast furnace was completed and it recommenced operating. Later in the year, modifications to No.2 blast furnace were completed and this was also brought into operation.

1872 April – County Rate Notice

In order to calculate the annual rates due from The North of England Industrial Iron and Coal Company, the Durham County valuer had estimated a Capital Value for the Township of the Carlton Ironworks which was itemised as follows:

> The Capital Value of the Ironworks, including blast furnaces, plant and 30 acres of land was given as a total of £22,500. The annual rates due on the works was calculated at 7½% of the Capital Value = £1,687.
> The Capital Value of workshops, stables (2 stalls and 1 engine), and the lodging house was given as £300 and £450 respectively.
> Rates due for these were based on 6% of Capital Value = £45.

The Capital Value was not shown for the remaining items but the Annual Rates due were as follows:

> Brick yard – 10 acres plus buildings and one machine £80.
> Two foreman's houses – £12 each. Total £24.
> 18 workmen's houses – £5 10s 0d each. Total £99.

> The above rates payable show that the two foremen's houses were rated superior to the eighteen workmen's houses in North Street.

This notice gives further confirmation of the state of development within the village at this time.

1872 Second Share Issue – 6,000 shares at £10 each

In order to attain some self sufficiency in the provision of raw materials, the North of England Industrial Iron and Coal Company purchased a colliery at East Howle and secured leases on the South Belmont ironstone mines near Guisborough, and on the Ailesbury ironstone mines from the Marquis of Ailesbury. To finance these items, the directors decided on a further issue of 6,000 shares which would raise £60,000 worth of new capital.

1872 Ecclesiastical Parish of Stillington formed (Reported in London Gazette)

William Cassidi, the vicar of Grindon, anticipated the potential growth of the Village of the Carlton Ironworks and decided a new parish was needed to provide the religious services required by its inhabitants. He therefore applied his energies to forming this new parish and on May 31st 1872 Queen Victoria ratified the

The Counte de Paris: The locomotive working on the site when the furnaces were being modernised was named after the Counte de Paris, who was an early shareholder of the newly formed North of England Industrial Iron and Coal Company. It was built in 1870 by Black Hawthorne and Company Limited of Newcastle, to be supplied new to the ironworks from where, at the end of its working life, it was sold for scrap. The author's great-grandfather, Mr George Bell, who was a first tenant in the first street built in the village (North Street), was employed by the company as loco driver and would almost certainly be the driver of the Counte de Paris.

North Street in relation to the Ironworks: This photograph shows the close proximity of North Street to the ironworks. The buildings running parallel and to the left of North Street are the engineering shops, which included a fitting shop, blacksmith's shop and joiner's shop. Running perpendicular to these are buildings which, it is assumed, are the houses built for the work's foremen in 1870.

necessary documentation. The new parish was named after the hamlet of Stillington, and encompassed Whitton, Stillington and the Village of the Carlton Ironworks. The existing parishes of Redmarshall and Grindon lost parts of their original jurisdictions in order that the new Parish of Stillington could be formed. The vicar designated to perform the necessary duties within the new parish was the Reverend John Allen Parker, who held services and carried out baptisms from its inception, but weddings continued to be performed at either Redmarshall or Bishopton until the church for Stillington parish was built in 1880. Funerals previously fulfilled at Redmarshall or Bishopton were carried out in the village after the consecration of a plot of land in October 1877.

The first baptism, carried out in the new parish on August 11th 1872, was that of Alice Maud Moore, daughter of James and Jane Moore of 18 North Street, Village of the Carlton Iron Works.

> With no church or other suitable building available until the Cassidi Hall was built in February 1874, it is not known where normal church services and baptisms took place, but the general opinion of the more elderly in the village would suggest that a section of the newly built fitting shop at the ironworks was used. This is highly probable, as the only houses in the village at this time were those in North Street and the two foremen's houses, all of which were less than 100 yards from the fitting shop.

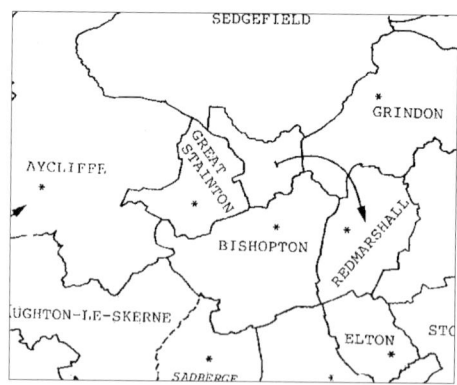

Parish and Chapelry Boundaries

Above are shown maps of the Parish and Chapel Boundaries local to Stillington before and after the formation of the Ecclesiastical Parish of Stillington. Most of the new parish was formed by taking over the segregated area of the previous Redmarshall Parish.

The left hand map has been reproduced from the Map of Parish and Chapelry Boundaries, c. 1800, produced by Durham Record Office. The right hand map is based on the Map of Parish and Chapelry Boundaries, c. 1800, produced by Durham Record Office.

1872 Malleable Iron Works

Malleable iron was quickly becoming of greater use to the engineering industry than pig iron because it could be used to form rail sections, bars and plates for shipbuilding, whereas the pig iron was only useful for casting products and was very brittle. Malleable iron could compete commercially for most markets but even it was coming under threat from steel which, at this time, could only be produced in quantity by the use of the Bessemer Convertor. Cleveland ironstone was unsuitable for steelmaking by this method because of its high phosphoric content and, as a result, many local companies including the North of England Industrial Iron and Coal Company, who were committed to the use of Cleveland ironstone, decided to concentrate on the production of malleable iron.

The company were intent on setting up their own malleable iron works as quickly as possible, in order to commence the manufacture of engineering sections and plates with the hope of getting a good return on their investments before steel and its products became preferred.

Plans and estimates for the setting up of a malleable iron works were completed and these included the use of six Danks' puddling furnaces which would further process the pig iron produced by the blast furnaces and convert it into malleable iron. The site of these works was to be the area which, in later years, was used by the North Eastern Iron Refinery.

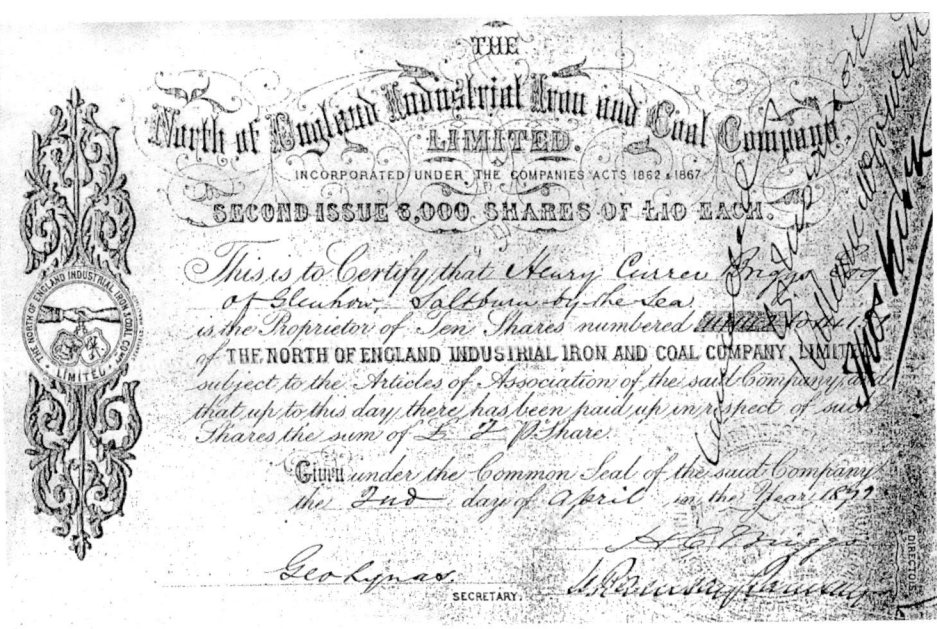

Second Share Certificates
Above is a copy of one of the second issue of shares issued by the North Of England Industrial Iron and Coal Company

Danks was an American who had developed and patented a revolving puddling furnace which converted pig iron into malleable iron. He allowed companies to use these furnaces under license, and an agreement between Danks and the North of England Industrial Iron and Coal Company allowed the company to construct and use six puddling furnaces in consideration for the sum of £1,500. Further royalties of one shilling per ton of iron puddled was to be an option for the licensee.

1872 More finance required

More capital was required by the North of England Industrial Iron and Coal Company to enable continued expansion and this was raised through a mortgage of £8,000 secured from Miss Sophia Henry of Hyde Park, London and indentured against the property of the ironworks.

1872 Rural Sanitary Authority of the Stockton Union

> The Guardians of the Poor of the Stockton Union had previously been formed to oversee the general governing of the area around Stockton, similar to a vestry but covering a whole district. Membership of the Guardians comprised local dignitaries such as landowners, wealthy farmers, doctors, vicars and solicitors. There was a hard-core of men representing Stockton, supplemented by at least one member from each of the Parochial Committees in the area which included Whitton, Redmarshall, Carlton, Thorpe and Wolviston.

The Parochial Committee representing Whitton was Clark Nesom, J Hunton (also a member of the Carlton Parochial Committee), J Blenkinsop, J Thompson, J Brownless, R Foster and D Parsons, all of whom were farmers from in and around Whitton. Clark Nesom and J Hunton were both active and influential members of the Guardians, being elected onto several committees.

> The Parochial Parish Committees were re-appointed each year but, in the main, there were never any changes unless someone died or retired voluntarily. This was certainly the situation at Whitton and the above persons were members of the Whitton Parochial Committee for many years.
> The Village of the Carlton Ironworks had no Parochial Committee of its own and was not represented on the Whitton Parochial Committee which, in consequence, meant they had no representative at the meetings of the Guardians.

In 1872 the Guardians also began acting as the Rural Sanitary authority of the Stockton Union and, from this juncture, they took on the responsibility of trying to ensure that all buildings in their district were fit for habitation and that adequate drains and sewers were installed. An Inspector of Nuisances was appointed, who would scour the district for any nuisance and report back to the Rural Sanitary Authority, who had the power to order the nuisance to be abated. A Medical Officer of Health was also appointed to oversee all health hazards within the district and advise on action to be taken during epidemics.

A planning committee, comprising all the Guardians, was formed to check all plans of new buildings or extensions which had to be submitted to ensure adherence to local by-laws and for the Guardians' approval.

The formation of this new authority meant that the directors of the ironworks now had to submit the plans of any new houses they were to build in the Village of the Carlton Ironworks to the Rural Sanitary Authority of the Stockton Union and be prepared for the inspection of their houses by the Inspector of Nuisances and to abide by his decisions on drainage and sanitation.

1872 July – Company purchase more land

The North of England Industrial Iron and Coal Company purchased 37 acres of land adjoining Moor Closes. The land was bought from Mr Anthony Wilkinson for £150 per acre.

The planned usage of this land was to allow more area for the tipping of slag and the eventual building of more workmen's houses.

1872 December – West Street and South Street

Because of the need for more workers to operate the third blast furnace, which was about to be commissioned, and the malleable works now being erected, the directors of the North of England Industrial Iron and Coal Company decided to proceed with additions and alterations to the Lodging House and the building of additional cottages. The cottages, already under construction, were 30 workmen's houses and one larger house in West Street and 16 houses in South Street.

West Street was built in two terraces comprising 16 and 15 houses with a central gap forming a roadway. The larger house, number 17, was built as the residence of a work's foreman, or some other staff member, and was situated at the top of the bottom terrace. Each house had a back yard with a coalhouse and privy. There were no gardens and shared water points were positioned in the street. The front of the houses faced west thus the name West Street.

South Street comprised 16 terraced houses similar in style and facilities to those in West Street. The downstairs of No. 10 was set aside for use as a chapel and therefore the adjoining houses were allotted the upstairs rooms. Chapel services were held at No. 10 until the chapel was built in 1884. South Street was so called because the front of the houses faced south.

1873 Mount Pleasant

Mount Pleasant was also built at this time and comprised six terraced houses, two large and four small. All were superior in quality, with a larger living area than the houses previously built in the village, and were built to accommodate senior personnel from the ironworks.

These houses had spacious back yards, each with its own water point, and the front of the houses looked out onto a field which ran down to the beck. This field

South Street: Built in 1872/73, South Street comprised 16 houses. The photograph taken in 1900, shows the end house in the process of being modified to provide suitable premises for Mr Thomas Fawcett, who had just been promoted as Company Secretary to the Carlton Iron Company. The house was almost doubled in size and was given two bay windows facing west and looking onto a newly laid fenced lawn which extended to form a line with West Street. When Mr Fawcett vacated the house it became used as a doctor's house and surgery until 1954, and then again for a period in the 1980s. The chapel built in 1884 is shown on the left of the photograph with West Street visible on the extreme left, Redmarshall Street and Kirk Street were not yet built. The ground upon which South Street was built has obviously been levelled to take off the natural slope of the land and the consequential drop at the front of the street was eventually buttressed by a thick concrete wall.

Top part of West Street: Photograph taken around 1900, shows houses numbered one to sixteen of West Street which was built in 1872/73. The Royal Hotel, built in 1876, is at the top of the street with the railway crossing just beyond and the signal box in the background. The village policeman, Mr John Metcalfe, lived in number 11 where the police insignia can been seen above the door. The road was not made up and remained in an unmetalled state until the 1950s.

Bottom part of West Street: Photograph, taken around 1900, shows houses numbered 17–31 of West Street that were built in 1872/73. The top house was originally number 17, which had an ornate front door surround, a larger house than the remainder built for a senior member of the ironworks. In 1874 the Cooperative Society were allowed to build a store with accommodation above adjoining number 17 and this is what the photograph shows. At the bottom of West Street, but not adjoining, is the Cassidi Hall and further down the pump house, which pumped water from the beck to the works. What appears to be a building to the left of the pump house is an unknown facility but may possibly have been the first pump house now replaced but not yet demolished.

Mount Pleasant (built c. 1873)

This photograph of Mount Pleasant, taken in 1998, shows almost the full extent of the original buildings. The end house on the right was where the first village doctor, Dr Bonnar, lived and held surgery. The photograph, taken from the garden of one of the smaller houses, shows that the houses have been extensively modernised with most of the original windows and doors replaced.

was later divided between the houses to provide them with large front gardens about 30 yards long.

When Mount Pleasant was built the two end houses were almost double the size of the other four, but when a new company secretary was appointed in 1878, numbers 3 and 4 were combined to make a suitable residence for him. This resulted in there being only five houses in the terrace, three large and two smaller.

As the name would suggest, Mount Pleasant was built on the side of a hill with the front of the houses facing west and overlooking the beck with pleasant countryside beyond.

> Dr Bonnar, the first doctor to live in the village, resided at 1 Mount Pleasant where he had a 'lean-to' built on to the gable end for use as a surgery. He was born in Scotland and came to the village in 1873 at the age of 28 and retired around 1908, when he moved to Whitton.

1873 Stable Row (later to become Office Row)

Stable Row was built adjoining a stable which had been on the site since 1870.

The stable had two stalls for the use of horses belonging to the ironworks with room for all the necessary equipment and carts.

Stable Row comprised three small houses, each having a back yard with the normal facilities for the period. Water was available from a shared stand pipe.

The exact date that these houses were built is not recorded although two facts are clear, they were not built in 1872 but were fully occupied in 1881. The 1881 census gives a clue to the date of erection by stating that one of Stable Row's resident families, (the Snowballs), had children aged 8, 6 and 2, all of whom were born in the Village of the Carlton Iron Works.

Making the presumption that all three children were born in Stable Row this would give 1873 as the date the row was built.

1873 Public House

In March the managing director of the ironworks was 'empowered to act' in the immediate erection of a public house but, despite this statement, no action was taken until 1876.

1873 June – Third blast furnace commissioned

The directors of the North of England Industrial Iron and Coal Company reported that the third blast furnace had been successfully brought into operation and that the malleable iron works were almost complete.

1873 Third issue of Shares

The North of England Industrial Iron and Coal Company issued another 5,000 ordinary shares at £10 each and 250 Debenture Shares at £100 each. The primary need for this money was to complete the malleable works, finance the development of a new coal seam and to erect new coke ovens at East Howle.

Charges on the leaseholds of South Belmont and Ailesbury ironstone mines were also due, making it imperative that more money was available to help the cash flow situation. The need for this money was especially urgent because the iron trade was currently unprofitable, with the price available for pig iron and manufactured iron having fallen by thirty shillings a ton during the previous six months.

1874 Feb 26th – The Cassidi Hall

The North of England Industrial Iron and Coal Company agreed to lease a plot of land to the Reverend William Cassidi, vicar of Grindon and the Reverend John Allen Parker, vicar of Stillington Parish, upon which they organised the building of a Mission House. The Mission House was situated approximately 20ft from, and directly in line with, the bottom of West Street and was named the Cassidi Hall. On completion, the hall was used for Sunday Services, Baptisms and Sunday School whilst part of the hall was used as a Library/Reading Room on Friday and Tuesday evenings.

A plan accompanying the lease showed that the North of England Industrial Iron and Coal Company had planned to build Lowson Street in the position where

The Mission House later known as The Cassidi Hall
The Mission House was built at the bottom of West Street on land leased from the North of England Industrial Iron and Coal Company and was later named the Cassidi Hall after its founder, the Reverend William Cassidi, vicar of Grindon. The sketch shows the hall in its original form, the extension which made the Cassidi Hall an L-shaped building was added some 10 years later.

Kirk Street was eventually sited and that the Cassidi Hall was initially a rectangular building 52ft 6ins long by 22ft 6ins wide.

1874 April – The Cooperative Stores

The North of England Industrial Iron and Coal Company leased a small plot of land to the Cooperative movement on which they built a Cooperative Stores. The term of the lease was 21 years and allowed the company to buy back the land and the property for a reasonable price after 7 or 14 years. The Cooperative Stores adjoined the large house at the top of the bottom half of West Street and included living accommodation above the store for the manager. There was a large cellar under the store and a back yard with the usual facilities.

> The Cooperative Stores occupied these premises until 1935 when they moved to Morrison Terrace.
> The property remained empty for many years but was re-opened as a shop in the 1950s and is still in use as a general dealers.

1874 Expansion of the Malleable Iron Works

The prospect of improved profits from the production of malleable iron persuaded the directors of the North of England Industrial Iron and Coal Company to expand this facet of their business in order to increase production capacity. The expansion would include the purchase of four additional Danks' puddling furnaces and the erection of two plate mills to produce plates for use in the shipbuilding industry.

1874 The Plate Mills

Tenders were invited for the erection of the two plate mills and Thomas Kirk of Kirk Brothers, ironmakers of Workington, was awarded the contract based on an estimated cost of £33,995. The 22 inch mill was to be completed first at a cost of £21,070.

The plate mills were housed in a building which became a familiar sight to the village folk, with its high corrugated sheeting roof of two semi circular spans, stretching back from the road approximately 60 yards with each semi circle spanning a width of 20 yards. The roof extended 30ft beyond the front face of the main building with three 12 inch diameter cast iron columns supporting it. This gave an area of open ground ahead of the building, but sheltered by the roof of 30ft by 120ft, and the children of the village used this as an excellent all-weather play area. All kinds of games were played here when the weather was inclement, including football, cricket and even cycle speedway, for which the columns made ideal track markers.

> This building became better known as the Blacking Mill when the Carlton Iron Company leased it to Thomas Wilkinson and Son for the purpose of manufacturing foundry blacking in 1912.

Plate Mills/Blacking Mill

Built in 1874 and fitted with two plate mills and all the ancillary plant necessary for the manufacture of plates for the shipbuilding industry. The plate mills never came into commercial use because of the slump in the iron and steel industry and the building and some plant were eventually leased to Thomas Wilkinson in 1912 for the purpose of producing foundry blacking. The building was 60 yards long by 40 yards wide with the front of the roof extending about 30ft beyond the main building. The roof comprised two large semicircular sections made from corrugated sheeting and supported by structural steel. The cost of the original mill was £30,000. The sketch depicts the compiler's memory of the building.c. 1945.

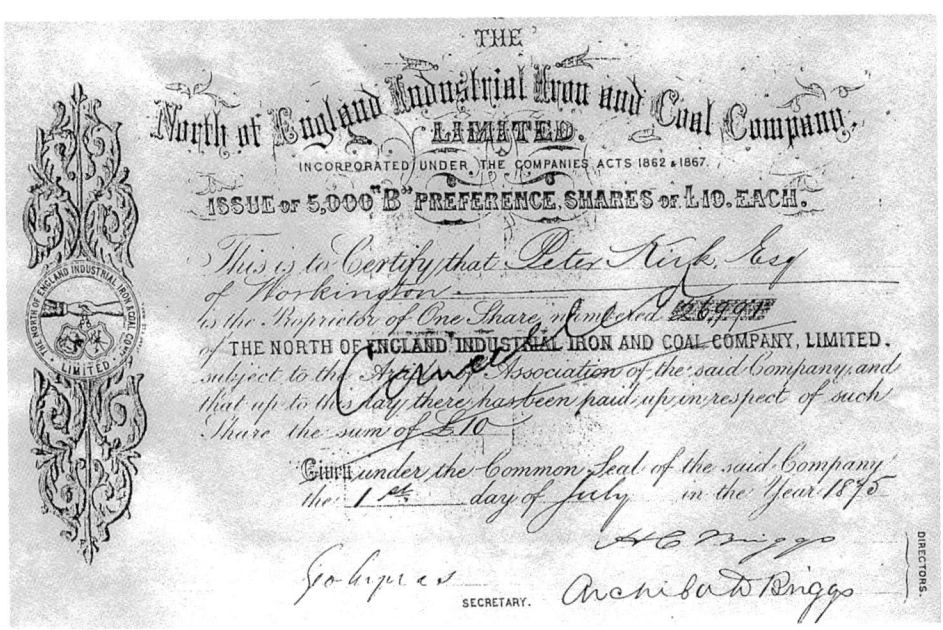

Preference Shares

The North of England Industrial Iron and Coal Co. needed money desperately and to attract more shareholders they issued preference shares that hold preference when dividend is paid. They were offered with a promise of 10% dividend per annum. Above is shown a copy of a Preference Share, note the logo on the side of the certificate now showing the handshake denoting the company's profit sharing scheme.

1874 June – More capital raised by a second mortgage

A second mortgage was obtained on the land and plant of the North of England Industrial Iron and Coal Company for the sum of £10,000 loaned by Captain Hill at an annual rate of interest of 5%.

1874 Cash flow problems

Despite the money raised through the second mortgage, lack of available finance was still a problem for the North of England Industrial Iron and Coal Company, and they were forced to raise a substantial amount by:
(a) the allotment of Debenture Bonds costing £100 each promising an annual rate of interest of 6%, and
(b) an issue of 5,000 'B' or Preference Shares costing £10 each and offering a 10% dividend per annum.

The directors hoped these actions would enable them to raise another £50,000.

> It should be noted that the directors themselves invested heavily in the company, especially Walter Morrison who, apart from buying shares, had recently advanced the company a £5,000 loan that was later converted to Debenture Bonds.

1874 July – School Board formed

Dignitaries associated with the Village of the Carlton Ironworks elected a school board to represent the United District of Whitton and Stillington with the eventual aim of building a village school. This was probably the consequence of the Elementary Education Act of 1870 that had given elected school boards the power to claim money from the local authority to help finance schools under their jurisdiction. The chairman of the School Board was Mr H C Briggs, chairman and managing director of the North of England Industrial Iron and Coal Company, with Reverend John Allen Parker as Vice Chairman. Other members included Thompson Gibbon, Clark Nesom (both local farmers) and Mr Worton a manager at the works. Mr Martin Best was appointed Clerk to the Board, at £15 per annum, and Police Constable Murdy became Warden to the Board, whose duties included visiting parents whose children were not attending school regularly. PC Murdy left the district and was replaced by PC Waitman.

1874 Temporary School organised in Ironworks Lodging House

The School Board proceeded to organise the opening of a school by seeking temporary premises, prior to building a new school in the village. The Rev Cassidi had been asked for his permission to use the Reading Room in the Mission House (Cassidi Hall) until such time as a school was built, but later the Board decided that the space offered by Rev Cassidi was not sufficient for the purpose, and Mr Briggs' offer of four rooms at the Workman's Home (The Lodging House), would be accepted. It must be presumed that the houses already built in the village had created vacancies in the Lodging House thus making this offer possible. The removal of partitions and other modifications, such as extra ventilation and the fitting of a new stove, would be costed to the School Board. Equipment was ordered that included four desks 9ft long at a cost of four shillings and sixpence per foot.

Having got the school premises and major equipment organised, the School Board placed an advert in the national and local papers asking for applications for the post of Headmaster. As well as the usual requirements, the advert also asked that the headmaster's wife or sister be capable of taking a sewing class and that a knowledge of singing was desirable. The salary quoted in the advert was £90 per annum, plus free house and coal and one-third of the Government Grant. The amount of Government Grant received depended on the number of pupils attending, the general condition of the school and the performance of the pupils when inspected by the authorised inspector.

Modified Lodging House used as temporary school
This sketch shows the Lodging House after it had been modified in 1873 to accommodate more workmen who were needed when the third furnace was commissioned. Notice the addition of the water storage on the roof. In 1874 the first school in the village was set up using four rooms of the Lodging House as temporary premises until the school was built in Lowson Street in 1877. Later more rooms were made available and a new toilet built to avert the school inspector stopping the Government Grant because of overcrowding and lack of sanitation. Immediately prior to the new school opening, 100 children were attending this temporary school.

1874 Danks' puddling furnaces fail to function

The North of England Industrial Iron and Coal Company suffered a major setback to the completion of their malleable iron works when it was found that the Danks' puddling furnaces were failing to function satisfactorily in their original form. They were having to be substantially modified at a great deal of extra cost in time, labour and money.

1875 January 11th – Temporary School opens

Mr Thomas Fenton of Huddersfield had been appointed headmaster and was removed from Huddersfield and rehoused in the village ready for the opening of the school on January 11th 1875. The School Board prepared a case for claiming a precept of £80 a year from the local overseers and the children were charged 3d a week for under-sevens and 4d a week for over-sevens. The government grant would also be forthcoming when the school achieved the required standard to pass the inspectorate.

Mrs Stephenson, the appointed cleaner, was paid three shillings a week to clean the school rooms.

The White House *Photograph taken 1988*
Built for the Residential Works Manager in 1875 and converted to the Company Offices when he vacated in 1878. An area at the rear of the house was retained as living accommodation. At this time, Stable Row became Office Row, with the White House accommodation becoming No. 1.

1875 Thomas Kirk comes to the area

Thomas Kirk, an experienced ironmaker, had been awarded the contract to build the rolling mills for the North of England Industrial Iron and Coal Company and, as part of his contract, he was to take charge of the production of all the company's malleable iron business for a period of not less than seven years.

Under these circumstances, he decided to remove from Workington and come to reside in Stockton, and so began a long and important association between the Kirk family and the Village of the Carlton Ironworks.

1875 The White House

The White House was built close to the goods yard on the north side of the Clarence Railway a few yards south of Stable Row. The White House was a big detached residence with double fronted bay windows facing south and a walled garden at the front and east side of the house. The yard was at the rear of the building with privy, coalhouse and water point included.

The directors of the North of England Industrial Iron and Coal Company had given their residential manager, Mr Worton, permission to build this house on land owned by the company. In the event of him leaving the company's employment, they would buy the house from him at a reasonable price. Mr Worton was appointed in 1872 and left the company in 1878.

The name, White House, was probably derived from the fact that the outside of the house has always been painted white.

1875 South Belmont Ironstone Mine

The quality and production of ironstone from the South Belmont Mine had deteriorated so badly that the North of England Industrial Iron and Coal Company terminated the lease by giving the required twelve months' notice.

1875 January – Railway Cottages and Goods Yard

The North of England Industrial Iron and Coal Company sold land to the North Eastern Railway Company upon which they built Railway Cottages and created a goods yard. The goods yard included warehouse facilities and was sited adjacent to the boarding halt. Its construction would indicate that a substantial amount of mineral and freight business was now being transacted at the Village of the Carlton Ironworks.

Railway Cottages comprised four houses, one of which was larger than the others.

They were built close to and on the south side of the Clarence Railway, about 80 yards east of the passenger halt. The large house, initially the residence of the station master, was detached from the other three houses and was self-contained with four bedrooms and a large yard housing a privy, an ashpit, a coalhouse and a water tap.

The other three houses had no yard and their facilities were in outbuildings in the back street. All the houses had adequate back gardens at this time, but these were lost when the railway was widened c. 1884.

1875 New School and School House planned

The school inspector acting on behalf of the government (who allotted the grants to help finance schools), reported that unless general conditions were improved at the village school no further grants could be recommended. The School Board reacted by advancing their plans to build a new school and when Mr Davison refused to sell land for this purpose The North of England Industrial Iron and Coal Company gave them half an acre that had previously been named 'Fattening Pasture'. The School Board henceforth requested tenders to be submitted for the building of a school and school house for the headmaster. These were received from John Perks, £2,014; Geo Lazenby, £1900 and Robert Stephenson, £1,170 for the school and £360 for the school house. The Lowson Street school and the school house were eventually built on this land in 1877 by George Lazenby who had reduced his price to £1,700.

1875 New Vicar for Stillington Parish

John Allen Parker died and Thomas Varley succeeded him as vicar of Stillington Parish and also as a member of the school board.

1875 The Danks' puddling furnaces modified

Specialist modifications were made to the puddling furnaces under instructions which had been patented by a Mr Crampton from Workington. The North of England Industrial Iron and Coal Company paid the necessary fee in order to carry out these modifications under license. The changes failed to bring the furnaces into a workable condition and Mr Thomas Kirk had to redesign and supervise further modifications before the puddling furnaces were able to function as intended. Mr Kirk was very angry with Danks and Crampton, both of whom were licensing designs which did not fulfil their claims, and he wrote to Crampton criticising his patented modifications in great detail.

The delay caused by these malfunctions denied the North of England Industrial Iron and Coal Company a place in the forefront of the malleable iron industry and were ultimately to prove very costly indeed to the shareholders.

To further assist in the production of high quality malleable iron, the company bought a nine and a half ton steam forging hammer to supplement the plant already existing in the malleable works.

1875 Mr W Lowson and Mr R A Hardcastle

Mr Lowson, one of the original directors of the North of England Industrial Iron and Coal Company, who lived in Dundee, resigned from the board of directors because of the long distances he was required to travel to attend meetings etc. Mr R A Hardcastle also resigned his position on the board. Mr Hodgetts and Mr Mcgowan were appointed as board members to replace Lowson and Hardcastle.

1875 June – 50 more houses

Mr H C Briggs, Managing Director of the North of England Industrial Iron and Coal Company was given authority, by the board, to arrange for the erection of 50 more houses in the Village of the Carlton Ironworks. These were necessary to accommodate the increasing numbers of workmen required by the ironworks and were to become the first thirteen houses to be built in Lowson Street and the first thirty seven to be built in Morrison Street.

Briggs arranged to buy the houses himself with the intention of leasing them to the company at a fixed annual rent and, in accordance with this, he drew up an agreement which received board approval.

1876 January – Shops, Hotel and Workingmen's Club

With the village expanding and the population growing, the North of England Industrial Iron and Coal Company urgently needed to improve the available amenities and arranged for the building of an hotel, a workingmen's club and three shops. They sold 3,540 square yards of land to a builder named Stephenson

A view of Morrison Terrace showing the Workingmen's Club with a double bay windowed frontage.

at a price of two shillings per square yard upon which he immediately commenced building the Royal Hotel and Morrison Terrace.

Morrison Terrace

Morrison Terrace, named after Walter Morrison, a director of the North of England Industrial Iron and Coal Company, comprised four properties, a workingmen's club and three shops.

The Workingmen's Club built on the corner site of Morrison Terrace, was a place where the workmen of the village could go and relax and enjoy the varied facilities provided. On the ground floor there was a billiard room, a bagatelle room, a snug and a club room where dances and other functions could be held. The first floor had six rooms which were used as living accommodation, initially for the steward of the club. A large yard at the rear of the building was enclosed by a high wall, which not only held the usual facilities such as a coalhouse and two privies, but also stables and a covered area where carts could be stored. Access to a large cellar was also available in the yard.

> When the ironworks closed in 1930 the building was used as a library until c. 1935 when it was taken over by the Cooperative Society and converted into one of their stores.

Morrison Terrace built in 1876, was named after Walter Morrison, a director of the North of England Industrial Iron and Coal Company, and comprised four properties, a workingmen's club and three shops with accommodation. The workingmen's club bcame the Cooperative stores in 1935. The photograph, taken around 1900, shows the size and proximity of the slag heap to good effect.

The other three units in Morrison Terrace were purpose built as shops with living accommodation, all had backyards with the usual facilities but no gardens. The water point for all of these premises was in the yard of the clubhouse.

1876 Lowson Street (initially named Church Street) and Morrison Street

These streets were named after William Lowson and Walter Morrison, directors of the North of England Industrial Iron and Coal Company. Lowson Street was initially named Church Street, but was later renamed to commemorate the work that William Lowson had given the company before leaving in 1875.

Thirteen houses were built in Lowson Street and thirty seven in Morrison Street, with the top of each street starting level with the other. Both streets were built in terraces running parallel to each other with a narrow back alley separating them. Morrison Street ended the width of an alley from the back of Morrison Terrace and perpendicular to it.

Residents shared strategically positioned water taps but eventually had water installed into each household.

All houses had a backyard with coalhouse and privy. They had no gardens but there was plenty of scope for allotments and 'places'.

Morrison Terrace
This photograph taken around 1920, shows that Morrison Terrace had been modified by having a tapered segment taken fron the end of the corner shop. The entrance to the shop had now had to be positioned at the side of the premises instead of the front. This modification was probably carried out to give a smoother and wider curve to the main road as it turned towards Carlton Bridge.

'Places' were set up by many of the menfolk who gained permission from the company to fence off an area of waste land, generally close to the slag heap, within which they would build a shed from wood and corrugated sheeting to house birds or animals. The 'places' were roughly built, with no regular shape or size and, when the corrugated sheeting began to rust, the area took on the look of a shanty town and the food being scattered for hens, pigeons and other livestock attracted rats. However the places afforded both the men and women of the village a great deal of pleasure and the animals and hens housed therein were, in some cases, a vital source of food supplement during times of unemployment and poverty.

These first houses in Lowson Street and Morrison Street were built in conjunction with each other and were completed at the beginning of 1881.

1875–77 Building of the viaduct at Thorpe Thewles

The viaduct carrying the Stockton to Castle Eden railway was built at Thorpe Thewles at this time.

Eight million bricks were used in its construction with the final cost being calculated to be £37,000.

Many casual workers were employed on this massive project, the majority of whom lived in temporary accommodation adjacent to the site. Their habitat followed the progress of the line, therefore any impact on the permanent population of Thorpe Thewles and its surrounding areas was minimal.

1876 May 24th
Archibald Briggs resigns – Thomas Kirk appointed as director

Archibald Briggs resigned as a director of the North of England Industrial Iron and Coal Company because of his wife's illness. He had been advised by the doctor to take her abroad to find a warmer climate and cleaner air.

Thomas Kirk was elected on to the board of directors as his replacement.

1876 The Plate Mills and malleable iron production on hold

The Plate Mills were complete and all heavy machinery installed. However, because of a depression within the industry, the use of the plate mills and the manufacture of malleable iron were put on hold.

The board of the North of England Industrial Iron and Coal Company were confident of an upturn in the iron and coal trades and made all preparations necessary in order to take full advantage of that situation when it occurred.

1876 Diversion of footpath

A long-standing double hedged footpath named Gypsy Lane, which ran from the railway crossing near the passenger halt diagonally across to the bottom of the Spring Field and on to Thorpe Thewles, needed to be diverted to allow an expansion of the slag tipping area.

The North of England Industrial Iron and Coal Company were granted permission to divert the path to a route that took it down the Black Bank, running parallel to the Clarence Railway then eastward behind the Little School to a stile at the top of the Spring Field. The path then followed the perimeter of the Spring Field to the stile leading to Swan's Lane, where it rejoined its normal route to Thorpe Thewles.

1876 September – Condition of school improved

Conditions in the original school rooms at the Lodging House were becoming totally unsuitable and insanitary for the number of children now attending school. As the North of England Industrial Iron and Coal Company were not using the Lodging House at this time, because work was at a low ebb and there were plenty of houses available to accommodate the workmen, they were able, in conjunction with the School Board, to arrange a new set of more spacious school rooms inside the Lodging House and also built a new outside toilet facility.

The children moved to their improved facilities in September 1886 with the headmaster being given a private room. The monitor, Joseph Robinson, who had commenced duties in August 1875 was moving towards becoming a Pupil Teacher.

The School Board now comprised: Thos Kirk, Chairman; Thos Varley, Vice Chairman; Thompson Hopps; John D Pipe; Dr T W Bonnar and Anthony Stephenson. They were hoping that this move would satisfy the inspectorate until the new school was built and so retain the grant. An extract taken from the school log book, September 1886, in which the headmaster wrote 'Great difficultly in getting girls from Slag Row into school at proper time, they excuse themselves by saying they cannot cross the railway line because of an engine standing', would suggest that using the Lodging House as school premises had become highly dangerous because of the network of lines leading to and from the furnaces.

1876 December
Mr Henry Currer Briggs resigns as Managing Director of the North of England Industrial Iron and Coal Company. Mr Thomas Kirk appointed to fill the vacancy

Mr Briggs resigned as Managing Director of the North of England Industrial Iron and Coal Company due to pressure of work. He remained as a director and Chairman of the Board. Mr Thomas Kirk was confirmed as the new Managing Director at the Half Yearly meeting of company shareholders on 18th January 1877.

1876 December – Invoice for erection of Plate Mills received

Kirk Brothers invoiced the North of England Industrial Iron and Coal Company for the erection of the plate mills and roofing. The roofing was additional because, during the erection of the building, a severe gale had blown all the corrugated sheeting from the roof. The invoice for £27,000 was accepted and passed by the board.

1877 January – Morrison Terrace completed

Mr Stephenson, the builder, completed Morrison Terrace and passed ownership of the Workingmen's Club to the North of England Industrial Iron and Coal Company.

He retained the ownership of the shops and, for several years leased them to interested clients, before finally selling them to the ironworks after many years of negotiation regarding the sale price.

1877 January – The Royal Hotel

The North of England Industrial Iron and Coal Company leased the Royal Hotel to John Redshaw for a term of 14 years, at a fixed annual rental of £52.

The lease documents included a plan which gave the area covered by the Royal Hotel and grounds as 750 square yards. A note on the plan denoted a 'Brick Field' to the east and adjacent to the hotel yard, thus confirming that the clay quarry had now extended almost to the Clarence Railway and was still being operated.

From the records it appears that Redshaw was declared bankrupt in 1878, and a brewery agent from Sunderland took over the lease. Redshaw remained as manager, presumably working for the brewery.

View of the Royal Hotel from the railway crossing.

The Royal Hotel: Built by the North of England Iron and Coal Company in 1876 to accommodate the businessmen who were visiting the ironworks.
photo taken 1998

1877 January 18th – Company name changed

Having found the previous name cumbersome and giving no indication of the location of the principal works, the Board of Directors decided to change the name of the company from:

THE NORTH OF ENGLAND INDUSTRIAL IRON & COAL COMPANY
to
THE CARLTON IRON COMPANY LIMITED

Approval of this change was obtained at the Half Yearly Meeting of the shareholders.
   The directors of the company did not change and were:
   Henry Currer Briggs, Esq., Chairman, Belvedere, Harrogate
   Thomas Kirk, Esq., Managing Director, West Villas, Stockton
   Walter Morrison, Esq., JP, Malham Tarn, Yorkshire
   Alfred Hodgetts, Esq., St. Bees, Carnforth
   John Stevenson McGowan, Esq., Whitehaven

1877 March – School and School House

The Carlton Iron Company finalised the conveyance of land, upon which the new school was being built, to the School Board of the United District of Whitton.

Lowson Street School
Opened in October 1877 when the first houses in Lowson Street and Morrison Street were still under construction.

School House
Built in 1877 as accommodation for the headmaster of the Lowson Street school. Sited adjacent to the top of the school yard.

The company subscribed £50 to the building fund and later agreed to help the School Board pay back the money they had borrowed to finance the building of the school. The company agreed to pay a minimum of one half of the amounts payable in instalments due to the interest and principal repayments.

The School Board ordered that the school and school house be completed within four months of this date and that members of the board should provide

Classroom in Lowson Street School
This classroom was used for Standard One and infant pupils. The room size was 28ft by 20ft with an officially approved capacity of 60 pupils. In 1885 the inspector's report stated that the average number in the class was 65, with as many as 105 children being crowded into the classroom on the day of his visit. This resulted in the Cassidi Hall being brought into use as a school later that year for the infants and Standard One pupils.

horses and carts to the contractor at not more than 8 shillings per day to assist completion. (The school opened in October).

The total site was just less than half an acre and gave ample room for the school, two play yards and a good sized house with rear garden and lawn for the headmaster. All were enclosed within a brick wall perimeter.

1877 July – Storage of pig iron

Due to the continued fall in demand for pig iron, the directors of the Carlton Iron Company decided that, in order to avoid the heavy cost incurred by 'blowing out' a furnace, they would buy and store the pig iron themselves.

4,000 square yards of the company's land, just north of the ironworks, was leased to the directors to use as a storage area for the pig iron they bought.

1877 October – Consecration of burial ground

An area of land above Lowson Street and Morrison Street was consecrated by the Bishop of Durham to allow burials to take place in the village. The burial of people from the Village of the Carlton Ironworks had previously been carried out at Redmarshall or Bishopton. St John's church was built on the site of the burial ground in 1880.

1877 25th October – New School opens

The new school in Lowson Street opened on Thursday, 25th October, with approximately 110 pupils attending. Mr Fenton, the headmaster, and Joseph Robinson, a pupil teacher, were the only staff although a new pupil teacher, Miss Margaret Palmer, aged fifteen, commenced in January 1878.

This was the first purpose-built school in the village and comprised a small classroom, 28ft by 20ft, and a large room which could be used as a hall or divided into two classrooms, 28ft by 20ft and 30ft by 20ft. A sliding panelled partition was fitted at a later stage which made the division of the hall a quick and easy operation.

Other facilities included a teacher's room, 15ft by 14ft, two cloakrooms, one for boys and one for girls, both fitted with wash basins and a water fountain and six outside privies, three for the boys and three for girls.

Classrooms were heated by large open fires housed in an ornate black cast iron casing and protected by metal fireguards which were firmly secured to the wall. The school was well built and is still a fine looking building, although it ceased to function as a school in 1959, and is now used as the village hall.

1877 December – Another financial crisis for the Carlton Iron Company

In order to keep the company viable and ready for the expected upturn in the demand for pig iron, the directors of the Carlton Iron Company urgently needed more capital and took the following actions to attain it.

(1) They applied to the banks for an increase in the borrowing power of the company. The figure required as an allowable overdraft was £35,000. This request could only be granted if the shareholders agreed to change the borrowing power of the company to one-half instead of one-quarter of the paid-up capital of the company. The shareholders agreed.

(2) They appealed to shareholders to purchase Debenture Bonds at £100 each up to a total of £10,000. If this figure was reached the directors would contribute a similar sum. It took several appeals and even threats of liquidation from the directors before the shareholders finally agreed to take up the offer in June 1878.

1877 Thinford Colliery

The Carlton Iron Company organised a lease which enabled them to mine coal at the Thinford colliery. This was a contingency measure because the severe flooding which had occurred at their East Howle colliery was proving very difficult to contain, even with extra pumping equipment.

1878 June
The White House becomes the offices of the Carlton Iron Company

The offices of the company were removed from No. 3 Exchange Place, Middlesbrough to the White House in the Village of the Carlton Ironworks. The White House, which had originally been built for Mr Worton, the company's residential manager, and had been vacated by him a little earlier in the year, was considered ideal for the purpose and has been used as office accommodation ever since.

A small living quarter was retained at the rear of the house for the accommodation of a staff member and became No. 1 Office Row. This would probably be the time that the address of the 3 houses adjacent to the White House was changed from Stable Row to Office Row.

1878 Typhoid fever in the Village

An outbreak of typhoid fever in the Village of the Carlton Ironworks was reported to the board by the managing director of the Carlton Iron Company, and they authorised a sum of up to £20 to bring relief to sufferers.

Water from the River Tees had been responsible for the outbreak of typhoid in Stockton and Middlesbrough, and similarly polluted water from the beck was deemed responsible for the outbreak in the village. The Medical Officer of Health, who was employed by the Guardians of the Poor of the Stockton Union, an organisation which also acted as the Rural Sanitary Authority, had reported that the Board School and headmaster's house had no proper water supply and the school was to be closed until the School Board could rectify the situation. The Carlton Iron Company made arrangements to procure water from a Mr Wilson, whom it is assumed had a well somewhere near the works. Several weeks later, the company were served with a notice from the Medical Officer instructing them to lay a water pipe from a well to their domestic supply system.

> The Ordnance Survey map of 1857 shows that the nearest well to the works was situated just beyond and west of the bottom corner of the Spring Field. By 1894 the well had been covered by the ever increasing fringe of the slag heap.

Dr Bonnar, the local doctor during the epidemic, was presented with a certificate by the committee of the Carlton Iron Works Sick Club in appreciation of his efforts during the crisis.

1878 New company secretary

Mr Hoggett was appointed company secretary to the Carlton Iron Company in place of Mr George Lynas. This in itself is of no great historical interest, but it affected the village in a minor way when, as part of his remuneration, Mr Hoggett received an annual salary of £200 and rent free use of a house. The house was situated in Mount Pleasant and Mr Hoggett was regarded with such esteem that the company arranged to have numbers 3 and 4 Mount Pleasant modified to make one house instead of two, and so afford him 'suitable' accommodation.

1879 February – Guardians of the poor of the Stockton Union

At a special meeting of the Guardians of the Poor of the Stockton Union, acting as the Rural Sanitary Authority of the Stockton Union, held at the Board Room, Exchange Buildings, Nelson Terrace, Stockton it was resolved all powers and duties of the Guardians as the Rural Sanitary Authority be delegated for the current year to a committee. The committee to consist of the ex-officio Guardians of the Union, plus the elected guardians from several Rural Parishes, and the following elected guardians for the Township of Stockton:- Joseph Dodds, William Bonnington, John Trotter, Thomas Nelson and J. Hunton. Clark Nesom of Whitton was elected onto this committee.

The Engine Shed
Built around 1880 by the Carlton Iron Company, the shed was still standing in 1998.

1879 January – Foundation stone of the church laid

The school closed on January 23rd 1879 to allow the holding of a luncheon where dignitaries of the church and invited guests could celebrate the laying of the church foundation stone.

1879 November 1st – Original Stillington station closed

The original Stillington station closed and all business transferred to the passenger halt in the Village of the Carlton Iron Works. The station's name of Stillington was also transferred to the passenger halt and the site of the original station became known as Stillington Weigh, with the two cottages situated there being named Weigh Cottages. The weighing machine at Stillington Weigh continued to be used for several years but eventually became obsolete and was removed. Weigh Cottages continued to house railway personnel until around 1942, when they were in such a state of disrepair that they were abandoned.

1879 August – New headmaster appointed

During the summer holidays Mr Fenton had been asked to resign and so, after the summer holidays, a new headmaster, Mr Thomas Kirtley, took charge of the school and took up residence in the school house. There had been no indication of this new appointment before the holidays and no explanation of the change given in the school log book. However, the school inspector had been very critical of the children's academic capabilities in his annual report and had threatened to recommend withholding the school grant unless there was an improvement. The loss of grant was a serious matter, and the School Board decided to be seen to rectify the problem by relieving Mr Fenton of his post.

This decision was very harsh on Mr Fenton, who had struggled manfully during the past few years in unsatisfactory surroundings and with virtually no physical help in the teaching of in excess of 100 children. Mr Fenton was given a reference, so the Board must have had some sympathy towards him.

1880 St John's church

The church, dedicated to St John, was erected on the hillside to the east of the arch and beyond the top of Morrison Street and Lowson Street. The church was of brick construction with Gothic style stone finishing and a grey slate roof. The interior consisted of a nave, a small side chapel, a vestry and an entrance porch at the west end of the south wall.

The nave was separated from the chapel by an arcade of bays supported upon stone pillars with beautifully carved caps, from which sprang the graceful moulded arches. The combination of stone and brick was employed to good effect and the interior of the church was well-balanced and had both aesthetic and reverential appeal.

St John's Church, Stillington
Consecrated by the Most Reverend Lightfoot, Bishop of Durham on 29th June 1880.

Interior of St John's Church
Photograph shows the interior when oil lamps were still in use.

The pulpit and seats were made from pitch pine and provided seating for over 200 people. A brass eagle lectern was installed as a memorial to those men of the village who died in the 1914–18 war, and this further enhanced the interior of the church.

The stained glass windows at the west and east end of the church were damaged and were replaced, around 1950, with plain glass at the east end and a patterned west window that was dedicated to the men of the village who had died in the 1939–45 war. Artificial light was originally provided by oil lamps but was replaced by electric light around 1930. The cost of the electric light installation was financed by the Kirk family, who also donated the funds with which to convert the lights in the chapel.

The church had a square tower that housed a single bell and supported a pyramid shaped, grey slated steeple with a distinctive weathercock mounted at its apex.

The architects of the church were Alexander and Henman and the total cost of building was £2,800.

The consecration of the church was carried out by the Bishop of Durham, The Most Reverend Lightfoot, on the morning of Tuesday, 29th June 1880, followed by a luncheon in the school.

The first baptism in the church was on July 11th 1880, and the first wedding on July 19th 1880. This was between John Airey of Halifax and Elizabeth Daniels from the village.

Interior of St John's Church c. 1920
Photograph shows that electric lighting has been installed and the brass eagle lectern is in place.

1880 February – Epidemic of measles

More than 60 children were suffering from measles and could not attend school.

The situation worsened and the Medical Officer of Health for the district ordered the School Board to close the school in an attempt to stop the spread of the disease. The school was closed for three weeks.

1880 April – Captain Hill

Captain Hill died and his executors asked for the repayment of the £10,000 mortgage that the Carlton Iron Company had negotiated with Captain Hill in 1874. With the company still in financial difficulty, Mr Morrison repaid the money personally and later negotiated a mortgage agreement with the company for the said amount.

1880 December – Lease of Royal Hotel

Problems relating to John Redshaw's bankruptcy were discussed between the Carlton Iron Company and the trustee in charge of the bankruptcy. The situation was resolved when the trustee agreed that if the existing lease was cancelled a new lease could be granted to any person advancing the money owed to the trustees from that existing lease.

Mr Hodgetts, a director of the Carlton Iron Company, advanced the sum due on the lease and took over a new lease. John Redshaw continued as manager at the Royal Hotel.

1881 Plate mill and malleable iron works to be sold or leased

With the industry still in a depressed state, the directors of the Carlton Iron Company deemed it unlikely that the malleable iron works and the plate mill would ever be used on a production basis. Without the prospect of any other return, it was decided to sell or lease all or any part of this plant and buildings.

At least £50,000 had been invested in these projects on capital expenditure alone. This, added to the cost of the labour involved over the past eight years, meant that the closure of these works amounted to a massive financial blow to the company and shareholders.

1881 Seaton Carew Ironworks

The directors of the Carlton Iron Company bought the failed West Hartlepool Iron Company and formed the Seaton Carew Ironworks.

Thos Kirk was appointed managing director and William Thomlinson was made general manager of these works.

> Thomlinson was to marry Thos Kirk's daughter, Hannah, and live in a house which dominated the green at Seaton Carew and is now converted into the Seaton Hall Hotel. He was a highly skilled ironmaster and very adept in the money market as

well as being a competent linguist. Thomlinson eventually became managing director of both Seaton Carew Ironworks and Carlton Iron Company.

Although Thomlinson was married to Thomas Kirk's daughter his progress through the company was due to his abilities rather than to nepotism. He was very active in other spheres, becoming Deputy Lieutenant of Durham County, and was knighted in 1936.

Part of the work carried out at Seaton Ironworks was a special iron refining process which, in 1926, they decided to close down. Thomlinson was aware of this closure and immediately created a company named the North Eastern Iron Refinery at the Village of the Carlton Ironworks, in order to take over this iron refining process.

This company created much needed employment in the village during the very desperate times of the late 1920s and onwards.

Directors of the North Eastern Iron Refinery, especially the Kirk family, were responsible for many other employment opportunities which took place in the village during the 1940s and 1950s, in particular the formation of Stillington Estates and British Refrasil, so the activities at Seaton Carew which, at first sight seem to be somewhat remote from the Village of the Carlton Ironworks, eventually had a large bearing on the future of the village and the employment of its inhabitants.

1881 Summary of the Village of the Carlton Ironworks

Data from the 1881 census showed that in the ten years since the last census, the number of houses in the village had increased by 123 to a total of 135 and the village now comprised the following:

North Street	18 houses.
West Street	31 houses and one shop with accommodation above.
South Street	16 houses. Downstairs of No 10 was used as a chapel.
Mount Pleasant	5 houses, one of which comprised two original houses combined.
Office Row	3 houses and the accommodation in the White House.
Morrison Terrace	3 shops/houses and Workingmen's Club with accommodation above.
Railway Cottages	4 houses.
Church Street	13 houses. Later to be named Lowson Street.
Morrison Street	37 houses. 23 unoccupied, including the last 15, which suggests that they had only recently been completed.

Other existing buildings and facts

The Royal Hotel, where John Redshaw was the manager, was extensively used by business men visiting the Carlton Iron Company. Wedding receptions and other functions were catered for in the hotel, which also served as the village pub.

School in Lowson Street, and the school house where Mr Kirtley, the headmaster lived.

The Cassidi Hall, used as a Sunday school and village hall.

St. Johns Church had been built and consecrated. The vicarage had not yet been built and Thos Varley, the vicar, was living in the accommodation above the Workingmen's club in Morrison Terrace.

The Rev J A Parker had carried out the duties of vicar since 1872 until just before his death in 1875.

Dr Bonnar was still practising from his surgery in Mount Pleasant, where he had been since around 1873, and had been highly praised for his work during the typhoid epidemic of 1878.

Mr John Dunn Pipe, the station master, lived in 2 Railway Cottages. Station House had not yet been built.

The village also had a local policeman, Thomas Applegarth, who lived in 5 North Street.

Population facts from census:
Total population was 611, comprising :
Adult males 201; Adult females 128; child males 140; child females 142.
These totals included 59 male lodgers, 27 of whom had come from Ireland.
Total number of working males was 192. Working females other than housewives was 14.

Female occupations listed were:
Dressmakers, club keeper, charwomen, general servants, grocer, pupil teacher, milliner's assistant and housekeepers.

Male occupations were mainly connected with the ironworks and included:
Furnace keepers, boiler cleaners, boiler superintendant, smelter men, blast enginemen, engine firemen, blacksmiths, boilermakers, stonemasons, bricklayers, loco drivers and stokers, weighmen, strikers, slaggers, fitters, moulders, engine fitters, patternmakers, cartmen, horsekeeper, draughtsman, engineer, clerks, time clerks, time keepers, commercial clerks, foremen, labourers and a company secretary.

Other occupations not connected with the ironworks were:
Police constable, shoemaker, grocer, draper, publican, railway clerk, porter, platelayers, signalmen, station master, farm labourer, school master, general practitioner and vicar.

Children listed as attending school totalled 144 and although full attendance was rarely achieved, the headmaster and his young assistants, pupil teachers Margaret Palmer and Joseph Robinson, had little chance of giving the children a proper education with such a high pupil/teacher ratio.

1881 Henry Currer Briggs dies

Mr H C Briggs, who with his brother had bought the ironworks in 1870, and had been chairman of the company since that date, died. His achievements should not be forgotten because it was he who, as managing director and chairman of the North of England Industrial Iron and Coal Company, had transformed two outdated blast furnaces into an industrial concern which now had three modern blast furnaces with updated ancillary plant and equipment, owned coal mines, and held leases on ironstone mines.

As well as being a shrewd hard working business man, Briggs cared about his workforce and had built good quality houses for their accommodation at all locations where the company were involved. This was especially the case at the Village of the Carlton Ironworks, where he had not only built houses but a hotel, a workingmen's club and shops, and had allowed the building of the Cassidi Hall on the company's land. As chairman of the School Board, he had helped to initiate the setting up of a school and he and the Carlton Iron Company had greatly assisted in the building and financing of the new school in Lowson Street.

Henry Currer Briggs Esq should be remembered as one of the main pioneers of the Village of the Carlton Ironworks.

1881 Carlton Iron Company appoint a new chairman

The person appointed to fill the vacancy left by the death of H C Briggs was Walter Morrison, who had been a director of the Carlton Iron Company since 1870, and who had invested a lot of his own money into the company. Thomas Kirk was re-appointed as managing director. He had had to change his title from managing director to general manager to satisfy some technical aspect of an earlier reorganisation of the Carlton Iron Company, although he had always retained the same salary and authority.

The Wesleyan Chapel: Built at the end of South Street in 1884, the chapel eventually closed in 1972 through lack of support. Demolished early in 1973.

1882 December – Wesleyan Chapel

The Carlton Iron Company received an application from the Reverend Vowles for the purchase of a building plot to be used for the erection of a chapel in the Village of the Carlton Ironworks. A site was offered at the east end of South Street at a cost of £100 per acre. This was accepted by the chapel trustees

1883 September – Chapel Memorial Stone

Members of the Methodist community celebrated the laying of the Memorial Stone of their new chapel by holding afternoon tea in the school.

1884 June – Wesleyan Chapel

The chapel was built on the plot of land at the end of South Street, which had been purchased by the trustees of the chapel from the Carlton Iron Company for £25. The company gave £25 towards the cost of building. The chapel was capable of holding up to 120 people and was organised and maintained by a group of people appointed as trustees, the first of these being listed below:

Name	Occupation	Address
Robert Robinson Bainbridge	Chemist	Stockton
Hatherstone Nattrass	Corn merchant	Stockton
Benjamin Robinson	Clothier	Stockton
John Wilson Watson	Brickmaker	Stockton
Christopher Bone	unknown	Stockton
Alexander Cameron	Draper	Stockton
Richard Hind	Plumber	Stockton
Arthur Bainbridge	Ironbroker	Stockton
Frederick Raines	Grocer	Stockton
Francis Sanderson	Accountant	Stockton
William Brayshay	Gentleman	Stockton
George J Groves	Draper	Stockton
Ralph Jameson	Accountant	Stockton
Thomas Scurr	Joiner	Village of Carlton Ironworks
John Dunn Pipe	Station master	Village of Carlton Ironworks
Micheal Urwin Mann	Signalman	Village of Carlton Ironworks
Thomas Scurr	Joiner	Village of Carlton Ironworks

Most of the original trustees came from Stockton but in 1896 there was an addition of seven men from the Village of the Carlton Ironworks and two from Stillington.

From the Village of Carlton Ironworks:
David Jacob, Blacksmith; Wilson Macintosh, Contractor; Charles Kibble, Ironworker
Robert Price, Labourer; Henry Bridges, Labourer; William Fletcher, Gasman;
George Fletcher, Blast Furnace Foreman.
From Stillington: James White, Platelayer; Joseph Gibson, Farmer.

For many years the chapel services were well supported and other activities like Sunshine Corner and Sunday school were very popular, with outings to the seaside by train being arranged each year.

Attendances fell dramatically during the late 1960s and, despite the efforts of one family, the Wells', all services and activities were suspended in January 1972 and the chapel was demolished in early 1973.

1884 Vicarage

The vicarage was built just beyond the church at a cost of £1250. It was completed in 1884 and opened by Bishop Lightfoot, the Bishop of Durham. Reverend Thomas Varley, the vicar, took up residence in the vicarage. He had previously lived above the Workingmen's Club in Morrison Terrace, where he had shared the living accommodation with Mr Joseph Roberts and his family.

1884 June – The Cassidi Hall

The increase in the number of children attending Sunday school made it necessary for the church authorities to extend the Cassidi Hall in order to accommodate them. Thomas Varley, vicar of Stillington, requested the Carlton Iron Company to sell the land upon which the Cassidi Hall was built and also an adjacent plot to allow the hall to be extended. The request was granted and the land was sold to the church for the sum of £20.

A section was added to the Cassidi Hall which made it L-shaped, and a small room and coke vault were built underneath the floor of the extension to utilise the

The Vicarage: Completed in 1884 at a cost of £1250, the vicarage was officially opened by Bishop Lightfoot, the Bishop of Durham.

THE DEVELOPMENT OF THE VILLAGE OF THE CARLTON IRONWORKS

The Cassidi Hall after being extended
Sketch shows the Cassidi Hall after being extended to make the building L-shaped. The extension was completed in 1884 at a cost of £200.

Downstairs Room of the extended Cassidi Hall
The sketch shows the use that was made of the steep slope upon which the extension of the Cassidi Hall was built. The cut away gives a view of a room that was probably used by the Sunday School teachers and school teachers. Vaults for coal and coke were to the left of the room and later a passage to the underside of the stage.

space created by the steep slope upon which it was built. A good area of land was encased within the L-shape of the building and this was extended to meet the South Street back alley and surrounded by a high wall.

1884 Widening of the Clarence Railway

Land owned by the Carlton Iron Company adjacent to the Clarence Railway was required by the North Eastern Railway Company for the purpose of widening the railway from two tracks to four. After much correspondence between the two companies, during which the railway company threatened compulsory purchase by use of the Railways Act, agreement was reached on the sale of the land at a cost of £150.

One of the consequences of widening the railway was the total removal of the rear gardens belonging to Railway Cottages. The new lines came within about fifteen feet of the bottom house and tapered away to five feet at the top of the street.

The height of the line was level with the bedroom windows of the cottages and this meant a support wall had to be built a few feet from the back of the cottages in order to retain and support the railway. This wall created a claustrophobic situation for the residents which was made worse by the thundering noise, the vibration, the smoke and the grime created by the almost continuous traffic of heavy goods and mineral trains using the lines. The North Eastern Railway Company compensated the residents of Railway Cottages by buying one rood of land at the front of the houses in order to provide them with front gardens.

The area used for the gardens had previously been part of the clay quarry and although it required substantial filling, the final result was very pleasing to the residents who had acquired good sized, south facing front gardens.

Before finalising the agreement to sell land to the North Eastern Railway Company for the widening of the railway, the Carlton Iron Company requested that the following actions were fulfilled:-

Photograph showing part of the front garden of No. 2 Railway Cottages after the widening of the railway. Mr and Mrs Sayers are standing on the doorstep.

1) Compensate Royal Hotel for loss of frontage.
2) Drain the railway goods yard to the company's drain, at a rent of one shilling per annum.
3) Pay £2 per annum for right to cross the company's private road for access to goods yard.
4) Repair brickwork of dry arch, Carlton Bridge, which was in poor condition.
5) Put a drain under the railway where surface water gathered and was unable to get through the rail embankment, in consequence the water ran down the company's road causing flooding and danger, especially in the winter.

As a result of these requests the following operations were completed:
1) The original Carlton Bridge which had been constructed of dry stone, was modified to a brick construction when being lengthened to accommodate the two extra railway lines. The width of the bridge remained the same, and became the subject of many long discussions in the years to come.
2) A culvert was put through the railway embankment which emerged as an open stream near the end of Kirk Street. The stream was then channelled under the road at the end of South Street, before draining into the beck through the natural

Railway Cottages c. 1945

Sketch showing the proximity of the Clarence Railway after it was widened in 1884. Previous to that date the cottages had decent sized back gardens but, as compensation for their loss, they were given ample front gardens. The back street was an ideal play area because balls could not be lost. The car in the foreground had to enter the street via an arduous route through gates at the top and centre of the front gardens. These cottages were demolished in 1980 and pensioners' bungalows built further from the line.

water gully. The original gully had run in an almost semi-circular path from the low point near Whitton Three Gates to the beck and, in order that the natural drainage of water was not interrupted, the Carlton Iron Company laid drains along the route of the gully before tipping slag over it.

In 1915 the 'Little Tip' was formed by slag being tipped adjacent to the railway embankment, just west of Carlton Bridge, to create a surface level with the railway where extra railway sidings could be sited. In unison with this operation, the road which ran alongside the railway, the Black Bank, was contoured to give a more gradual slope and a better surface by filling with and distributing crushed slag. The little tip and the road also had drains fitted before slag filling commenced and these linked the drains under the main slag heap to the culvert fitted under the railway, thus retaining the uninterrupted flow of water to the beck.

> When Stillite Products Limited were blasting for slag in the 1940s, the drains under the main slag heap were damaged and the natural water course became blocked. The trapped water formed a large pond, known as Clarkies' Bottoms, in the low lying fields adjacent to the north east fringe of the slag tip. When the slag heap was removed in 1969, the pond drained and a smaller pond formed about three hundred yards south west of the original and has, at the time of writing (1993), become a haven for frogs and provides a high percentage of the frog spawn registered in the county. This area could turn full circle and become a future nature reserve.

1884 Station, Station House, signal box and subway

During the addition of the new lines, a new island type passenger platform was erected to replace the wooden halt at the Village of the Carlton Ironworks. The station master's house, a signal box and a subway were also built in the general

Stillington Station Goods Yard and Signal Cabin c. 1945

THE DEVELOPMENT OF THE VILLAGE OF THE CARLTON IRONWORKS

Stillington Station c.1945
Sketch of the station showing its position relative to West Street and the Royal Hotel.

Wesleyan Chapel c.1900
View of inside of chapel decorated for the Harvest Festival. Notice the oil lamps.

upgrading of the station and its surrounds. The subway replaced the footpath which had crossed the railway by means of a level crossing, except at the final line on the north side of the railway that still had to be crossed via the crossing. The subway was upgraded and taken the whole width of the railway in 1909, although the crossing was retained for the use of vehicles which were too high or too wide to pass through the Carlton Arch.

1885 May – Telephone Line

Probably the first telephone line in the village was installed between the Carlton Iron Company and Middlesbrough after agreement had been reached between the company and the Postmaster General.

1885 August – Cassidi Hall used as Infants School

The school inspectorate had for two years been very unhappy about the number of children attending the Lowson Street school and had made it clear that an average attendance greater than the approved capacity of 162 would not be tolerated without the school grant being affected. To alleviate the problem the Infants and Standard One (whose ages ranged from 4 years to 8 years old) were rehoused in the Cassidi Hall. Standard One children returned to the Lowson Street school in 1900.

Miss Knott was appointed as head teacher at the Cassidi Hall that had been extended and improved and was quite suitable for use as a school. Apart from the internal facilities it possessed a good area of enclosed land that created an ideal playground for the children. Miss Knott received a salary of £60 per annum.

1885 Ironstone Mines

The rental being paid for the Aislesbury mines was thought by the Carlton Iron Company to be too high considering the depressed state of the industry and the poor quality of ironstone available therein. They therefore terminated their tenancy and sought other sources of iron ore.

The East and West mines at Rosedale in North Yorkshire had been abandoned after the failure of the Rosedale and Ferryhill Iron Company, even though rich deposits of ironstone remained. The Carlton Iron Company obtained the lease for the East Mines and reopened them at moderate expense and on better terms than had been available at Aislesbury.

1885 Coal Depots

The Carlton Iron Company purchased the coal depots in Mary Street, Stockton, adjacent to the railway line and 200 yards south of Stockton station.

> When the company went into decline in 1920 the depots were bought by Thomas and Oswald Fawcett, sons of Thomas F Fawcett, the company secretary, who resided in South Street. The conveyance described Thomas as a coal merchant and Oswald as a farmer.

THE DEVELOPMENT OF THE VILLAGE OF THE CARLTON IRONWORKS 65

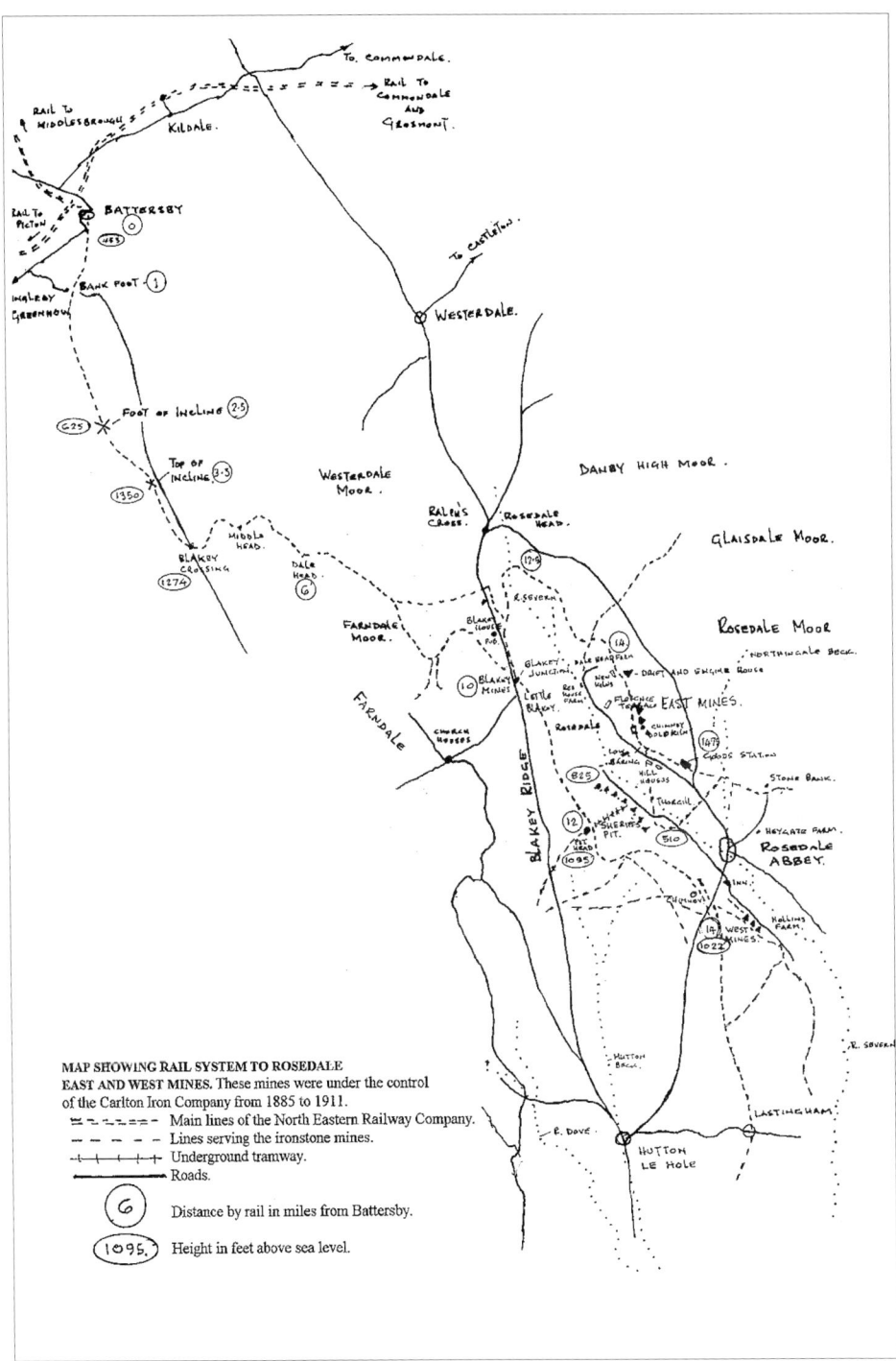

MAP SHOWING RAIL SYSTEM TO ROSEDALE EAST AND WEST MINES. These mines were under the control of the Carlton Iron Company from 1885 to 1911.
- ╪═╪═╪═ Main lines of the North Eastern Railway Company.
- ─ ─ ─ ─ Lines serving the ironstone mines.
- ┼┼┼┼┼ Underground tramway.
- ─── Roads.
- (6) Distance by rail in miles from Battersby.
- (1095) Height in feet above sea level.

The pithead at Sheriff's pit – Rosedale West Mines
Sheriff's pit had been abandoned after the failure of Rosedale and Ferryhill Mine Company. The Carlton Iron Company re-opened the pit in 1887 and worked it until 1911. Ironstone from seven drifts were taken by tramlines to a central drift that was connected to the pit shaft and hauled 270 feet to the surface by the pit elevator and loaded directly into rail trucks for transportation. Photograph shows the pithead with manager's house on the left. (*photo © from the Hayes collection, Rydale Folk Museum*).

Drift entrance at Rosedale West Mines
Miners at one of the seven drift entrances that fed the Sheriff's Pit. The drifts were all linked by a tramway with one of them extending to the foot of the pithead where the ironstone would be hauled to the surface. (*photo © from the Hayes collection, Rydale Folk Museum*).

Ruins of the old calcinating kilns near Rosedale Station
photo © from the Hayes collection, Rydale Folk Museum

Ruins of more modern calcinating kilns near High Barking
photo © from the Hayes collection, Rydale Folk Museum

General view of Rosedale East Mines
Re-opened by the Carlton Iron Company in 1885 and abandoned by them in 1911
Photo © from the Hayes collection, Rydale Folk Museum

1886 Briquette Plant

The directors of the Carlton Iron Company decided to build a Briquette Plant within the confines of their works, in order to manufacture briquettes using waste iron dust and finely ground slag as the main ingredients.

1886 October – Measles epidemic

The schools were closed for two weeks because of an epidemic of measles.

1887 July – The Basic Phosphate Company

Part of the Plate Mill and Puddling Furnace area, together with buildings and machines, were leased to William Barclay Peat. His company, the Basic Phosphate Company, was to produce fertiliser at the plant using finely ground slag as the main ingredient. The basic slag had to be purchased from the Carlton Iron Company.

1887 Rosedale Ironstone Mines

Such was the success of the reopening of the East Mines at Rosedale that the Carlton Iron Company decided to lease and reopen the section of the West Mines known as Sheriff's Pit.

The ironstone at Sheriff's Pit was mined using seven drifts cut into the hillside. These drifts were linked by narrow gauge railway lines to a vertical shaft. The shaft

Briquette Plant
Set up by the Carlton Iron Company in 1886 to produce briquettes from finely groung slag. The briquette plant was sited near to where the North Eastern Iron Refinery cupolas were built up in 1926.

was 270 feet deep and had a lift which brought the ironstone to the surface and deposited it directly into railway wagons for transportation. This method of direct loading meant that the ironstone from Sheriff's Pit was not calcinated at source but needed to be calcinated at its destination.

> Calcination is a process whereby the raw ironstone is 'roasted' in kilns to burn off the waste materials and leave a higher percentage of pure ironstone. This was usually carried out at source to reduce cost of transportation.

Two kilns were built by Carlton Iron Company at their works in the Village of the Carlton Ironworks to calcinate the ironstone from Sheriff's Pit which was to be used in the company's blast furnaces. However a lot of the ironstone from Sheriff's Pit was sold to other companies.

The company introduced a unique feature into the East Mines when, in 1900, they installed an electric generating plant which produced the electricity used for lighting the mine drifts and for drilling and haulage. The generator was removed when the mine closed in 1911 and was installed at the Village of the Carlton Ironworks to provide lighting in and around the ironworks, and eventually for the street lighting around the village.

Whilst they were working the Rosedale mines, the Carlton Iron Company did much to help the community of Rosedale Abbey, including helping to finance and repair the school.

1887 John S Mcgowan, a director of the Carlton Iron Company, dies

His brother, William, from Whitehaven was elected to replace him. Another director, Alfred Hodgetts of St Bees, Carnforth, also died during this year. He was not replaced.

1888 Selling of Rosedale Ironstone

The directors of the Carlton Iron Company showed their resourcefulness and forward thinking when they decided to buy 125 shares in the Acklam Ironworks at £100 each share. This move came to fruition when the Acklam Iron Company agreed to buy from the Carlton Iron Company all the ironstone they required, for any number of furnaces, over a period of not less than 7 years.

1888 Forty coke ovens erected

The Carlton Iron Company erected forty coke ovens, just north of the blast furnaces, at their works in the Village of the Carlton Ironworks. The coke ovens were of the type invented and patented by Dr Von Bauer an Austrian engineer. They were chosen after much investigation and were the first of their type used in England, although William Baird had some in use at his Ayrshire Collieries in Scotland.

The erection of coke ovens adjacent to blast furnaces was a novel idea within the industry at this time as most were built at the head of a coal pit.

1888 East Howle colliery band

The Carlton Iron Company, who were mining coal at East Howle, were asked if they would lend the colliery band £100 in order that they could purchase some musical instruments. The company agreed and the loan was organised.

1888 June – More houses needed – extension to Lowson Street

The board of the Carlton Iron Company decided that there was still a shortage of houses for the company's work people and resolved that houses would be built during the summer to a value of £1,000, exclusive of land.

These houses were to be an extension to the 13 houses existing in Lowson Street.

1888 Managing director's salary

As a matter of historical record the annual salary of the managing director of the Carlton Iron Company was at this time £1250 plus £250 for expenses.

A table showing other salaries at various dates is shown in the Appendices.

1888 July – Water supply to the Village of the Carlton Ironworks

The water supply, which up to this point had been taken from the beck via the Pump House at the bottom of the 'Donkey Bank' (presumably named after the type of engine originally used to pump the water from the beck, ie a Donkey Engine), was not sufficient to meet the increasing needs of the Carlton Iron Company and required to be supplemented by some other source. The directors of the company contacted the Stockton and Middlesbrough Water Board to see if they could help.

The domestic water supply had for some time after the outbreak of typhoid fever in 1878 come from a local well. Later, the water from the beck was used again but was passed through filter beds, which were sited just north of North Street, before being piped to standpipes around the village.

After several discussions between the two companies, the Water Board sent a letter to the Carlton Iron Company setting out their proposals for the supply of water to the works and the village.

The letter, dated 19th July 1888, was handwritten and read as follows:

(1) The Water Board to lay a line of 9" water mains from the Sadberge reservoir to a point on the Carlton Iron Company's premises adjoining the subway near the railway station where a meter will be fixed for the purpose of measuring the water supplied to the works, and also such mains as shall be necessary for supplying the houses on the south side of the railway and adjoining the road leading from the subway to the highway from Whitton. Any pipes necessary to carry the water from the meter to various parts of the works to be laid by the Carlton Iron Company.

(2) The water supplied to the cottages to be paid for at the ordinary scale of domestic water rents, applicable to premises outside the Boroughs.
(3) The water supplied for the works to be paid for at the following rates.
First 5,000,000 gallon per quarter at 4½d per 1,000 gallon.
Second 5,000,000 gallon per quarter at 4d per 1,000 gallon.
all above 10,000,000 gallon per quarter at 3d per 1,000 gallon.
(4) The Chairman of the company or some other responsible person satisfactory to the Water Board shall enter into an agreement that lasts for 10 years after the commencement of supply. The annual payment shall not be less than £450 and he shall agree to make up any deficiency to this amount after deducting any previous years in excess of £450.
(5) After the expiration of the 10 years aforesaid the supply to be continued at the ordinary scale of water charges in force at that time.
(6) The Water Board to provide proper meter for measuring supplies for the use of the works for which the company shall pay the usual meter rents. The company shall also provide a proper housing for the protection of the meter.

D D Wilson,
General Manager

The Water Board explained that, from their experience with other users, 3 furnaces would use nearly 5 million gallons of water each quarter.

The Sadberge reservoir was used as the water supply source because the Elton reservoir, although closer, was too low to allow a gravity feed supply to the Village of the Carlton Ironworks.

The terms set out by the Water Board in the above letter were accepted by the Carlton Iron Company in September 1888.

1888 August – Assessment of tax for inhabited houses

An Assessment of Tax for the inhabited houses in the Village of the Carlton Ironworks was issued by the Surveyor of Taxes.

The Tax Assessment Forms for the various streets gave the following information.

Mount Pleasant
owned by Carlton Iron Company and inhabited by the following tenants:

No.	Tenant	Annual rent	Occupation
No. 1	Anthony Stephenson	£12	Engineer at ironworks.
No. 2	Francis Ross	£12	Draughtsman at ironworks.
Nos. 3 and 4	Henry Hoggetts	£24	Company secretary from 1878–1898
No. 5	John Scobie Barnacle	£12	
No. 6	T W Bonnar	£12	Local doctor.

THE DEVELOPMENT OF THE VILLAGE OF THE CARLTON IRONWORKS

Other properties owned by the Carlton Iron Company:

North Street	18 houses	Annual rent £5.10s each
Office Row	4 houses	Annual rent £5.10s each (incl. accommodation in White House)
West Street	31 houses	Annual rent £5.0.0 each
South Street	16 houses	Annual rent £5.10s each
Morrison Street	37 houses	Annual rent £5.0.0 each
Lowson Street	13 houses	Annual rent £5.0.0 each

Morrison Terrace
owned by Stephenson's Mortgages and inhabited by the following tenants:

House and shop	Bartholomew Stephenson	Annual rent £14	General dealer
House and shop	John Dawson	Annual rent £13	Fruit and Vegetables
House and shop	Joseph Bulmer	Annual rent £14	Draper
House over club	Joseph Daniels	Annual rent £7	

Rates were chargeable at 6d per annum for every £1 of annual rent.

This was the total number of houses in the village except for Railway Cottages, station house, school house, Royal Hotel, vicarage and the house above the Cooperative Stores in West Street.

> The Assessment Forms were endorsed by C Nesom, a farmer from Whitton, who was one of the Guardians of the Poor of the Stockton Union and a member of the Rural Sanitary Authority.

1889 September – Lowson Street

The building of sixteen additional houses in Lowson Street was proceeding and in November it was decided to increase this number to twenty one.

This brought the total in Lowson Street to thirty four with the last house forming an alley between itself and the Workingmen's Club in Morrison Terrace.

1890 November – Scavenging the Village

The Carlton Iron Company wrote to the Stockton Union, Rural Sanitary Authority, offering to do all the work involved in the regular cleaning out of privies, ashpits and cesspools for all of the houses in the Village of the Carlton Ironworks at a cost of £45 per year.

The offer was accepted by the Sanitary Authority and the company carried out the work which had previously been done by a local farmer.

1891 Summary of the Village of the Carlton Ironworks using data from the census

The number of houses in the village had increased from 135 to 157 since the 1881 census.

The additions were 21 houses built in Lowson Street and the vicarage. Only 2 houses in the village were unoccupied at this time.

The Village of the Carlton Ironworks now comprised:
18 houses in North Street
31 houses and one shop in West Street
16 houses in South Street
5 houses in Mount Pleasant
3 houses in Office Row. Plus one accommodation in White House
3 shops/houses and Workingmen's Club with accommodation above in Morrison Terrace
4 houses in Railway Cottages
34 houses in Lowson Street
37 houses in Morrison Street
The vicarage, the schoolhouse and the Royal Hotel

The station house was built but was counted in the Stillington census and not the Village of the Carlton Ironworks' census, because of its position just inside the Sedgefield RDC border. The Stillington census also showed that the station master, Mr John Dunn Pipe, now resided at Stillington Station and not at 2 Railway Cottages where he had lived in 1881, which would confirm that the station house was now in existence adjacent to the newly sited Stillington Station.

Total number of houses in the Village of the Carlton Ironworks was 158, including the station house.

Buildings and people of note were:
School and schoolhouse in Lowson Street. Headmaster, Mr Thomas Kirtley.
The Cassidi Hall, being used as a school for children between 4 and 8 years old.
St Johns Church and the vicarage. The vicar was the Reverend Thomas Varley.
The Wesleyan Chapel.
The station and station house with Mr John Dunn Pipe as station master.
Dr Bonnar was still practising from Mount Pleasant.
Mr Walter Thompson the local policeman, lived at 11 West Street.
Mr John Redshaw, publican at the Royal Hotel.

The total population of the Village of the Carlton Ironworks was now 976, and comprised 541 males and 435 females.

With 156 houses occupied the average number of persons per household was 6.3.

Further breakdown of population: Adult Males 331, Adult females 246, Child Males 210, Child Females 189.

These totals include 80 male lodgers, 21 of whom came from Ireland and 2 from Wales.

All adult males were working and about 10 females did work other than housekeeping.

Occupations of the female workers:

7 dressmakers, 1 grocer and 2 elementary teachers.

Occupations of male workers was still mainly connected with the ironworks and included: furnace keepers, boiler cleaners, boiler superintendent, smelter men, blast engine men, engine firemen, blacksmiths, boilermakers, stonemasons, bricklayers, loco drivers and stokers, weighmen, strikers, slaggers, fitters, moulders, engine fitters, joiner, millwright, patternmakers, cartmen, horsekeeper, draughtsman, engineer, clerks, time clerks, coke burner, time keepers, commercial clerks, foremen, labourers and company secretary.

Others not connected with the ironworks were; police constable, shoemaker, grocer, draper, publican, railway clerk, porter, platelayers, signalmen, station master, cordwainer, farm labourer, school master, elementary teacher, pupil teacher, general practitioner, vicar and servants.

Scholars listed totalled 221, 127 boys and 94 girls, being taught in the Cassidi Hall (infants up to 8 years old) and the school in Lowson Street.

Whitton village housed another 12 ironworkers and a further 18 scholars.

The scholars, 11 boys and 7 girls, also attended the schools in the Village of the Carlton Ironworks.

In 1874 the Carlton Iron Company had bought, from Mr Anthony Wilkinson, about eight acres of land in Whitton together with cottages. These were Millbank Terrace and possibly the cottages opposite including Rosedale House. Six ironworkers lived in these cottages as the 'head of the household' with six other ironworkers living with them as lodgers.

1891 School proposed to be built at Redmarshall

The Rev E C Richardson submitted a plan to Stockton Rural Sanitary Authority for the proposed building of a school at Redmarshall. The plan was approved.

1891 Summary of the Carlton Iron company's main activities within the Village of the Carlton Ironworks

Three blast furnaces each producing 500 tons of pig iron per week.

Forty coke ovens, making coke and gas sufficient to fuel the blast furnaces with excess which was sold to local institutions.

A briquette plant, producing briquettes from finely crushed slag and iron dust.

The Basic Manure Mills producing fertiliser from crushed slag. Although these were not controlled directly by the Carlton Iron Company the directors had a major shareholding in the company.

The number of men employed at the above works was between 350 and 400.

The famous Slag Heap was now well established with the slag from the ironmaking being tipped over a large area adjacent to the works. Slag was tipped as close to existing houses as possible coming to the very limits of North Street, the school in Lowson Street, and later to the back street of little Lowson Street. The sky would be lit up almost continually by the blaze of fire caused when the molten slag was being discharged from the slag bogies and allowed to run down the side of the tip sending fumes, smoke and intense heat into the atmosphere.

1891 Employers Liability Insurance

An Employers Liability Insurance was taken out by the Carlton Iron Company on behalf of its workers. Information supplied to the insurance company included some interesting points which are shown below.

> Occupation of workers, fitters, smiths, masons, joiners and apprentices, engineers, firemen and blast furnacemen.
>
> Workers in connection with Basic Manure Mills, coke ovens and by-product plant assemblies.
>
> Wages estimated to be paid:
> By subcontractors; £6,000, by employers direct, £14,000. Total £20,000.
>
> In 1897 the total was £20,000 and in 1899 the total was £24,000.

1891 September – School fees abolished

The Free Education Act abolished school fees and children could now attend school free of charge.

However, the School Board responsible for the schools in the Village of the Carlton Ironworks decided to retain some charges to assist the cost of supplying books and materials for use in the schools. On the first Monday of each month the children in Standards 5, 6 and 7 had to pay threepence, those in Standards 3 and 4 had to pay twopence, and each child in Standard 2 had to pay one penny. All charges were abolished in 1892. The School Board at around this time were receiving, to help run the schools, a precept of; £10 every 6 months from the Stillington overseers, £70 every 6 months from Whitton overseers and a Government Grant of approximately £165 annually.

1892 January – Fire Insurance policy

A Fire Insurance Policy was taken out by the Carlton Iron Company for their works and property in the Village of the Carlton Ironworks. The policy specification gives a comprehensive list of houses and buildings existing and belonging to them at this time.

Details are described in the following text.

THE DEVELOPMENT OF THE VILLAGE OF THE CARLTON IRONWORKS

The Caledonian Insurance Company

Sum assured – £11,825 Annual Premium – £12.10s.
Assured – The Carlton Iron Company as owners and Sophia Susan Henry as Mortgagee, of 7 Gloucestor Terrace, Hyde Park, Middlesex.
Dates of coverage – Between 25th December 1892 and 25th December 1893.
See below for full specification.

Specification for Fire policy

(1) In equal proportions on the buildings of 18 private cottages situate North Street, Carlton Iron Works, near Stockton-on-Tees. (£1250.) (The remainder of the specification was set out in similar terms but is condensed for easier reading).
(2) Boilersmith's Shop (£50).
(3) Blacksmith's Shop (£50).
(4) Joiner's Shop, inc. 3 double benches, 2 wall benches, small circular saw and a turning lathe. The shavings are removed weekly. An open fireplace therein. (£50).
(5) Fitter's Shop, adjoining last mentioned and divided therefrom by an entire wall up to but not through the roof. Containing Steam Engine, the steam is brought from a distance. (£150).

Reduced copy of Fire Insurance Policy heading

(6) On timber scaffolding and supports, and railway gearing over Coal, Coke, Limestone and mine depots. Timber built and being all in line with Coke Ovens but at a distance of several feet from. (£750).
(7) On the building of New Coal Bunker adjoining Coke Ovens. Detached from last. (£500).
(8) On Loco-Shed. (£50).
(9) Weighing Machine House, Time Office, and store for general goods. 2 casks of paraffin oil and 3cwt of clean cotton waste kept separate and therefore allowed to be kept therein. (£200). (This was the building initially used as the lodging house).
(10) On the general offices and small house communicating therewith. (£200). (The White House)
(11) 3 cottages in Office Row to rear of Item 10. (£150).
(12) Small stable and loft over adjoining Item 11. (£50).
(13) Royal Hotel in the tenure of John Redshaw. (£800). (Rated as equal to about 10 or 11 cottages.)
(14) 16 private cottages adjoining each other in West Street. (top). (£1280).
(15) Dwelling House and Shop in the tenure of Whaley, situated in West Street. (£100).
(16) 15 private cottages, adjoining each other, in bottom half of West Street. Adjoining Item 15. (£1120).
(17) 16 private cottages, adjoining each other, South Street. (£1280).
(18) On the following 5 buildings in Mount Pleasant all adjoining each other:
Doctor's dwellinghouse with Lean-to used as a communicating surgery. (£120).
Single house adjoining thereto. (£100).
Double house adjoining Item 19. (£200).
Single house adjoining Item 20. (£100).
Double house adjoining Item 21. (£200)
(19) Pumping Engine House with Boiler inside adjacent to stream. (£15).
(20) 34 private cottages adjoining each other in Lowson Street. (£1700).
(21) 37 private cottages adjoining each other in Morrison Street. (£1850).

General notes on policy stated: Said buildings are all stone or brick and slated or tiled and forming part of the Carlton Ironworks. Coal Bunker is supported by Iron Pillars and protected by corrugated iron on the side of and next to the coke ovens, the wall of which is 6' thick.

> Properties not included in the policy are: Morrison Terrace because it was not owned by the Carlton Iron Company at this point but by Stephenson's Mortgages. The company did buy the terrace within the next few years after a long dispute over the price. The final settlement was in the region of £800.
> Railway Cottages not included as they belonged to the Railway Company.

Notes regarding Fire Insurance Policy covering December 1898 to December 1899

The Fire Policy for 1898–99 had exactly the same schedule as the policy for 1892–93 except for the addition of the Engineer's Drawing Office, which was built in 1894. (Became the Stillite Offices in 1939).

Premium at 1898 was £15.4s.9d with the sum assured being £12,525.

1892 February – Bauer Coke ovens leased to S A Sadler & Company

The Bauer coke ovens were leased to S A Sadler and Sons with an adjacent acre of land on which they built equipment to process the by-products created during the manufacture of the coke.

The building which had been the model lodging house was now being utilised by the Carlton Iron Company as a weigh house, with the upper storey unused except as a storage area. Sadlers were also granted a lease on this area in order to set up a laboratory where they could carry out tests and check the chemical analysis of their by-products. The by-products of coke making are tar, ammonia, gas and some light oil, all of which was produced and marketed by S A Sadler and Company from this site.

> Sir Samuel A Sadler, a neighbour of Thomas Kirk at The Avenue, Eaglescliffe, was a person of some importance in Middlesbrough for he was one of the founder members of the town and became its mayor three times. He was also the first Conservative Member of Parliament for Middlesbrough and his statue now stands in the gardens opposite Middlesbrough Town Hall. He founded his company S A Sadler & Company in 1868 and, although the company is now involved mainly in the transport of bulk liquids, the name Sadler has survived.

1893 December – Royal Hotel

The Royal Hotel was leased to J D Ingram by the Carlton Iron Company.

1894 Engineer's and drawing offices

The Carlton Iron Company built an office block opposite the blast furnaces and close to the engine shed. A two storey building with spacious offices on both floors where the engineers and draughtsmen of the company were housed. These offices were abandoned, but not demolished, after the ironworks closed.

They were given a new lease of life when Stillite Products Limited commenced operations in 1939 and, after a little renovation, used them as their main offices. When Stillite Products closed their factory in 1965 the offices were again abandoned and were eventually gutted by fire and demolished in the 1980s.

1895 February – Royal Hotel

The Royal Hotel was leased to William Robert Wardle by the Carlton Iron Company.

Engineer's and drawing offices

At this time the Royal was being used by businessmen who were visiting the Carlton Iron Company and staying overnight or longer. It had all the usual hotel facilities such as an ample number of bedrooms, dining rooms, function rooms, lounges and bars.

Local girls were employed as cooks, waitresses, chambermaids, cleaners and barmaids.

> Since the closure of the ironworks around 1928, the Royal has been used only as a public house, with little or no modernisation carried out to improve its appeal and encourage custom from outside the Village. With modernisation carried out at most village pubs throughout the country, the Royal Hotel is one of the few remaining pubs where local customers are not outnumbered by motorists or passing trade.

1894 February – water tap to be provided to each house

The Clerk of Stockton Rural Sanitary Authority wrote to the Carlton Iron Company requesting them to provide a water tap in each of their dwelling homes at the Village of the Carlton Ironworks, as suggested by the Inspector of Nuisances.

No action was taken and the clerk wrote again in April and May. In October notice was given to the Carlton Iron Company requiring them to provide a proper and sufficient water supply to the dwelling houses belonging to them in the Village of the Carlton Ironworks within one calendar month, in default of which legal proceedings would be taken to compel the said company to do so.

The company replied on the 31st October, stating that the work required for providing a proper water supply would be proceeded with and completed.

At this time only the houses in Mount Pleasant had individual water taps in their yards – all other houses shared water standpipes.

1894 Drainage of back alley between Lowson and Morrison Street

The main drain in Morrison Street was referred to in the District Surveyor's report and he was authorised by Stockton Rural Sanitary Authority to carry out any necessary work to alleviate the problem. He proceeded to lay a main drain down the centre of the back alley between Lowson Street and Morrison Street in the Village of the Carlton Ironworks

The dwelling houses in Morrison Street were inspected by the Inspector of Nuisances and he reported to the Sanitary Authority that there were some defects in need of urgent repair and that the Carlton Iron Company had been instructed to take any necessary action.

A notice was served by the District Council on the Reverend Newsome and Dr Bonnar, as trustees of the Cassidi Memorial Mission Room, requiring them to abate the nuisance reported to exist on these premises by the Inspector of Nuisances.

> There was no specific explanation in the relevant documents as to what the nuisance was, but generally these complaints were linked with drainage or hygiene and, as the Cassidi Hall was still being used as an Infants School, the inspector would be keen to abate any such problem.

1894 Henry Kirk and Thomas Kirk (Junior)

Henry and Thomas, Jnr were the second and third sons of Thomas Kirk, Snr, the managing director of the Carlton Iron Company. Both were given positions within the company – Thomas Jnr being appointed works manager, and Henry coke ovens manager.

1894 June – Measles epidemic

Another epidemic of measles swept through the village and forced the closure of the school for four weeks commencing June 15th. The School Board ruled that this period be deducted from the annual summer holiday to curtail the school time lost by the children.

1895 Renewal of coke ovens

The coke ovens were in urgent need of renewal but the Carlton Iron Company were unable to finance a scheme to replace them. However Walter Morrison, chairman of the company, was willing to expend £20,000 of his own money on the project, provided some security could be assured. To this end a mortgage was arranged between him and the company which allowed the erection of new coke ovens to proceed.

1895 January 4th – First Parish Council meeting. Whitton Parish Council formed

In accordance with the instructions of Local Government Act 1894, parish councils were inaugurated throughout the nation in order that the governing of small communities could become more democratic. It was also ordered that the election of councillors would take place every three years.

One Parish Council member to be elected to represent the parish at the meetings of a higher Local Authority, in the case of Whitton Parish this was the newly formed Stockton Rural District Council which had replaced the Stockton Rural Sanitary Authority, and was responsible for governing all the parishes within its district.

A prominent member of each community was asked to convene a meeting in order that a Parish Council could be elected to represent the people therein.

In consequence of the above instructions a meeting was held in the Lowson Street school to elect a Parish Council which would be responsible for governing Whitton Parish, which included Whitton village and the Village of the Carlton Ironworks.

Dr Bonnar, who had been chosen to convene the meeting, took the chair until a chairman had been elected by the assembled company, after which Dr Bonnar left the meeting.

Nine councillors were required and, with only nine persons present at the meeting, all were duly elected. They were:

Clark Nesom	Wealthy farmer from Whitton, who had been a member of the Whitton Parochial Committee and a former guardian of the Stockton Union
Thomas Kirk, Jnr.	Works manager, Carlton Iron Company
Thomas Kirtley	Headmaster at village school
Joseph Dixon	Fitter, Carlton Iron Company
Walter Bearman	Blacksmith, Carlton Iron Company
George Moore	Engine driver, Carlton Iron Company
William Harrison	Patternmaker, Carlton Iron Company
Thomas Dawson	Traffic manager, Carlton Iron Company
James Duncan	Signalman

Clark Nesom was elected chairman
Thomas Kirk, Jnr. was elected vice chairman and treasurer.

Robert Barker, an ironworker's clerk, who had acted as overseer during the election of officers and councillors, was appointed to the position of assistant overseer and clerk to the council at an annual salary of £8.

From this time onward the representation on Whitton Parish Council was mainly from the Village of the Carlton Ironworks, thus giving the Whitton representatives much less control than they had enjoyed previously.

1895 September – Drainage at the Village of the Carlton Ironworks

Although most of the village was lacking in proper drainage facilities, the area which caused most concern was the alley between Lowson Street and Morrison Street, which was considered by the District Surveyor and the Medical Officer of Health to be an health hazard, especially on the days that the ash privies were emptied.

> The ash privies were used by the householders to discard ashes and all other rubbish, including human waste, which had accrued during the previous week. They were emptied by men raking the rubbish from the ash privy directly into the back alley through a purpose-built access hole, after first removing its sliding cast iron cover. The waste was left in piles adjacent to each ash privy from where it was shovelled into a horse drawn cart by the men following the rakers up the alley. The whole process became known as scavenging. The rough surface of the alley made it impossible to remove all trace of the waste and, although the District Surveyor had laid a central drain between the streets, the dirt and smell of the ash privies contents still caused a problem especially when children were playing there and housewives used it for hanging out their washing. This alley had come in for particular attention because it divided Lowson Street and Morrison Street, whereas all other streets in the village at this time had their ash privies facing open areas.

1895 October – Paving of back alley between Lowson Street and Morrison Street

The Carlton Iron Company wrote to Stockton Rural District Council stating that they had decided to pave the back street between Morrison Street and Lowson Street with slag bricks and that they would complete the work as soon as possible, thus enabling any residue waste from the ash privies to be washed into the central drain. The slag bricks with which the Carlton Iron Company were to pave the alley would come from the Briquette Plant that they had formed in 1886 to make briquettes from crushed slag. These were ideal for the purpose, with a smooth surface finish and very hard wearing. Eventually all the back streets in the village were treated in the same manner, with the council laying drains which, before the erection of the sewerage works, ran into settling tanks positioned around the village.

1896 March – First Triennial Parish Council Elections

The first Triennial Meeting of Whitton Parish Council and the election of new councillors took place but there was still a limitation on persons holding franchise and the existing councillors were usually automatically re-elected. If a new councillor was needed, because of a resignation or some other reason, the replacement would be an associate of the existing councillors.

Persons elected as parish councillors: C Nesom, T Kirk jnr, J Dixon, F Walkington, W Bearman, T Kirtley, J Dawson, G W Callender.

Carlton Ironworks, Glykoline Terrace and the Glykoline Chimney c. 1900
This is a view looking north eastwards from the station house garden showing the three houses in Glykoline Terrace relative to the ironworks. On the right of picture is the Glykoline chimney and part of the Glykoline works. A public footpath to Foxton ran between the Glykoline properties and the ironworks.

Carlton Bridge
This bridge was built to provide a path for horses and carts when the Clarence Railway was constructed in 1833 and became almost the central point of the Village of the Carlton Ironworks. The bridge was extended when the railway was widened to four lines from two in 1884. After years of negotiation for the bridge to be widened, it was finally replaced in 1965 by a new bridge that was wider and higher, in order to cope with modern traffic. The stile on the right is the start of the top footpath to Whitton.

Officials elected: Thomas Kirk, Jnr – Chairman and treasurer; Clark Nesom – Vice Chairman; A Bell and T Dawson – Overseers.

The assistant overseer and clerk to the council, R Barker, had resigned and Mr Thomas Fawcett was appointed as his replacement at a later meeting. His annual salary was £20 for the assistant overseer's post, and £8 as clerk to Whitton Parish Council.

> Fawcett was at this time an ironmaster's accountant living in 1 South Street, a house which was later to be extensively modified and extended for him by the Carlton Iron Company when he became their company secretary.

1896 March – Glykoline Lubricant Company

The Glykoline Lubricant Company Limited bought a piece of land from Merton College, Oxford, at a price of £100 per acre. This land was immediately north of the station master's house and on it they were to build a factory where they would refine grease and produce grease blocks which were used to lubricate the hot bearings of the rolls in the steel rolling mills. To gain access to their works they had to cross land

First Workers at the Glykoline Lubricant Company c. 1898
This photograph shows the first workers to be employed at the Glykoline and probably the first occupants of Glykoline Terrace. Second from left, with the pipe, is Albert Amos Johnson with his son, Amos, aged 12, directly in front of him. Albert Amos Johnson lived in Glykoline Terrace and was married to a Swedish lady named Beda Elfreda and he was very soon to be appointed as foreman. The names of the other workers are not known, but tenants of Glykoline Terrace at the time were Dave Daniels and Richard Ingle. The two gentlemen in suits were probably the manager and the foreman, who would have been based at the company's Middlesbrough factory helping to establish the Stillington works.

belonging to the Carlton Iron Company and asked permission to do so. In return they gave the Carlton Iron Company a strip of their land four feet wide by approximately 150 yards long, and constructed a fence to form a boundary between the two properties. The fence ran adjacent to the footpath to Foxton, starting at the station house and ending at Glykoline Terrace, and was made from used railway sleepers.

1896 New Headmistress for Infant's School

Miss Margaret Blair took over as headmistress of the infants in place of Miss Knott. This appointment coincided with the children in Standard One being transferred back to the Lowson Street school leaving only the infants, aged four to eight, at the Cassidi Hall. The school inspector's report of 1898 was highly critical of the discipline and teaching of Miss Blair and her two assistants, Miss Dixon, pupil teacher and Miss Hodgson, monitor. In an attempt to improve the situation, the School Board installed a wood and glass panelled partition to segregate the very young children from the older ones. The partition reached from floor to ceiling, about seventeen feet, and divided the L shape area into two good sized rooms with a connecting door. It was mounted on slides at top and bottom which made it easy to open or close depending on the immediate requirement. The glass in the panels commenced four feet from the floor and went to the full height of the partition, each pane of glass was patterned with delicate pastel shade figures and scenes, which were very beautiful and a fine work of art.

1898 Glykoline Terrace

After the factory was established, the Glykoline Lubricant Company built three terraced houses for their employees. These were about 100 yards north of the factory

and had three bedrooms, a spacious back yard with coal house and privy, and a good sized, privately fenced front garden with only countryside beyond. These houses were very well built and had an exceptionally fine outlook from the front garden.

The first tenants of Glykoline Terrace were Albert Amos Johnson and his Swedish wife Beda Elfreda. She is seen here standing in the yard of their house almost immediately after moving in. She was well pleased with the house and, on the 5th May 1898, she wrote a letter to her mother in Sweden stating 'that her husband had a good job in the oil factory and they had got a new fine house with one living room, two kitchens and three bedrooms. There is lots of activity with two ironworks just outside our kitchen window and I have had company every night since we moved in one week ago.'

This last sentence would suggest that the houses were completed at this time ie. May 1898.

1898 April Election of Stockton Rural District Councillors

Elections took place in the parishes for the selection of Rural District Councillors and below are the results for Carlton, Redmarshall and Whitton.

	Candidate	*Address*	*Elected*
Carlton	William Knowles Hunton	Greystones, Carlton	W K Hunton
Redmarshall	Thomas Bell	Oxbridge	Thos Bell
Whitton	Thomas Kirk, Jnr 79 votes	Mount Pleasant CIW	Thomas Kirk Jnr
	Clark Nesom 57 votes	Whitton	

Clark Nesom lost his place on the council after many years as a member of the Guardians and a councillor for the last three years.

1898 Houses for company officials at end of South Street and North Street

Two further dwellings were required by the Carlton Iron Company which were suitable for accommodating officials of the company, and these were gained by modifying existing houses in South Street and North Street. The official's house in South Street was achieved by extending the existing end house to double its original size, and including two large bay windows facing west and overlooking a garden, which was created by extending the boundary of the property until it was level with the side wall of the Cassidi Hall, thus giving the house a good size garden which was fenced and hedged around its perimeter.

These modifications and the extension were carried out to provide a suitable residence for Mr Thomas F Fawcett who had been appointed to the post of company secretary.

The end house in North Street was modified to a lesser degree and was used as a foreman's residence.

1898 July – Completion of Lowson and Morrison Streets

Owing to the increase in operations at the Carlton Iron Company and the consequent requirement for more workmen, the board resolved that more dwellings be built at the top of Lowson and Morrison Streets. Seven more houses were built at the top of each street bringing them to within the width of an alley from the churchyard wall.

1898 Settling tanks for sewage disposal

Since around 1894 settling tanks had been situated at one or two points around the Village of the Carlton Ironworks, with drains from the streets carrying the sewage to them or, where more convenient, the drains were allowed to discharge directly into the beck.

In October 1896 it was recorded that the Carlton Iron Company had covered one of these settling tanks with slag and were ordered to replace it by Stockton Rural District Council.

After this incident there were many discussions on drainage. It was decided to build a central area of settlement tanks to where the whole of the village would eventually be drained. A quarter of an acre of land, situated about 400 yards south of Mount Pleasant, was leased by the District Council from Sherburn Hospital, upon which the settling tanks were sited with the residue from the tanks being discharged into the nearby beck.

1898 Coke ovens built at Seaton Carew

The Carlton Iron Company built fifty coke ovens adjacent to their ironworks at Seaton Carew and Henry Kirk was given the task of managing them. His brother Harold replaced him as coke ovens manager at the company's works in the Village of the Carlton Ironworks.

Harold lived with his brother Thomas, Jnr at 2 Mount Pleasant.

1899 February – Another change of Headmistress at the Infant's School

Despite the changes made to the layout of the school rooms in the Cassidi Hall, the school inspector continued to be critical of the teaching and discipline therein. As a consequence the headmistress, Miss Margaret Blair, was replaced by Miss M J Harrison.

Average pupil attendance at the infants school was 125, which gives some idea of the problems facing the headmistress and her two young assistants – a pupil teacher and a candidate pupil teacher.

The problem of numbers was aggravated by children of all ages transferring from other schools with little or no previous educational training.

1899 May – 'Little' Lowson Street

Even with the fourteen houses now being built at the top of Lowson and Morrison Streets, there was still a shortage of houses for the men being employed by the Carlton Iron Company, especially when all three blast furnaces were working.

The company decided to build seventeen more houses opposite and parallel to the existing Lowson Street houses. They were built in a terrace positioned between the school house and the church wall and officially named Lowson Street but soon became more commonly known as 'Little' Lowson Street. The contract for building these houses was awarded in June to John Davison, a builder from Stockton on Tees, at a price of £174 per house which included house drainage, water closets and the laying of all the cobblestones for the end and back streets.

All work carried out was inspected by the company and the Local Authority to ensure satisfactory adherence to regulations.

View of a house modified for a company official at the west end of South Street
Photograph shows the bay windows and part of the garden of the house modified in 1898 to house the ironworks' company secretary. In later years, several village doctors used the house as their residence-cum- surgery. Photo taken 1998.

'Little' Lowson Street

Built in 1900 'Little' Lowson Street comprised 17 houses that were numbered 42 to 58 Lowson Street. The photograph, taken just after the completion of the houses, shows the relative position of little Lowson Street to big Lowson Street, the church and the school house on the left of the picture.

'Little' Lowson Street

This photograph shows the rear of little Lowson Street, possibly on a Monday with the clothes hanging out to dry. The corrugated sheeting on the left of the picture is part of the 'places' that the villagers built to house hens, rabbits, pigeons and, in some cases, although positioned further from the houses, goats and pigs. Taken in the 1970s, this photograph still shows some of the sliding covers which covered the hole from where the ash privies were raked out and the coal house access doors which were used by the coalman to tip the coal into the coalhouse from the back street.

Carlton Bridge

Photograph taken from Morrison Terrace gives a good view of the bridge running under the Clarence Railway and the end of the little tip on the right hand side.

'Big' Lowson Street

'Big' Lowson Street, named after William Lowson, one of the original directors of the Carlton Iron Company, comprised a total of 41 houses. The first 13 were built in conjunction with the first 37 houses in Morrison Street in c. 1880, with the bottom 21 being added in 1889. In 1899 another 7 houses were built at the top of the street, bringing the total to 42. The photograph, taken c. 1975, shows the street at a time when demolition was being considered, and it is fitting that darkness is falling on the scene. The church tower can be seen in the centre of the photograph, whilst the little school and the outline of the tip are visible on the left hand side.

Morrison Street. Photo c. 1900
Morrison Street – named after Walter Morrison, a director of the Carlton Iron Company – comprised 44 houses. The bottom 35 were built c. 1880, with the top 7 being erected in 1899.

Top of 'Big' Lowson Street showing its proximity to St John's church
The photograph also gives a good example of the washing lines strung across the road between 'Little' Lowson Street and 'Big' Lowson Street, which meant that the washing had to be lifted or removed when any delivery vans came into the street. Photograph taken c. 1969.
Reproduced courtesy of the Evening Gazette, Middlesbrough

1900 Electric Supply Cables

The North Eastern Railway Company allowed the Carlton Iron Company to lay three electric cables under the railway through the subway. The cables were laid to carry power from the company's generating plant to the Royal Hotel and, possibly, some of the houses on the south side of the railway.

1901 Analysis of census information

Complete statistics for the 1901 census will not be available until the year 2001 and only general information has been released to date.

The preliminary census details for Whitton and the Village of the Carlton Ironworks are integrated and some of the information concerning the Village of the Carlton Ironworks is also included in the Stillington census. An accurate analysis of the 1901 census is therefore difficult, but local knowledge used in conjunction with the census, helps to give a reasonably accurate assessment of the situation at that point.

The 1891 census gave the following details regarding the Village of the Carlton Ironworks:

Number of houses 158 – Population 976
Additional houses built since that date:
Three in Glykoline Terrace
Seven at the top of Lowson Street
Seven at the top of Morrison Street
Seventeen in 'Little' Lowson Street
Total of additional houses = 34
Total number of houses now in village = 158 plus 34 = 192

In 1901 the combined population of Whitton and the Village of the Carlton Iron Works was given as 1099. In 1891 the population of Whitton was 105, and with no significant change at Whitton over the last ten years, it can be assumed that the population at 1901 was still about 105.

The Village of the Carlton Iron Works population in 1901 would therefore be 1099 minus 105 = 994.

We then have to add the occupants of houses included in the Stillington census which were, three houses in Glykoline Cottages, one accommodation in the White House, and the station house. Assuming 4 persons per household we can add 20 to the previous total of 994 giving a final population count for the Village of the Carlton Ironworks of 1,014 in 1901. Although no breakdown of the ratio of males to females is given, this is usually 54% male, 46% female.

To summarise, the Village of the Carlton Iron Works now comprised 192 dwellings with a total population of 1014 (548 males and 466 females).

Whitton Council Infant School (Class One) 1908
Teachers: Miss Dora Holder (left) Miss Olive Dixon (right)

Whitton Council Infant School (Class Two) 1908
Back row: Miss S Iley (Headmistress); G Buckley; Alice Gell; B Dixon; Fred Allison; Tom Wills; L Jackson; J Chandler; Jeanette Jackson; May Moore; Olive Dixon (Teacher).
Middle row, 4th left: Violet Bell, (b. Jan 1903), Author's mother.
Front row: Mildred Fawcett; Emma Borrett; Jessie Chandler; Gladys Wills (b. July 1903); Kate Allison; Flossie Wills (b. April 1902); unknown; Hilda Wills (b. 1903).

1901 April – New Headmistress for Infant's School

Miss Harrison, the headmistress, left in February and Miss Iley was appointed to replace her. There were three other staff at the school, – one certificated teacher, Miss Hill, and two pupil teachers, Miss E H Dixon and Miss D E Holder. The compliment of children attending the Infants' School in the Cassidi Hall was around 140.

1901 October – New water supply pipe

The Carlton Iron Company was granted permission by the North Eastern Railway Company to lay a 12" water pipe under the Clarence Railway for an easement cost of £1 per year.

The pipe followed a path parallel with West Street turning slightly at the top of the street to bring it just west of the railway crossing, where it went under the Clarence Railway, before continuing to the east of the goods warehouse and the station master's house and onwards to the works via the footpath to Foxton. It is presumed that the original 9" diameter water mains pipe, laid by the Water Board in 1898, was being replaced by the 12" diameter pipe because of the need for a greater volume of water to serve the works and the houses now existing in the village.

A map showing the path of the new pipe also showed the station, the subway (under three lines only with access steps to station and southern end of subway), the station master's house, the goods yard and a signal cabin sited in the goods yard. The signal cabin was the latest addition to the station complex.

1903 September – Measles and whooping cough epidemic

Both measles and whooping cough were regular complaints amongst the children of the village and these became more prevalent in September when 80 children were absent from the Mixed School, with 95 out of a possible 135 absent from the infant's school.

Dr Blandford, the Medical Officer for Health, had visited the village during the early part of September and refused a request from the local doctor, Dr Bonnar, to close the schools. However, with the situation worsening, he did order the schools to close at the end of September, for at least three weeks.

1904 April – Schools come under the jurisdiction of Durham County Council

The schools in the Village of the Carlton Ironworks came under the jurisdiction of Durham County Council Education Committee instead of Whitton and Stillington School Board. The existing School Board was asked to act as the Local Sub Committee which they did. The School Board at the time comprised:

Thomas Farrer Fawcett, Chairman, 1 South Street; Company Secretary;
Joseph Thos. Dixon, Vice Chairman, 5 South Street, Engineer;
George Callender, 15 North Street, Timekeeper;
William McIntosh, 2 Morrison Terrace, General Dealer;

Thomas Swann, Whitton Three Gates, Farmer.

The name of the schools changed from Whitton Board Schools, Mixed and Infants, to Whitton Council Schools, Mixed and Infants.

1904 August – School managers appointed

Durham County Council Education Committee asked Whitton Parish Council to appoint two managers for the Whitton Council Schools to oversee their general management. If the managers were dissatisfied with any aspect of the school they could influence the situation by discussing the problem with the head teacher or, if necessary, reporting the matter to Durham County Education Committee.

Parish councillors Joseph Dixon and Thomas Kirk, Jnr. were appointed as school managers.

With the change of authority passing to Durham County Council they, and not the government, would send an inspector to carry out the annual inspection of the schools and children. The inspector would prepare a report, based on his findings, and send it to Durham County Education Committee dealing with the academic progress of the children, the capability of the teachers and the general condition of the schools.

Impression of the Carlton Ironworks c. 1900

1905 February – More problems with sewage disposal

Despite spending much time and effort on the drainage of sewage, Stockton Rural District Council received a letter from Durham County Council which referred to a nuisance at Stillington Beck and informed the Council that the River Pollution Sub-Committee of the County were of the opinion that Sewerage Disposal Works was necessary at the Village of the Carlton Ironworks in order to solve the problem. A sub-committee was formed comprising Councillor Thomas Kirk, Jnr and Councillors Micklejohn and Hunton, who were to investigate and report.

1906 Improvements to the Lowson Street School

The number of children attending the Mixed School in Lowson Street was causing the school inspector some concern. Officially sanctioned to accommodate 160 children there was 194 on the school register. To combat some of the problems, he advised that a partition should be fitted to the hall, which would enable it to be converted to two classrooms, that the yard and toilets be improved and that the teachers be given a private toilet.

All these improvements were carried out during the summer holidays, which had to be extended to allow the work to be completed. The yard was asphalted, extra toilets were built and converted to water closets, a partition was fitted in the hall, the teacher's room was extended to accommodate a toilet and all the floors in the school were repaired.

1907 The Top School

Durham County Education Committee proposed that a new elementary school suitable for approximately 250 children should be erected in the Village of the Carlton Ironworks. The Parish Council agreed and cooperated with the Education Committee in finding a suitable site for the new school. The site selected was at the top of the hill above Morrison Street and just beyond the vicarage, with the proviso that a suitable water supply could be made available.

1907 Carlton Iron Company buy Mainsforth Colliery

The colliery at East Howle had been closed and heavy financial losses incurred because of a serious fire. In consequence, a new source of coal had to be found. The Carlton Iron Company had been negotiating the right to mine coal and fireclay in the Mainsforth area for several years and, having obtained important leases on these rights, they decided to purchase Mainsforth Colliery. Leases were obtained from Colonel Surtees, who was the 'Lord of the Manor' at Mainsforth, the Ecclesiastical Commissioners, Lord Eldon and several others, the leases were for a period of 42 years and covered about 1000 acres.

The cost of purchasing the colliery was £152,290 which was paid for by two mortgages provided by Walter Morrison the chairman of the company, one for

View of the Carlton Ironworks looking north. c. 1900
This photograph gives a clear view of the regeneration stoves positioned around No. 3 Blast Furnace. The Lodging House at the centre of the picture appears to be in a state where it was no longer being used to accommodate workers and had probably become the weigh house, a purpose for which it was used for many years after the closure of the Carlton Iron Company. At bottom right of the picture can be seen piles of briquettes manufactured at the Briquette plant, which was situated a little further to the right.

Carlton Iron Company c. 1900
View of the ironworks looking west with North Street at the bottom right of picture. The engine shed and the engineer's office are just to the left of centre with the slag heap being formed on the extreme left of the picture.

£133,015 and the other for £42,218. The excess amount, above the purchase price of the colliery, would cover the cost of any ancillary equipment and the building of houses for the workers.

A couple of years later the company gained the royalties to mine 160 acres on the west side of Bishop Middleham and, in 1910, they linked the Bishop Middleham and the Mainsforth coalfields underground. To ensure an adequate workforce to work the mine, the Carlton Iron Company had to provide housing in the vicinity and accordingly they leased, bought or built approximately 500 houses in the areas surrounding the Mainsforth Colliery. These houses were acquired in places such as Chilton, Chilton Lane, Thrislington, West Cornforth, Thinford Bridge, Metal Bridge, East Howle and Mainsforth. They also bought the Christian Lay Church in East Howle and a villa named Glencragg in Mainsforth at a cost of £700 to be used as the mine manager's residence.

1907 August – Sewerage disposal works to be built at the Village of the Carlton Ironworks

Since receiving the opinion of Durham County River Pollution Sub-Committee on February 1905, Stockton Rural District Council had only tinkered with the problem and received another letter from the County Health Inspector, dated November 1906, complaining about the pollution at Stillington Beck and asking what course of action the council proposed to adopt. Following this, Stockton Rural District Council leased an acre of land from Sherburn Hospital, which included the quarter acre already leased, and the surveyor was ordered to immediately draw up plans and specifications for a Sewerage Disposal Works to be built on this land.

Tenders were invited for the construction of the works and the following were received.

A E Hobbs £100.11.5; G A Revell £115.9.9; S Walker £119.14.0
Goodall Bros. £125.8.10; J Pearson £131.0.11; W Robinson £134.15.3;
R Wilson £142.19.0.

A E Hobbs was awarded the contract and entered into a bond with two sureties for the fulfillment of the contract.

When the work was completed, a man was engaged to attend the sewerage works and keep them in good working order.

1908 Thomas Kirk, Managing Director of the Carlton Iron Company since 1876 dies – William Thomlinson, Thomas Kirk's son-in-law, takes over as Managing Director

William Thomlinson, a director at the works since 1906, had previously taken over Thomas Kirk's position as managing director of the Seaton Carew Iron Company and was now responsible for both organisations.

1910 Bridge over beck at bottom of the 'Donkey Bank'

An agreement between the Carlton Iron Company and Slingsby Duncan Shafto of Beamish Park, Co Durham was reached regarding a bridge over the beck at the bottom of the Donkey Bank.

The agreement read as follows:

> The company hereby agrees to demise and grant to S D Shafto (Lessee) full right and liberty for him and his tenants, servants and licensees, by day or night with or without horses, cattle, carts and carriages etc. except traction engines, for all purposes connected with the use and enjoyment of the lessees land, to pass and repass over and along the road of the company in the Township of Whitton which lies between South Street and the stream known as Bishopton Beck, and which said road is nine feet wide.
>
> Lease for 20 years and from year to year. The lessee shall also have the right, so far as the company can grant same, of erecting a cart bridge over the said stream and so connect with said road. The bridge shall be erected of such material and design as shall be approved by the company. The lessee to pay the company five shillings per year.

Signed by: W Thomlinson for the Carlton Iron Company, and S D Shafto.
Witnessed by: Thomas Fawcett and T Lister Clark.

1911 March – Manor Farm (in some documentation this was called Whitton Farm but, judging by the fields shown on the map accompanying the conveyance, it was Manor Farm)

West House Farm and Manor Farm at Whitton had been put on the market and the chairman of the Carlton Iron Company, Walter Morrison, bought Manor Farm, which included 120 acres of land, from Mr Anthony Wilkinson and others, with most of this newly bought land bordering the north and east areas of the company.

Morrison leased the farm to the Carlton Iron Company for a period of 21 years permitting them to utilise the land as required. The lease was however terminated in 1915 when the company bought the farm.

1911 Census – Housing and population

No housing development had taken place in the village since the 1901 census and therefore the number of houses in the Village of the Carlton Ironworks remained at 192.

The combined population of Whitton and the Village of the Carlton Iron Works was quoted as being 1113 which was an increase of 14 on the total given in the 1901 census. The 1901 population of the Village of the Carlton Iron Works can in consequence be increased by around ten giving a population of 1024 in 1911.

Summary of situation in 1911:
Number of dwellings in the Village of the Carlton Iron Works = 192
Population of the Village of the Carlton Iron Works = 1024

Rosedale East Mine Generator House

In 1900, the Carlton Iron Company installed a generator at the East Mines to provide power for lighting and haulage. Around 1910 it was dismantled and transferred to the Village of the Carlton Ironworks and enabled the provision of some street lighting in the village.

Photo© from the Hayes collection, Rydale Folk Museum

Boiler Room of the Generator House
Photo © from the Hayes collection, Rydale Folk Museum

1911 July – Basic Phosphate Company closes

The Basic Phosphate Company ceased all operations. The Carlton Iron Company held one third of the shares issued by the Basic Phosphate Company and acquired the remainder of the company for its written down capital value of £450.

The £450 allowed the Basic Phosphate Company to clear their liquidation debts, principally owed to Barclay's bank, and the Carlton Iron Company took total possession of the premises and plant.

1911 Thomas Kirk, Jnr resigns

Thomas Kirk, Jnr resigned his position as the work's manager at the Carlton Iron Company.

He continued as chairman of Whitton Parish Council, a position he had held since 1895, until he left the village in 1913.

Mr P C Bune was appointed as the new works' manager with a salary of £400 per annum.

> Bune was a strict disciplinarian not only at the works but around the village and was quick to admonish anyone not behaving in a suitable manner. His power as work's manager was immense, and his wishes had to be respected by company employees both in and out of work time, otherwise the result could be the loss of both job and house tenancy.
>
> Bune used his power to influence the local policeman and virtually instruct him to stop children playing in some areas of the village, especially those close to his house in Mount Pleasant. This attitude caused a lot of stifled resentment among the villagers, especially as there was no designated play area for children. Eventually the Parish Council took a hand and wrote to Mr Thomlinson, managing director of the Carlton Iron Company, in an attempt to arrange an area where the children could play. They were offered the waste land below the Lowson Street school and although they deemed this area not totally suitable it was, for the time being, accepted.

1911 Rosedale Ironstone Mines abandoned

Due to heavy losses at the East Mines and the poor quality of ore now available at both East and West Mines, it was considered useless to continue further and the directors of the Carlton Iron Company decided that operations at Rosedale be stopped and the mines abandoned.

All useful equipment was salvaged from Rosedale and included the electricity generator, which had supplied the East Mines with light and energy. The generator was transferred to the works at the Village of the Carlton Ironworks, where it was used to boost existing plant in supplying electric power to the works. Agreement was reached between the Carlton Iron Company and Whitton Parish Council that the generator would also provide power for the lighting of paths approaching the works, in particular the 'Black Bank' and later some limited street and house lighting in the village.

1911 More financial help needed

The Carlton Iron Company were in urgent need of money and Walter Morrison, chairman of the company, was kind enough to give £5,000 in order that pressing accounts could be paid.

1911 September – The Top School

A new school was erected at the top of the village just beyond the vicarage and, because of its position at the top of the hill, it became generally known as the Top School.

The school was formally opened on September 11th when all the teachers and children from the Lowson Street school took possession. They were joined by 32 infants and one uncertificated teacher from the Cassidi Hall school. Mr Kirtley, the headmaster, was at this time assisted in the new school by five teachers and one pupil teacher. The teacher who accompanied the infants from the Cassidi Hall to the Top School was Miss Mary Liverseed, who became quite a celebrity in the late 1990s because of her longevity – she was 107 years old in 1998. She left Stillington in November 1912 to take up a teaching post at Eaglescliffe.

The remaining teachers, infants and equipment from the Cassidi Hall were transferred to the Lowson Street school on December 11th. The infant school teachers were pleased with the change to a purpose-built school and greatly improved conditions, especially as there had been three different occasions during the year when rats had been sighted in the Cassidi Hall during lessons. Two of these rats had been caught by a dog being brought into the school, whilst the third escaped to the beck after running through the children in the classroom.

The Cassidi Hall was never to be used as a school again, except for Sunday school, and took on the role of village hall.

1912 Miner's strike

The miners at Mainsforth, which was owned by the Carlton Iron Company, joined the Mining Federation's call for a national stoppage of work in support of a guaranteed minimum wage.

The strike lasted from February 29th until April 11th and, as a result, two furnaces at the Village of the Carlton Ironworks had to be shut down, one on March 3rd and the other on March 27th. Although the strike ended on April 11th it took until the end of May to get the furnaces working normally again, which caused a loss of earnings for the men and a financial loss of about £6000 for the company.

Morrison, the chairman, again helped with a loan of £15,000 to assist the company through the difficulties caused by the strike.

THE DEVELOPMENT OF THE VILLAGE OF THE CARLTON IRONWORKS

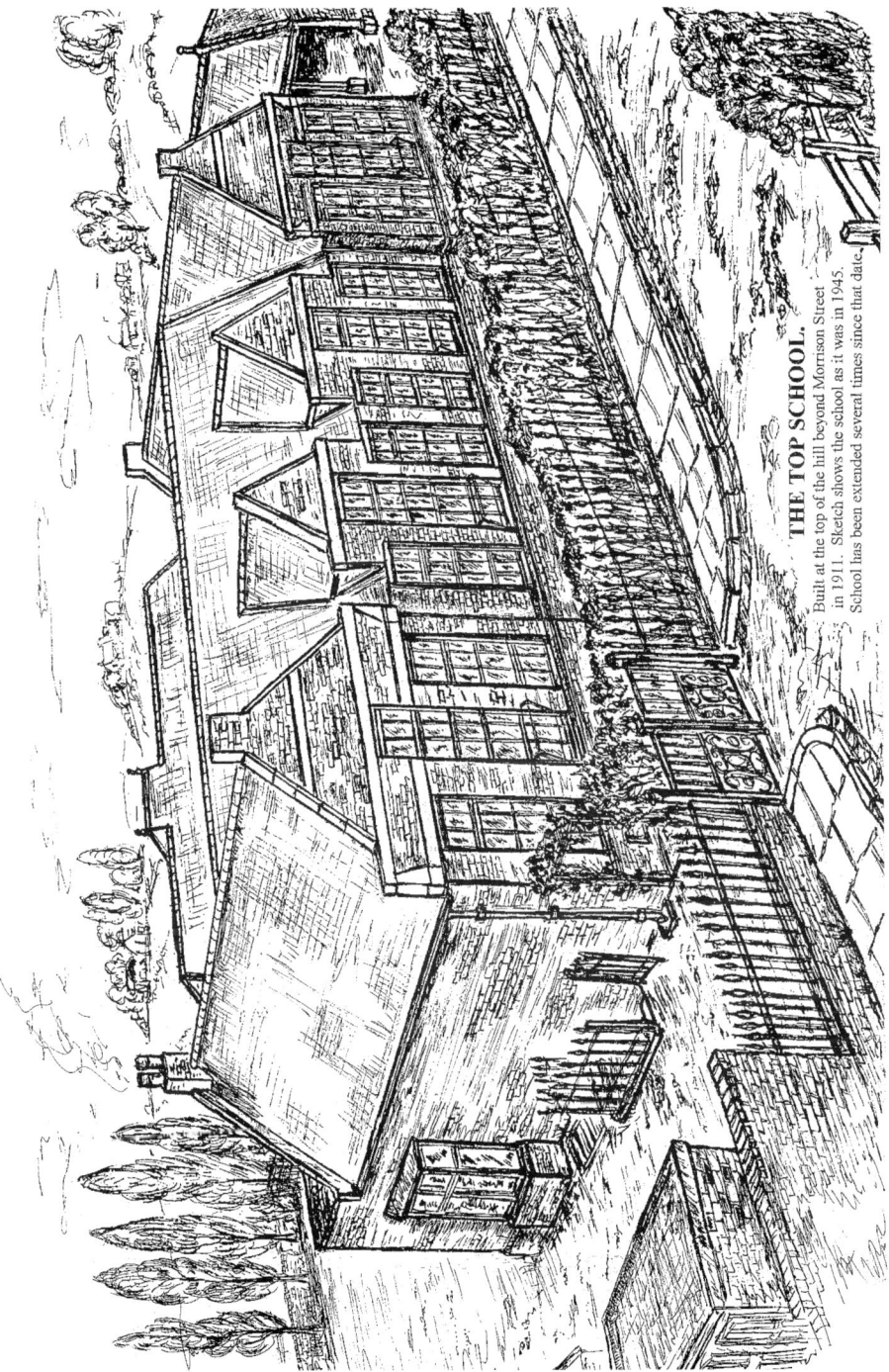

The Top School
Built at the top of the hill beyond Morrison Street in 1911. Sketch shows the school as it was in 1945. School has been extended several times since that date.

By the end of May output from Mainsforth Colliery had reached 1,500 tons average each full working day and this was reported as being favourable.

1912 Redmarshall Street

The building of ten houses had commenced at the top of Redmarshall Street but the need for more houses was apparent, and the managing director of the Carlton Iron Company reported that he had under consideration sites for a total of thirty more houses, five of which would be for officials of the company.

Ten more houses were eventually built in Redmarshall Street, and fourteen in Kirk Street.

1912 Allotment for the Top School

The Education Committee had decided that the school needed an extra interest in its curriculum and authorised the lease of an allotment where gardening could be taught, in a practical manner, to the older boys attending the mixed school. The allotment chosen was one of those in existence on the south side of Morrison Street and situated about fifty yards east of the school.

1912 December – Blacking Mill

Thomas Wilkinson leased the building, which had housed the rolling mills, from the Carlton Iron Company for the purpose of manufacturing foundry blacking and related products. From this time the building was known as the Blacking Mill.

The term of the lease was thirteen years at an agreed rental of £70 per annum.

1913 February – Bathrooms and water closets for houses in Mount Pleasant

The Carlton Iron Company submitted plans for alterations to their houses in Mount Pleasant, which included the fitting of bathrooms and water closets. The Planning Committee of Stockton Rural District Council approved the scheme for the water closets but withheld further approval.

1913 December – Water closets to be fitted to new houses

An instruction was sent out by Durham County Council that all new houses were to be fitted with water closets and old privies converted when possible.

1913 Redmarshall Street

The building of Redmarshall Street was completed and comprised two groups of ten terraced houses running parallel and forming a narrow back alley with West Street. They were good sized houses with a large backyard and a small but private front garden, a facility not enjoyed by any of the previous houses except those in Mount Pleasant and the end house of South Street.

> The improvement in quality of these houses was due to the Public Works Loan Board offering privileges to anyone building an improved type of 'workingman's

the blast furnaces at the Village of the Carlton Ironworks in production, despite the enormous competition then prevailing not only in the area, but worldwide.

1914 Slag Crushing Plant (The Cracker) and closure of the Briquette Plant

Mr Benjamin Maughan leased a plot of land from the Carlton Iron Company on which to build a slag crushing plant.

It is probable that the equipment used in the crushing of slag for the manufacture of briquettes was also leased to him, until he erected suitable plant of his own, which would mean that the Briquette Plant had already closed (this fact is not recorded).

He was permitted to use the slag from the company's slag heap at a rental based on the amount of slag used. The plant was sited between the Blacking Mill and the slag heap and became known as 'The Cracker' because of the noise created by the crushing and cracking of the slag that was then used for road making. The removal of slag over a long period created a large hole in the slag heap and this was named the Cracker Hole. The Cracker Hole became home to a large colony of jackdaws who used its sheer, cliff-like faces as a safe nesting place.

1914 Outbreak of war

The outbreak of the First World War halted all further development in the Village of the Carlton Ironworks and most of its young men volunteered for active service.

149 of the village youth volunteered for active service. 36 were killed in action.

1914 Ministry of Munitions takes control

The Government, seeing no early end to the war, created a Ministry of Munitions to control the iron and steel industry in order to achieve the maximum output of metals to the specifications most urgently needed for the manufacture of armaments.

The Carlton Iron Company worked under this restraint throughout the war.

1915 Headmaster dies

Mr Thomas Kirtley, who had been headmaster at the village school since 1879, died after what was described as a short illness, although in reality he had suffered long periods of illness during the last few years. Thomas Kirtley had been a parish councillor since the formation of Whitton Parish Council in 1895 and was its chairman for many years.

Mr John Buchan took over as headmaster in October 1915 but had to report for war service in August 1916, when a temporary head took charge for the duration of the war. His name was Arnold Russell Binns.

1915 December – The Little Tip

Following agreement with the North Eastern Railway Company, the Carlton Iron Company contracted the railway company to build extra sidings alongside those which already existed. The Carlton Iron Company paid all the costs of construction, including fences, gates and signals. Slag and other solid waste was tipped alongside the north side of the railway, starting about 100 yards east of the station to form a piece of land which was level with the railway and stretched to the Carlton Bridge. Sidings were built on this land and when they were completed more slag was tipped, and later the area became a favourite play area for the village children, which they named the Little Tip.

> In 1953 the Little Tip was to become the site of the first buildings to be erected and used by The British Refrasil Company for the manufacture of prototype high temperature insulation blankets. These blankets were designed to insulate the exhaust pipes of aircraft and so protect the structure of aircraft from the heat created by their engines. Modern aircraft engine developments ensured the success of this type of high temperature insulation and enabled the company to expand into other areas of insulation, such as that of nuclear pressure vessels, and to become the main source of employment within the village for many years.
>
> The history of The British Refrasil Company, later to be named Darchem Engineering, requires a book of its own to explain how it expanded to become a major producer and supplier of insulation and other engineering products to all types of industry worldwide.

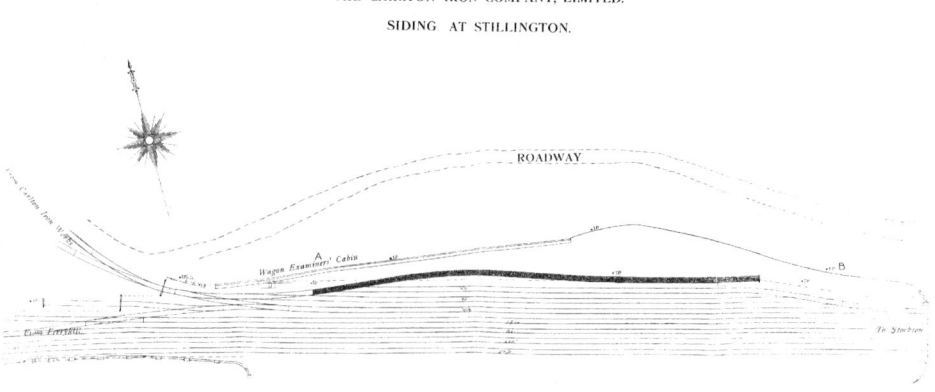

The above map shows the position of the siding built by the North Eastern Railway Company for the Carlton Iron Company in December 1915. The Carlton Iron Company paid all the cost of construction, including fences, gates and signals. Slag and other solid waste were tipped to form the basis of the siding and the excess created what was to be named the Little Tip. The Carlton Bridge can be seen on the extreme right of the map and the retaining wall which formed the back street of Railway Cottages can be seen on the lower left of the map. The 'roadway' was the Black Bank leading to the ironworks.

1917 June 27th – Postmaster and Post Office

Mr Tom Jackson, the station master, left the village because he had been appointed as station master at Heaton, near Newcastle. His duties as the village station master included those of village postmaster with the station office also being used as the post office. The Parish Council decided that his departure was an ideal time to separate the two functions and find suitable premises for a post office away from the station and also appoint an independent postmaster. In accordance with this decision, Mr Burchley the Darlington postmaster, who was in charge of the district post offices, was requested to attend a meeting of the Parish Council to discuss the matter.

At the meeting, Mr Burchley agreed to do all in his power to find a suitable postmaster and the clerk to the parish council, who was also the company secretary of the Carlton Iron Company, promised that the company would assist in finding suitable premises for the post office. Further discussion took place regarding suitable candidates for the position and it was resolved that Mr Burchley would approach Mr Joseph Parry with a view to his son, William, taking up the work and arranging for the post office to be within his premises. This arrangement was completed and the post office was transferred to 43 Morrison Street, where the Parry's lived, and William Parry was appointed as postmaster.

When housed in the station, the post office was known as Stillington post office, because the station was named Stillington, and it continued under that name at its new address. This meant that, sited in the Village of the Carlton Ironworks, was a post office and a station both bearing the name of Stillington.

1918 Influenza epidemics and School closures

Two epidemics of influenza occurred during the year, one in July the other in November, and both caused the school to be closed. In July, the closure was for two weeks, whilst the November epidemic closed the school from November 19th 1918 until January 7th 1919. Influenza continued to persist throughout the village during early 1919 and, in February, the schools were forced to close again for another month.

Other reasons for the school closing during the year were, one week in February to allow the teachers to help in the distribution and collection of ration cards, one week in March to allow the teachers to help the Rural District Council Food Control Committee with a meat distribution scheme, and a further week to celebrate the end of the war after the signing of the Armistice on November 11th. These closures, plus the normal holiday periods, caused the pupils to be very unsettled and obviously their education suffered through loss of school time.

1918 War against Germany ends

The Armistice was signed on November 11th 1918 and the war with Germany came to an end. The village men returned home to much celebration which, however, was tempered by the loss of 36 menfolk who had been killed in action.

One man from the village, Lance Corporal J T Tingle, had been awarded the Distinguished Conduct Medal for bravery at Neuve Chapelle in France where his

A HERO'S RETURN.

ENTHUSIASTIC RECEPTION FOR A BRAVE SOLDIER.

Lance-Corporal J. T. Tingle, who has been awarded the Distinguished Conduct Medal for gallantry at Neuve Chapelle, reached his home, Carlton Ironworks, Stillington, about 6.30 last night. The people of the village turned out en masse to welcome him. Amongst those who met him on the station platform were Mr Harold Kirk, M. P. Bune representatives of the firm of the Carlton Ironworks Co., Ltd., and Mr Thos McKenna, general secretary of the Cleveland and Durham Blastfurnacement's and Cokemen's Association.

He had the protection of a strong bodyguard to save him from the too demonstrative enthusiasm of the men who wanted to carry him shoulder high, and was assisted into gaily-decked vehicle, and accompanied by the local body of boy scouts, with their bugle, band, and drums, a procession was made around the village, where loud cheers of welcome greeted him.

Later a smoking concert was held in the Station Hotel, over which Mr T. McKenna presided. Mr Percy Bune, on behalf of the people of Carlton Ironworks, said they were all delighted to have Lance-Corporal Tingle amongst them again, and congratulated him upon his splendid action at Neuve Chapelle, whereby he probably saved the lives of his whole company, and was instrumental in capturing a number of Germans who were in greater numbers than their captors. He was also delighted that his feat had received official notice, and that he was to be awarded the D.C.M.

Mr Kirk associated himself with the remarks of Mr Bune. Mr McKenna also added a few words of welcome and congratulation, and said the Blast-furnacemen of the district were proud of the honour which their colleague had won, the glory of which was reflected upon the village he belonged to, and upon the Association which he had so lately served as a works representative.

Lance-Corporal Tingle, in an unpretentious manner, thanked everybody for the grand reception which had been given him. He alluded, with restraint, to the deed which had been spoken about, and said that he had only done a soldier's simple duty.

The rest of the night was spent in harmony, Lance-Corporal Tingle enjoying to the full the company of his old friends and neighbours.

Above: A newspaper cutting describing the return of Lance Corporal J T Tingle to the Village of the Carlton Ironworks after his exploits during the 1914–18 War, which had earned him the Distinguished Conduct Medal. *Photograph below* shows Mr Tingle (the Prince), with Mrs Atkinson in Stockton High Street during the late 1940s.

action had saved the lives of his whole company and was instrumental in them capturing a number of Germans when they themselves were completely outnumbered. He was given a hero's welcome when the whole village turned out to greet him home and see him met by local dignitaries and paraded around the streets in a gaily decked vehicle accompanied by the local boy scouts and their band.

The celebrations continued into the evening with a smoking concert being held at the Royal Hotel on his behalf.

Prince Tingle, as he became known, lived and worked in the village for the remainder of his life and was a well known character whose voice could be heard ringing around the ground during the home football matches.

1919 Mr Buchan returns

Mr John Buchan, the appointed headmaster of the mixed school, returned from war service on April 29th and resumed his duties. Mr Arnold Russell Binns, who had been acting headmaster during Mr Buchan's enforced absence, left the school the following day.

1920 Dorman Long and Company take over the Carlton Iron Company

Dorman Long and Company had grown to be a major world producer of steel and its engineering products by keeping ahead in the field of development. The introduction of the Bessemer Convertor had made it possible to produce steel in commercially viable quantities but ironstone from the Cleveland Hills was unsuitable

Village Celebration March
Celebrating the end of the 1914–18 War. Danny Cornwall is riding the white horse and Mr E R Newcomb playing the big drum.

for use in this process because of its phosphoric content which, in the early stages, could not be burnt off in the convertor. Many local companies, such as the Carlton Iron Company, were committed to the use of Cleveland ironstone and therefore continued with the production of pig iron and malleable iron whilst Dorman Long and Company decided to import ore from Europe in order to manufacture steel by the use of Bessemer Convertors. This decision proved vital and allowed Dorman Long and Company to flourish when steel overtook malleable iron as the preferred material for many engineering components. They remained in an excellent position to expand when the high cost of development forced the industry to be rationalised and less successful companies were forced out of business or were taken over.

This then was the background to Dorman Long and Company taking over the Carlton Iron Company, a takeover which included nearly all of the houses in the Village of the Carlton Ironworks and a substantial amount of the land surrounding the village. The only properties not included were Railway Cottages, the station house and Glykoline Terrace.

The nominal capital value of the Carlton Iron Company at the time was £325,000 and initially Dorman Long and Company obtained seventy per cent of the shares, and gained control of the company, by paying the sum of £540,000 on January 31st 1920.

A further sum was paid by Dorman Long and Company for existing stocks of ores, minerals, flue dust, all scrap, the machinery in the malleable works, the rolling mills and plate rolls, horizontal reversing engines, five mills and plant, an air compressor, a Ford motor car used by Colonel Thomlinson and a motor bus which had been used for the transportation of workmen. All of these items were valued at prices existing in January 1920 and the appropriate sum paid at a later date.

Dorman Long and Company appear to have been quite generous in the price they paid shareholders for control of the Carlton Iron Company, and their attitude to the village and its development was also one of goodwill, until the depression of the mid-1920s caused a decline of the iron and steel industry and all its dependencies.

Colonel William Thomlinson was retained as managing director of the Carlton Iron Company, but the remainder of the board was replaced by members of the Dorman family.

  Sir Arthur J Dorman KBE. became Chairman;
  J Dorman and A Dorman were appointed as directors.

1920 Village development continues

The development of the Village of the Carlton Ironworks was continued by Dorman Long and Company with the building of more houses in West Street.

A further twenty-nine houses were added to West Street and these were built in small terraced blocks comprising four, three, six, eight and eight houses. The

THE DEVELOPMENT OF THE VILLAGE OF THE CARLTON IRONWORKS

West Street c. 1925

Photograph taken from the railway crossing gates showing both old and new houses in West Street and the Royal Hotel. The older houses on the left were built in 1872, whilst the new houses on the right were not built until 1920. The trees in front of the new houses still have their trunks supported, which suggests that they had only recently been planted.

West Street (North)

The top two blocks of West Street were turned to run parallel with the railway and were consequently facing north. Initially they were named West Street North but this was later changed to a continuation of West Street. This view shows West Street from near the subway and gives a good idea of the quality of the houses and the pleasant outlook provided by the trees. The Cricket Field can be seen mid left of the picture. *Photo taken 1998.*

West Street

Above: A photograph of West Street (north) taken from the end of the Cricket Field and showing the Royal Hotel in the background. The end house in the foreground was first occupied by the Hindley family and Mrs Annie Hindley baked cakes and pies etc and sold them from a shed in the yard, along with sweets and chocolate. She also sent her family around the streets to sell her produce. Around 1936 the Featherstone family moved into the house and Mr Featherstone set himself up as the village cobbler utilising the shed as his workshop.

Right: The bottom block of houses in West Street with South Avenue just visible beyond the end house. The end house was the home of the Norman family from c. 1935 and it was from here that Mr Norman operated his taxi service during the '30s and '40s.

first two blocks faced north, and were opposite the station, whilst the remainder were built opposite the houses already existing in West Street and were separated from them by a wide road, a grass verge lined with trees and a pavement. All the new houses had a good sized front garden, with the first two groups having bigger backyards than the remainder, although all the yards were of a decent size.

> In the late 1940s the owners of these houses were given the opportunity of buying the field at the rear of their houses, which afforded them a generous plot of land to transform into gardens with plenty of space for sheds and garages.

The new West Street houses were of exceptional quality with plenty of space at both front and back and symbolised the good intent shown by Dorman Long and Company towards the future of the village.

1920 Street Lighting

A further street light was erected just beyond the south side of Carlton Bridge in the Village of the Carlton Ironworks. This brought the total of street lights in the village to eight, with five on the path to the works and one at each end of Morrison Terrace erected around 1910. All were powered by electricity supplied by the works generator.

South Avenue
South Avenue from the new Workingmen's Club on Bishopton Road. This picture shows the extensive gardens in front of the houses and also gives a perception of the view from the houses. *Photo taken 1998.*

1920–21 South Avenue

The final phase of the housing programme to be undertaken by Dorman Long and Company was the building of two blocks of four terraced houses at the bottom of, and perpendicular to, the new houses in West Street. These were high quality houses with an ornate stone front terrace and a balustraded wall with steps leading down to the garden. With the front of the houses facing south, the street was named South Avenue.

Initially, only senior personnel from the ironworks and other local dignitaries were allotted these houses, because of their high quality and fine outlook.

The long front garden which now exists was not a feature until the 1950s, when the field in front of the houses was sold to the occupants and subsequently made into the extensive gardens now in place and well established.

1921 Boundary Problems

> The boundary line dividing Stockton Rural District Council and Sedgefield District Council ran directly between new West Street and old West Street and northwards to the east of Station House and Glykoline Terrace.

South Avenue
Photograph of South Avenue looking west showing an ideal view of the frontage and quality of these houses. *Photo taken 1998.*

In July 1920, after the exchange of much correspondence, Sedgefield Rural District Council and Stockton Rural District Council decided to hold a joint meeting to resolve the situation regarding the new houses (new West Street and South Avenue) being built in the Village of the Carlton Ironworks, which were just inside Sedgefield RDC but just outside Stockton RDC's jurisdiction under which the remainder of the village was governed. At this meeting, it was resolved that Sedgefield RDC would pay Stockton RDC fifteen shillings per house per annum for the connecting of their drains to the existing Stockton sewer, and that the scavenging of the houses including the Station House and Glykoline Cottages would be the responsibility of Sedgefield RDC. However, the matter of the boundary being altered to enable the new houses and existing houses inside the Sedgefield border to be brought inside Stockton RDC jurisdiction was unresolved. This move would affect approximately 160 acres of land and it was agreed to let the matter stand for three years. If during this time there were no further material developments, then Sedgefield RDC would agree to a certain portion of the Parish of Stillington being added to the Parish of Whitton and consequently to Stockton RDC. The word 'material' was defined as meaning the erection of more than 50 houses or an increase in rates of £500.

In consequence South Avenue, new West Street, Glykoline Terrace and Station House remained under the jurisdiction of Sedgefield District Council and Stillington Parish Council and not Stockton Rural District Council and Whitton Parish Council, who controlled the remainder of the village. However it became policy in major issues concerning the whole of the village that the two parish councils would hold joint consultation meetings to agree a common policy.

Despite the promise of a boundary change after three years, the above situation continued until the formation of Cleveland County in 1974, when the whole of the village came under the jurisdiction of Cleveland County Council and the parish councils united to form Stillington and Whitton Parish Council.

1921 Sir Hugh Bell becomes chairman of the Carlton Iron Company

In 1921 Sir Hugh Bell (Baronet), a well known ironmaster, who had given his name to the Hugh Bell school in Middlesbrough, was appointed chairman of the company.

In 1853 Hugh Bell and his brothers (Bell Brothers), had created an ironworks on the northern bank of the River Tees at Port Clarence. These works had already been taken over by Dorman Long and Company.

Sir Hugh Bell's wife, Lady Florence, became famous when her book 'At the Works' became a social and historic record of the lives of ironworkers and their families. Although originally published in 1907 it was much later, in the 1980s, that the book's historic value became apparent.

'At the Works' was an illuminating look into the lives and conditions that the ironworkers' families endured during the period dating from around 1870 to 1900. Even though she was the wife of an ironmaster, Lady Bell was obviously sympathetic to the workers and their families, and was the founder of the Clarence Workingmen's Club.

1921 The Park

In keeping with their policy of bringing better housing and amenities to the Village of the Carlton Ironworks, Dorman Long and Company constructed a park on the site of the now abandoned clay quarry. Clever use was made of this ugly scar on the landscape, by creating different levels of lawns and sloping areas of shrubs and gardens from the uneven ground, resulting from the ad hoc removal of clay over many years.

The park comprised a wooded area, eventually named the plantation, many immaculate lawns, an abundance of shrubs, plants, flowers, some particularly graceful willow trees, and an exceptionally fine monkey puzzle tree. Seats were sited at various positions throughout the park, with one of these being named the Shady Seat, because an adjacent hawthorn bush was trained to provide a complete overhang of foliage which gave ample shade to occupants of the seat from the sun and shelter from the rain. Another feature was the Roundie, a circular seat positioned at one of the highest levels of the park and surrounded on three sides by a neat low hedge which retained a mass of shrubs and small trees. The official village flag pole was sited at the centre of the Roundie with the War Memorial close by.

The Park
Sketch showing steps leading to the Messines Road gate with Railway Cottages at top right.

The Park
Constructed by Dorman Long and Company soon after they had taken over the Carlton Iron Company in 1920. The site was set between the Clarence Railway, Redmarshall Street, Kirk Street and the Chapel Bank. The area used had previously been the site of a clay quarry and brickworks and great use was made of the differing levels created by the clay cutting. The park was a wonderful asset to this industrial village and allowed villagers an area of extreme beauty and tranquility that was unfortunately lost in the 1950s through lack of community finance. View taken from the steps in the central path leading to the Kirk Street gate. Kirk Street can be seen in the centre of the picture. *Photograph c. 1925.*

The park was a very scenic, interesting and relaxing place which was kept in immaculate condition by a full time park keeper, firstly Mr Chandler and later Mr Alf Kendall, and was in stark contrast to the scene on the opposite side of the Clarence Railway where the blast furnaces, the blacking mill, the coke ovens, the glykoline and the slag heap all combined to create a grimy industrial environment.

1921 May – Name of schools changed

The name of the schools was changed from Whitton Council Schools to Stillington Council Schools, Mixed and Infant's Departments. County number 353. Board of Education number 344.

1921 Messines Lane

In order to gain access through Carlton Bridge to the shops, schools and church on the north side of the railway, the south side residents of West Street, Redmarshall Street and Railway Cottages had created a footpath which ran between the embankment of the Clarence Railway and the north edge of the clay quarry. When the park was constructed, this path was upgraded to form a road which was named

Typical views of Stillington Park c. 1946

Messines Lane. This unusual name probably derived from Messines Hill in France, where the British army battled for weeks during the 1914–18 war before successfully ousting the Germans from this coveted high ground and thus made further advances possible in the long running Battle of the Somme. The majority of soldiers from the village would certainly have been fighting in this area, if not being actually involved in the battle for Messines Hill, and naming the road after the hill was a fitting tribute to those who died and those who came home from that horrific battlefield.

1921 Bell Square

Bell Square was constructed in conjunction with the park, and included an oval enclosure sited in the middle of the square which was created by the area between the two blocks of Redmarshall Street, the back of West Street, and the double park gates.

The oval enclosure was planted with poplar trees which were fine for many years but, by the 1950s, they had grown too large for this confined area and when rooks formed a rookery in the trees, the nuisance they caused became to much for the adjacent residents. These two factors led to the eventual felling of the trees in the 1960s, when the oval area was paved to maintain the presence of a roundabout.

There is a slight doubt about whom the square was named after. Candidates included the wife of Thomas Kirk, the former managing director of the Carlton Iron Company, whose maiden name was Mary Bell, and a lady friend of Walter Morrison, the former chairman, whose name was Bell. Both of these persons claim some support but, at the time the oval enclosure was being created and the poplars planted, the chairman of the Carlton Iron Company was Sir Hugh Bell and it is highly probable that the square was named after him.

1921 Census – number of houses and population

The census information regarding the population of the Village of the Carlton Ironworks was integrated within that of Whitton and Stillington parishes, which is detailed below.

Census data for the Parish of Whitton
Population = 1153
Number of dwellings = 231 (including 222 from Village of Carlton Ironworks).
This would give an average number of persons per dwelling = 4.99.

Census data for the Parish of Stillington
Population = 269
Number of dwellings = 51 (including 41 from the Village of Carlton Ironworks)
Giving an average number of persons per dwelling = 5.2.

Data relating to the Village of the Carlton Ironworks
Number of houses in village at 1911 census was 192.

Additions since that date have been: Redmarshall Street 20; Kirk Street 14; West Street (new) 29; South Avenue, 8.

Total of additional houses = 71 giving a new overall total of 263

In calculating the population of the Village of the Carlton Ironworks, the data detailed above with regard to the parishes of Whitton and Stillington, the majority of which relates to the Village of the Carlton Ironworks, would make it reasonable to assume that five persons was the average number residing in each dwelling.

To summarise we had: Number of dwellings in village = 192 + 71 = 263.

Estimated population = 263 multiply by 5 = 1315.

1921 East Farm at Stillington

William Gibbin, who was managing East Farm on behalf of Merton College, bought the farm from Merton College for the sum of £5,500 and immediately transferred ownership to Dorman Long and Company.

The area of land involved in the sale was 258 acres and included the Cricket Field and the allotments adjacent to it.

Evidence suggests that Mr Gibbin bought the farm on behalf of Dorman Long and Company and this is substantiated by one of the minutes of a director's meeting which took place on October 12th 1921. The minute states: 'The managing director reported the conclusion of the purchase of East Farm, Stillington, through Mr W Gibbin the present tenant, from the warden and scholars of Merton College, Oxford, in consideration of the sum of £5,500'.

1921 Sherburn Hospital selling their Whitton Estate

Sherburn Hospital had decided to sell their Whitton estate and offered Stockton Rural District Council the opportunity to buy two acres of land, including the area which they were currently using for the sewerage works in the village of the Carlton Ironworks.

The council ultimately agreed to purchase four acres of land to allow for any required expansion to the sewerage works and paid Sherburn Hospital a total of £500.

1921 Summary of the first fifty years

It was now just over 50 years since the first houses were built in the Village of the Carlton Ironworks and below is a summary of what existed in 1921, including some of the works buildings.

18 houses in North Street

31 houses and a cooperative stores with accommodation above in old West Street

29 houses in new West Street

16 houses in South Street

5 houses in Mount Pleasant

3 houses in Office Row. Plus one accommodation in White House

3 shops/houses and Workingmen's Club with accommodation above in
    Morrison Terrace
  4 houses in Railway Cottages
  41 houses in big Lowson Street
  17 houses in little Lowson Street
  44 houses in Morrison Street
  3 houses in Glykoline Terrace
  20 houses in Redmarshall Street
  14 houses in Kirk Street
  8 houses in South Avenue
  The vicarage, schoolhouse, Station House and Royal Hotel
  The total number of dwellings = 263.

Other buildings worthy of note were: the infant's school in Lowson Street, the mixed school above Morrison Street, the Cassidi Hall, St Johns Church, the Wesleyan Chapel, the engineer's offices, the White House offices, the engine shed and the former lodging house now being used as a weigh house. The station is supplemented with a ticket office, a signal cabin and a goods yard equipped with crane and warehouse. A subway allows pedestrians passage under the railway and access to the station. Passenger, freight and mineral traffic make the station and the adjacent sidings a bustle of activity.

No more houses were built in the Village until 1949 when a council estate was commenced.

1922 February – Number of men working at the Carlton Iron Company

The following information was given by the company secretary to the Minister of Labour concerning the ratio of disabled personnel employed at the Carlton Iron Company.

  Total number of people employed by the company = 460.
  These comprised 405 men and boys and 51 women and girls
  Number of disabled on the payroll in receipt of a disabled pension = 23.

The secretary stated that numerous other workers who had been wounded in the war had not been asked if they were in receipt of a disabled pension because the company regarded this as being too inquisitive.

The twenty-three disabled represented five per cent of the workforce and was in keeping with a pledge previously made by the company to the Minister of Labour with regard to the employment of disabled persons.

1922 Influenza Epidemic

The Medical Officer of Health ordered the schools in the Village of the Carlton Ironworks to be closed for three weeks in January due to an epidemic of influenza.

1922 March 13th – Triennial Parish Meeting and election of Parish Councillors

At triennial meetings, parish councillors were elected to serve on the parish council for the following three years. The administration of Whitton Parish Council required nine councillors to be elected and previous triennial meetings had only been attended by sitting councillors or their selected nominees. Nominations for councillors had only exceeded the number of councillors required once in the last five meetings, which meant that the existing council or their selected nominee was almost certain to be returned unopposed.

This triennial meeting took a major step towards attaining some democracy in the election of parish councillors, because it was attended by forty-three villagers who were able to prevent the election being controlled by the sitting councillors. The proceedings of this triennial meeting deserve to be reported in some detail therefore the following text gives a full account of the happenings that occurred therein.

> Mr R A F Bell opened the meeting as chairman but, as he was a candidate for the council, he gave way to Mr H W Mills who was not a candidate.
>
> Mr Mills asked that any nominations for councillors be handed to him.
>
> The names of the eighteen nominations were received and put to the meeting and voted upon by show of hands. Nominees Callender and Dawson had to be put to the meeting twice, because they had received an equal number of votes at the first count, on the second count Callender was elected.

At this juncture Mr Johnson demanded a poll, and he was immediately supported by Messrs Spence, Butler, Wrigby and McWilliams – the necessary number of electors required to enforce this request.

Mr Johnson stated that the reason they wanted a poll was because they had promised some of their fellow men, who were working and could not attend, that they would demand a poll. He also stated that a show of hands was unsatisfactory and almost a farce in a place like the Village of the Carlton Ironworks. (Presumably meaning that people were afraid to be seen to vote freely in the presence of works officials and other village dignitaries who made up most of the existing council).

Mr Bell proposed that no poll be taken, but the chairman stated that no amendment could be put to the meeting unless the demand was withdrawn and he had no option but to declare a poll unless a withdrawal was made within the stipulated time of 10 minutes.

At the end of the ten minutes a poll was still demanded and the chairman declared that a poll would be taken, which meant that all the people in the parish who were eligible to vote would get the chance to do so.

Candidates and Results

Show of hands	Candidate	Poll	Show of hands	Candidate	Poll
8	Bell, RAF	35	9	Bune, Percy CH	53
36	Butler, Wm.	111*	17	Bury, Rev. RV	70
22	Callender, Fred	84	26	Carlton, Robert	94*
28	Cleary, Dr John P	135*	22	Dawson, John Geo.	114*
2	Dodsworth, Ben	49	33	Johnson, Wm.	121*
19	Marshall, John	64	38	McWilliams, Anthony	181*
20	Moore, Robert	70	38	Rigby, Geo. Wm.	140*
27	Stephenson, Thos.	114*	19	Stibbard, Thos.	65
26	Thurston, Wm.	105*	5	Waring, John W	70

*The persons elected were Dr John Cleary, William Johnson, John Geo. Dawson, Geo. Rigby, Wm. Thurston, Wm. Butler, Robert Carlton, Anthony McWilliams and Thos. Stephenson

The result of the poll was almost exactly the same as that of the vote taken at the meeting, with the only change being Dawson favoured to Callender. This would suggest that the forty-three people who attended the meeting generally knew the feelings of the rest of the villagers, and had reflected this in their voting, with the main objective being to get the senior works personnel removed from the council.

The ruling council previous to this meeting had been, Bune, Bell, Callender, Dawson, Hopper, Johnson, Stephenson, Waring, and Stibbard with only Johnson, Stephenson and Dawson surviving. Of the others Bune was works manager, and Bell, Hopper and Waring all held senior staff positions at the Carlton Iron Company. This was the first time a poll had been demanded, and one can only assume that the men of the village were tired of being domineered by the same people, both at work and in their leisure activities.

Another change that occurred immediately after this meeting was that the venue for the parish council meetings was changed from the work's offices to the Lowson Street school. This however was probably coincidental with the company offices being moved from the White House to Middlesbrough.

1922 April – The Carlton Iron Company offices transferred

The head offices of the Carlton Iron Company were transferred from the White House in the Village of the Carlton Ironworks to Zetland Place, Middlesbrough.

1922 April – Children's Recreational area

Children were no longer allowed to play on the waste ground in front of South Street and the policeman was continually driving them off the streets, generally at the instruction of Mr Bune, the work's manager at the Carlton Iron Company, who had been voted off the parish council at the last meeting. They had been allowed to play

STILLINGTON WAR MEMORIAL
Sited in the park near the 'Roundy Seat' (now demolished) and the Flag Pole.
Erected to the grateful memory of the men of this parish who gave their lives
in the Great War. (1914–18).

Make them to be numbered with thy saints in glory and to everlasting God.

Also to commemorate the return of 113 men

Argyle, A V	Barr, J R	Blenkinsop, F	Challis, A	Cowans, S I
Cummin, J G	Daniel, W	Durrant, A	Fawcett, N	Fenny, W
Gell, C	Goodman, H	Hardy, G H	Harper, B	Harper, H
Harris, T	Hill, A	Jackson, E	Johnson, A	Metcalfe, M
Parker, W	Robinson, G H	Stewart, A	Tait, J	Townsend, E A
Walkington, G H	Ward, M	Whitewell, R	Wills, H L	Wilson, W
Wilson, W O	Wood, G	Wood, H	Wright, A	Wyeth, R
Young, G				

The war of 1939–45

Britton, E	Charlson, G	Hardy, R	Kendrew, J
Lupton, J	Stewart, W	Tingle, A	

in the field opposite the station when this was managed by Mr William Gibbin, but the field was now in the ownership of Dorman Long and Company who had recently given permission to the men of the village to relay the turf in order to make the field suitable for use as a cricket field. The men guarded the field zealously and did not allow the children to play there. This field henceforth became known as the Cricket Field, and a disused wooden railway carriage was mounted on a brick base at the top corner of the field to act as a cricket pavilion. This was used until around 1952, but gradually fell into total disrepair and was removed, although the brick foundations remained for many years afterwards. The parish council were exasperated by Mr Bune's continual harassment of the children and wrote to Colonel Thomlinson, the managing director of the Carlton Iron Company, in an attempt to resolve the problem of a play area. Colonel Thomlinson gave permission for the children to play on the waste ground between the Lowson Street school and the Clarence Railway, but this was not totally satisfactory and the lack of a suitable recreation ground continued to be the subject of debate for many years.

1922 May – The Unveiling of the War Memorial

The following is part of a transcript from the *Stockton and Teesside Herald* dated 20th May 1922.

> "The Dean of Durham, Bishop Welldon, dedicated a beautiful Gothic cross in Yorkshire stone, which had been erected in the Village of the Carlton Ironworks, in memory of the 36 men of Stillington Parish who gave their lives in the war and to commemorate the return of 113 men who served. The unveiling ceremony took place on Saturday afternoon and was performed by Col. Thomlinson the Managing Director of the Carlton Iron Company. The cross costing £250 is enclosed in a miniature park laid out in a commanding spot in a new part of the village, and a large crowd witnessed the proceedings. Wreaths were laid on the memorial by relatives of the dead and the Last Post was sounded. The Reverend R Bury, vicar of Stillington and the Reverend H A Hodgson, Wesleyan Chapel Superintendent, assisted in the service and the Carlton Ironworks Band tendered the National Anthem to conclude the ceremony".

The statement regarding a miniature park in a new part of the village would suggest that this was the first area of the Park to be prepared. The band referred to would be that shown in the photograph in Appendix 12

The Reverend Bury had also requested that a brass eagle lectern and a Roll of Honour be placed in the church to the memory of those who died in the 1914–18 war. As a consequence, a brass eagle lectern (shown left), and a brass plaque were placed in the church. The plaque was sited on the north wall of the church on a base of black marble. The inscription on it reads: 'The brass eagle lectern in this church was erected by the parishioners and is dedicated to the service and glory of God and is a memorial in honour of those men who gave their lives for King and country in the Great War 1914–1918'. Followed by the names of the fallen.

A private memorial brass plaque was mounted in the church by the Fawcett family in loving memory of their second son, Norman, a sergeant in the 18th DLI (PALS), who fell in action on May 3rd 1917 when aged 25 and was buried at Gavrelle, France. Also in memory of their adopted son, Frank Blenkinsop, a lieutenant in the 19th DLI regiment, who fell in action at St. Quentin, France on May 16th 1917, aged 31. 'They died the noblest death that man can die Fighting for God and Right and Liberty'. Mr Fawcett was the company secretary to the Carlton Iron Company, who lived in the house modified for him at the west end of South Street.

After the Second World War of 1939–45, a grey marble plaque was erected and inscribed 'In thanksgiving for those who returned in safety and in memory of the fallen'. This is followed by the names of those killed in the war.

1922 July – Colonel Thomlinson retires as Managing Director

Colonel Thomlinson, at the age of seventy, retired as the managing director of the Carlton Iron Company and also as the colliery agent at Mainsforth. In order to take advantage of his vast experience, the company retained him as a director acting in an advisory capacity.

1922 October – Coke ovens

The coke ovens at the Carlton Iron Company were updated and the bye products plant improved.

1923 April 17th – Company 'Wound Up' Voluntarily

At an Extraordinary General Meeting it was resolved that the Carlton Iron Company would be wound up voluntarily and Thomas Duncan Henlock Stubbs, the company secretary of Dorman Long and Company, was appointed as the liquidator. This resolve was confirmed at a further Extraordinary Meeting held on May 2nd and it was also agreed that some work would be carried out under the jurisdiction of the liquidator. The available work was given to the workforce on a rotational basis, thus enabling as many workers as possible to earn a little money and thereby allow more of the villagers to pay the rent due on the houses that, with a few exceptions, were owned by Dorman Long and Company.

1924 Headmistress of Infant's school retires

Miss Iley, the headmistress of the Infant's School, retired on the 31st October and Miss Mary G. Lowden was appointed to replace her. The headmistress was at this time assisted by Miss Olive Dixon, an uncertificated teacher, who was suffering from nervous strain and only able to teach about 20 of the 75 children who were attending the school. Miss Dixon retired in 1925 and was replaced by Miss Ann Maria Taylor.

1925 March – Mr P C Bune re-elected to the Parish Council

Mr P C Bune, works manager at the Carlton Iron Company, who had lost his place on the parish council during the memorable meeting of 1922, was re-elected at the 1925 triennial meeting. This is mentioned because of his extraordinary reaction to his re-election. Towards the end of the meeting, and under the heading of Any Other Business, he gave an explanation of his attitude to requests he had received from the outgoing parish council. Quote.

> 'Amongst other requests received was one recently asking that the village be lit with electric lighting supplied by the work's generator. I had not deigned to reply to this, owing to the attitude at the last election of the electors in throwing me off the council. Now that they have seen fit to re-elect me, I promise that the village will be supplied with lights before the autumn. Also, whilst I am on the council, I will do my utmost for the benefit of the community.'

It was agreed that lights were urgently needed in some streets and the clerk to the parish council was directed to write to Mr Bune with reference to getting more electric street lights installed. They were duly installed later in the year.

1925 Blacking Mill

A new lease for the hire of the Blacking Mill was drawn up between Dorman Long and Company and Thomas Wilkinson and Company. The lease was for five years at an annual rental of £150.

1925 Street lighting for the Village of the Carlton Ironworks

Dorman Long and Company agreed to supply and erect more street lights around the village and also supply the necessary power from the work's generator. In response to a request from the parish council, twelve more lights were added to the existing eight that were erected in 1910 and 1920.

1925 May 1st – Whitton water supply

The water pump at Whitton was not working and residents were having to obtain their water from the well sited at the bottom of 'Cobbler's Bank'. The parish council were urged to organise a mains water supply to Whitton and, in consequence, sent a letter to Tees Valley Water Board requesting a quotation for the required work. Tees Valley Water Board communicated with Mr Heslop, the Durham County surveyor, and outlined the cost involved in laying a water main from the archway at the Village of the Carlton Ironworks to Whitton village via the public footpath. The cost was estimated to be £920 plus an interest charge of 10 per cent that the Water Board were legally bound to charge. Differing methods of payment were discussed, with the agreed system being £400 when the work was completed and the remainder to be paid over a ten year period. Whitton Parish Council accepted this offer and, although Stockton Rural District Council agreed to pay the initial £400, the money would be recovered from Whitton Parish Council through their rates.

Map prepared by Dorman Long & Company showing the extra street lighting agreed between them and Whitton Parish Council in 1925.

1925 October – Road from Sedgefield to the Village of The Carlton Ironworks

Sedgefield Rural District Council proposed to build a road from Sedgefield to the Village of the Carlton Ironworks that they would fund at a cost of £16,470. They wrote to Stockton Rural District Council asking if they would like to contribute towards the scheme, but were refused any offer of help. They wrote again, asking that representatives of Stockton RDC met Sedgefield RDC representatives on site. It was eventually agreed that a meeting would take place on April 22nd 1926 at the Board Room, Stockton. Harold Kirk and W Mclaren were two of four Stockton councillors who met the Sedgefield councillors. At this meeting, the two councils agreed on certain items but no details were recorded.

1926 Whooping cough epidemic – Infant's School closed

Attendances were severely affected by children suffering from whooping cough and for several weeks the headmistress appealed, without success, to the Medical Officer for the school to be closed. The Medical Officer finally agreed that the incidence of whooping cough was increasing and closed the school on July 12th until after the summer holidays.

1926 Formation of the North Eastern Iron Refinery Company Ltd

The idea and most of the capital required for the formation of this company came from William Thomlinson, who had succeeded his father-in-law, Thomas Kirk senior, as the managing director of the Carlton Iron Company. Thomlinson had retired from that position in 1922, at the age of seventy, but was still seeking to be active in the business world and was appointed as the first Chairman of the Chemical and Insulating Company that was being constructed on the outskirts of Darlington at around this time. In 1953 this company was to play a major role in the future prosperity of the village. As the major shareholder, Thomlinson became Chairman of the newly formed North Eastern Iron Refinery with the sons of Thomas Kirk senior, Peter and Harold, being appointed as Managing Director and director respectively. Mr F F Sharpe, an iron merchant from Wolverhampton, also became a director and completed the board. A lease was agreed between Dorman Long and Company and the North Eastern Iron Refinery that allowed the refinery use of the land and buildings that had originally been built as the malleable works for the Carlton Iron Company. This area was situated at the north end of the buildings now being used as a Blacking Mill.

Dorman Long and Company supplied the water to the refinery from their 'beck supply' and not from the mains water supplied by the Water Board, which meant the pump at the bottom of the Donkey Bank was still in working order.

The North Eastern Iron Refinery Company was formed with the intention of taking over the production and marketing of a specialised refined pig iron that the Seaton Carew Works had produced for many years. Thomlinson became aware that the Seaton Carew Works were about to cease production and seized the opportunity to bring the work to the Village of the Carlton Ironworks. He also brought Mr J K Smithson, a metallurgist, and other skilled workers from the Seaton Carew Works to enable a smooth transition of the process. The capital involved in setting up the company was approximately £10,000, an investment that not only gave a good financial return, but also gave employment to about 35 villagers for many years. During the 1939–45 war, and for some time after, output from the refinery was controlled by the government. Materials were allocated which enabled refined iron to be produced which, when further processed, was suitable for the production of armaments. Throughout this period the plant worked to its maximum output of about 10,000 tons per year. Sir William Thomlinson died in 1941 and the Chairmanship of the company passed into the hands of Peter Kirk, but the major shareholders were the inheritors of Thomlinson's shares – his daughter and her husband C L Wainwright, who became a director. The company was generally being managed by J K Smithson, who had been appointed as a director in 1938.

1927 Headmistress of Infant's School leaves

Miss Mary J Lowden terminated her contract as headmistress of the infant's school to take up a similar position in Warrington. She had had a difference of opinion with Durham Education Authority over arrangements for the children's Christmas treat, which had upset her deeply and caused her to be unsettled enough to look for employment outside the area. Miss Elizabeth Blair was appointed headmistress on November 1st, a position she would hold until around 1958 when she retired.

1928 October – Quarries opened in Whitton

Mr A F Hobbs of Stockton opened a gravel quarry on the north side of the village green at Whitton. He was allowed to make a temporary access road across the green to his quarry and undertook to make good all resulting damage when he had completed excavation. The parish council, in good faith, agreed to this arrangement, but Mr Hobbs made no repairs to the green and, with no written agreement, it was impossible to force him to do so. Help to resolve the matter was sought by the parish council from Stockton Rural District Council but none was forthcoming.

Quarry workings in the 'Honeypots' field was also causing problems by quarrying across the footpath between Carlton from Whitton. A deep hole about forty yards wide was created where the path should have been, causing danger to walkers especially at night. After many protests from Whitton Parish Council to the quarry owner, Mr Maughan, Stockton Rural District Council instructed him to reinstate the path. He dumped about 300 tons of soil into the excavation to create a platform to carry the path but this was still a danger to walkers, especially at night, because of the steep sloping sides each side of the path. A fence was built along this area of the path and, at some point, a fenced wooden bridge was erected, but Whitton Parish Council was still not satisfied and was gravely

Stillington Infants School, Lowson Street. 1925

Back row: Roland Swinbank; Billy Craggs; George Dixon; John King; Albert Carlton; Bobby Robson; Gus Gent; Jacky Minto; Wilf Lonsdale; Miss Lowden.
Centre: Rushford; Alf Harrison; Marion Pernie; Bessie Harding; Mary Butler; Kathy Fox; G Reevell; Emily Hudson; Edwin Hopps; Stan Butler.
Front: Billy Stewart (standing); Horace Dodds; Lal Wills; Ella Hardy; Elsie Bean; Jenny Peakman; Eva Wyeth; Frank King. The Headmistress, Miss Lowden, married Frank Dixon of 17 West Street.

Stillington Infants School, Lowson Street. Class 2. 1925

Rear: John Stokell; n/k; George Mitchell; Maurice Scurr; Wm Trotter; Lol Harper; Geo. Nevison; Jack Atkinson *Back left:*Irene Storey; John Bell.
*Centre:*Laurie Sirrell; Ernie Clayton; n/k; n/k; Mary Pannett; Manna Stephenson; n/k; Madge Argyle; Ede Henderson; Irene Barr; Eva Gent; Ken & Harry Kennedy; Frank Pernie
*Front:*Marie Hodgson; Eva Purchase; Doris Kendal; Daisy Pinch; Marjorie Linsdell; Peggy Warner; Nancy Stewart

concerned for the safety of persons using this path. Eventually Stockton Rural District Council withdrew their support and, in fact, chastised the Parish Council for making a fuss.

1928 Telegraph Office

The Postmaster General stated that provision had been made for telegraph facilities at the Village of the Carlton Iron Works. No guarantees of minimum use were now required and the service would commence on September 26th 1928.

This facility had been provided after much negotiation with the Parish Council over many months, during which time the Postmaster General had always previously insisted on a guaranteed number of users.

1928 October – Royal Hotel

The Royal Hotel was leased by Dorman Long and Company to John Smith's Tadcaster Brewery. Lease to run for five years at an annual rent of £150.

1929 April – St John's Churchyard

The churchyard was almost full of graves and more land would be required in the near future if burials were to continue in the village. The Parish Council agreed that if the church authorities could not provide the necessary land, they would provide a cemetery with a special rate levied for its upkeep. The Reverend Douglas, vicar of the parish and also a parish councillor, was given the task of resolving the matter by first approaching owners of adjacent land and then contacting the church authorities to see if they could afford to buy it.

1929 Formation of Boy Scouts Group

On 14th August an application was made to the Boy Scout's Association for the registration of a Boy Scout Group under the title of Stillington St Johns. The group headquarters was the Cassidi Hall and the controller was named as the Reverend J C Douglas, Vicar of the Parish of Stillington. The two officers in charge were, Mr Ronald Thompson of 1 Redmarshall Street and Mr Sydney Sayers of Weigh Cottages. The application was approved on 2nd September and the group was given the registration number 10090. Sadly, the group was disbanded and registration cancelled in 1931, since which time the village has not been involved with the scout movement again. There is photographic evidence that the Village of the Carlton Ironworks did have a scout group in 1913 which was still in force at the end of the 1914–18 war when they were reported to be greeting the homecoming of a local hero, Lance Corporal J T Tingle, who had been awarded the Distinguished Conduct Medal for bravery at Neuve Chappelle. Unfortunately no records are available regarding when they were formed or when they were disbanded.

1930 January – Final blast furnace 'blown out' at Carlton Iron Company

Since 1923 the liquidator had allowed one furnace to remain working in the hope that the industry would pick up and also to allow some work for the village men on a rotational basis. This hope had not been realised, and Dorman and Long decided that all work would cease forthwith, thus dealing the villagers another devastating blow.

Blowing out of the last Blast Furnace, January 1930
Since the Carlton Iron Company came under the control of the liquidator in April 1923 he had allowed the working of one of the three blast furnaces to give a little work to the village menfolk on a rotational basis. The above are pictures from the *Evening Gazette* dated January 24th 1930 reporting that the last furnaces had finally been blown out. Picture bottom left is of the park. Picture on bottom right is of South Street. *Reproduced courtesy of the Evening Gazette, Middlesbrough.*

1930 March – Electric supply since the closure of Carlton Iron Company Works

Dorman Long and Company had written to the Parish Council stating that, now the works were closed down completely, they had installed a temporary source of electric sufficient for the houses and shops, and thirteen of the twenty street lights installed. The charge would be £30 per annum paid quarterly, exclusive of breakages and repairs. The company reserved the right to terminate this agreement at anytime and at short notice. After a long discussion, the Council was still deadlocked about whether or not to agree to the terms offered by Dorman Long and Company and the chairman settled the issue by using his casting vote to accept the agreement.

1930 November – Road to Foxton from the Village of the Carlton Iron Works

It had been proposed to build a road from the Village of the Carlton Ironworks to Foxton that would have joined the existing road at Foxton. This would have given a direct route to Sedgefield, but the closure of the Carlton Iron Company caused Durham County Council to abandon the scheme, despite appeals from the Whitton Parish Council.

1930 Parish Council request a change of District Authority

Several incidents during the last ten years had made relations between the Parish Council and Stockton Rural District Council quite strained. Lack of support from the District Council on various issues prompted the Parish Council to apply, during a review of all districts by the County Authorities, to leave Stockton Rural District Council and be placed under the jurisdiction of Sedgefield Rural District. To this end, Whitton Parish Council sent a resolution to Durham County Council which read as follows:

> It is felt in this parish that the time has come when a re-arrangement is necessary. We feel instead of being attached to Stockton Rural District Council the boundary of this parish and that of Stillington Parish, which is already in the Sedgefield Rural District Council, be so arranged with a view to the Village of the Carlton Iron Works and Whitton being solely within the Sedgefield Rural District Council. The part of the Whitton Parish, which is known as the Village of the Carlton Iron Works, ought to be renamed Stillington and attached to the Parish of Stillington. This in view of the fact that the Carlton Iron Company works, after which the village was originally named, are now being demolished. The village of Whitton in this parish should retain its name and be created as a separate parish, which should also be included in the Sedgefield Rural District Council. The Parish Council feels our best interests would be served by being attached to the Sedgefield Area which, in the main, is industrial, instead of being attached to a small and purely agricultural Rural District. We trust that the County Authorities

THE DEVELOPMENT OF THE VILLAGE OF THE CARLTON IRONWORKS

Demolition of the Big Chimney
After surviving several attempts to demolish it, the biggest chimney on the site finally succumbs. Although there are a few spectators, the majority had gone home because an earlier attempt had failed and its final fall came unexpectedly.

take these matters into consideration. We as members of Whitton Parish Council hereby append our signatures in support of the foregoing resolution.

J C Douglas, J G Dawson, A McWilliams, R Carlton, Wm Thurston, R Lonsdale, Dr D McLister, G Rigby.

Durham County Council responded many times to this resolution but no action resulted.

1930 November – Church Yard extension

Dorman Long and Company had given land to the Church Authorities for the extension of the churchyard. The extension necessitated the diversion of a right of way across the Spring Field by three or four yards. When the diversion had been approved, the extended area was enclosed within the churchyard perimeter wall.

1931 Conversion to water closets

The Parish Council received a letter from Mr Bailey, the Sanitary Inspector, stating that he had been in touch with Dorman Long and Company who had forwarded specifications to various contractors for the conversion of the privies in Nos. 2–16 South Street and 1–3 Office Row to water closets. Number 1 South Street would have been fitted with a water closet during its extension in 1898 and the privy at 4 Office Row, the accommodation at the rear of the White House, was probably already converted to water flushing .

1931 Census and Summary of existing workplaces

The number of houses and other significant buildings in the village had not altered since the summary of 1921. However, the employment situation was very different. With the closure of the ironworks, the main employers in the village were: the North Eastern Iron Refinery, the Glykoline, the Blacking Mill, the Cracker and the quarries at Whitton, Thorpe, Stillington and Bishopton. The iron refinery was only working three days a week and, with the other employers only requiring a handful of men to fulfil the necessary work, there was widespread unemployment throughout the village and some families left to seek work elsewhere, mainly to the other steel areas such as Scunthorpe and Royston. A few of the village men found work in Stockton and others were employed by the railway company. Seasonal work on local farms provided a little extra money for some, but the general outlook in the area was poor and unemployment in the village remained at a high level for many years, giving the obvious problems and frustrations associated with enforced idleness and poverty. The closure of the Carlton Iron Company's ironworks and coke ovens had had a devastating effect upon the village but, despite this, the population data given in the 1931 census would indicate that the majority of families remained within the village awaiting better times.

THE DEVELOPMENT OF THE VILLAGE OF THE CARLTON IRONWORKS

General Layout of Back Yards

Photograph, top left, shows a typical privy before conversions to water closets began. These would usually be positioned at the end of the back yard. The privy was fitted with a lid which would lift up to enable ashes and other rubbish to be put in, whilst the small circular lid, visible in the photograph, would be removed to uncover a hole for use when the privy was used as a toilet. The coalhouse would be sited alongside the privy and the door adjoining the privy door on the photograph would give access.

Photograph, bottom left, shows the outside of the back yard with the yard door leading into the back street. The smaller square door alongside would give access to the coalhouse and enable the coalman to deliver the coal directly from the back street.

Photograph, below, shows the remains of the sliding cover which would be removed to allow the scavenge men access to the privy contents in order to rake them into the back street. A following team would shovel up all the contents and deposit them into a horse drawn cart. When the cart was full, it would be taken to an allotted site, usually in one of the farmer's fields, and tipped.

A drop of around 200 in the overall population, since 1921, is indicated and it would therefore be reasonably accurate to state that the population of the village in 1931 was around 1,130 and, although there were still 263 dwellings, some were unoccupied.

1931 Village postal address changed

The Postmaster General was approached by the Parish Council with a view to changing the postal address of the Village of the Carlton Ironworks to Stillington. Now that the ironworks of the Carlton Iron Company had been demolished, there was no reason for retaining the aforementioned name. The Postmaster General accepted this as a sensible suggestion and promised the changes would be incorporated as soon as possible.

> Henceforth postal addresses were changed as noted below:
> **The Village of the Carlton Ironworks** was renamed **Stillington**
> The original **Stillington** was renamed **Old Stillington**
> *From this juncture the new names will be used in the text.*

1931 Stillington branch of Women's Institute formed

The Stillington branch of the Women's Institute was formed in order to create another interest for the women of the village. Visiting speakers and education in handicrafts and cooking were features of their weekly meetings. A prominent member and a true stalwart of the Stillington Women's Institute was Mrs Nan Trotter, who took over as president in 1935 and continued in this position until the early sixties, when she retired. Members of the Women's Institute were

Front cover and two sample pages from the Women's Institute annual programme for 1959

THE DEVELOPMENT OF THE VILLAGE OF THE CARLTON IRONWORKS

The Demise of the Ironworks
These views show the ironworks in stages of demolition. The blast furnaces and the regeneration stoves have gone and only chimneys and brick buildings remain. The engine shed in the centre of the top picture survives until the present day.

always involved when events needed to be arranged in the village and were continually organising or taking part in dances, whist drives, concerts and plays in order to raise money for charity, pensioner day trips and any good cause of the day.

1931 October – Fire Hydrant in West Street

Mr C E Faber, Clerk to Stockton Rural District Council, confirmed that his council had decided to site a water hydrant near the Cooperative Stores in West Street at a cost of £7.10s.8d. The Chief Officer of the Fire Brigade suggested that a hydrant should also be sited at the top of Lowson Street to give easier access to water in the case of fire on the north side of the Clarence Railway. The old cast iron water hydrant that was attached to the original water main, running from the beck to the ironworks, remains as a monument to that early period.

1931 Stillington Nursing Association formed

Members of the village formed a Nursing Association and successfully applied for affiliation to the Durham County Nursing Association. The Stillington Nursing Association comprised Mrs J Carter Hon Treasurer, Miss N Douglas Hon Sec., plus nine committee members, who were dedicated to providing a service to the poor and working-class of Stillington and others within a three mile radius. They appointed Sarah Gertrude Robinson, who had completed her training as a 'Village Nurse and Midwife', to serve the district at a salary of £140 per annum. Miss Robinson was to serve as District Nurse for many years before leaving to become matron at the Hardwick Maternity Hospital.

Fees of twenty-one shillings for members and thirty shillings for non-members, plus a grant from the Durham County Association, were the source of financing the scheme. Mr G K Smithson was soon to take over as the Hon. Secretary, followed by Mr Filby, both of whom worked very hard to uphold a competent nursing service. The local doctor, Dr McLister, although not enthusiastic, was stated as being 'neutral' about the setting up of this service. The doctors had had a nurse under their jurisdiction for some time previous to this.

1931 October – New Lighting Agreement with Dorman Long and Company

A new agreement with Dorman Long and Company with regard to lighting throughout the village was agreed after a long discussion within the Parish Council. It relaxed all liability from the council for the poles carrying the main cables for house lighting. The Parish Council had withheld all lighting payments due to Dorman Long and Company until this new agreement had been forthcoming and they now paid the outstanding amount of fifteen pounds.

The majority of parishes in the area had already adopted the Lighting and Watching Act of 1833 and a general meeting was called where the Whitton Parish Council obtained the approval of the electorate to follow this policy.

THE DEVELOPMENT OF THE VILLAGE OF THE CARLTON IRONWORKS

1933 September – Use of sidings by the Blacking Mill

Dorman Long and Company informed Thomas Wilkinson and Sons of Stockton Street, Middlesbrough, that they would be charged each time their company used the railway network and sidings at Stillington. The charge was threepence a ton for shunting and weighing, and included the hauling of empty wagons into position and of loaded wagons to the point where they were accepted by the North Eastern Railway Company. Thomas Wilkinson and Sons were to indemnify Dorman Long and Company from accidents to their workmen whilst on the sidings.

The Slag Heap
This spectacular view of the slag heap is taken from the top of the Black Bank. The houses of Big Lowson Street shown on the left, gives some idea of the height of the tip and the amount of slag tipped during the fifty odd years that the ironworks were functioning. Before its removal in 1969, the tip dominated the village on the northern side of the Clarence Railway and was a superb adventure play area for the children.

1933 February – West Street Privies

Complaints were made regarding the stench arising from the earth closets in the older houses of West Street and the clerk to Whitton Parish Council was instructed to determine the cost for water closets to be substituted.

1934 Mains Electricity for the village street lighting

It had been proposed to install mains electricity to power the village street lighting, in preference to the present supply provided by Dorman Long and Company from their generator. The cost of this provision had been calculated at £194 that would have to be found by the Parish Council, and the only way they could finance this scheme was by obtaining a loan which would have to be repaid by collecting extra rates from the villagers. A general parish meeting was held in the Cassidi Memorial Hall on June 13th to discuss the matter and this was attended by ninety-one people. After some preliminary discussion, the following resolution was proposed by Mr Tingay and seconded by Mr Orwin. 'The Parish Council be empowered to obtain sanction to raise a loan, not exceeding £194, to be repaid over 20 years or longer, for the purpose of carrying out a scheme of street lighting by mains electricity in the parish of Whitton. That they also be empowered to call for a rate of fivepence in the £1 per annum to meet the cost of the loan, the interest charges and the running cost of the installation'. The resolution was carried by sixty six votes to sixteen and, in consequence, the sum of £194 was borrowed, in accordance with terms sanctioned by the Ministry of Health and Durham County Council, from the Public Works Loan Board, repayable over 20 years.

1934 September – Conversion of privies to water closets

A letter received from Stockton Rural District Council advised the Parish Council that toilet conversions throughout the village must be carried out as soon as possible, to be paid for by the parish council. This was discussed at a Parish Council meeting, during which it was decided to press for the conversions and to also apply pressure to the railway company to convert the privies in Railway Cottages to the water flushing system. The residents of these cottages had complained that their privies were even worse since the installation of pans. This comment refers to the fact that human waste and ashes were originally mixed together within the privy and the collectors raked the mixture into the open before they shovelled it into the scavenge cart. To make their jobs easier, metal pans had been provided for the human waste, whilst the ashes were tipped in a separate pile. The collector would carry the full pan to the cart and empty it whilst the ashes were cleared separately. The clerk to the Parish Council was instructed to write to Mr Faber, Clerk to Stockton Rural District Council, to ask if the cost of the conversions could be spread over as long a period as possible. In June 1935, the Parish Council were still pressing for these conversions to be carried out. The older houses in West Street

THE DEVELOPMENT OF THE VILLAGE OF THE CARLTON IRONWORKS

The Slag Heap
This view of the slag heap is from the back street of Little Lowson Street. The tip came within feet of the back alley and then cut back to allow some waste land where the villagers built their 'places' and where Mrs Florrie Argyle started her first fish shop in a wooden hut opposite No. 58 Lowson Street.

were eventually converted during the last quarter of 1935 by J C Watson at a cost of £8.9s.6d each house. The chapel privy was converted to the water flushing system in November 1936 by Wilfred Wilkinson of Sedgefield but Railway Cottages, which were the responsibility of the North Eastern Railway Company, were not converted until 1953.

1934 Formation of voluntary fire brigade

The local authorities considered that it would be advantageous if Stillington had a volunteer fire brigade that could act swiftly to deal with small fires and limit the larger fires in the village until the Stockton Fire Brigade arrived. The names of 12 volunteers had to be submitted to Mr W Darley, 20 Finkle Street, Stockton, for his attention and for him to make arrangements for their training.

The names given were: Messrs J E Fowler, G H Newton, A Jaques, P Cahalone, T H Atkinson, G A Hodgson, Wm Watts, C E Eldridge, Jos O Donnell, G E Pipe, R Carlton, W Thurston.

The volunteers would receive two shillings and sixpence for each training session they attended at Stockton.

1935 January – Fire Appliances

The volunteer fire brigade asked Dorman Long and Company if they would give the appliances held by them at Stillington to this brigade. This equipment had been obtained during the 1914–18 war and included lengths of hose, a trailer pump, a cart and hydrant keys. Dorman Long and Company agreed to give their fire appliances and a hut for storing to Whitton Parish Council, with the stipulation that the brigade would attend any fires that might occur in both Whitton and Stillington parishes. (Dorman Long and Company owned the houses in West Street and South Avenue that came under the jurisdiction of Stillington Parish Council) and this was agreed.

The council had to find a new site for the hut and they arranged to re-erect it a few yards from the north end of Mount Pleasant.

1935 May 15th, Noon – The end of the Carlton Iron Company

The final meeting of the Carlton Iron Company was held at the registered offices of Dorman Long and Company in Zetland Road, Middlesbrough. Dorman Long and Company, as sole contributors, were represented under Section 116 of the Companies Act 1929 by Mr R S H Capes, the liquidator. Mr Capes had been appointed as liquidator after the deaths of Mr T D H Stubbs and his successor, Mr S W Rawson.

The Liquidator read the notice calling the meeting that had been convened under Section 195 of the Companies (Consolidation) Act 1908, the notice having been advertised in the London Gazette on the 12th April 1935. It was resolved that the Statement of Accounts submitted by the Liquidator, showing how the winding up had been conducted and the property of the company had been disposed of, be approved and that a report of the meeting be forwarded to the Registrar of Companies for registration.

The minutes of this meeting were signed by R S H Capes (Liquidator).

This was the final meeting and the end of the Carlton Iron Company.

1935 Cooperative Stores move to Morrison Terrace

With the demise of the Carlton Iron Company, the workingmen's club in Morrison Terrace, which the company had built for its workforce, became unused and the Cooperative Society moved their stores from West Street into the club building. This gave the store more floor area and allowed the sale of a greater variety of groceries and also a spacious hardware section.

1936 May – Conversion of privies to water closets

A minute in the records of Whitton Parish Council reported that all conversion of privies to water closets in the houses under their control were complete except for the school house.

They were still pressing the North Eastern Railway Company to carry out the conversions to the privies belonging to Railway Cottages.

1937 February – Stillington slag works close down

Stillington Slag Works (The Cracker), was desperately short of work and faced closure if more orders were not forthcoming. In response to their plight, the Parish

Workers at the Slag Crushing Plant (The Cracker). c. 1935
Jim Swales; Fred Swales; Albert Gilbert. After 23 years of producing road materials from crushed slag, the plant had to close in 1937 due to complete lack of orders.

Council urged Sedgefield Rural District Council, Stockton Rural District Council and Durham County Council to give consideration to the slag works when placing orders for their road materials.

A few weeks later there was no significant change to the workload and consequently the works were closed, creating further unemployment in the village.

1937 October – Cricket Field (playing field)

Dorman Long and Company offered to sell the Cricket Field to Whitton Parish Council and, although the Reverend Douglas proposed that the council accept the offer, he did not receive a seconder. His proposal was not acceptable to the remainder of the council because it would mean further charges to be covered by a special rate at a time when the villagers could ill afford any extra financial burden.

1938 June – Telephone Kiosk

The Post Office wanted to erect a telephone kiosk in Stillington and, although the Parish Council had no objection, they informed the Post Office that permission must be sought from Dorman Long and Company, the owners of all the land available in the village, before any site could be used.

The kiosk was eventually erected on the waste land opposite Lowson Street, about fifty yards west of the Infant's School.

1939 June – The Park

Dorman Long and Company wanted Stockton Rural District Council to take over the responsibility of the park. They declined and said that it was a matter for Whitton Parish Council.

Whitton Parish Council also decided to reject the idea because of the cost to its ratepayers. This would have amounted to a rate increase of 1s.1d. in the £1 if the full burden had fallen on the villagers themselves. No help was offered by Stockton Rural District Council to assist the village in retaining the park.

This area of beauty and tranquility was in stark contrast to the industrial dereliction left behind by the closure of the ironworks, and failure to preserve it gives a sad reflection of the environmental attitudes of Stockton Rural District Council at that time.

1938 October – Licence to tip

The North Eastern Iron Refining Company was granted a licence by Dorman Long and Company that allowed them to tip slag and similar waste products at a position towards the north end of the existing slag heap, and also the right to use the route and track constructed thereon. The annual rent for this licence was £10. If any difference or dispute arose, it would be referred to arbitration, in accordance with the Arbitration Acts 1889–1934.

The agreement was signed by:

For Dorman Long and Company: Arthur Dorman, director, and R S H Capes, company secretary.

For North Eastern Iron Refinery: Peter Kirk, director, and G P Kirk, company secretary.

A map, accompanying the agreement, outlined the area allocated for tipping and also showed that the coke ovens, the blast furnaces and most of the works that had belonged to the Carlton Iron Company had been dismantled.

1939 Stillite Products Limited open a factory at Stillington

Mr H A Mackay, a true entrepreneur and sole owner of Stillite Products, leased an area of the old ironwork's site, approximately where the coke ovens had been, upon which he built a factory. The land was leased from Dorman Long and Company, from whom he also leased the offices adjacent to the engine shed which had been built to house the engineers of the Carlton Iron Company.

The factory was designed to produce slag wool, an efficient insulating material, by processing good quality slag. The slag was available in abundance from the nearby slag heap, formed by the Carlton Iron Company depositing slag from their blast furnaces for over fifty years.

A hole in the slag heap created by the Stillington Slag Company had been nicknamed the Cracker Hole and Stillite Products used the same area when they commenced quarrying. A team of men was employed to quarry the slag, which they did by planting explosives in the face of the slag heap and blasting the slag loose. The loose slag was loaded into bogies and winched up the slope from the bottom of the Cracker Hole to a turntable situated near the winching shed. The bogey would be turned on a turntable and then allowed to run down a slight incline on the rails leading directly to the boiler house and furnace just inside the factory gates. The man controlling or 'riding' the bogey had a unique system of slowing it. This comprised of a solid piece of wood, usually a pattern for the pigs used at the iron refinery, that he jammed and levered between the bogey frame and the wheel. When he needed to slow the bogey, he applied pressure to one end of the wood, thus levering it against the wheel and creating a very effective, if somewhat dangerous, braking system.

The blasts and rumbling vibrations caused by the explosives were a constant reminder of the work being carried out, and these were always accompanied by a loud screeching and cawing as hundreds of jackdaws took to the sky after each blast. Despite these constant interruptions to their existence, this colony of birds lived and nested in the face of the Cracker Hole until the tip was totally removed in 1970.

When the slag reached the factory it was made molten, and a controlled flow of the molten slag would be converted into a mass of fine fibres by converging it with a high pressure jet of steam. When cool, the fibres settled and formed the slag wool that could be used as insulation in its loose form or sewn into a cloth covering to create a blanket. Further process enabled the slag wool to be moulded into shapes that would fit components requiring insulation such as pipes and valves.

> After the closure of the Carlton Iron Company's ironworks and coke ovens the village folk had suffered years of hardship and unemployment and the opening of the Stillite Product's factory gave a tremendous boost to their morale that was, unfortunately, soon to be tempered by the outbreak of the Second World War. Many of the younger men were called up for active service and so the factory utilised a great deal of the available female labour. This would be the first time many of the women in the village had worked in a factory environment. By the end of the war in 1945 Stillite Products was employing about 160 people, including 60 women and girls.
>
> By 1965 modernisation of plant and machinery in the factory had become an absolute necessity but Mr Mackay felt he was too old to embark on a factory regeneration scheme. This, combined with the poor quality of the slag now remaining in the slag heap, led to his decision to close the factory. Mr Mackay amalgamated with a Middlesbrough company and moved to a factory in South Bank where a good supply of suitable slag was assured. He did transfer a few of his Stillington workforce to the new site, but travelling to South Bank on a daily basis was inconvenient and costly and eventually most found jobs elsewhere.

1939 September – War with Germany declared

With the outbreak of war, all able bodied men between the ages of eighteen and forty who were not working in jobs considered to be essential to the nation were called to active service. The girls had to join the services or some other organisation that assisted the war effort, such as the Land Army or nursing. The Land Army girls were sent to work on farms throughout the country to replace the men who had been conscripted and they became a familiar sight in their green jumpers and fawn breeches. Quite often, however, the farmers did not respond favourably to their presence and often the girls lived in very rudimentary conditions on the farm and usually took second place to the Italian prisoners of war who were latterly sent to help the farmers.

Another alternative for girls over eighteen was to work in a munitions factory, one of which was built at Aycliffe. This was named the Royal Ordnance Filling Factory and it covered an area of 867 acres with 1000 buildings all camouflaged by earth mounds and vegetation. A few girls from Stillington decided to work at this factory and special trains running from Middlesbrough direct to the factory were organised to stop at Stillington station to take them to work and bring them home. The work was very dangerous for, as the name of the factory suggests, the main task of the girls was filling shells and bombs with explosive powder, then assembling the detonators and fuses. Many deaths were caused through accidents occurring during this process, but no great publicity was given to these events and the girls remained the unsung heroes of the war.

As the war continued, the shortage of miners became so acute that, in 1943, the government decided that some of the new conscripts would have to work in the coal mines instead of going into the armed forces. These men were named the

Bevin Boys, after the minister who created the scheme, and even after the war ended the majority were kept in the mines and not allowed to leave until around 1948. Some village men were drafted into the mines, and although maybe not as dangerous as being in the forces, they were living away from home and had to work long hours in difficult conditions for very little pay.

1939 Ministry of Supply takes control of the North Eastern Iron Refinery

The Iron and Steel Industry came under the control of the Ministry of Supply and the village industry most affected was the North Eastern Iron Refinery. For the duration of the war, and some time afterwards, the refinery was allocated materials that enabled the production of the types of refined iron required in the manufacture of armaments. The cupolas worked at maximum output for the whole of the war producing around 10,000 tons of refined iron per year. Scrap metal of every description was sent by rail to the refinery and unloaded into piles alongside the network of railway lines that covered the site, until eventually every conceivable area around the works was stacked with high piles of rusty scrap iron. An important constituent of

Group of Stillite Girl workers c. 1940
back: Vera Savage, Ena Britton, Dora Goldie, Mary McWilliams.
centre: Eveleyn Milton, Jennie Peakman, Queenie Bunker, Olive Goodman.
front: Bessie Stewart, Dolly Bean, Helen Featherstone, Doreen Cooke.
These girls would be among the first employed by Stillite Products Limited to work in their slag wool factory at Stillington.

the refined iron was silicon and this was delivered by rail in wooden barrels. The wood from the empty barrels was used by the villagers for all types of construction such as sheds, rabbit hutches, fences and of course it was the major source of fuel at a time when coal and coke were very scarce.

The refinery had two cupolas into which the scrap metal, silicon and other elements were tipped in measured loads to be melted down. When a load was completely molten, it was tapped from the cupola and guided into casting moulds to form pigs of refined iron that were distributed to steel manufacturers throughout the country. The cupolas were used on alternate days, one in use whilst the insulation in the other was being fettled and generally made good. This was the task of one man, Mr George Jobling, who also prepared the cupola for lighting by loading it with oil soaked rags, railway sleeper wood, coal and coke. The cupola was then able to be lit and brought up to temperature before the start of the morning shift.

Delivery of the scrap and silicon to the refinery and the distribution of the pigs meant a high level of railway traffic to and from the village with shunting going on continually around the refinery and the remainder of the site. The rail network and sidings constructed during the heyday of the Carlton Iron Company were once again being used to their full capacity.

The refinery employed about thirty men and the company was now controlled by Peter Kirk, chairman, J K Smithson, managing director, G P Kirk and K C Sharpe, both of whom were non executive directors and sons of two of the original directors.

1940 Defence of Village and other war related activities

The war necessitated defensive activities be undertaken in the village and these included the formation of an Auxiliary Fire Service, a unit of the Home Guard, and the formation of Air Raid Wardens, all of which were manned by men who had not

Photograph shows the wreckage of the German Dornier that crashed at Great Stainton after being shot down. The crew of four bailed out and parachuted to the ground, where they were apprehended by the Stillington Home Guard.

Ernst Schneiderbaur, the pilot of the Dornier that crashed at Great Stainton. He was taken prisoner by the Stillington Home Guard.

been called up to serve in the armed forces or seconded to the mines as Bevin Boys. The village escaped the main brunt of the enemy air raids and so these organisations were not needed to any great extent and were only brought into action on very few occasions.

The Home Guard, under the leadership of Mr Norman Young, kept a constant vigil from a specially constructed hut on top of the slag heap. One of their major actions was carried out on March 11th 1943 when a German aircraft, a Dornier on a mission to mark bombing targets around Newcastle, had been intercepted and shot down by an RAF Beaufighter. The Dornier crashed near Great Stainton but the crew of four had managed to evacuate the plane and parachute to safety. The Stillington Home Guard observed this action and were instructed to send a unit to help capture the parachutists. When they arrived on the scene three of the crew had already surrendered but the fourth was missing. They organised a sweep search of the area and found him badly injured with his parachute caught in a tree.

The group that apprehended this fourth crew member included Norman Young, Jackson Wilson, Cyril Butler and Alan Argyle. Cyril Butler, only seventeen at this time, was later called to serve in the army and became the first allied soldier to enter the German city of Bremen when it was captured during their advance through Europe. Alan Argyle was a sixteen year old when carrying out this operation and he was later conscripted to serve in the coal mines as a Bevin Boy.

Towards the end of the war the Home Guard hut caught fire and the Auxiliary Fire Service was called upon to extinguish the fire. Although a useful exercise it was a futile operation, made impossible by the difficult access up the side of the tip to reach the blazing hut. Hoses were fixed from a water hydrant to the trailer pump and from the pump up the side of the tip to the hut. This completed, the pump was started and everyone waited for the water to surge from the nozzle of the hose and extinguish the fire. Unfortunately, the height of the hut in relation to the pump created a back water pressure almost equal to the pump capacity, with the consequence that the water barely trickled from the nozzle. The hut was completely destroyed and the fire burnt itself out, despite the efforts of the local children to keep it going long enough for some boost to the pump pressure to be made available.

The Air Raid Wardens were responsible for ensuring that all lights were 'blacked out' after dusk and for raising the alarm if an air raid was imminent. This they did by going around the village blowing three short blasts on a whistle when the raid started and one long blast when the raid was over. This method was eventually replaced by a siren mounted above the warden's office, which made an undulating whine at the start of a raid and a continuous whine at the end. The warden's office, nicknamed the warden's hut, was one of the outbuildings in the yard of the old workingmen's club in Morrison Terrace that the Cooperative Stores had taken over in 1935. The Air Raid Wardens were also responsible for issuing everyone in the village with a gas mask and, every six months, the school children were taken to the hut by their teachers in order to have their gas mask checked by one of the wardens.

A government campaign was started under the heading Dig for Victory where everyone was encouraged to grow their own food. To promote this scheme, the government asked local councils to ensure that anyone requesting an allotment should be given one. Mr Waring was, at this time, managing the affairs of Dorman Long and Company in Stillington and was also a member of Whitton Parish Council. He was able therefore to liaise between the two organisations and ensure that enough of the land owned by Dorman Long and Company was made available to the council for conversion to allotments. Further encouragement was given to allotment holders when the government issued free vegetable seeds for them to plant.

Members of the Stillington Women's Institute contributed to the war effort by knitting socks, gloves, balaclava helmets and woollen patchwork blankets, all of which were sent to the Red Cross for distribution among the servicemen.

1940 Searchlight Unit

A searchlight unit was sited half a mile west of Stillington, alongside the road to Old Stillington, and was used in conjunction with the anti-aircraft guns positioned at 'Kiora' near the Two Mile House as part of the area defences. The searchlight was manned by a unit of army personnel who became well known to the villagers. They joined in most social activities, used the Royal Hotel as their local and organised football matches against the village menfolk. Two or three later married village girls.

1940 January – Playing Field

Dorman Long and Company asked Stockton Rural District Council to buy or lease about two acres of land situated in front of South Street which they suggested could be used as a playing field for the village. Stockton Rural District Council asked Whitton Parish Council if they were interested but the Parish Council did not want to increase the rates burden of the villagers and therefore rejected the offer.

THE DEVELOPMENT OF THE VILLAGE OF THE CARLTON IRONWORKS

Stillington Auxiliary Fire Service *c. 1940*
Photographs taken outside headquarters in Mount Pleasant

Back (centre): Tom Britton. *Back*: Mr Savage; Jim Swales; Peter Gaffney; Cliff Moore
Centre: Mr Irvin; Freddy Bell; Margaret O'Donnell; Margaret Moore.
Front: Norman Fletcher; Harry Wells; Bertie Clayton; Stan Smith; Wilf Wells.

Back: Tom Britton; Peter Gaffney. *Centre*: Jim Swales; Freddy Bell; Cliff Moore; Ces Challis; Len Oliver
Front: Harry Wells; Bertie Clayton; Mr Irvin

1941 British Plane Crashed

A British plane crashed in the fields to the left of Whitton road and three airmen were severely burnt. After being treated by Dr McMahon, the local doctor, they were taken to the Military Hospital in Sedgefield. This incident exposed the inadequate resources the doctor possessed for such emergencies in the form of bandages and general first aid equipment. He informed the Parish Council of this deficiency and they contacted Durham County Council and requested a list of supplies that the doctor had compiled in order to create a suitable First Aid resource.

1941 November – Communal Air Raid Shelters

One shelter had already been built in Lowson Street and three more were to be sited around the village. They were eventually built in the following locations: one in Morrison Street, one in the shrubbery opposite the west end of South Street and one at the top of Redmarshall Street. Shelters were also built at the bottom of the play-yards in the Infants and Mixed Schools for the use by the children during school hours. Fortunately, these shelters were only used on about half a dozen occasions. When the warning siren sounded, the teachers would hustle the children into the shelters, which was thought to be great fun by the majority of the children, as most of the time in the shelter was spent singing nursery rhymes and playing other group games.

The only hardship occurred when teachers decided to carry out a gas mask practice. The wearing of these masks was unpleasant with the pungent smell of rubber and difficulty in breathing. The practices were probably a good ploy used by the teachers when the children were getting over-excited, although discipline was well maintained in the schools of this era with the threat, and often the use of the cane. Such punishment was always fairly administered at the Stillington schools and no one suffered too much. However, the threat did create an environment of discipline that is essential to the smooth running of any organisation and indeed society.

1942 November – Diphtheria

There were three reported cases of diphtheria in Stillington and the school teachers were warned that any pupil complaining of a sore throat was to be sent home immediately and the doctor informed. Diphtheria was a very infectious and life threatening disease and, in order to combat any spread of the disease, the houses belonging to the infected persons were fumigated.

1943 June – Fund Raising to help the War Effort

The national government instructed local councils to attempt to raise money to assist the war effort and two such events were named Wings for Victory and Salute the Soldier Week. Stockton Rural District Council were asked to raise $40,000

THE DEVELOPMENT OF THE VILLAGE OF THE CARLTON IRONWORKS

PROGRAMME (Continued)

STILLINGTON (Target £2,500)

SATURDAY, 19th JUNE.
  GRAND PARADE at 2.30 p.m.
  OPENING CEREMONY, by R.A.F. Officer, at 3.30 p.m.
  Dance at 7.30 p.m. Admission 1s.
SUNDAY, 20th June.
  COMBINED OPEN AIR SERVICE, at 2.30 p.m.
MONDAY, 21st JUNE.
  WHIST DRIVE, at 7 p.m. DANCE, at 9.30 p.m. Lofsdon, Whist 1s
  Dance 6d.
WEDNESDAY, 23rd JUNE.
  Badminton by Rotale Admission 4d
  FOOTBALL MATCH at 6.30 p.m.
  DARTS AND DOMINOES at 8 p.m. Admission 3d.
THURSDAY, 24th JUNE.
  GRAND DANCE. R.A.F. Dance Band (by kind permission of Group Capt.
  M. Kelly). Admission 2s. CINEMA VAN, 5 p.m.
FRIDAY, 25th JUNE.
  BRING AND BUY SALE at 2.15 p.m.
  WHIST DRIVE, at 7.30 p.m.
  Social at 9.30 p.m.
  Admission : Whist 1s. Social 6d.
SATURDAY, 26th JUNE.
  CHILDREN'S SPORTS at 2 p.m.
  DANCE, at 7.30 p.m. Admission 1s.

THORPE THEWLES (Target £1,000)

SATURDAY, 19th JUNE.
  OPENING CEREMONY, in the Parish Hall, by the Chairman of the Wings
  for Victory Committee, 2.30 p.m.
  Children's Sports, Games, Competitions and Side Shows, 2.45 p.m.
MONDAY, 21st JUNE.
  FILM SHOW, in the Parish Hall, 7 p.m. - 9 p.m.
TUESDAY, 22nd JUNE.
  CONCERT in the Parish Hall, 7 p.m. - 9.30 p.m.
THURSDAY, 24th JUNE.
  BRING AND BUY SALES, on the Vicarage Lawn, at 2.30 p.m
  WHIST DRIVE, on the Vicarage Lawn, at 3 p.m. CINEMA VAN.
FRIDAY, 25th JUNE.
  DANCE, in the Parish Hall, 9 p.m. - 1 a.m.
SATURDAY, 26th JUNE.
  GRAND TOTAL of amount raised during the Week to be announced in the
  Parish Hall, at 6 p.m.

STOCKTON RURAL DISTRICT WINGS FOR VICTORY WEEK
JUNE 19 - 26

STOCKTON RURAL DISTRICT   JUNE 19 - 26, 1943

Wings for Victory Week

TARGET: £40,000 for 8 FIGHTERS

 3d

Programmes for fund raising weeks, Salute the soldier and Wings for Victory

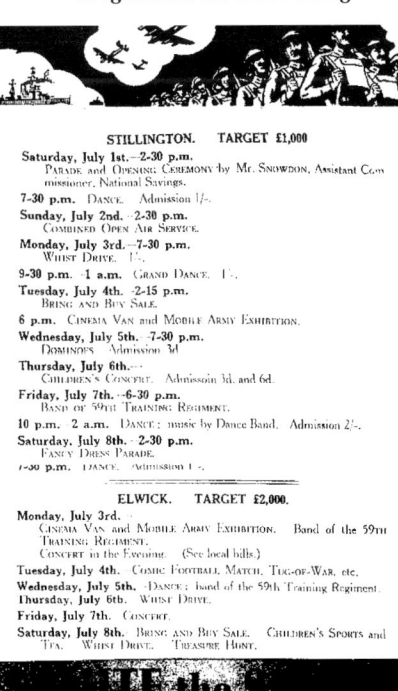

STILLINGTON.   TARGET £1,000

Saturday, July 1st.—2-30 p.m.
  PARADE and OPENING CEREMONY by Mr. SNOWDON, Assistant Commissioner, National Savings.
7-30 p.m. DANCE. Admission 1/-.
Sunday, July 2nd.—2-30 p.m.
  COMBINED OPEN AIR SERVICE.
Monday, July 3rd.—7-30 p.m.
  WHIST DRIVE. 1/-.
9-30 p.m.—1 a.m. GRAND DANCE. 1/-.
Tuesday, July 4th.—2-15 p.m.
  BRING AND BUY SALE.
6 p.m. CINEMA VAN and MOBILE ARMY EXHIBITION.
Wednesday, July 5th.—7-30 p.m.
  DOMINOES. Admission 3d
Thursday, July 6th.—
  CHILDREN'S CONCERT. Admission 3d. and 6d.
Friday, July 7th.—6-30 p.m.
  BAND OF 59TH TRAINING REGIMENT.
10 p.m.—2 a.m. DANCE; music by Dance Band. Admission 2/-.
Saturday, July 8th.—2-30 p.m.
  FANCY DRESS PARADE.
7-30 p.m. DANCE. Admission 1/-.

ELWICK.   TARGET £2,000.

Monday, July 3rd.—
  CINEMA VAN and MOBILE ARMY EXHIBITION. Band of the 59TH
  TRAINING REGIMENT.
  CONCERT in the Evening. (See local bills.)
Tuesday, July 4th. COMIC FOOTBALL MATCH, TUG-OF-WAR, etc.
Wednesday, July 5th. DANCE; band of the 59th Training Regiment.
Thursday, July 6th. WHIST DRIVE.
Friday, July 7th. CONCERT.
Saturday, July 8th. BRING AND BUY SALE. CHILDREN'S SPORTS and
  TEA. WHIST DRIVE. TREASURE HUNT.

pounds during the Wings for Victory week which would pay for eight fighter planes, and the following year £60,000 was requested to equip and feed a Parachute Battalion. Stillington was set targets of £2,500 and £1,000 respectively by organising dances, whist drives, jumble sales, fancy dress parades, sporting events, concerts and street collections. No details of what was actually achieved have been found, but the task of raising such large amounts from such a small community would seem impossible, even though everyone would give wholeheartedly.

1943 July – Holidays at home

War weariness was overtaking the nation and, with travel being limited, even if it could be afforded, the government instructed local authorities to organise a Holidays at Home week and gave permission for a sensible amount of funding to be raised through the rates. The parish councils of Whitton and Stillington called a Joint General Meeting to discuss this project and thereby obtained approval to raise £20 through an increase in the rates.

This money was used to sponsor events that included sports meetings, dances, whist drives, football matches, cricket matches and fancy dress parades, all organised to take place during the week of August 9th–14th.

1943 August – Playing Field (Cricket Field)

Whitton and Stillington Parish Councils were intent on acquiring a playing field for the children of Stillington and, to this end, they invited Mr Spedding of Durham County Playing Field Association to attend one of their meetings. Mr Spedding was able to explain the procedure to follow in the quest for a playing field and advised that the first step to be taken in this instance was the compilation of a joint resolution, to be agreed by the parishes of both Whitton and Stillington.

Mr Carlton and Mr Smithson, respective chairmen of Whitton and Stillington Parish Councils, therefore proposed and seconded the following resolution.

> The united councils of Whitton and Stillington deplore the circumstances attending the position as it at present affects the Cricket Field and hereby give the clerk authorisation to immediately communicate with the owners, Messrs Dorman Long and Company, with a view to securing, on behalf of the said councils, a free gift of land to be held in perpetuity as a playing field. Failing the receipt of the land in gift form, Dorman Long and Company to be asked to either lease the land to the said councils at a reasonable annual rental for 99 years, or sell the land to the said councils for a reasonable price per acre.
>
> The said councils to guarantee that such land if secured will always be used as a 'playing field'.

The above resolution was voted upon and passed by the meeting.

Dorman Long and Company responded to the resolution by agreeing to sell the Cricket Field, which covered an area of 5.2 acres, for the sum of £260. The Parish

THE DEVELOPMENT OF THE VILLAGE OF THE CARLTON IRONWORKS 163

STILLITE PRODUCTS EMPLOYEES c. 1945

Councils thought the price was reasonable but needed the authority of a Public Meeting before finalisation.

In November a Public Meeting decided that as no monies could be borrowed during wartime, and the increase to the rates required to raise the money would be 1s.6d. in the £1., the Councils should ask Dorman Long and Company if they would rent the field for a 5 year period with the option to buy after this period.

Note: A 1d rate in the £1 for Whitton Parish would yield an annual sum of £10.8.0.
    A 1d rate in the £1 for Stillington Parish would yield an annual sum of £3.13.2.

Dorman Long and Company refused this compromise.

1944 July – Playing Field (Cricket Field)

Dorman Long and Company asked the combined councils of Whitton and Stillington to make them a final offer for the purchase of the Cricket Field. They explained that this and other land owned by them at Stillington would be put up for Public Auction at the end of August if no reasonable offer had been received. The Councils decided to offer £130 and Dorman Long and Company accepted this.

As previously stated, no money could be borrowed during wartime and the villagers could not afford the burden of a rate increase, so the money for the purchase of the Cricket Field had to be raised by other means. A Playing Field committee was formed and made responsible for the raising of the money. They organised functions such as dances, concert parties, whist drives and sports days, and wrote to individuals and companies for contributions. Money remaining from the Holidays at Home Fund was being held for future projects and it was agreed that this should be transferred to the Playing Field Fund.

All members of the Women's Institute were on the Playing Field committee and they played a major role in organising all the events and also carried out a door-to-door collection. These fund raising events continued until enough money had been collected to buy the field and cover the legal expenses involved.

1944 October – Final Acquisition of Playing Field (Cricket Field)

A full attendance of the Playing Field Committee met to witness the inspection and agreement of the Deeds of Conveyance for the playing field. Mr Scurr of Whitton Parish Council and Mr Trotter of Stillington Parish Council were selected to sign the Deeds.

Mr Lodge, a solicitor from Sedgefield who was handling the conveyance on behalf of the parish councils, was handed a cheque for £136 as payment for the field and his services.

1945 February – Conveyance of Playing Field (Cricket Field)

Mr R Carlton of Whitton Parish Council and Mr J W Trotter of Stillington Parish Council duly signed the conveyance document that finalised the sale of the playing field from Dorman Long and Company to the parish councils. This meant that after

TEES-SIDER'S TREK THROUGH THE JUNGLE

UNITED STATES MARINES on the island of Guadalcanal, in the Solomons, recently told how the Rev. Leslie Stibbard, a northerner, had burst in on them at their headquarters with an account of his trek through the jungle and over the mountains to escape the Japanese invaders.

This adventurer is the 34-year-old son of Mr. and Mrs. T. M. Stibbard, 11, Lawson-street, Stillington, Co. Durham. He was headmaster of Maravovo Boys' School until the Japanese captured the island, when he and his pupils had to flee.

"To stay meant eventual starvation," he said. "So we decided to try to trek to the Marines' base.

Took Everything

"We had planted vegetable gardens to supply us with food, for we had been cut off from the outside world for eight months, but the Japanese took everything, including the boys' bugles and drums."

During the trek, which lasted for weeks, the party often almost blundered into Japanese troops.

"Some Japanese soldiers coming out of the combat zone looked as if they had been through hell," continued Mr. Stibbard. "Once I lay near three of them, hardly daring to breathe. After a time we abandoned the native trails and cut our way through the jungle and waded rivers."

An old boy of Stockton Secondary School, Mr. Stibbard studied theology at St. Augustine's College, Canterbury. Immediately after his ordination in 1937 he took up missionary work in Melanesia.

Until they received a letter this week, his parents had had no news of him since August last year.

Mr. Stibbard is now at Sydney, Australia.

Leslie Stibbard
Photo shows Leslie during his years as a chorister at Stillington St Johns', c. 1926

years of debate regarding a recreational area for the village, the joint councils of Whitton and Stillington had finally acquired a field for that sole purpose. A sub-committee of Whitton Parish Council was formed to oversee its usage and maintenance. The playing field, commonly known as the Cricket Field, was officially opened by Mr Peter Kirk with various functions such as sports, a fancy dress parade and charity stalls organised to mark the occasion.

1945 May 8th – Victory in Europe Day

The Germans unconditionally surrendered on the 7th May and Mr Albert Dixon was so delighted he toured the village playing his accordion and spreading the good news. Festivities were quickly organised in the village to celebrate the end of the war in Europe. Dances, fancy dress parades and street parties were arranged and two huge bonfires were built to be lit at nightfall. One bonfire was at the top corner of the cricket field and the other on the waste land adjacent to the school in Lowson Street. An old tradition of friendly rivalry existed between 'our side' and 'yon side', depending on which side of the Clarence Railway one lived, to see which side could build the biggest bonfire with both ending up around fifteen feet in diameter by twelve feet high.

Mr Calvert, a local grocer, usually came to the Lowson Street bonfire with a box of fireworks and treated the onlookers to a mini firework display. This was much appreciated because fireworks were scarce and, even when available, few people could afford them.

A Victory Sports Day was organised with £10 contributed from Whitton Parish council precept and £3.13s 2d from Stillington Parish Council precept. These monies were given to the Celebration Committee who were given the responsibility of organising the Sports and Field Day. Any money remaining from these celebrations were to be put aside for the purpose of having the names of those killed in the war added to the cenotaph, and having the cenotaph cleaned and generally upgraded. The total cost of adding the seven names to the cenotaph, cleaning and putting stone curb stones around it, was estimated at £46.10s. The work was carried out in 1948 by Mr Malthouse of Norton Sand and Gravel and a precept rate of 2.5d was agreed on both parishes to cover the necessary shortfall in finances. Mr Malthouse did, in fact, give the curbstones free as a gift to the parishes.

1945 June – The Park

Dorman Long and Company were keen to dispose of all their property and land in and around Stillington and had given Bradford Property Trust Company the responsibility of doing this on their behalf. Through the Bradford Property Trust, they asked Stockton Rural District Council if they would take over the park. This request was passed to Whitton Parish Council, who called a joint meeting with Stillington Parish Council to discuss the matter. After what was reported as a 'thorough discussion' the two councils decided it was impossible to take over the park due to the extra burden

THE DEVELOPMENT OF THE VILLAGE OF THE CARLTON IRONWORKS 167

Redmarshall Street c.1945
View from Kirk Street showing Bell Square, (the poplar trees in the centre), and Railway Cottages at the top of the street. Part of the perimeter hedge of the park can be seen on the right.

South Street c. 1945
This street is now part of the road taken by through traffic. The embankment on the opposite side of the road has been buttressed with a concrete wall and trees are now well established between the fence and the wall giving the houses a pleasant outlook.

The 'Cracker Hole Gang' c. 1946
from left: Matt Taylor, John Swales, John Scott, Alan Farley, Johnnie Gudgeon, Wilf Wilkinson, Walter Norris.

The 'Cracker Hole' was started by the Stillington Slag Company when they were removing slag from the tip to crush in their factory and sell as road building material. The cracking of the slag gave the factory the nickname of 'The Cracker' and in consequence the hole they created in the slag tip became known as the 'Cracker Hole'. In 1939 Stillite Products Ltd set up a factory in Stillington to manufacture slag wool and they recommenced the removal of slag from the 'Cracker Hole'. The slag was loosened by planting explosives as deep as possible into the face of the hole and blasting. It was then loaded into bogeys and hauled to the top of the hole and then taken down to the factory for processing. The above team were responsible for this work with Matt Taylor being the foreman and explosives expert.

that this would place on the village ratepayers. Once again, the chance to retain this area of extreme beauty and peaceful charm on behalf of the villagers was lost without them being consulted. A general meeting would have given the village people the opportunity to express their opinions, but the Parish Councils did not deem this to be necessary. These two councils had fought a long, hard and determined battle to obtain a playing field for the village and yet made no attempt to bargain for the retention of this established and well loved area of relaxation.

Stockton Rural District Council had also distanced themselves from any responsibility of seeking to retain the park by merely transferring the problem to the Parish Councils. The park was eventually bought from Dorman Long and Company by Stillington Estates who sold it off piece-meal as building plots.

The area of land where the cenotaph was sited and access to it was given to the Parish Council free of charge by Stillington Estates with the inclusion of the erection of a fence around the allotted area. They also gave the council the small triangular plot on the opposite side of the road and offered them the eastern side of the park (the Plantation), also free of charge.

The council decided to reject the offer of the eastern side of the park on the basis that it would give rise to liabilities beyond their resources.

1945 Dorman Long and Company sell all their Village houses

Dorman Long and Company continued to dispose of their assets in Stillington and sold all their houses (251 in Stillington and 6 in Whitton), to the Bradford Property Trust Company for £45,500. The aforementioned disposals included the Royal Hotel that was sold to John Smith's for £6,000.

Bradford Trust then offered the houses for sale to sitting tenants, and later to anyone who wished to buy them. Many people bought their own houses and, when given the opportunity, some bought two or more.

Typical of the price being asked for the houses are those in Redmarshall Street that were being offered for sale at around £300. (See picture on pp 167) and Mount Pleasant at around £700.

1945 August 15th – Victory in Japan Day

When the Japanese surrendered on August 14th the way was clear for the demobilisation of the armed forces, affording great relief to the families of men and

Schematic sketch of the 'Cracker Hole' 1945
Sketch shows the 'Cracker Hole' with the winching shed at the top and one of the gang taking a full bogey to the Stillite factory. The remains of the Stillington Slag Company works can be seen opposite the North Eastern Iron Refinery cupolas with the Blacking Mill stretching towards the Clarence Railway.

women serving abroad and especially to those with relatives who had been taken prisoner by the Japanese. Seven village men had died in action during the 1939–45 hostilities.

The village celebrations of this victory matched those that had been organised for Victory in Europe Day.

1946 German Prisoners help clean up the industrial site

At the end of the war, the industrial area on the north side of the Clarence Railway was littered with ruins, scrap and waste of all descriptions, that made it look worse than a bomb site. It is impossible to describe the sight that unfolded as one walked through this area, but a few examples of the things that contributed to the general chaos are cited here.

Firstly, the demolition of the ironworks and the coke ovens, previously part of the Carlton Iron Company, had been carried out but no attempt had been made to clean up the debris which included the ruins and bases of the big chimneys. Part ruins of all types of buildings, blocks of brickwork and loose bricks were scattered throughout the site; the old winch house was still almost complete and much of the blast engine houses remained. The man-made incline and the wall that retained it was intact, the walls that were built to enclose the pig beds were almost untouched and stood for many years hence. The pig bed walls, built in 1870,

North Street (Slag Row). c. 1945
Sketch shows how North Street had become enveloped by slag from the ironworks. Most of the tenants had a place where they kept pigeons, hens and other livestock and these can be seen beyond the houses. The reservoirs, on the left, have been re-opened by Stillite Products and one of the Cracker Hole gang can be seen taking a bogey full of slag to the factory. North Street became surrounded by so much scrap and dirt that the houses were demolished in 1949 and the tenants rehoused in new council houses.

were ten feet high and three feet thick with integrated brick steps going up one side to give access to the pig beds from the ground.

Twisted pieces of boiler plate, girders, old bogies and winch cables made from multiple strands of twisted wire, were littered all round the area. The frayed ends of these cables were as sharp as needles and extremely dangerous to the children who used the area as an adventure playground.

The reservoirs, the cooling ponds and the filter beds, once used by the Carlton Iron Company, had dried up and were full of debris among which frogs, newts and lizards were prevalent. The reservoirs were eventually cleaned out by Stillite Products and used by them as cooling ponds.

Adjacent to the reservoirs was North Street (Slag Row), and although most of the houses were still inhabited they were surrounded by slag, industrial waste and rubbish. They were also subjected to the grime and dirt emitted from the iron refinery cupolas and the Stillite factory, along with the dust and noise caused by the intermittent blasting of slag in the Cracker Hole. This combination of factors, plus the fact that electricity had not been installed into their houses, made the environment of these North Street residents almost unbearable.

Secondly, although Stillite Products had cleaned out the reservoirs, they added to the general chaos by continually tipping waste slag wool among the ruins of the old ironworks. This waste eventually developed a green mould on its surface resulting in great areas of dark green slime occurring throughout the tipping area, with the added problem of rats nesting in the waste slag wool.

They also threw out reject insulation blankets wrapped in wire netting, with the consequence that irregular shaped sheets of wire netting were strewn about the site and, although useful to the villagers for fencing, rabbit hutches and animal pens, this added to the general unsightliness of the site.

Thirdly, there was pile upon pile of scrap metal, at least six feet high, that had been and was being tipped in every available space pending its use at the iron refinery. All types of scrap would arrive daily in railway trucks that would be shunted to a point where the workmen would unload the scrap and throw it onto the piles, from where it would eventually be barrowed to the cupolas. However, the scrap arrived at a much greater rate than it could be used, with the consequence that barely any ground local to the work's rail network was free from these piles of rusty scrap metal.

Wooden barrels packed with silicon also arrived in trucks and, when being unloaded, the barrels would be rolled from the trucks to the ground. The barrels would split on impact and the silicon, the wood and the metal bands, which had held the barrels together, would spread at random over the surrounding area.

The North Eastern Refinery directors allowed the villagers to collect the wood and use it for firewood, fencing and the construction of animal hutches. Unfortunately the villagers would leave the metal bands lying where they had released them from the wood, with the consequence that these were littered not

Day's end at the North Eastern Iron Refinery c. 1941
The men rake out the cupola that has been working all day while the second cupola is fettled ready for an early start next morning. When raking out is completed and the half burned coke has cooled, the waiting youngsters collect a bagful to take home to supplement their household's fuel supply. This was very helpful during the winter months of the war, when the supply of coal was very erratic. Mr George Jobling of West Street, was employed full time fettling furnaces and preparing them for lighting by the use of oily rags and railway sleepers. In the background, barrow-loads of coke and scrap metal are being prepared as the first load for the early morning shift.

only at the site of the works but throughout the village until the Parish Council asked the works to ensure the barrels were dismantled on site.

The extent of the area covered by scrap metal was further increased by Edward James who set up a scrap works between the iron refinery and the Glykoline factory. James proceeded to cover this area, which included the man-made incline, with his scrap metal. He installed magnetic cranes that were supported on three long legs set into concrete bases in a triangular pattern. The cranes were employed to empty the scrap metal from the railway trucks and, with the long reach of the jib, were able to deposit it over a much greater area than the manual methods being used at the refinery. The noise of heavy scrap being moved was almost continuous throughout the day.

Fourthly, dominating the whole scene was the massive towering heap of slag left as a legacy of fifty years of ironmaking and, in its shadows, the large black semi circular corrugated roofed building of the Blacking Mill and a little further north, the two cupolas of the iron refinery.

Finally there was the rancid smell of grease being processed at the Glykoline, the black dust created by the pulverising of coal in the Blacking Mill, the fumes and grime emitted from the cupolas of the iron refinery, the wisps of slag wool drifting from the slag wool factory, the explosions caused by the slag being blasted in the Cracker Hole followed by the screeching of the disturbed jackdaws, the general noise of scrap metal being thrown and tipped, the constant clanking of trucks shunted by the diesel shunting engine and the main line steam engines with all their associated smoke, steam and noise.

Paradoxically, there was something here which bonded the people of Stillington into a closely knit community and created within them a peculiar sentimental affinity for this unsightly industrial creation.

The necessity for a 'clean up' was obvious and the service of a group of German prisoners was organised to help in making up the roads, in particular the Black Bank, and a general tidying up of the site.

Edward James' scrap yard c 1948
View of Edward James' scrap yard showing the magnetic cranes used for loading and unloading scrap from railway trucks.

Remains of the Big Chimney c. 1945

Sketch shows what remained of the big chimney after demolition. Children used the wind tunnels as a camp area where they would light a brazier on which they could roast potatoes and boil birds eggs for a mock feast. Stone fights would be fought by friendly rivals for possession of this premium spot for gang headquarters.

1946 Parish Meeting – First Triennial meeting since the war commenced

The purpose of this meeting was to select parish councillors for the next three years and a good attendance was reported.

Mr Buchan took the chair and asked for nominations for councillors.

Sixteen nominations were received and voting took place with the following result.

Mr S Britton	19	Mr S Butler	23	Mr R J Calvert	9	Rev J C Lockyer	17
Mr G Lowes	23	Mr R Moore	20	Mr R J Carlton	26	Mr P Carr	18
Mr J Henderson	14	Mr T W Newcomb	17	Mr G Pipe	36	Mr J T Scurr	24
Mr O Smithson	15	Mr W Thurston	24	Mr W Trotter	21	Mr G T Tingle	21

The nine persons elected were: George Pipe, Bob Carlton, Jack Scurr, William Thurston, Stan Butler, George Lowes, Tommy Tingle, R Moore and William Trotter.

The assistant counters were Mr Buchan, Mr Sydney Sayers and Mr Arnold Wells.

Mr Trotter was elected chairman.

Mr Carlton was elected vice chairman.

Messrs Thurston and Scurr were appointed as school managers and rate authorities.

Mr Oliver, of Barclay's Bank, was re-appointed as treasurer.

Mr Tom Stephenson was retained as clerk to the council on a salary of £25 per annum.

1946 July – Whitton Duck Pond

The pond had become a collecting point for rubbish and the water was beginning to stagnate due to the natural water flow being blocked. Following complaints about its condition, the Parish Council asked Stockton Rural District Council to fill the pond and direct the water course to a nearby drain.

Mr Brown, the sanitary inspector, investigated this proposal but rejected it, on the basis that the pond was used for watering cattle owned by John Hall, the tenant farmer of Manor Farm. The pond had been used for this purpose since the farm

Group of Stillington infants c. 1947
Photo taken in front of the air raid shelter at the bottom of the school yard, showing the slag heap in the background.
back row: John Hardy; Keith Wilkinson; n/k; Bell twins, Cedric and Trevor; Dennis Littler.
centre: Margaret Barret; Dorothy Simpson; Kathy Bremner; Jean Cutler; Bessy Bell.
front: Maureen Ferguson; ? Burnett; Maureen Fox; Olga Durham; Doris Scurr; Elizabeth Tingle; Margaret Hodgson.

had been formed and an alternative supply of water would need to be provided if the pond was filled in. Durham County Council was responsible for finding a new supply of water and they refused to do this.

Whitton Parish Council then wrote to Captain Parlour, the owner of Manor Farm, seeking permission to fill in the pond. However, it was not until around 1952, that a compromise was reached and part of the pond was filled in. A year later the problem of rubbish and stagnating water still persisted and finally led to the pond being filled completely and the area grassed to form an extension to the village green.

1946 Mr John Buchan retires

Mr Buchan retired as headmaster of the Mixed School after over 30 years in that position, only interrupted by compulsory service during the 1914–18 war.

Mr Mather commenced at the school but only as senior teacher and, although the Parish Council pressed the Director of Education many times to appoint a new headmaster, no replacement was found until August 1948, when Mr Harold Maddison took over.

Mr Mather was then transferred to another school.

1946 July 25th – Schemes for New houses in Village

A plan of a proposed housing scheme had been sent to Whitton Parish Council from Stockton Rural District Council and, after much debate, the Parish Council decided to press for the scheme shown on Plan No. 90. It is presumed that this plan showed the houses that were erected as Whitton Grove and Park Crescent during 1949 and onwards.

1947 August 11th – Formation of Workingmen's Club

Whitton Parish Council received a request, signed by 6 local government electors, asking for a Public Meeting to be called to debate the setting up of a Workingmen's Club.

The request was submitted by Messrs Joseph Henderson, John Trotter, Edward Drury, Harry Harper, Robert Bellerby and Oswald Smith.

A Public Meeting was held in the Cassidi Hall and a very large attendance was recorded.

Mr W Trotter took the chair and immediately declared a personal interest in the establishment of a club and therefore asked that another chairman be appointed. However a vote was taken and Mr Trotter was voted back into the chair.

He explained that anyone wanting to raise objections about the setting up of a workingmen's club would be allowed time to do so before a vote was taken. A vote, taken by show of hands, resulted in overwhelming support in favour of a club.

Mr A Wells and Mr O Smithson counted the votes that showed 125 in favour and 8 against.

The Stillington Workingmen's Club was therefore formed and a committee appointed to run its affairs. The first task of the committee was to find suitable premises for the club and, coincidentally, the church wanted to dispose of the Cassidi Hall. The club bought the hall and, by carrying out a few modifications, such as the installation of a bar, they converted it into their first home.

The Cassidi Hall proved to be admirably suitable for its dramatic change of purpose, whilst the room downstairs provided an ideal club committee room.

The large cellar under the extension of 1884 was used for the storage of beer, and the stage that had been fitted by local volunteer craftsmen in the late thirties was ready made for the staging of entertainment.

The existing sliding partition made it easy to divide the L-shaped room into two for differing functions, whilst being able to return to full size for larger functions such as dances.

The Cassidi Hall remained the home of the Workingmen's Club until a new club house was built near the Donkey Bank in 1968, costing about £90,000.

1947 December – Electric Lighting for the Schools

Whitton Parish Council requested the Director of Education to organise the installation of electric lighting and power into the village schools.

1948 April – Lighting for Whitton Village

The North Eastern Electric Supply Company was asked by the Parish Council to install lighting in the farmhouses and other private dwellings in Whitton and also consider the lighting of the village with three street lights. The council was informed that, since they had turned down a previous offer to install electricity at Whitton, they would have to wait two years until other villages had been completed.

The council sought the help of the War Agricultural Committee to contest and maybe improve on this timescale.

1948 April – Glykoline Terrace

Mr Brown, the sanitary inspector, was asked if the toilet water disposal system for these cottages could be connected to Stockton Rural District Council's sewer near the White House.

The request was refused because, with the additional waste due to come from the new houses now being built in the village, the sewage system would be working at full capacity.

1948 Stillington Estates formed

The directors of the North Eastern Iron Refinery feared that the nationalisation of the iron and steel industry could lead to the takeover of the iron refinery, together with the site and all of the company's assets.

As a precaution against this they formed another company, comprising the same directors, and named it Stillington Estates. They then transferred the site and all other assets of the North Eastern Iron Refinery, with the exception of the refinery itself, into the ownership of Stillington Estates.

In the event of the government nationalising, only the iron refinery would be affected, with the site and other assets being able to be developed free from government control and under the auspices of Stillington Estates. The site included the total area covered by the works of the old Carlton Iron Company, the slag heap and the village park, all of which had been bought by the North Eastern Iron Refinery when Dorman Long and Company were disposing of their holdings in the village.

Companies already working on the site such as the Blacking Mill, Stillite Products and Edward James' Scrap Metal had their leases transferred to Stillington Estates ownership and allowed to continue their activities as normal.

The Glykoline factory had bought their land directly from Merton College and was, therefore, independent of this arrangement.

In an attempt to develop diversification of work in the village, Stillington Estates built a welding fabrication unit, opposite the Blacking Mill, with the intention of carrying out any available sub-contract work. They did some work for a company named Cosely Engineering based in Wolverhampton and owned by K C

The North Eastern Iron Refinery workforce c. 1957
Back row: unknown; unknown; Alan Argyle; Ian Parker; unknown; Bill Beadle; Ron Swainston;
3rd row: unknown; unknown; Frank Breckon; George Nevison; Jack Lockey; John Bremner; Geo. Jobling;
2nd row: J Moran, (*General Manager*); Ali Peekman; Ralph Snowball; unknown; Peter Carr;
Ernie Dilks; Ewie Lavelle; Bob Robinson; Geo. Snowball; E Crangle, (*Fabrications Manager*);
Ron Littler; Frank Hart, (*Chemist*)
Front: Bob Wilks; Frank Pernie; Ali Hodgson; Jack Copeland; John Lockey; Billy Fletcher; Jack Carr;
Bert Rutter; Nelson Argyle; *Chemist standing on right, unknown.*

Sharpe, who was also a director of the North Eastern Iron Refinery and Stillington Estates.

In 1953 Cosely Engineering was contracted to build the first workshops used by the British Refrasil Company and some of the extensions that were to follow as that company expanded.

1948 Stillite Products and the Chemical and Insulating Company (Darlington)

Equipment and plant at the Stillite Products factory were in urgent need of modernisation in order to keep pace with developments taking place within the insulation industry. This would require a substantial amount of capital investment and Mr Mackay, the sole owner of Stillite Products, felt the financial requirement was too much for him to bear at this late stage of his career and, as an alternative, sought the association of another company.

The Chemical and Insulating Company of Darlington was already well established in the manufacture of an insulation named Magnesia and agreement was reached between the two companies with regard to the development of the slag wool industry at Stillington. In furtherance of this agreement, the Chemical and Insulating Company purchased from Stillington Estates the site already being leased by Stillite Products, plus the slag heap and some land to the north of the existing slag wool factory. As negotiations of a merger between the two companies entered their final stages, Mr Mackay blocked the deal and decided to carry on without any modernisation to the slag wool factory. This decision left the Chemical and Insulating Company with a considerable area of land adjacent to the slag wool factory, plus the slag heap itself with no immediate plans for its development.

Five years later the Chemical and Insulating Company were preparing to manufacture a high temperature insulation suitable for application to the exhaust pipes of jet aircraft. They required an engineering solution to the encapsulation of this insulation in order that it could be fitted to the exhaust pipes in a practical manner. Mr Geoffrey Kirk was asked to consider the problem and he submitted a design scheme that encapsulated the insulation in very thin stainless steel to form an insulation blanket. The Chemical and Insulating Company accepted this as a practical solution and gave Mr Kirk complete financial backing to set up a workshop in order to develop his ideas. The workshop was built by Stillington Estates in conjunction with Cosely on the the Little Tip that had previously been purchased by the Chemical and Insulating Company when seeking a merger with Stillite Products.

The manufacturing development and trials proved so successful that the Chemical and Insulating Company formed the British Refrasil Company to manufacture these high temperature insulation blankets on a production basis, and appointed Mr Kirk as their Technical Director.

The company grew rapidly and the land owned by the Chemical and Insulating Company now became very useful in allowing the factory buildings to be extended, without them having to search for suitable sites

1948 Stillington Parish Players formed

In 1948 the Rev R C D Jasper had taken over as vicar from the Rev C J Lockyer and he quickly made an impact on the village with his energy and resourcefulness. Apart from enlivening the church community, he did other things around the village to enhance the community spirit.

One such activity was the formation of an amateur dramatic group named the Stillington Parish Players, who began by performing Nativity Plays at Stillington and other churches in the district. Initially, the major players were drawn from the Stillington church choir and the regular congregation, but gradually others were recruited and the 'Players' went on to perform about two plays a year. The plays were generally staged in the Infant's School where the stage and lighting had to be erected, by a team of volunteers, each time a new play was performed. Each play would usually run for two or three nights and always to a full house. Jasper's ambitions for the Parish Players grew and, before he left the parish, he had directed a couple of Gilbert and Sullivan's operas with an accompanying small orchestra. These were a great success and the cast, which had now grown tremendously, included the members of the chapel with whom Reverend Jasper had forged a much greater understanding than had previously been enjoyed. The Reverend Jasper left Stillington in 1955 to take up a position in Exeter Cathedral and was later appointed as the Dean of York. The Parish Players carried on and staged another Gilbert and Sullivan under the auspices of Reverend Smith, Jasper's replacement, but no one had the drive necessary to retain the required interest and the players disbanded.

1948 Modernisation of the North Eastern Iron Refinery

After working to its full capacity during and after the war, the original cupolas were almost beyond repair. With the plant still under governmental control permission was sought from the Ministry to refurbish and modernise the cupolas and other plant. Permission was granted and three new cupolas were built to replace the two 'old faithfuls' and a general modernisation of the pig moulding process was completed, which dispensed with the need to prepare moulds in a sand bed. These modifications were sufficient to carry the company through the next ten years but in 1957–8 the improvements in production techniques were demanding fundamental changes to the existing plant in order to remain competitive in an increasingly difficult market.

A new general manager, Mr John Moran, had been appointed and he urged the directors to instal electric furnaces and generally modernise the whole plant. The finance required to fulfil these modifications would necessitate a loan or debenture being secured against all of the company assets including Stillington Estates and possibly the existing directors would need to invest more money. Peter Kirk had died in 1957 and Geoffrey Kirk, who was acting as chairman, decided to sell his and his mother's shares to C L Wainwright, along with others including K C Sharpe, thus giving total control to the Wainwrights.

Modernisation went ahead under the new management team, with electric furnaces being installed and, although the labour force was reduced, the plant still remains in production. John Moran bought the company from the Wainwrights around 1970 and remained in charge until his death in 1992.

Photograph shows the 'new look' Iron Refinery with an N N Argyle wagon being loaded with the specially refined pig iron.

Photograph shows the new look Iron Refinery with an N N Argyle wagon being loaded with the specially refined pig iron.

Whitton Grove
The first group of houses built by Stockton District Council in Stillington. Built in 1949/50 adjacent to the Chapel Bank and opposite the wooded area of the park. These were the first homes without any connection to the Ironworks and started a new era in housing availability in the village. The initial priority tenants were residents of North Street, that was demolished soon after.

Park Crescent
View from Carlton Bridge of second group of Council houses built in the village in 1953.

1949 December – New Housing Estate

The building of a new housing estate by Stockton Rural District Council was now under way and Whitton Parish Council wanted the first group of houses to be named Park Crescent. This request was overruled by Stockton Rural District Council and the estate was named Whitton Grove. However, the second batch of houses was named Park Crescent.

Whitton Grove comprised 26 semi-detached houses built in an elongated oval. They were the first houses in the village to be owned by the council and afforded tenants modern accommodation. They were also the first houses in the village to have a purpose-built bathroom, although some of the older houses had at this stage had bathrooms added and kitchens modernised. Generous gardens at both the front and rear of the houses provided much greater privacy than the traditional terraced houses that led directly on to the street. North Street was condemned and its residents were rehoused in Whitton Grove that provided good modern housing and catered for all the needs of the average family.

North Street c. 1950

Rear view of North Street houses showing the back yard leading out to the waste land adjoining the reservoirs. The photograph was taken shortly after the residents were rehoused in the new council houses of Whitton Grove, leaving North Street free for demolition. The top houses with larger back yards were modified to an improved design by the Carlton Iron Company, c. 1900 in order to house a couple of their foremen or similar personnel. The ironworks have been demolished and the works in the background belong to Stillite Products Limited. One remaining feature of the ironworks is the wall directly above the end house. This is the retaining wall for the pig iron beds of one of the furnaces. In the centre of the picture are two posts, these are the survivors of the washing posts provided to allow washing lines to be strung between the posts and hooks attached to the back yard wall.

1950 and onwards

The council housing developments began a new era in the history of Stillington because, from now onwards, many changes overtook not only the physical characteristics of the village but also the outlook and aspirations of the people living there. The attitudes of the 'good old days' were slowly replaced by a totally new set of values as the villagers became accustomed to a better standard of living in a materialistic sense. Sadly, however, some of the camaraderie and community spirit, which had carried the villagers through many desperately hard times, was allowed to die among the debris of North Street when it was demolished in 1950.

This then would seem an ideal point at which to conclude the early history of Stillington and, although the story of the village from 1950 onwards is worthy of record, I feel it should not be integrated with the early history because of the vast contrasts dividing the periods.

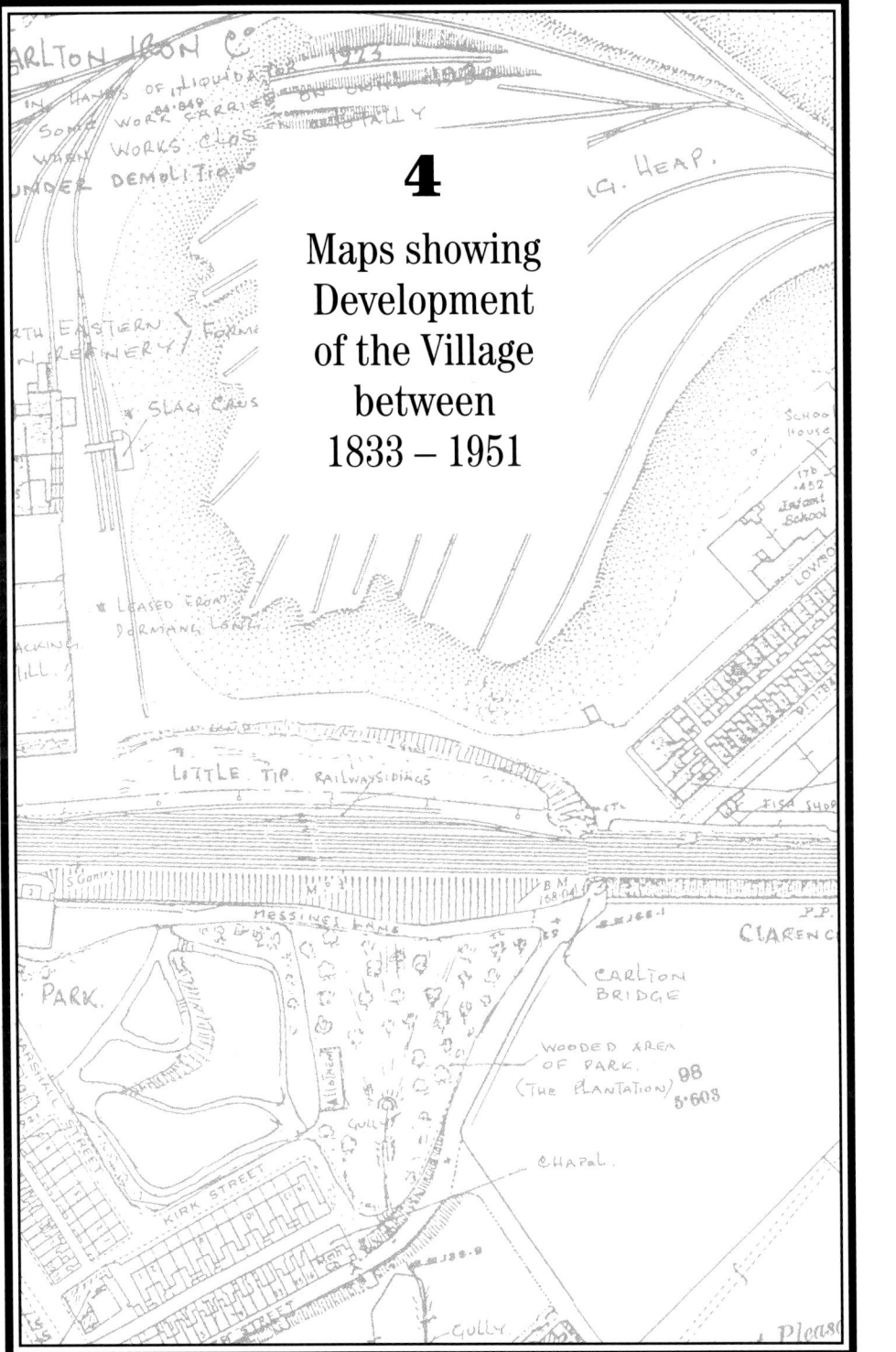

4
Maps showing Development of the Village between 1833 – 1951

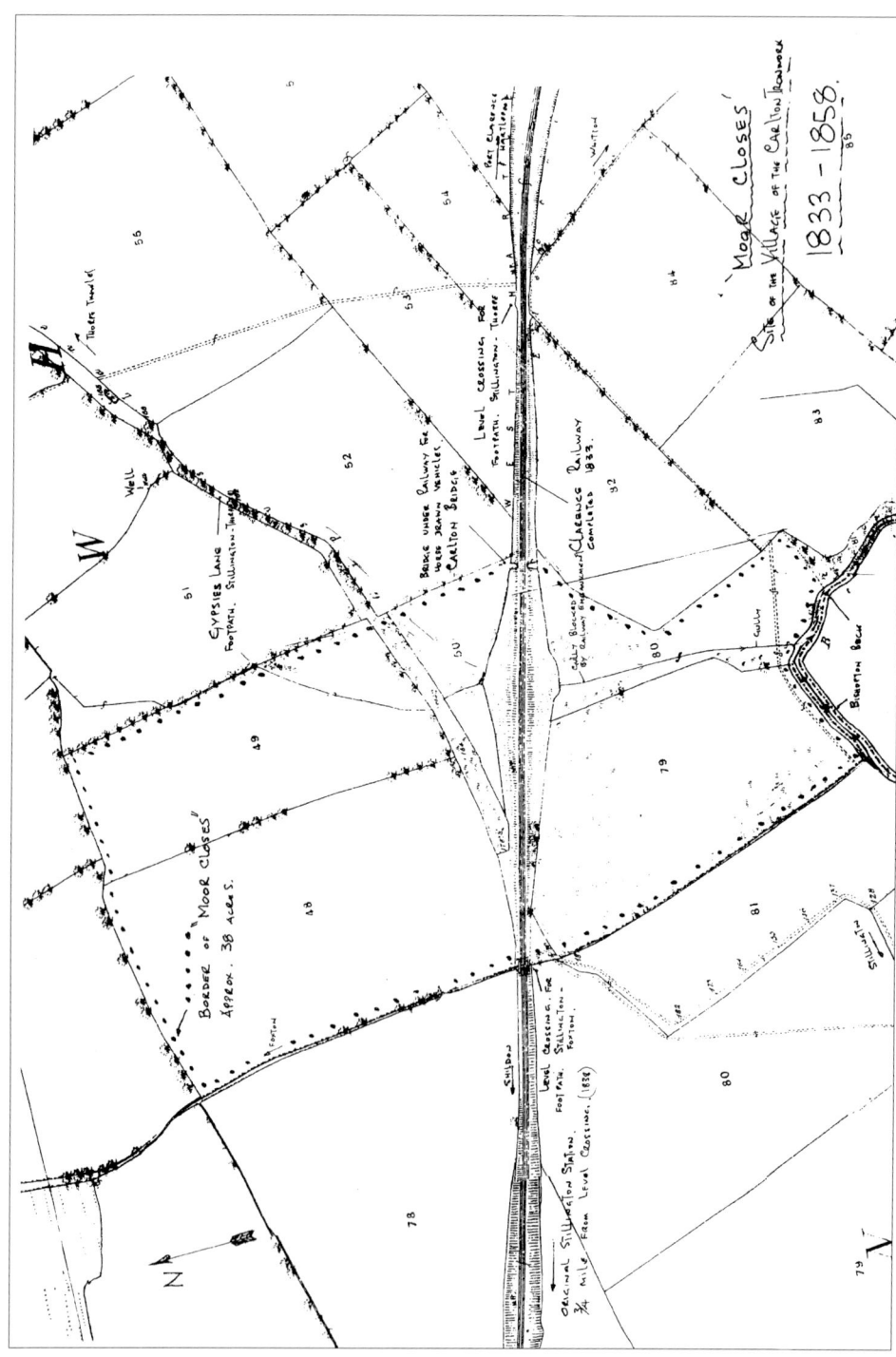

Moor Closes
Site of the Village of the Carlton Ironworks 1833–1858

DEVELOPMENT OF THE VILLAGE BETWEEN 1833–1951

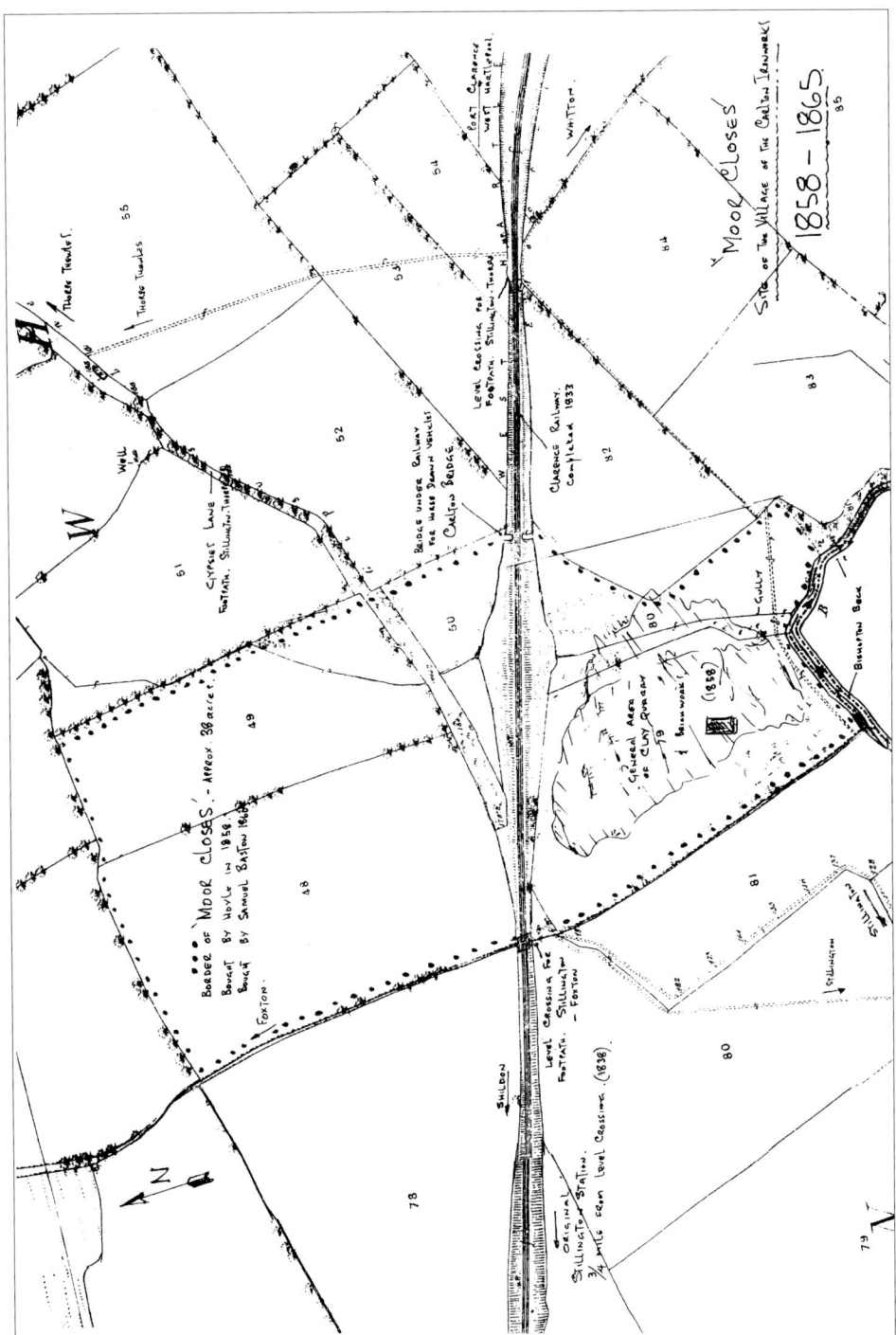

Moor Closes
Site of the Village of the Carlton Ironworks 1858–1865

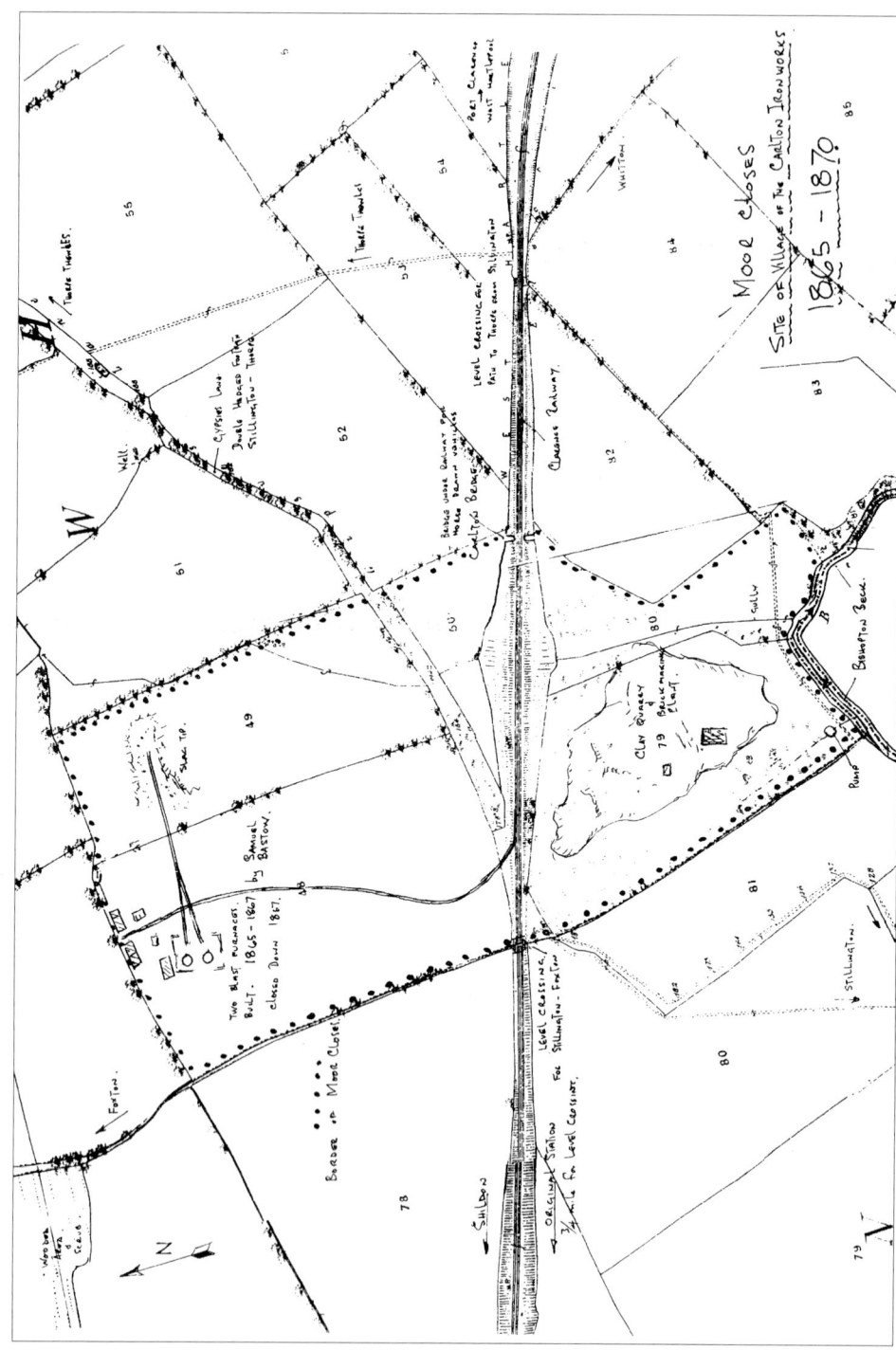

Moor Closes
Site of the Village of the Carlton Ironworks 1865–1870

DEVELOPMENT OF THE VILLAGE BETWEEN 1833–1951

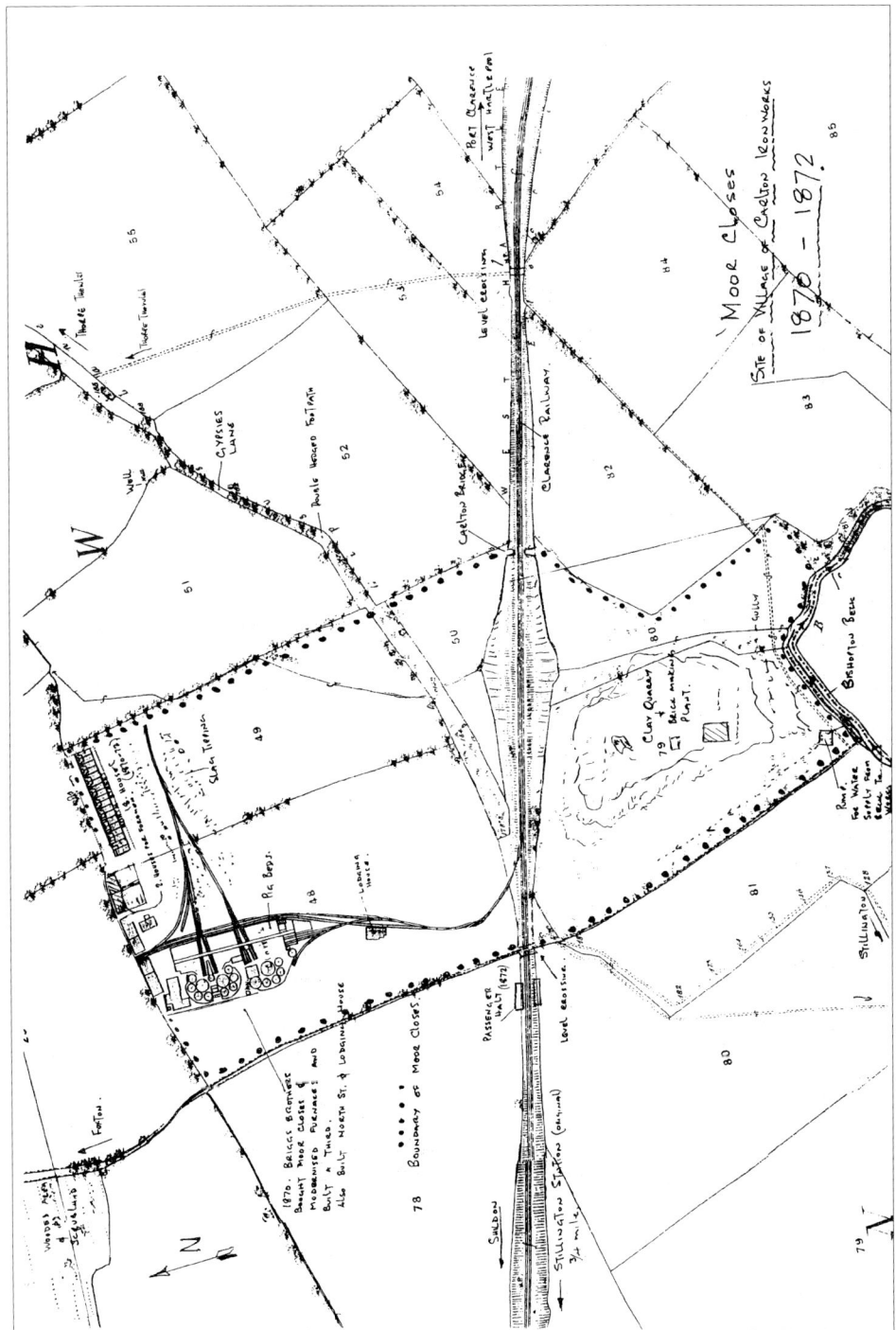

Moor Closes
Site of the Village of the Carlton Ironworks 1870–1872

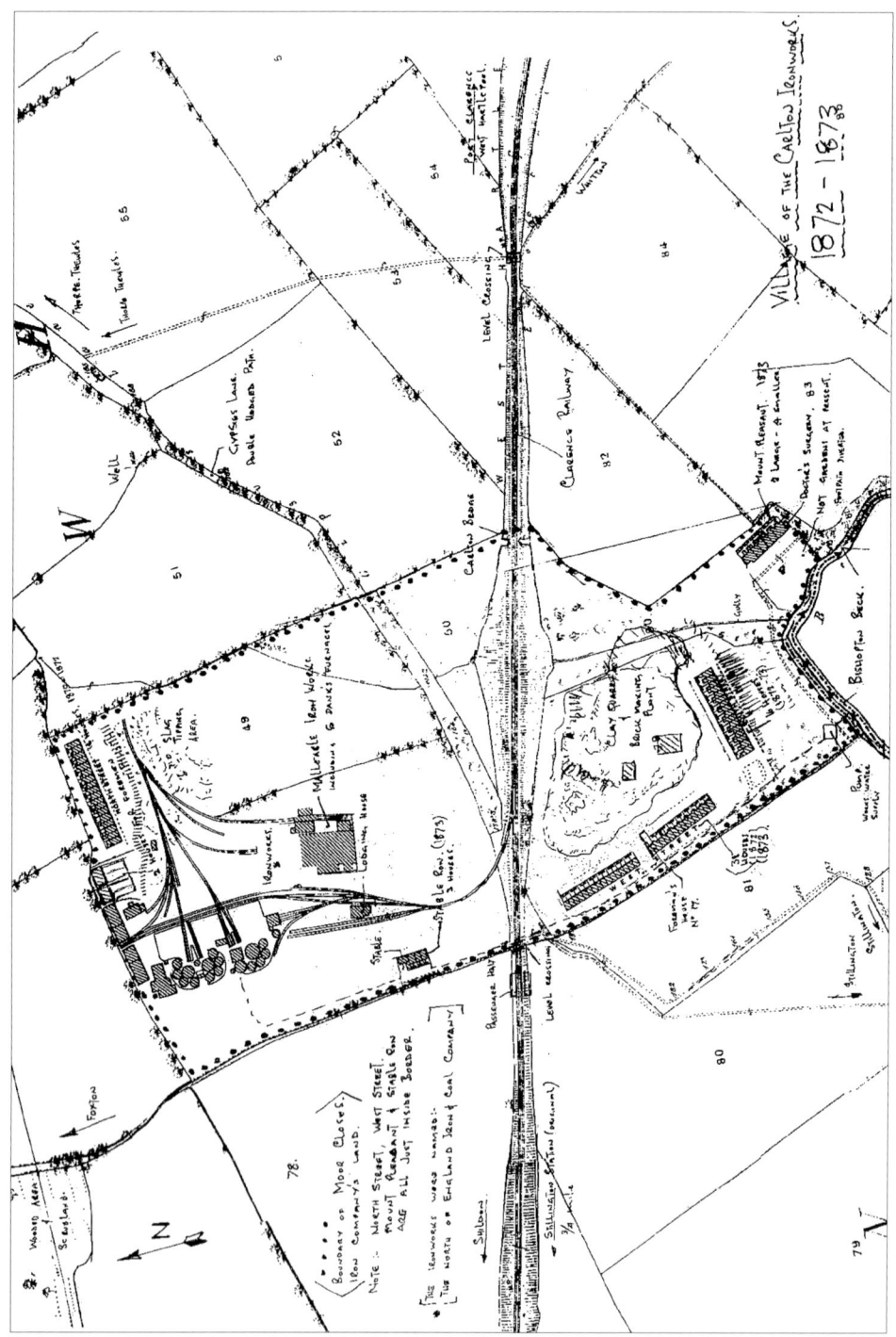

Village of the Carlton Ironworks 1872–1873

DEVELOPMENT OF THE VILLAGE BETWEEN 1833–1951

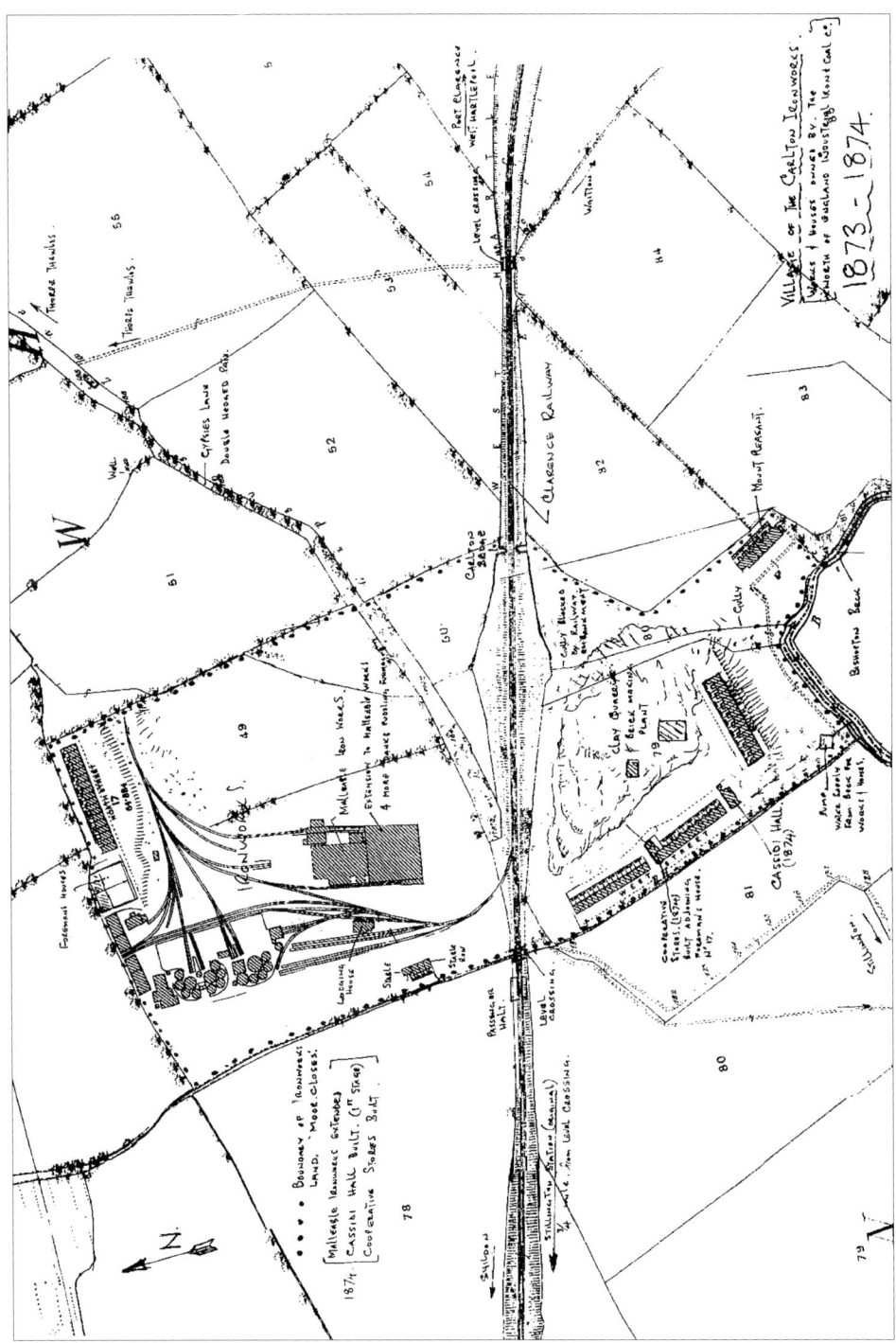

Village of the Carlton Ironworks
Works and houses owned by the North of England Industrial Iron & Coal Co. 1873–1874

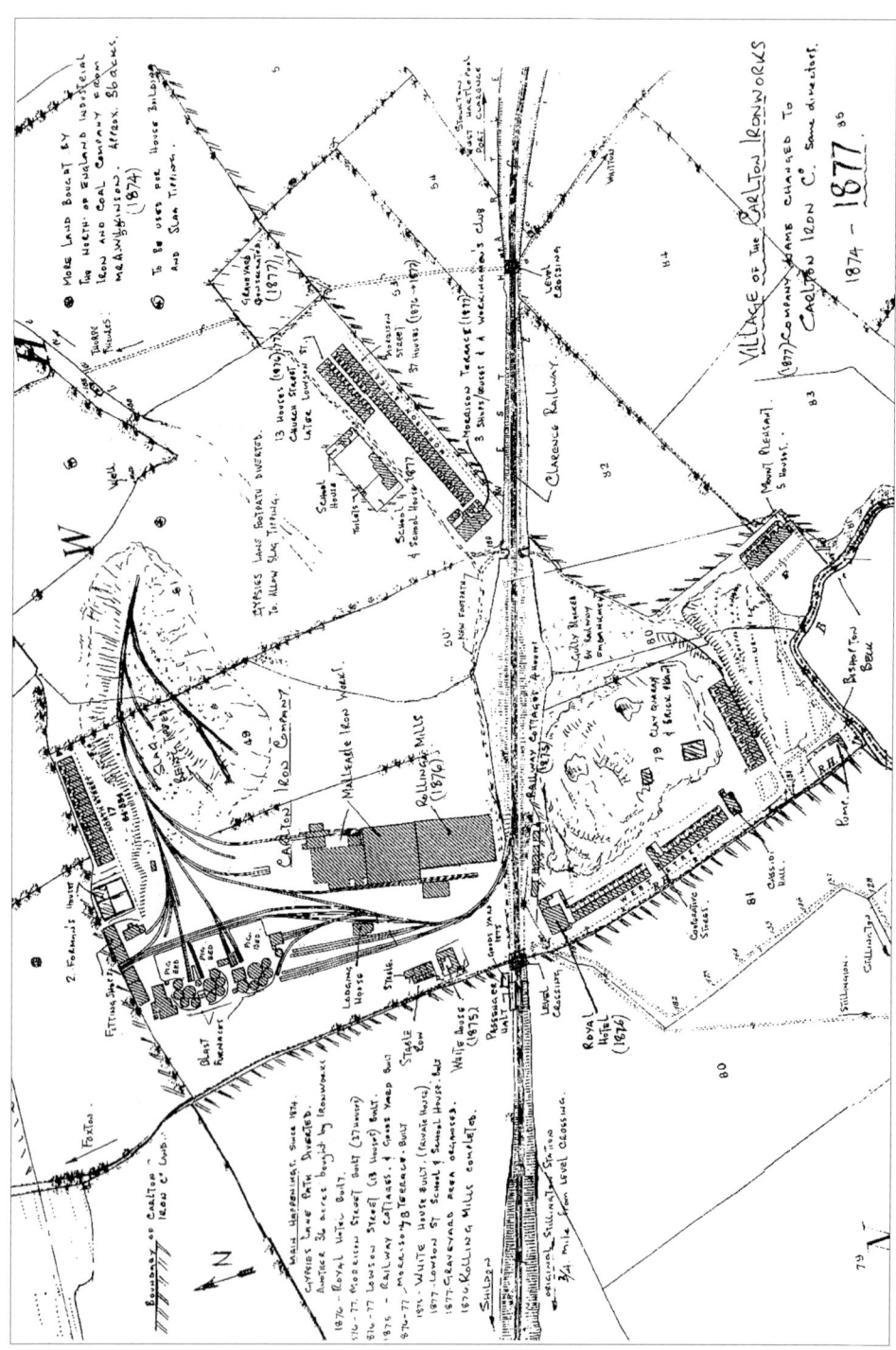

Village of the Carlton Ironworks 1874–1877
(1877) Company Name changed to Carlton Iron Co., same directors

DEVELOPMENT OF THE VILLAGE BETWEEN 1833–1951

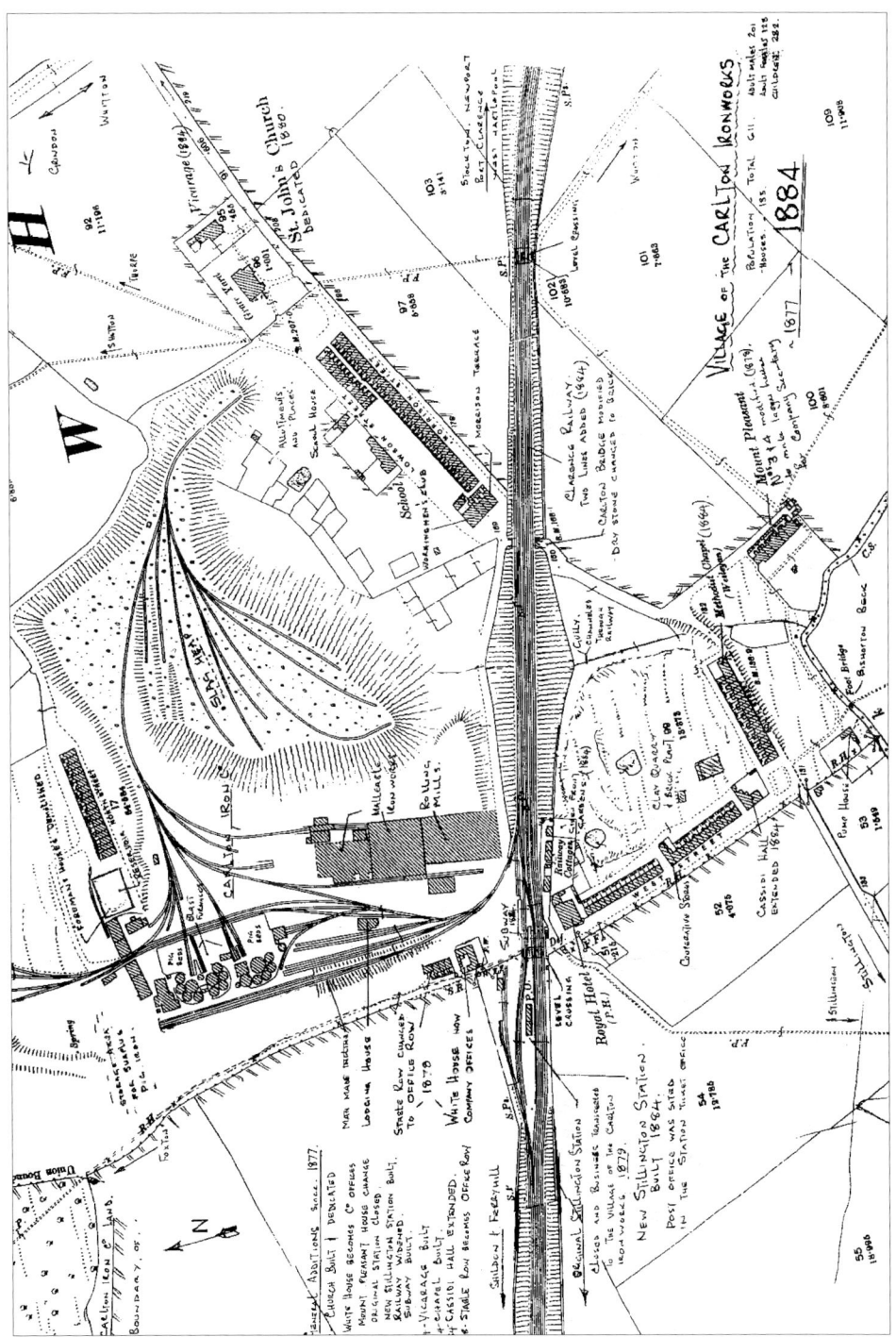

Village of the Carlton Ironworks 1877–1884
Population total 611; Houses 135

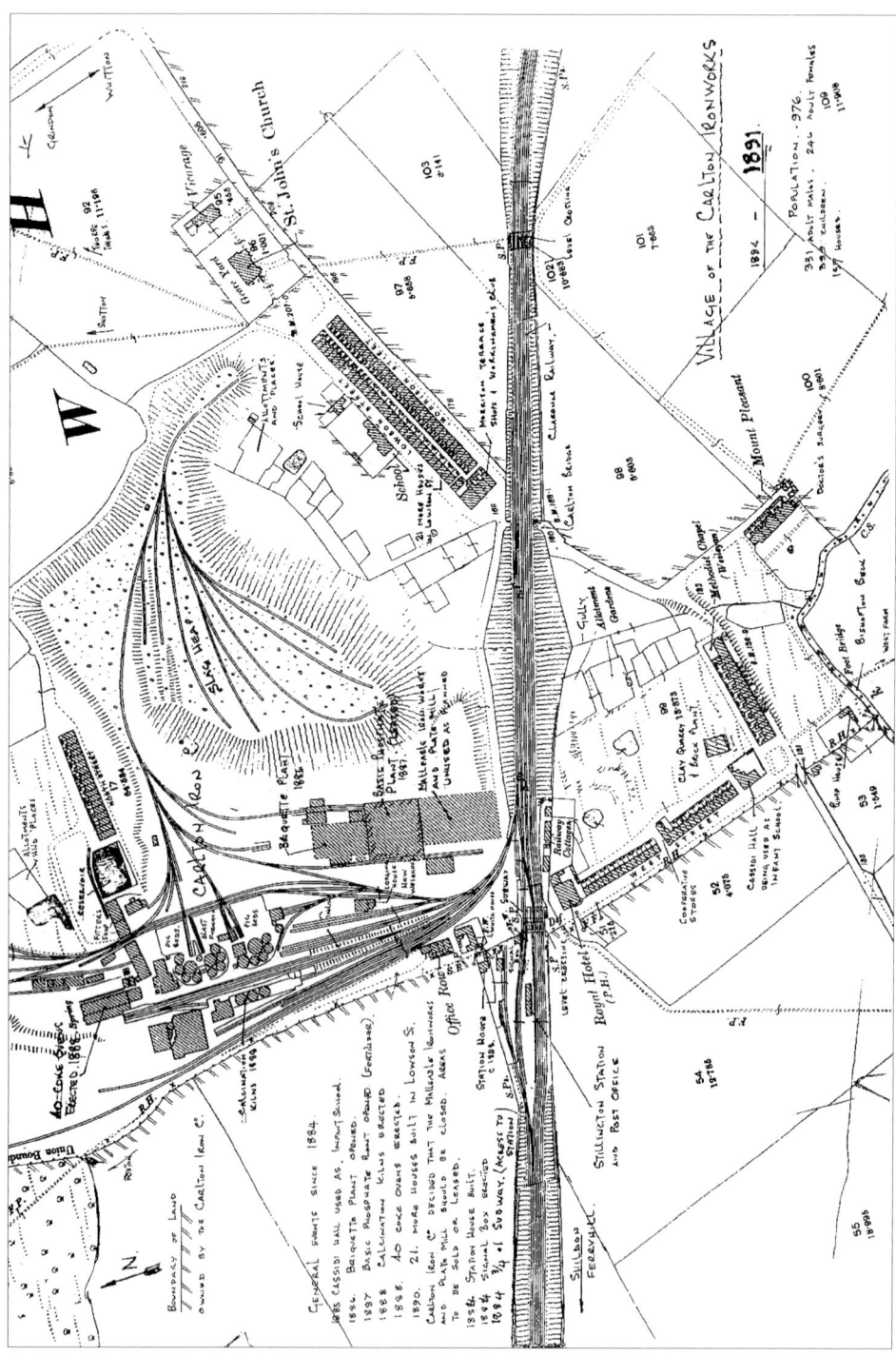

Village of the Carlton Ironworks 1884–1891
Population 976; Houses 157

DEVELOPMENT OF THE VILLAGE BETWEEN 1833–1951

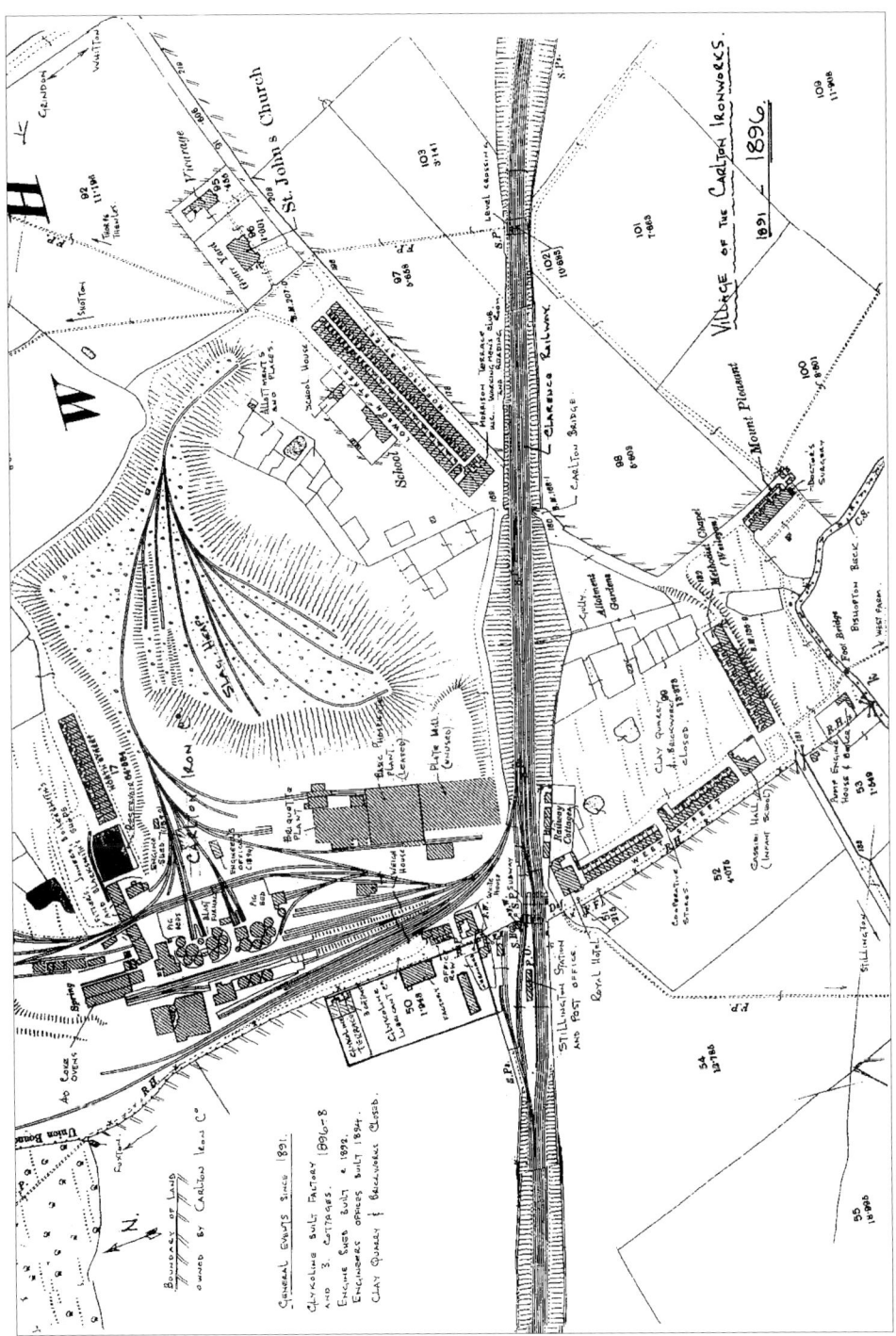

Village of the Carlton Ironworks 1891–1896

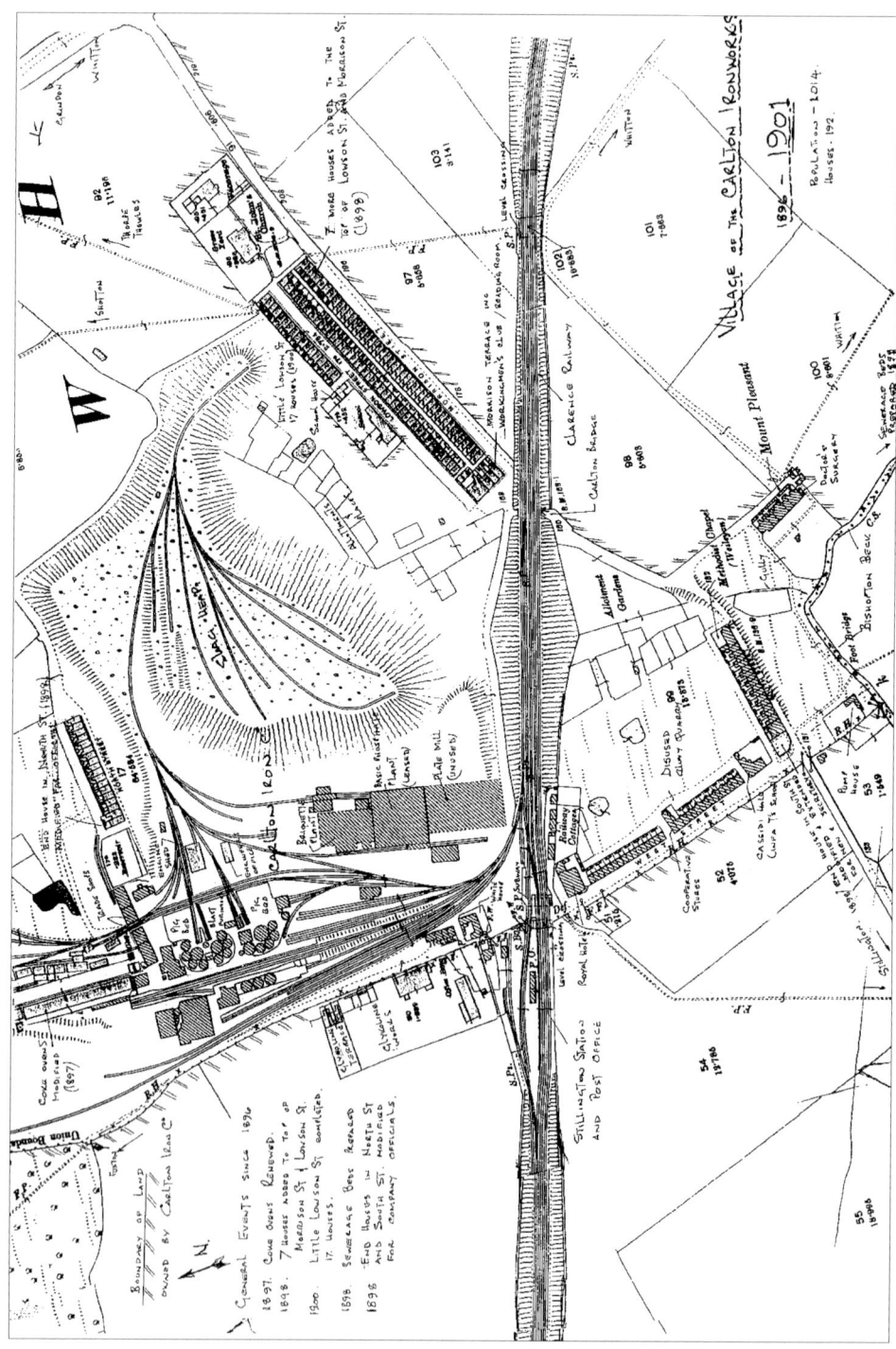

Village of the Carlton Ironworks 1896–1901
Population 1014; Houses 192

DEVELOPMENT OF THE VILLAGE BETWEEN 1833–1951

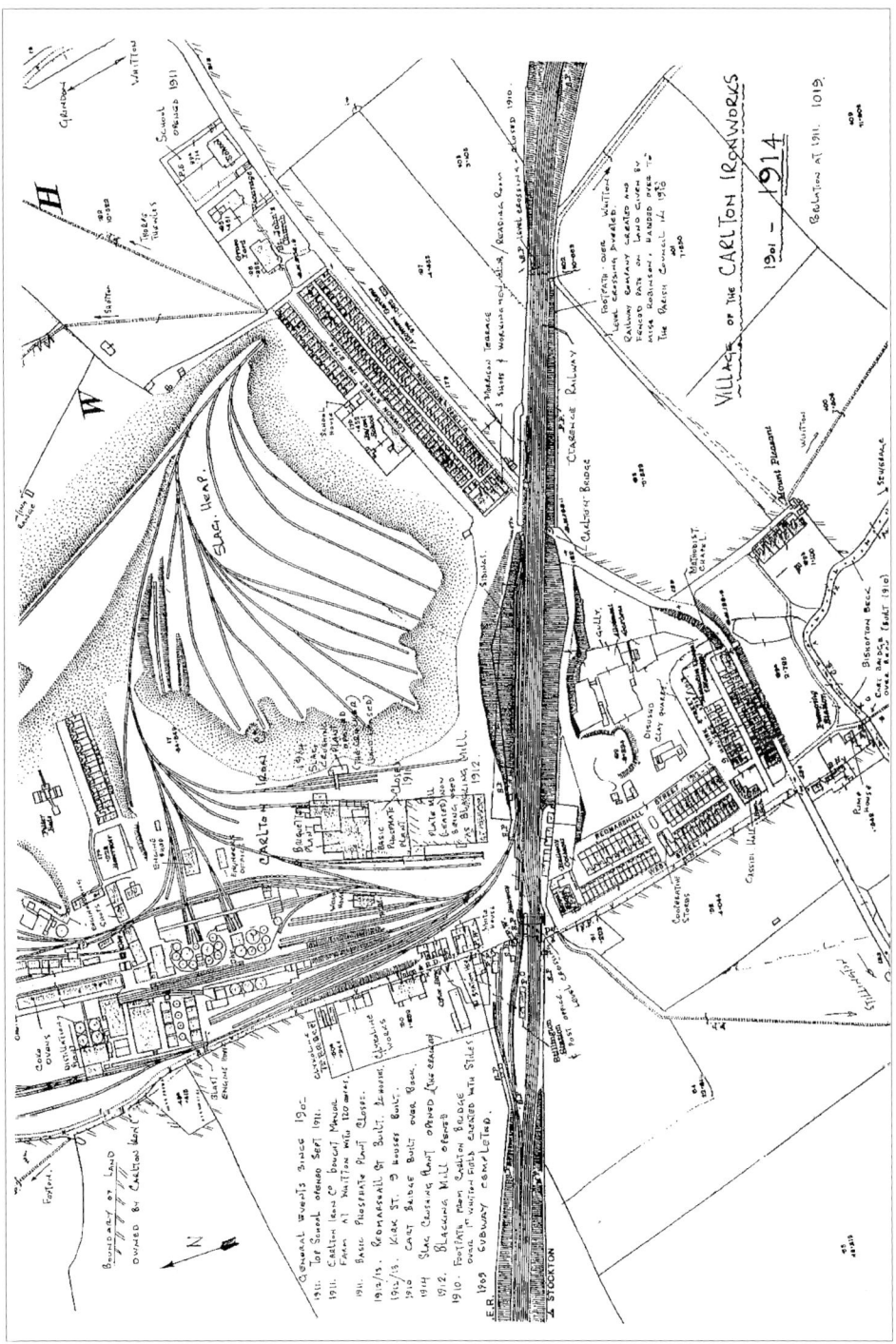

Village of the Carlton Ironworks 1901–1914
Population at 1911; 1019

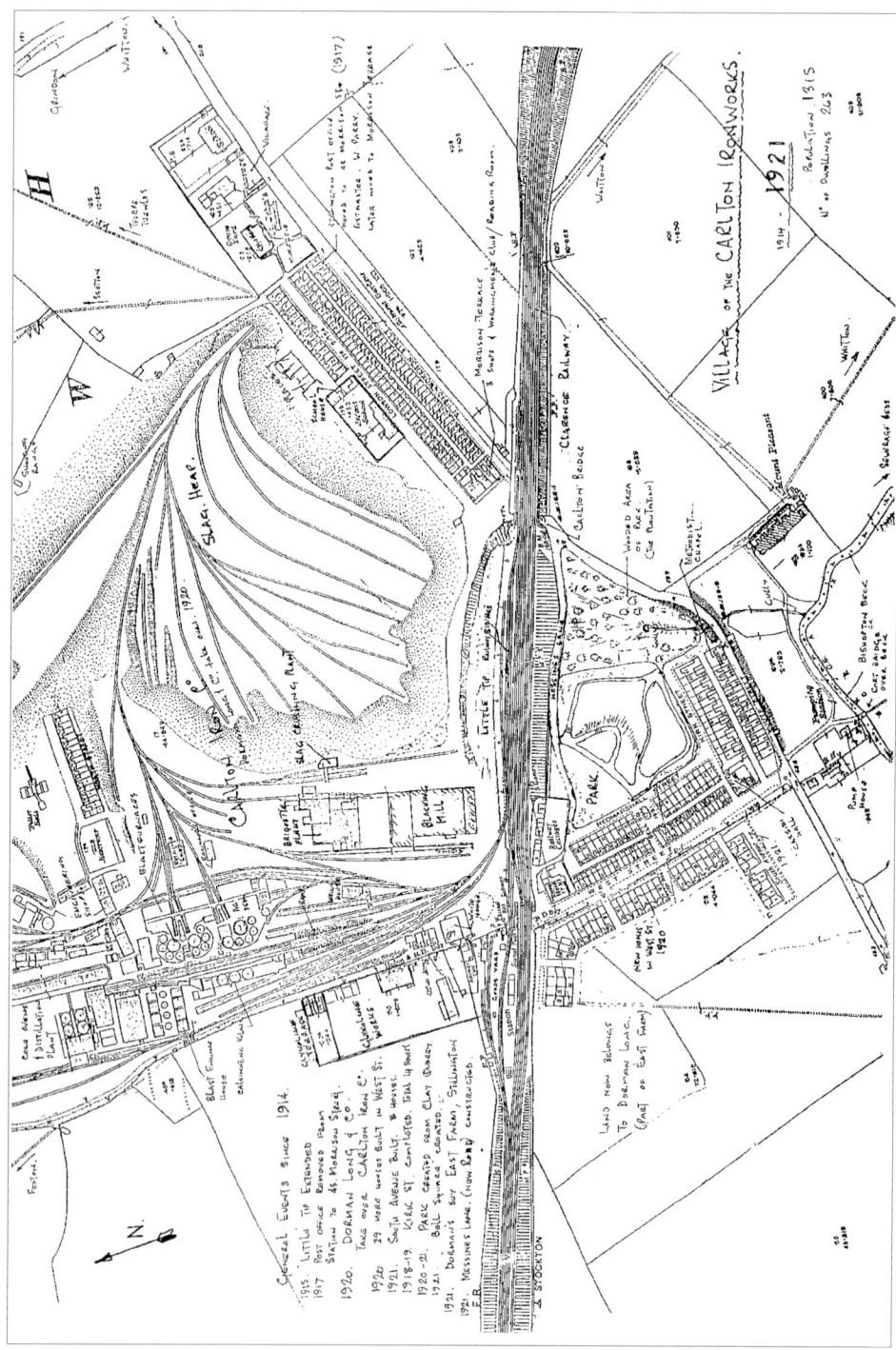

Village of the Carlton Ironworks 1914–1921
Population 1315; No of Dwellings 243

DEVELOPMENT OF THE VILLAGE BETWEEN 1833–1951

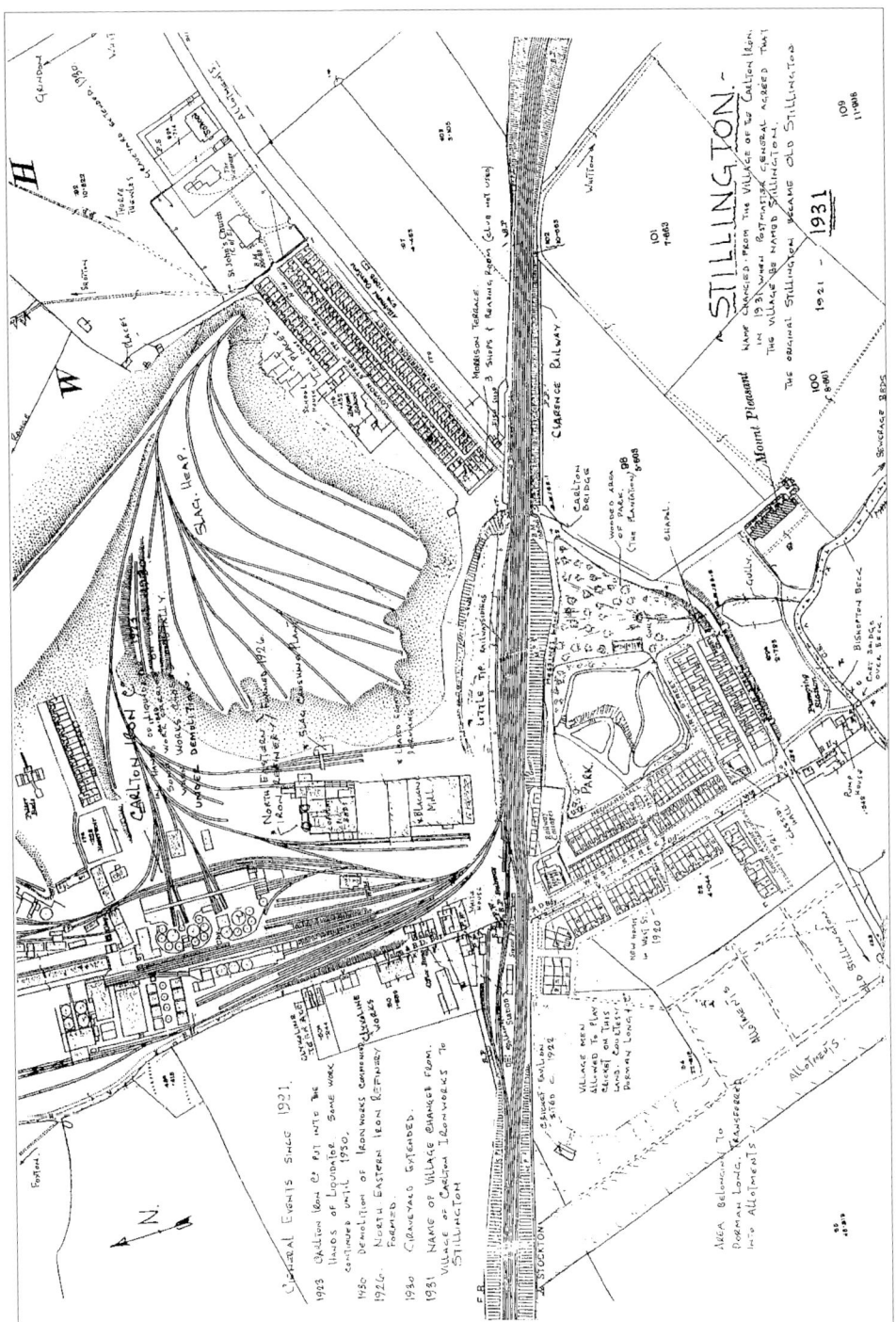

Stillington 1921–1931
Name changed from the Village of the Carlton Ironworks in 1931

Stillington 1931–1941

DEVELOPMENT OF THE VILLAGE BETWEEN 1833–1951

Stillington 1941–1951

5
Influx and Expansion of the Village Population

The first workers came to the site of Stillington village in 1859, and were employed by Mr Hoyle to quarry clay and produce bricks on land he had bought on the south side of the Clarence Railway. These men were never afforded any permanent accommodation and, therefore, no records exist as to who they were, or where they came from. The probability is that they had previously worked for Samuel Bastow in West Hartlepool, where he owned an engineering company and had also built the Cliff House ironworks in 1858. Bastow had arranged the purchase of the land where quarrying started and, although not recorded, it would seem that Hoyle was managing the quarry and the brick making plant on his behalf.

Bastow took total control of the site in 1860 and, in 1865, brought in extra workers to build two blast furnaces on the north side of the railway, in order to produce pig iron. Although they were successfully brought into operation, the blast furnaces, the ancillary plant and the brick works were all abandoned in 1867 when Bastow ran out of money.

In consequence of this, the workmen returned to the West Hartlepool district without contributing to the social structure of Stillington in any way. The only remaining proof of their existence was the clay quarry, the brickmaking plant, the two blast furnaces and other ancillary iron making equipment. These were to remain unused until 1870 when two brothers, Henry and Archibald Briggs, bought the works and the site for £13,300.

The brothers were part of a family business that owned several coal mines in Yorkshire and traded under the name of Briggs Brothers. They formed a new company named the North of England Industrial Iron and Coal Company, under which they immediately commenced the expansion and modernisation of the blast furnaces and brought the brickworks and quarry back into production.

The North of England Industrial Iron and Coal Company recruited men to the site who were skilled in the erection of blast furnaces, boilers, blast engines, blast engine houses, pig beds, chimneys and all other facets of an ironmaking plant. Tradesmen such as boilersmiths, bricklayers, engine fitters, blacksmiths and joiners came from Middlesbrough, Staffordshire and South Wales where ironmaking was well established and where they had gained vast experience in the building of ironmaking plant.

Unlike Samuel Bastow, the Briggs brothers and their fellow directors had clear long-term strategies for the ironworks and issued shares in the company to ensure sufficient finance was available to complete these. Although hard task masters, they were anxious to provide decent accommodation and a reasonable environment for their workforce, and one of their first projects was the building of a brick lodging

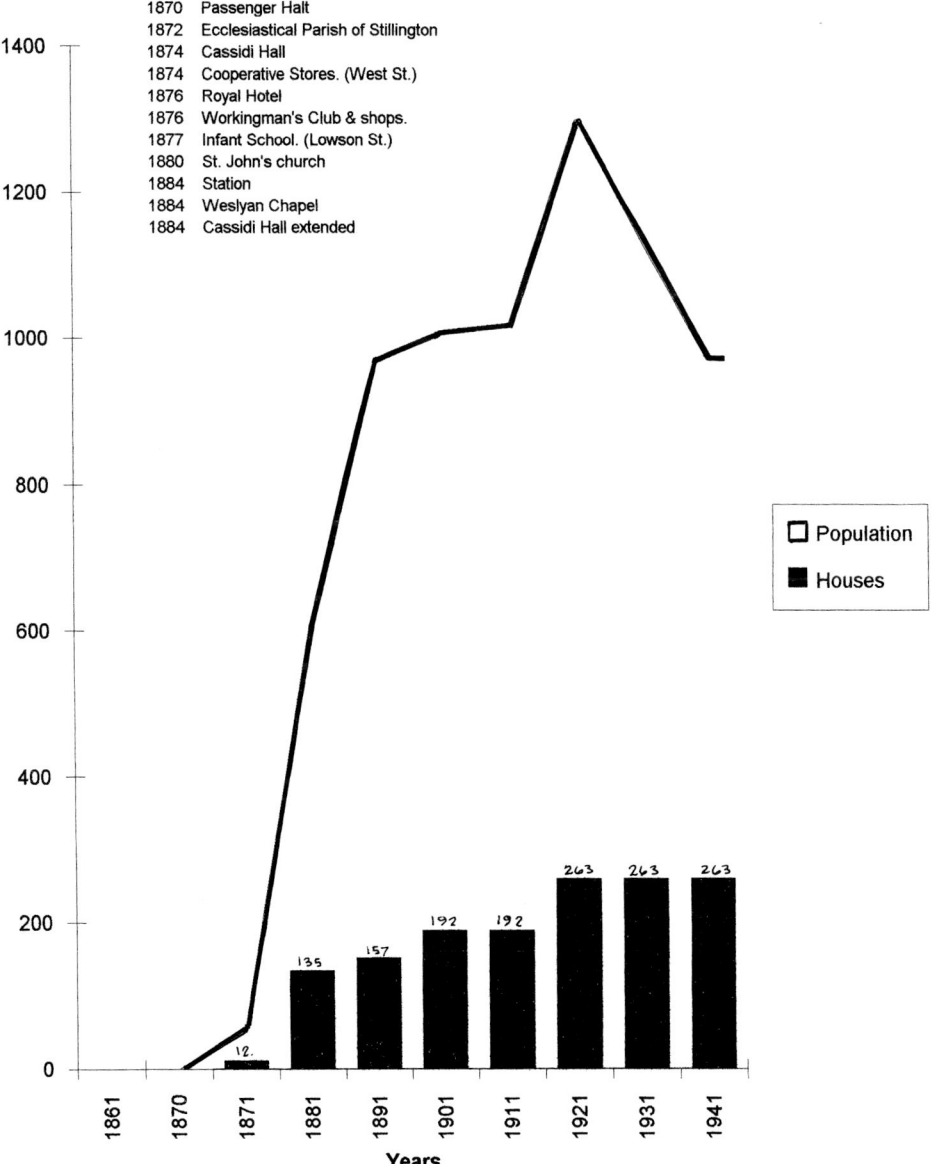

Population and housing graph for Stillington, formerly the Village of the Carlton Ironworks

house, two foremen's houses and 18 terraced houses close to the works. These houses (North Street), formed the embryo of the village of Stillington and enabled the workmen to bring their families to the site and set up a permanent home.

The two existing blast furnaces were quickly modified to an improved standard and brought into operation, whilst erection work continued on a third blast furnace and the development of a malleable iron works. The company, whilst continuing the expansion of the works, had also to recruit a workforce that would ensure the safe and efficient operation of the blast furnaces that were already producing pig iron.

Recruitment of labour continued, with men now being brought to the site from the local counties of Durham, Yorkshire and Northumberland, whilst others came with their families from Lancashire, Westmorland, Lincolnshire, Hertfordshire, Staffordshire, Cambridgeshire, Scotland, Wales and Ireland.

A great diversity of people with differing education, creed and culture were thrown together, with possibly their only common interest being the work they had been selected to perform. Houses were provided by the directors of the ironworks at a rate that attempted to keep up with the rising influx of manpower, although initially many of the houses were overcrowded, with tenants having to take in lodgers as a condition of being allotted accommodation.

The population and number of houses in the village continued to increase as the third blast furnace was brought into service and the malleable works were completed. Meanwhile, the site construction workers gradually left to seek erection work elsewhere and, by 1881, only a couple of the original resident families remained, these being the Scurr's and the Bell's, whose families remained in the village for two or three more generations.

Example of the number of occupants sharing one household

Below is an example of the number of people who lived in one house – the detail of which has been copied directly from the 1881 census forms.

The house was No. 29 West Street, a small two-bedroomed terraced house with a privy in the back yard and a shared cold water point in the back street. No electricity was available at this date.

Occupants	Relation to hd	Age	Occupation	Born
Mrs Fitspatrick	Widow	54	Householder	Co Fernanagh, Ireland
James Fitspatrick	Son	19	Labourer	Northumberland
John Fitspatrick	Son	17	Labourer	Northumberland
Hugh Fitspatrick	Son	15	Labourer	Northumberland
Margaret Fitspatrick	Daughter	13		Durham
Sarah O'Bryan	Niece	8		Durham
James O'Bryan	Brother	63	Labourer	Co Fernanagh, Ireland
James Nugent	Lodger	30	Labourer	Co Monaghan, Ireland
James Woods	Lodger	22	Labourer	Co Tyrone, Ireland
James Brunty	Lodger	26	Labourer	Co Fernanagh, Ireland

It is difficult to imagine how 10 individuals (7 working males, 1 woman and 2 young girls) could survive in such a small house, but this situation was not unusual during the early years of village development.

Growth of population

From a population of 79 in 1871, the population of the Village of the Carlton Ironworks had grown to a total of 611 by 1881, comprising 201 adult males, 128 adult females and 282 children. The adult males included 59 lodgers, 27 of whom had come from Ireland.

The census taken in 1891 showed that the population of the Village of the Carlton Ironworks had grown to almost 1000, with 331 of these being listed as adult males, including 80 lodgers, all of whom were working. From 1891 until 1918 the population remained fairly constant and then began to increase again, due to the natural expansion of the inherent families, few of whom moved away. More houses were built in 1920 and 1921 to cope with this increase, and these reduced the average number of people occupying each residence from seven to five. The village population reached 1300 in 1921, but gradually reduced after the closure of the works to around the 1000 level, where it remained until 1951. The residents of the village were by this time fully integrated, with many being related through marriage, and a fine community spirit had been developed.

6

Hardships endured by the families of the Village

The early inhabitants of the Village of the Carlton Ironworks had two things in common: the ironworks, which was the only reason they were there, and the general hardship, that was a feature common to all working-class families in the Victorian era.

Some of the hardships endured by the men of the Village

Most of the hardships endured by the men were related to their work at the ironworks, where the work was heavy and general conditions were arduous. They worked twelve-hour shifts, seven days a week, and on each alternate Sunday, a 24-hour shift was worked to ensure continuity of duties during shift changes. This practice survived unchallenged until 1894.

Workers had no holiday or sick pay entitlement, a situation that forced many to attend work when not in a fit condition to do so. To alleviate total hardship during a period of sickness, families could pay a few pence a week to the village doctor who, in return, would administer a certain amount of medicine and treatment.

The men could also join a Sick Club, such as the Shepherd's Club, and for a weekly subscription earn an entitlement of money paid when they were absent from work through illness. Strict rules applied to these entitlements. For example, if during his illness a claimant was seen outside after 7.30 in the evening, his allowance would be stopped, on the basis that if he were well enough to be out at that time of night, he could attend work.

In the early days of the ironworks, it was commonplace for men to walk from between 10 to 15 miles to work whilst waiting to be housed in the village. One such example was Billy Waites, who daily walked from Sedgefield, worked a 12-hour shift, and then walked back home. Eventually he was given the tenancy of a house in Lowson Street, where he and his wife Sally lived happily for many years hence.

Until around 1880, the top wage of the ironmaking industry was earned by the furnace-keepers who received ten shillings and ninepence per week, a sum which diminished pro rata, depending upon the workman's skill, down to three shillings and sixpence a week for the labourers.

Some of the hardships endured by the women of the Village

The hardship endured by men was generally work related, but the women of the village suffered just as much, if not more, for in many cases, they not only had large families to bring up, in less than ideal conditions, but also had to look after as many as 6 lodgers. The taking in of lodgers was not an option, but one of the conditions imposed by the company, when allotting the tenancy of a house to the workmen.

It can hardly be imagined what strain the women underwent in trying to cope with all the cooking, washing and cleaning in a two or three-bedroomed house with no electricity, and water having to be carried from a communal standpipe. The sanitary arrangements were horrendous with so many people using the ash privy, and the custom of keeping the 'jerry' under the bed for use during the night. The organisation of sleeping arrangements in these crowded households remains a mystery, but it was a regular practice for beds to be shared alternately by night-shift and day-shift workers, whilst 3 or 4 children shared a bed, sleeping top to tail in order to fit the confines of space.

Washday

Along with all her other chores, the full burden of washday was regarded as the woman's responsibility, and was a day of incredible hardship for the housewife. Firstly, the outside boiler had to be filled with water, that was carried from a standpipe situated somewhere in the street. Then the fire under the boiler had to be lit in order to heat the water which, when hot enough, was transferred to a large wooden washing tub by the use of a ladle tin. Some coarse soap was added to the water and the clothes were then put into the tub and washed by pounding continuously for about 10 minutes with a heavy wooden dolly stick, a process known as possing. When thoroughly possed, the clothes would be passed through the wringer, a big cast iron affair with 6" diameter wooden rollers geared to a cast iron wheel with a wooden handle, via which the woman could manually turn the rollers and thus squeeze the bulk of the water from the clothes. The washing process would be repeated, with fresh loads of clothes being processed, until the water in the tub became dirty. Whilst the tub was being emptied, the water would be used to swill the yard before being allowed to drain away. The tub was then filled with clean, cold water that was used to rinse the washed clothes, before they went through the wringer again. The clothes would then be pegged out to dry on the rope washing line that the housewife had previously fastened to hooks fixed to either side of the back street. The hooks were generally fastened to the walls either side of the back street but, if no wall existed, then six inch square wooden poles were provided for the purpose. This whole process would be repeated until all the dirty clothes had been washed, rinsed and dried. Greasy dirt on shirt collars and cuffs was removed by rubbing soap into the affected area and scrubbing with a hard bristled hand

Memory of Monday – the weekly washing day

Regardless of the weather, washing always took place in the yard, at best under some corrugated sheeting that the husband had suspended over part of the yard. If the housewife was lucky and the day was fine, she would get the clothes dried outside, if not, they would be draped all over the house and especially on lines suspended across the kitchen near and on the mantelpiece. Monday was always classed as washday, nobody ever washed on Sunday, and if the coal man or the scavenge men came on a Monday, all the washing in the back street had to be lifted to give them access to the coalhouses and ash privies. Even though fully occupied with the washing, mother still had to get the children ready for school, prepare lunch and tea for the children and others in the house, such as men on night shift, prepare meals for the day shift and arrange to have them taken to the works, make the beds, empty the 'jerries', clean the house, shake the mats, wash the dirty dishes, empty the ash pans and keep the fires refueled.

brush before rinsing. During the rinsing of white clothes, a 'blue bag' would be suspended in the water, giving the whites a bluish tint that supposedly enhanced their whiteness.

It became common practice to prepare and cook extra meat, potatoes, vegetables and Yorkshire puddings on a Sunday in order to simplify cooking on a Monday. This was achieved by putting all the Sunday left overs into a frying pan and reheating them for the main meal on Monday, a meal that became known as a fry-up.

Traditional daily tasks

The previous text gives a general description of a typical Monday facing the housewife and, although it was probably her hardest day of the week, the remainder were far from easy and most were filled with traditional duties. The family bread and cakes were baked on Tuesdays and Thursdays; ironing, with the old flat irons which had to be heated on the open fire, was carried out on Wednesdays; general cleaning and the polishing of the kitchen grate with black lead was Friday's main activity, although generally combined with washing the windows and scrubbing the stone doorsteps. After scrubbing, it was the usual practice to rub sour milk into the main surface of the step, in the belief that it darkened the stone and gave a greater contrast to the whitening used on the vertical surround.

Shopping for the weekly groceries had to fitted into this busy schedule, and it was in this area that older children helped their mother by running any necessary errands to the local shops.

> The older children were also responsible for taking father's 'bait' to the works, a practice that caused a young girl to lose her foot. She had been returning home across the slag tip when her foot slipped into a joint in the railway lines, and an oncoming shunting engine loaded with slag for tipping was unable to stop and sheared off her foot. The story goes that this happened early afternoon, and the girl had to catch the five-thirty train from Stillington to Stockton in order to receive hospital treatment. The young girl's companion when the accident happened, was Mrs Emma Collins who still lives in the village. The driver of the engine, Mr Hunt, suffered so badly with shock, he never worked again.

Friday night was usually bath night, when again the boiler would have to be lit to heat the water and a tin bath would be placed in front of the kitchen fire and filled with the heated water. Pans of water would be boiled on the kitchen fire and used to supplement the hot water in the bath as required. After two or three of the family had used the water, the remainder were using hot, but generally dirty water, and some probably never had a bath but would make do with a regular, good washing down.

Sunday, the day of rest, was anything but for the housewife who spent all morning cleaning and stoking the oven and preparing and cooking vegetables, Yorkshire puddings and the Sunday joint.

If the dinner was ready before the man of the house came back from having his Sunday lunchtime drink at the 'pub', then the family would generally have to wait for his return before their dinner was served. This situation was a source of many arguments between tired parents, and the main meal of the week was often spoiled by a hostile atmosphere.

Then came the Sunday's washing up, a pile of dirty, greasy plates, cast iron pans with vegetables hardened on to their side, and the greasy pudding and meat dishes all had to be washed without the modern facilities of hot water from the tap and an efficient washing up liquid.

Even after these full days, the mother would still have to get the children ready for bed before settling down to spend the remainder of the evening darning socks, patching clothes, knitting and even making 'hooky' or 'prodded' mats, all of which engendered the saying, 'women's work is never done'.

If times were really hard in terms of family finance, some women would seek employment for a few hours emptying trucks of ash and iron dust on to the slag tip. This was desperately hard and dirty work, but it brought a few extra shillings into the household.

When the works closed down, around ninety per cent of the men folk were thrown out of work and, although this was very depressing for them, the women still had to worry about the meals, clothing and all other household problems related to raising a family. These problems were made even worse through lack of financial sta-

Potato picking c.1935
This picture shows women scratching the potatoes from the soil after the farmer had ploughed the rows to expose the potatoes as much as possible. The buckets into which the potatoes were originally put, would have been brought from home by the women. When full, the buckets would be emptied into sacks, that when filled, would be loaded onto the cart and taken to the potato pile for storage. The women would generally have to walk to the picking field, work an eight hour day with one hour for lunch, and walk home again. It was usual for the farmer to supply tea and cake at ten o' clock and three o' clock and a can of tea at lunch time. Teams of up to ten women could often be seen in the fields but, during the war, most of the women were replaced by schoolchildren who were given time off school at potato picking time. The time off school could extend to several weeks, provided the farmer signed your card to prove you had actually been potato picking. The advent of the 'scratter' around 1944 that unearthed the potatoes and spread them over an area about six feet wide, was a great improvement, and saved having to scratch for them, but the work was still hard and poorly paid.

bility, and many of them sought work on the local farms in an attempt to supplement the meagre money paid by the state. Potato picking was one of the favourite jobs that women sought during October and early November, even though the work was terribly hard and back breaking and often carried out in harsh weather with the farmer urging them on to greater efforts. Pay for the job was pitiful, but one of the 'perks' the farmer allowed was that the women could take a bucketful of potatoes home at the end of the day. Even this so-called perk was a great hardship, when you consider that the tired women had to walk maybe a couple of miles home.

It is now difficult to imagine the working conditions that these men and women had to bear but, in general, working-class men and women were forced to endure these hardships until the social climate of the nation changed, with working conditions and household amenities gradually improving after the 1939–45 war.

7

Development of Village Amenities and Services

The directors of the North of England Industrial Iron and Coal Company, along with other organisations, were intent on providing the amenities and services essential to the daily lives of those workmen and their families who had come to work and settle in the village being formed around the ironworks. Soon after building North Street, West Street and South Street, the company directors invested time and money into creating an environment which would lead to the eventual consolidation of the village and the people therein.

Formation of the Ecclesiastical Parish of Stillington

William Cassidi, the vicar of Grindon, was alert to the potential growth of the Village of the Carlton Ironworks and, in 1872, he instigated the formation of the Ecclesiastical Parish of Stillington, that encompassed the Village of the Carlton Ironworks and the hamlets of Whitton and Stillington. In the same year, a vicar was appointed to perform the necessary parish services and ceremonies, except weddings and funerals, that were currently held at Bishopton or Redmarshall.

In 1876 a piece of land was consecrated at the top of the village where burials could take place, but weddings continued to be performed at Redmarshall or Bishopton, until the church of St. John's was built on the consecrated land in 1880.

The Cassidi Hall

In 1874, the Reverend Cassidi organised the building of a Mission Hall on land leased from the ironworks at the bottom of West Street. The Mission Hall was named after him and used for church services and baptisms until the church was built in 1880. It was also used to house the Sunday School, for which purpose it had, by 1884, become too small and, as a consequence, was extended to form an L-shaped building with a large yard enclosed within a high wall. The extended hall was used as the Infant School between 1885 and 1911, and afterwards became the social centre of the village, where most of the functions were held. In 1946 the Cassidi was converted into a workingmen's club, a situation that existed until 1968 when a new club was built near the Donkey Bank.

Cooperative Stores

The Cooperative Society bought a small plot of land from the North of England Industrial Iron and Coal Company in the middle of West Street and built a shop, with accommodation upstairs for the manager. The store opened in 1875, and continued to function as a grocery store until 1935, when the Cooperative moved their business to the building which had been the workingmen's club in Morrison Terrace. With the larger premises, the Cooperative was able to extend their range of goods and became a general store selling confectionery, hardware and a greater variety of groceries.

Workingmen's Club

The North of England Industrial Iron and Coal Company built the workingmen's club in Morrison Terrace in 1876 to provide an area of relaxation for their workmen. The ground floor included a billiard room, a bagatelle room, a club room and a snug, whilst upstairs provided ample accommodation for the club steward and his or her family.

An adjoining spacious yard contained outbuildings such as coalhouse, privies, stables and cart sheds, all enclosed within a high perimeter wall. The club room was used for dances, whist drives and many other social functions and, whilst the presence of a snug room suggests that ale was available at the club, there is no evidence to confirm this. After the closure of the ironworks, the club was used as a library and reading room until 1935 when, as stated above, the Cooperative Society transferred their stores into the building.

Other shops

Three shops were built in conjunction with, and adjoining the workingmen's club, forming the remainder of Morrison Terrace. These shops were leased to individuals who, once the type of goods they intended to retail were agreed, were bound by the terms of their lease to sell nothing else without prior permission. This fairly stringent measure was taken in an endeavour to ensure that a variety of food and goods was always available to the villagers and to avoid the retailers damaging each others' trade. Among the first tenants of Morrison Terrace was a draper, a grocer and a butcher, with later businesses including the village Post Office and a newsagent.

The newsagent's business was inaugurated in 1887 by the Butler family at their home in 14 West Street, and transferred to the shop in Morrison Terrace in 1924, where it was managed by Mr Stan Butler. When Stan retired, his son, Cyril, took over and when Morrison Terrace was demolished in 1978, he moved the business to the shop in Redmarshall Street opposite Bell Square.

Mr Philip Egerton lost a hand during the 1914–18 war and moved to Bradford for a time. On his return to the village he opened a small grocer's shop in his home at 26 Lowson Street. The business flourished, and he took over the house next door from where he, and eventually his sons, Laurence and Philip, traded until the 1960s. One feature always to be remembered about Phil, was that when he was weighing out a quarter of toffee for a customer, he did not need the traditional toffee hammer to break the large slab of toffee into smaller pieces, for he would just use the end of his false hand.

Most of the shopkeepers enhanced their trade by delivering the goods ordered by their customers, and by sending helpers round the village with a handcart loaded with groceries, sweets, fruit and vegetables. The last of these helpers was Billy Hoskins of Morrison Street, who helped Phil Egerton in this manner until the 1950s, when he took a job as a storeman with the British Refrasil company.

The Royal Hotel

In 1876 the North of England Industrial Iron and Coal Company commissioned a builder to build the Royal Hotel that, when completed, was used extensively by businessmen visiting the ironworks. The lessee of the hotel was allowed to manage

The Bar in the Royal Hotel c. 1905
The Landlord, Wilf Wardle, took over in 1895, when the Royal was a residential hotel with a large dining room and employed village girls as waitressess, cooks, chambermaids and barmaids. Wilf died in a shooting accident around 1924, and his wife Hilda continued to manage the Royal until 1928. The regular customers shown are Tom Britton, standing, and Mr Walkington. In 1993 the bar has changed very little from the above photograph.

without interference and he employed cooks, waiters, waitresses, chambermaids and barmaids to help him provide all the normal services expected of a good residential hotel. The bar and snug areas of the 'Royal' were open to non-residents for the sale and drinking of beer and spirits, with the usual pub games such as darts and dominoes being encouraged. Initially only the men of the village used these facilities, because any women seen drinking in public were ostracized and few risked this humiliation. It was not until after the Second World War that attitudes became more liberal in this respect.

An occasional drink at home was not frowned upon in the same way, and mothers would send children to the pub with a large jug or an enamelled tea can to be filled with beer or stout by the landlord, and taken home for mother to enjoy in private.

Chapel, School and Railway Station

In 1884, a chapel was built at the end of South street, a school was built in Lowson Street and a permanent railway station was constructed, which meant that within fourteen years of its inception, the village had most of the amenities necessary to be totally functional and reasonably self sufficient.

Other Services

In unison with the services and goods provided by the local shops, a host of travelling retailers would come to the village carrying their wares on a horse and cart or hand carts and, in the case of the ice cream vendor, a specially adapted three-wheeled bicycle.

Weekly visits were made by fishmongers, usually from Hartlepool, butchers and even a hardware and pottery salesman. The latter would set out his goods at the bottom of Lowson Street and, whilst his assistants were trading, he would give the village children a penny ride up and down Lowson Street on the horse and cart.

Butchers continued to come to the village until the 1960s, with the Cooperative Stores leading the way with a specially adapted van that was large enough for customers to stand inside whilst being served. The last butcher to come with a horse and trap was George Callender from Bishopton, an extremely jolly person who possessed the ideal personality and build for his trade. In the late 1940s, whilst on his rounds, George's horse bolted in West Street and when he attempted to hold it, the wheels of the trap ran over him causing an injury which prevented George from fully sustaining his business from then onwards.

Another butcher who came to the village for many years was Mr Aitkin from Fishburn. He only had a small van, but was a good butcher, and many people traded with him. Aitkin would buy rabbits from the local men in order to retail them from his van. The men were happy to supply them and gain a few extra shillings, and he was happy to buy and make a small profit by selling fresh rabbits.

Travelling traders seek a more permanent base

Some of the travelling traders decided to set up a more permanent base and were given permission to build huts close to the railway embankment opposite Morrison Terrace. These included a fruit and vegetable vendor, who resided at Whitton but eventually moved into one of the Morrison Terrace shops, from where he sold groceries whilst still retaining his fruit and vegetable hut. His name was John Dawson, who also worked at the ironworks, and in 1910 became instrumental in setting up the first Stillington football team to play in the local leagues.

Others who established themselves in one of these huts included a cobbler and a fishmonger.

The cobbler, named Tommy Watson, came from Stockton and was reported to be a very brusque man who refused to cobble shoes or boots that had been previously repaired by anyone else. After this gentleman retired in the 1930s, two people took up the service. One was Mr York, a blind person who lived with his sister, Mrs Milton, and did his cobbling in one of the outbuildings in the yard of the Royal Hotel. The other was Mr Featherstone, who had lost a leg in the 1914–18 war and eventually set up his shoe repairing business in a shed situated in the back yard of his home at 60 West Street. This shed had been built by the previous tenants, the Hindley family, to enable Mrs Hindley to sell sweets, cakes, bread and pies, most of which she made herself. As well as selling from the hut in the yard, Mrs Hindley would send her daughters Nellie, Phylis and Dorothy, round the village selling her wares. She began this small business at her previous home in little Lowson Street, and continued when the family moved to West Street.

The first recorded fishmonger to trade from a temporary lock-up shop was Mr J Lonsdale of 25 Morrison Street, who applied to Stockton Rural District Council for permission to build this shed/shop in January 1923. He was granted permission to trade, with the proviso that all fish cleaning and dressing was to be carried out in the shop, and that a proper water supply and adequate draining facilities were available.

These premises were later occupied by a heavily built lady fishmonger from Whinney Hill, who eventually started cooking fish and chips to sell alongside the wet fish she brought daily to the shop on her donkey and cart. Legend has it that she regularly sent her son, Jack, to the pub to get jugs full of beer that she consumed almost continuously whilst working, so that by the evening, she would be quite 'tipsy' and, on many occasions, relied solely on her donkey to get her home.

Many years later, a man from Whinney Hill would come to Stillington to sell wet fish from his three-wheeler van. This was Percy, who had only one leg but was a very jolly character well liked by the villagers. It is possible that he was some relation to the above fishlady, as they both came from Whinney Hill.

The pottery salesman and a barber from Stockton also occupied huts on this site, but most of these traders and the huts had gone by the late 1930s with only the fish shop surviving and taken over by Mr Fordham of West Street until he retired in 1940.

It was then bought by Mrs Florrie Argyle, who had started her business by cooking chips in the boiler of her house at 58 Lowson Street. She then opened a fish shop in a wooden hut opposite this house, where she made her name as the provider of delicious fish and chips. It was wartime when she moved into the Morrison Street shop and fish was very scarce so when her son, Harry, was seen coming from the station on his bicycle, with a box of fish on his shoulder, the villagers would attempt to get to the fish shop early, knowing that there was a chance of getting some fish before the meagre supply ran out. With no fish available, the fishcakes, or patties, as the townies called them, would have fish paste positioned between the two slices of potato, instead of a nice piece of fish, but even these were popular when cooked in batter and served with a few scraps for good measure. With the help of her eldest son, Norman, Mrs Argyle modernised and extended this shop and continued to run it until she retired in the 1950s.

When Norman Argyle was demobbed from the army, at the end of World War Two, he provided another service to the folk of the village by becoming the local bookmaker. 'Off course' betting was illegal at this time, and Norman ran the business from his home in Lowson Street with the occasional help of neighbours in calculating the bets and counting the money. A constant stream of men, women and children would visit his house each morning to place bets for the afternoon's racing or to collect winnings. The bets would be written on any slip of paper, but each was signed with an individual nom de plume that Norman would become familiar with, but which would not be recognised by the authorities in case of a raid on his premises. Other men, working on Norman's behalf, would take bets from the men at the works by using a bag fitted with a timed locking device to prevent fraud. One person who liked a bet, but did not always have sufficient money, was allowed to bet in bricks, which meant that if he lost, he had to pay Norman by cleaning the appropriate number of bricks from the demolished houses in North Street that Norman had contracted to remove.

It must be assumed that the local policeman turned a blind eye to these proceedings, for there was no way he would not be aware of the situation. He probably thought it would be almost impossible to prevent people betting and this was, in any case, a useful and trouble free service to the community, if carried out discreetly.

When 'off course' betting became legal in 1960, a betting shop was built adjacent to the new council houses and Norman passed the business to his cousin, Alan Argyle, whilst he concentrated his efforts on the thriving haulage business he had set up.

Coal Deliveries

Coal was delivered, not free, to the villagers by the ironworks company, presumably from their own pits, until the works closed down when a local man,

Freddy McWilliams, took over as the village coal merchant. The coal was brought to the village by rail and the coal truck was shunted into a siding near the subway. Mr McWilliams would position his flat cart alongside the truck and use it as a platform upon which to weigh the coal into one-hundredweights, put it into individual coal sacks and arrange the sacks on the cart ready for delivery throughout the village. Freddy's horse, a grey, lightly-built, good natured animal named Captain, was well liked by all the villagers, especially the children, and he was a familiar sight hauling the loaded flat cart round the back alleys with their slippery cobblestones causing him to tread carefully. The task almost looked beyond him, but he was a good servant to Freddy for many years before, to the great sadness of all, he collapsed and died in harness c. 1948. Mr McWilliams himself died shortly afterwards and Mr Tommy Tingle took over for a few years, using an old motor wagon to deliver the sacks of coal from his depot in Morrison Street to his customers.

Tommy had a few irons in the fire, including a petrol station in Morrison Street and, in 1957, he sold both these businesses and opened a newly built shop/residence he had had built in the park opposite Bell Square. Two or three merchants from outside the village then took over as coal suppliers to the village, bringing the coal in lorries from their base on a weekly basis.

Freddy McWilliams the Village Coalman
Freddy is seen here loading his flat cart with bags of coal for delivery around the village. The coal would be transported to the siding by the North Eastern Railway Company and weighed and bagged by Freddy directly from the truck. His grey horse, Captain, pulled the cart for many years before finally collapsing during one of his rounds. He was a loyal servant, well loved by all the villagers.

The sketch depicts a period in the 1940s and the houses shown on the other side of the railway are the Railway Cottages with the Royal Hotel on the centre right.

Delivering Milk
Olive Goodman, Vera Watts and Doris Waites, measuring out the milk for one of Walter Young's customers. Photograph taken adjacent to the Cassidi Hall wall.

Milk Deliveries

Until the late 1930s, milk was delivered daily by local farmers, who brought it to the village fresh from their dairies, carried in milk urns loaded onto a horse-drawn cart. As the farmer went round the village, the housewives would take a jug to the cart and the farmer would pour the appropriate amount of milk into the jug using a pint or gill tin measure.

Three people who delivered milk in this way were Mr Wheldon from Whitton Three Gates, Mr Raine from Whitton Moor and Walter Young, who owned a few cows that he grazed in fields directly in front of South Avenue and milked in the byres he owned near the beck.

Mr William Warner of 7 Lowson Street had built a temporary dairy in Lowson Street, presumably at the back of little Lowson Street, and was registered as a purveyor of milk in 1932. In 1936 he was granted a licence, costing £2 2s 0d, allowing him to bottle Grade A milk at his dairy.

Around 1938, the Cooperative Stores commenced doorstep delivery of bottled and pasteurised milk, and gradually took over the whole of the village milk trade. Every morning their milk wagon would bring crates of pasteurised milk from Stockton to the Morrison Terrace store, from where it was delivered by the local

Early form of transport – George Watson with his pony (Scamper) and trap
George lived in North Street, where he and his wife had twelve children including Herbert, affectionally known as Chunney, who was born with a club foot but was always well liked in the village and acted as mascot to the 1910–11 football teams. George moved from North Street to Glykoline Terrace, and this photograph was taken just beyond the top house in the terrace c. 1905. He bred pigs and hens in the 'places' that can just be seen in the background. In addition to being used for family transport, the pony and trap would be used to carry any produce that was ready for sale at Stockton Market.

milk lady, who would use a handcart to take the crates round the village. This handcart was a low, heavy affair with motor car wheels connected to a bulky axle and low chassis, that was difficult to push when empty let alone when filled with crates of milk. Mrs Donaghy did this job for many years, winter and summer, which was amazing when one considers the steep inclines she had to negotiate around the village and the frailty of her own frame. The lady who took over from Mrs Donaghy was Mrs Dorothy Turner, who was of similar physique but again managed this tough task amazingly well.

After the closure of their store, the Cooperative gradually lost custom and a local lad, Terry Wells, took over the majority of milk deliveries in the village and surrounding areas.

Early Medical Services

A doctor came to the village in 1873 and held his surgery in a 'lean-to' attached to the gable end of his house in Mount Pleasant and, although practising from several different venues, the village has had a resident doctor ever since that date. Families who could afford it, would pay the doctor a few pence each week that would entitle them to partake of his services when necessary, a system which continued until the introduction of the National Health Service. Some of the doctors would employ a nurse to help them with certain tasks, such as home care of patients.

The Stillington Nursing Association was formed in 1931 and became affiliated to the Durham County Nursing Association, with the purpose of providing a nursing service to the poor and working-class of the village. Their first appointment was Miss Sarah Gertrude Robinson (Nurse Robinson), who served the village and the surrounding areas as District Nurse for many years. The district nurse, who was paid by the Nursing Association, would help with childbirths, bandaging of wounds, the administration of some medicines and help in the tending of disabled and long-term sick. This service was separate from the doctor who, at the time the Association applied for affiliation to the Durham County Nursing Association, was stated on the Affiliation Form as being 'neutral' about the scheme. When the National Health Service came into being, the Nursing Association was disbanded and the services of doctor and nurses became amalgamated under the doctors supervision.

Transport – Bus Services

Several individuals attempted to provide a bus service between Stillington and Stockton with various picking up points on the way. Harewood's of Thornaby was

Later form of transport. Harewood's Buses of Old Thornaby c. 1930
Harewood was one of the first companies to provide a bus service between Stillington and Stockton. Above is one of the early buses used on this route.

One of Harewood's Buses at the Allison Street Bus terminus in Stockton c. 1930
Allison Street remained the terminus for the Stillington service until around 1950, when it was moved adjacent to the cattle market in Church Road. The driver is Bob Hutley, and the conductress Maude Charleson.

initially the most successful, with others such as local men, Mr McWilliams and Mr Jones, starting a service but giving up after a short period of time. However, one villager, Mr Jack Scurr, started and carried on until he was the only person able to successfully supply a regular service. Jack had, for a few years previously, run a cycling club, which encouraged him to build a hut at the bottom of Lowson Street and start himself up in the business of repairing bicycles. In around 1929 he bought himself a bus and started a successful passenger service between Stillington and Stockton. In 1932, a slag fall crushed his garage at the bottom of Lowson Street and he moved to a site in Morrison Street, where he built an improved garaging facility. The bus service improved and business continued to expand when, in the late forties, he was taken over by the partnership of Mr George Pipe, himself a Stillington person, and Mr G R Thompson. The buses still carried the name of Scurr's Motor Services and the new owners developed it into a company that not only provided a regular local service, but also successfully organised holiday excursions throughout Britain and Europe, before they themselves were taken over by Trimdon Motor Services.

Side view of the Harewood Bus at the Allison Street terminus
The clippie in this view of the Harewood bus service, shown in Ashton Street, Stockton, is Lil Swales, a stalwart of village life, who lived in the village all her life and joined in all events with enthusiasm. The driver is Ted Pritchard.

Other Road Transport

The only car in the village before the Second World War belonged to Mr Samuel Norman, who used it as a taxi. With mass unemployment and poverty prevalent in the village during the 1930s, the hiring of a taxi was rarely considered, though occasionally necessity prevailed and the help of Mr Norman and his taxi would be gratefully sought.

One other car seen regularly in the village belonged to Miss Cruddace, a school teacher at the Stillington Mixed School, who travelled from Bishopton to Stillington, each school day, either on her bicycle or in her green sports car. At some point in the 1940s, Miss Cruddace had been forbidden by her doctor to ride her bicycle or walk to school and so, for the convenience of travelling to school independently, she used her car. Buying a car was beyond the financial capability of most people but

Photograph shows Jack Scurr's first garage built on the site where he had previously had his bicycle repair shed at the base of the tip near Morrison Terrace. A slag fall demolished the garage in 1932 and Jack moved his premises to a position about halfway up Morrison Street. Unfortunately, in 1938, a fire destroyed this garage, all the buses and two cars. However Jack rebuilt his garage, bought new buses and continued to run a successful bus company for many years. In the foreground are Bob Cole and his nephew, Cyril Butler.

The Austin Swallow
The type of car that Norman Trotter bought for £85 with his war gratuity in 1946. This was one of very few cars in the village at this time.

One of Scurr's 'new' service buses in the Morrison Street garage area, c. 1946

Below is a copy of a return ticket from Stillington to Stockton. Ninepence was the cost of this journey from c. 1938 to 1950.

The original ticket was purchased by Mr Cyril Butler on his outward journey from Stillington to join the army fighting in Europe during the 1939–45 war. The ticket has been retained by him ever since.

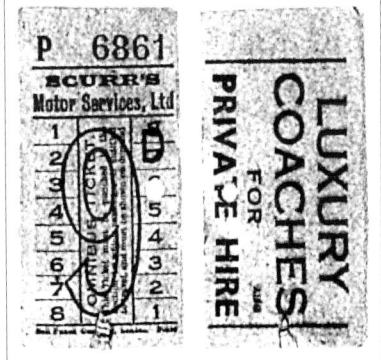

View looking up Morrison Street from the Clarence Railway showing on the right hand side the huts, which housed the fish shop and Tommy Watson's cobbler's shop. This had been the site of several other trades people but, by the late 1930s, only the fish shop remained. The thick hedge hides allotments which run from the fish shop to the junction with the Whitton to Grindon Road. Jack Scurr's new garage site can be seen about mid-picture. Photo c. 1946.

Royal Enfield motor bike and side car. 1928–29
Mr Stan Butler on his motor bike and sidecar photographed in South Street. This was probably the first motor cycle in the village. Stan garaged the bike in the outbuildings of the vicarage.

Miss Cruddace's father was a Master Mariner and probably he would have helped her buy what was then considered to be an item of extreme luxury. In 1946–47 four small cars appeared in the village. These belonged to John Scott, Norman Trotter, Cliff Wells and Harold Sayers, some of the single men of the village who had been demobbed from the services and were able to buy a car with their wartime gratuity. These small second-hand cars were the beginning of a gradual rise in car ownership in the village, which would now see almost every family owning at least one car.

Road Maintenance and Haulage

Mr Syd Britton bought a wagon c. 1944 that he used to do all types of work for Stockton Rural District Council, such as haulage, pushing the snow plough when the roads were blocked with snow, and carrying salt and grit that the road men shovelled on to the road from the back of his wagon when the roads were icy. When Mr McWilliams and his horse and cart were not available, Syd and his wagon would be called to carry the rubbish gathered from the Friday morning street sweeping and drain cleaning around the village. Other wagons, such as those belonging to Henry Peacock of Norton, and Tommy Tingle of Bishopton, became a regular sight

Roadmen's equipment

Photograph above taken around 1953, shows the snow plough and mobile home once used by the driver of the steam roller, who would need to travel to whichever district road repairs were being carried out. During the 1940s and early fifties, if there was a heavy fall of snow, the snow plough would be fastened to the front of Syd Britton's wagon and pushed around the district whilst the roadmen, Bob Robinson and Arthur Warner, would be in the back of the wagon shovelling grit and salt on to the roads to keep the ice under control. The mobile house was at this time only used by the roadmen as a place to shelter or have their lunch. Initially it would have been fitted out with a solid fuel cooking stove, a table, built-in cupboards and built-in beds. The plough and the mobile home were usually parked on the wide roadside verge near Whitton Bridge or down Swann's Lane, and the tethered goat served not only to save its owner feed but also kept the grass under control, at a time when the roadmen had to cut the verges with a scythe.

Photograph below shows the typical arrangement inside the roadman's mobile home.

and a source of work for some village men. Most of their haulage was involved with delivery of the sand and gravel from the local quarries.

Rail Services

A passenger train running a shuttle service between Ferryhill and Stockton stopped at the village from around 1871, and provided the villagers with a means of reaching the local towns. The service was initially arranged by the directors of the ironworks for the use of their work's personnel or visiting businessmen, but gradually came into more general use, especially by villagers who had obtained work in Stockton after the ironworks had closed down. Unfortunately, the eventual competition of road transport in the form of cars and buses caused the rail passenger service to be terminated in 1953, although it was estimated by the then station master, Mr Artley, that 100 people were still using the train each day.

Passenger train passing under Whitton Bridge c. 1900
Photograph shows a passenger train passing under Whitton Bridge on its way to Stillington. This would be part of a regular passenger service that ran between Stockton and Ferryhill stopping at Redmarshall, Stillington and Sedgefield. A connection to Spennymoor was available at Ferryhill.

The Steam Autocar
This type of single carriage steam car replaced the conventional passenger train in the early 1940s and continued until the termination of the passenger service in 1953. A familiar sight pulling into the station, and a good indicator of the time to men in their allotments and people playing on the Cricket Field.

Stillington Station c 1964
Sad sight of the abandoned railway station awaiting demolition. Gone are the busy days of the passenger trains, with porters and passengers milling around the station, with a welcoming fire in the waiting room. The signal box survived a little longer but even the tip, seen in the background was soon to go.

TRAIN SERVICE

FERRYHILL and SPENNYMOOR

3rd MAY 1943 until further notice

Table 143

WEEKDAYS (One class only)

		am	am	am	pm	pm					
FERRYHILL	dep	8 20	9 30	10 25	4 30	6 40	...	...	...	...	...
SPENNYMOOR	arr	8 30	9 40	10 35	4 40	6 50	...	...	...	...	...

WEEKDAYS (One class only)

		am	am	am	pm	pm					
SPENNYMOOR	dep	7 40	9 50	11 35	4 45	6 57	...	...	...	...	...
FERRYHILL	arr	7 48	10 0	11 45	4 53	7 5	...	...	...	...	...

FERRYHILL and STOCKTON

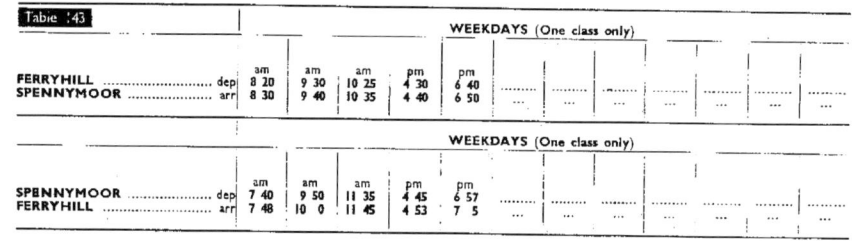

Full particulars of all L·N·E·R services can be obtained on request at stations

BRITISH RAILWAYS

TRAIN SERVICE

FERRYHILL and SPENNYMOOR

27th SEPTEMBER 1948 until further notice

Table 60

WEEKDAYS (One Class only)

	am	am	am	pm	pm	pm B				
FERRYHILL .... dep	8 20	9 30	10 45	4 26	6 45	8 42	......	......	......	......
SPENNYMOOR .... arr	8 30	9 40	10 55	4 36	6 55	8 52	...	...	...	...

WEEKDAYS (One Class only)

	am	am C	am	am	pm A	pm				
SPENNYMOOR .... dep	7 30	10 0	10 20	11 15	4 55	7 20	......	......	......	......
FERRYHILL .... arr	7 38	10 8	10 28	11 23	5 3	7 28	...	...	...	...

A—Through Train to Stockton arrive 5-36 pm   B—Through Train from Darlington depart 8-20 pm
C—Through Train to Darlington arrive 10-30 am

FERRYHILL and STOCKTON

Table 64

	WEEKDAYS (One Class only)							WEEKDAYS (One Class only)				
	am	am	pm	pm					am	am	pm	pm
Newcastle .... dep	6 50	10 35	2 45	7 10	......	......	Middlesbrough .... dep	5 25	8 25	3 20	5 20	......
							Thornaby .... ,,	6SX31	8 32	3 27	5 27	...
FERRYHILL .... dep	8 0	11 58	5 8 A	8 15	...	...						
Sedgefield .... ,,	8 7	12 5	5 15	8 22	...	...	STOCKTON .... dep	7 7	8 50	3 43	5 45	......
Stillington .... ,,	8 15	12 13	5 23	8 30	...	...	Redmarshall .... ,,	7 16	8 59	3 52	5 54	...
Redmarshall .... ,,	8 19	12 17	5 27	8 35	...	...	Stillington .... ,,	7 21	9 4	3 59	5 59	...
STOCKTON .... arr	8 27	12 25	5 36	8 43	...	...	Sedgefield .... ,,	7 30	9 13	4 6	6 8	...
							FERRYHILL .... arr	7 37	9 20	4 13	6 15	......
Thornaby .... arr	8 41	12 40	5 47	9 40	......	......						
Middlesbrough .... ,,	8 47	12 46	5 53	9 46	...	...	Newcastle .... arr	8 51	10 46	5 7	7 19	...

A—Through Train from Spennymoor depart 4-55 pm   SX—Saturdays excepted

Full particulars of all North Eastern Region services can be obtained on request at stations
Other communications regarding train services should be addressed to the District Passenger Manager, Newcastle
The train services shown here are subject to alteration or cancellation at short notice and do not necessarily apply at Bank and Public Holiday periods

Views of Morrison Terrace (the one time hub of the village).

Top: View showing the relationship between Lowson Street and Morrison Terrace. The Cooperative Stores, on the corner of Morrison Terrace, was built by the ironworks as a Workingman's club. The Infant School, now the Village Hall, can be seen towards left centre and the church is just visible at the top of Lowson Street.

Below: Some of the village lads assemble outside the Post Office, some maybe waiting to catch the bus to Stockton, whilst Mr Calvert loads his van with groceries for delivery around the village. Mr Calvert owned the grocers shop on the corner of Morrison Terrace.

Morrison Street c. 1950
Photograph of Morrison Street from Clarence Railway showing Florrie Argyles fish shop at bottom right, and Jack Scurr's garage mid right. The allotments run the full length of the street on the right hand side. These were taken over to build the new private estate in the 1990s.

Stan Butler and his son, Cyril, pause for breath after clearing the snow from the pavement of Morrison Terrace during the winter of 1947. Stan owned the village Post Office and newsagents, and Isa Parry owned the General Stores next door. The slag heap tinged with snow can be seen in the background.

8

The Governing of the Village

The organisation and general management of village affairs was, from 1870 until the mid 1920s, under the domination of the directors of the ironworks. The total dependence of the villagers on the works for their livelihood and accommodation made it imperative that they did not upset anyone in authority at the works. Every street in the village, except Railway Cottages and Glykoline Terrace, was built and owned by the ironworks and each had a manager, a foreman or some senior staff person living in it, usually in a larger end house. These people would report to the work's manager or the company directors any misdemeanor committed by a workman or his family, the result of which could have meant dismissal from the works and the loss of the tenancy of his house. No evidence exists of unfair treatment or over-zealous disciplines being applied and, although frowned upon, a certain amount of drunkenness was tolerated. With so little leisure time available, drinking was probably the only relaxation the men could enjoy, along with pub related games. This system of control was very effective in maintaining order and discipline, even before a village policeman was appointed c. 1875, and in any event the early policemen were almost completely guided by the work's managers and always responded to their requests to prevent or investigate some happening.

In 1894 the national government decided to standardise and improve the system of local government, and to this end, they decreed that parish councils should be formed to oversee the affairs of parishes. These, in turn, would be responsible to a higher authority such as a County or District Council. Accordingly in January 1895, the Whitton Parish Council was formed, which comprised of senior personnel from the ironworks plus the village headmaster and the local vicar. In the early years of this parish council vacancies were filled by friends or colleagues of the existing council, but despite this clique domination the council did seem to act fairly in their quest of a better environment for the people of the parish. This situation continued until the 1922 Triennial Meeting, where councillors who would serve the parish over the next three years were to be elected. In contrast to previous Triennial Meetings where very few people, if anyone other than the serving councillors, turned up, there were over forty villagers in attendance. The parish council comprised nine councillors and whereas in previous years only nine nominations were put forward, the electors had in 1922 nominated sixteen candidates.

A vote was taken by the usual method of a show of hands, but dissatisfaction was immediately expressed with regard to this way of voting, and a poll was demanded by a section of the meeting. The established council tried to block this move but the demand was not withdrawn and, therefore, a poll had to be taken giving all the electorate in the village the opportunity to cast their vote, which resulted in most of the work's orientated councillors losing their place on the council.

The poll had been demanded because people attending the meeting had stated that some of their workmates could not attend because they were at work, and those who were in attendance, felt intimidated by the presence of the senior work's personnel and could not vote freely with a show of hands in case of some future reprisal. This signalled the end of a council dominated by senior work's personnel and other members of the upper class society, and thereafter Whitton Parish Council was a more democratic mixture of personalities.

South Avenue and the new houses in West Street were built in 1920, causing a slight complication in the running of village affairs because these houses were outside the area covered by Whitton Parish Council. This meant that the majority of the village was under the jurisdiction of Whitton Parish Council and Stockton Rural District Council whilst the remainder, new West Street, South Avenue, Glykoline Terrace and Station House, was governed by Stillington Parish Council and Sedgefield Rural District Council.

This situation remained until the boundaries were reorganised in the 1970s when the two Parish Councils amalgamated and the whole of the village came under the one local authority of Cleveland County Council.

(See also Local Government explained in Appendix 11.)

9

Community spirit and activities

Good planning, and the monetary resources of the directors of the ironworks, ensured that the formation of the village continued apace until about 1890, when most of the physical requirements of a village were in position. The creation of a community is, however, a much more difficult and abstract problem, especially when the inhabitants have been brought together from many different areas and with widely varying interests and standards, which was the case here at Stillington.

The majority of the people living in the village had, for many years, only sufficient means to acquire the basic essentials of life but, despite this, a community spirit gradually became a genuine component within the village and prevailed throughout the hardships of war, unemployment and poverty. Continuous hardship formed a bond between the villagers that gave them a sense of comradeship, friendliness and security that has now declined in proportion with their materialistic expectations and achievements.

One of the first organisations in the village was the tennis club formed around 1890, with courts and changing area, built close to the beck near the site of the present workingmen's club. The tennis club was, however, to become a facility for the 'elite' of the village, with their dances being formal and by invitation only, which gave rise to some envy among a few of the other villagers.

Mr Thomas Kirk the managing director of the Carlton Iron Company, was an avid tennis player who had a tennis court at his home in Eaglescliffe and it was undoubtedly at his instigation that the tennis club was formed. Although he did not allay himself to any form of class distinction, the cost of joining the club automatically precluded the lower order of workman from participating.

A little later, a shooting range was set up close to the east side of the slag heap, but this again was only relevant to people who could afford to join and purchase the guns, ammunition and clothing necessary to enjoy the sport.

The natural defence mechanism of the workers led them to relate to their children that tennis and shooting were sports only played by sissies and, consequently, the youngsters had no wish to partake in either. This attitude continued until the late 1940s and also applied to games like golf and rugby.

Marriages were officiated in the village immediately after the church had been consecrated in 1880, and records show that of the 130 weddings that took place up to the year 1910, over 60% of them were between persons living in the village and the vast majority of the remaining 40% were between a villager and a partner who lived within a 10 mile radius. This gives some idea of the close-knit community that had developed within the village and also the lack of opportunity for people to integrate beyond their own immediate vicinity. Most of these married couples remained in the village and started families of their own and even though some shared house with parents others moved into new houses that the ironworks built to accommodate them.

Within 30 years of the building of the first house, families were raised by couples who had been born and bred in the village, a process that continued to predominate until well into the 1950s. The villagers were, therefore, not only bonded together by life-long friendships, but by relationships through marriage, all of which gave added strength to the community spirit and loyalty bonds that were growing between them.

The population of the village began to stabilise from 1890 onwards and people began to look for interests outside their working environment, organising social functions and thus making life more enjoyable, although still arduous in terms of work and general conditions. In around 1910 six brothers of the Britton family who lived in Lowson Street, teamed up with eight other villagers to form a brass band that became well known in the area for its musical ability and smart presentation. They played at dances in places as far afield as Spennymoor and this encouraged their fans from those areas to visit Stillington and vice versa.

The church gradually developed a good sized congregation and a choir of over thirty choristers. The chapel was also very well supported and the Sunday schools of both organisations had Christmas parties and a rail trip to Redcar each year. Both the church and chapel had their own organists and would tour the village at Christmas time stopping at key points to sing carols.

The generally accepted sports for the lower classes was football and, to a lesser extent, cricket, with all the village teams well supported and successful within their own level of local football. It is intended to go more deeply into the history of these two sports in a separate book, because of their tremendous value to the village community over many years, but it is noteworthy that the first records of organised football games are in 1910 when Stillington St. John's had teams entered in the Stockton and District Minor League and the Stockton Junior League. They headed these leagues and also won the Stockton Junior Challenge Cup and the Howard Gritten Challenge Cup, successes which typified the history of football teams which represented Stillington over many years.

A troop of scouts was formed in the village and, although they were in existence from at least 1913 until 1918, all records of this organisation are lost. They registered for membership of the Scouts Association again in 1929 under the name of

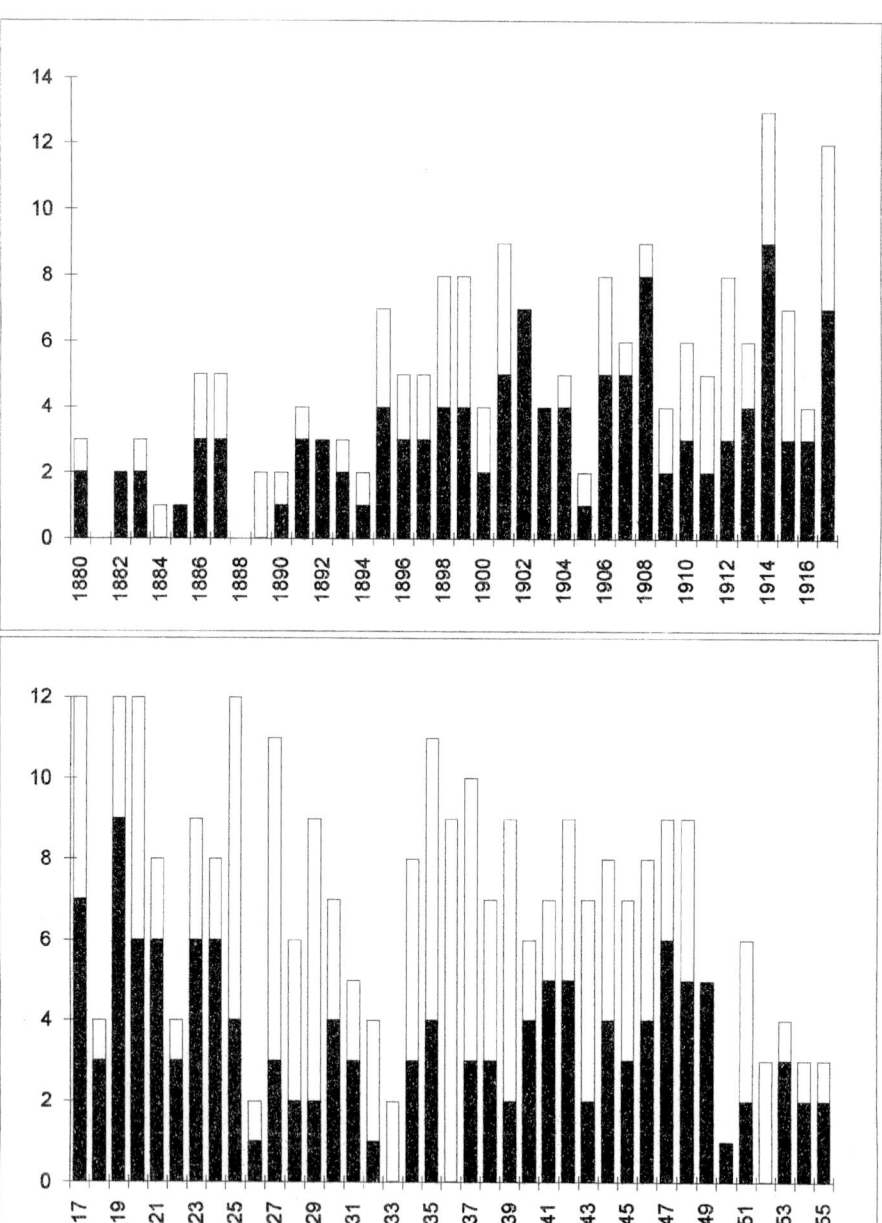

The above diagram shows the number of marriages which took place in St John's church, Stillington during the years shown. Marriages between couples both of whom lived in the village are shown in black.

in percentage terms	1881–91	1891–1901	1901–11	1911–21	1921–31	1931–41	1941–51
Both living in village	59%	59%	71.6%	60%	48%	40%	56%
Couples living within 3 mile radius	9%	0%	5%	8.4%	10%	12.5%	3%
Couples living between 3 & 10 mile radius	18%	22%	11.6%	18%	13%	33%	11.6%
Remainder	14%	19%	11.8%	13.6%	29%	14.5%	27>4%

Stillington St. John Scout Group with their headquarters in the Cassidi Hall and Reverend Douglas as controller but, after functioning for only two years, they were disbanded.

Supplementary to these organisations and events were the normal social activities of the village pub, the Royal Hotel, and the Morrison Terrace workingmen's club which, although managed by a steward, had its social events organised by a committee who were also responsible for the discipline of members.

The Royal Hotel became a regular rendezvous for the local 'hunt', who would assemble outside the pub dressed in their traditional finery and here they would be served drinks whilst the hounds milled around waiting for the signal to start. This tradition continued for several years after the 1939–45 war, but gradually died out.

The 1914–18 war brought with it a period of quiet on the social scene and dampened the spirits of the village folk with 150 young men from a total population of 1,000 volunteering for active service and 36 of them being killed in action. During the sadness of war and immediately afterwards, the village people drew comfort from the blanket of well being and camaraderie that enveloped the village and helped them come to terms with their individual tragedies.

Once again social functions became an important part of life in the village with dances, whist drives, concert parties, social evenings, plays and sports days organised on a regular basis. All functions were well attended and everyone joined in with a friendly and unselfish attitude that ensured total enjoyment of even the most minor events.

Cricket was introduced as a competitive sport around 1922, when an area of the cricket field was relaid in an attempt to provide a suitable pitch. The body of a wooden railway coach was mounted on a foundation in the top corner of the field to act as a pavilion, and a water pipe was laid to a standpipe positioned inside the field to assist the watering of the pitch, and the allotments on the south and west sides of the field. A heavy roller and a light roller, made from one inch thick steel plate were produced at the ironworks and these remained in the cricket field as momentoes of the past until the 1980s, when one of the village lads decided they would make him some money on the scrap market. The heavy roller required six to eight men to pull it over the wicket and, to add extra weight, young children were allowed to sit in the box like top and enjoy a ride. Although the team was reasonably successful and some fine individual players emerged, cricket never overtook football as the major sport of the village.

Another crippling blow struck the village in 1923 when the ironworks was forced into a gradual closure which, by 1925, put most of the men out of work. In the grip of unemployment and poverty for the next ten to fifteen years, with little money available for food and clothing, the ability to remain cheerful was of paramount importance to the general welfare of the village folk. Once again the community spirit was put to the test and but for their ability to respond to the hardship with friendliness and cooperation, the life of the villagers would have been tragic.

All of the functions previously mentioned were maintained by organisers keeping costs to an absolute minimum, and it seemed that a greater bond developed as people supported each other in any way possible. With the closure of the works, the Morrison Terrace workingmen's club ceased to function as a place of entertainment and became a library and a reading room, until the Cooperative Stores took it over in 1935. Indoor activities were then held in the Lowson Street School or the Cassidi Hall.

Dressmaking, knitting, shoe repairs and even mat making were carried out in most homes, and patched trousers and darned socks were commonplace among the school children as the money situation made the cost of buying new clothes more and more difficult.

Mats were a particularly cheap item to make, and important to the cosiness of the home at a time when wall-to-wall carpeting was unheard of. The lady of the house would obtain a empty sackcloth sugar bag, free of charge from the Cooperative Stores, open it up and wash it to form the backing of the mat. A simple pattern would be drawn onto the sackcloth and then it would be fastened into a wooden mat frame. The children of the house would be given the task of cutting clips from old discarded clothes. These clips were about one inch wide by three inches long and, of course, the colours depended upon the clothes that were being used. When the day's chores were over, the mat frames would be brought out and suspended over a couple of chair backs and the clips would be prodded into the sackcloth using a pointed piece of steel with a solid wood handle called a prodder. The colours of the clips were integrated into the pattern, usually forming a black border with an inner multi-coloured circle and then any make up patterns that seemed suitable. Anyone could join in the mat making and on a winter's evening with a cheerful fire blazing, the family could spend a couple of pleasant hours helping in the production of something that would serve and enhance the household for two or three years.

On the food side of things, some enterprising villagers started producing and selling certain items in their homes such as pies and peas, chips, roast potatoes, cakes and scones, toffee apples and sweets, that not only helped them to make a little money, but allowed the less able to buy very cheaply.

The men for their part would, if they had a 'place', keep hens, rabbits, pigeons and maybe a pig to help the food situation. Allotments became a strong feature and not only were vegetables grown for food, but also to enable the men to compete in the annual Leek Show that was held in the Cassidi Hall. This developed into a show for a variance of items such as cake making, embroidery and even the school children's handwriting. Prizes were keenly contested, especially among the gardening section, where the major prize was given to the owner of the best leeks. After the show all the vegetables were auctioned, thus allowing non gardeners to buy very cheaply. However, getting vegetables was not a problem as most of the gardeners were very generous to their friends and neighbours in the distribution of their produce.

PEGGY HUTCHINSON AMONG

THE GIANT LEEKS AT STILLINGTON.

CARLTON IRONWORKS SOCIETY'S SHOW: FEATURES OF THE WOMEN'S SECTION: CLEVER CHILDREN.

Sept 1934

LIKE THE WORLD AND HIS WIFE, I went to Stillington Show. Cheery Mr. Scurr was filling up his 'bus, and seeing him recalled the happy time I spent in Baldersdale. So I asked how the folks up at Hury were standing the drought. But he has had no word from the Dale for some time.

Travelling to Carlton, I saw that a lot of new houses have been built up this pleasant lane. Its popularity lies in its seclusion and quietness, and the easy access to the town.

Carlton is just as picturesque in the golden mellow September as it is in the colourful days of June. It has a sleepy atmosphere as though the hustle of the present-day and generation troubled it little. What a beautiful view we had of Thorpe Thewles. We missed the ducks by inches, and speculated on the possibility of a cheap and tasty dinner had we been the quicker.

But here is Stillington. I understand the big refuse heap is to be used for road material. I hope the Town and Country Planning Committee will visit Stillington and see for themselves the dignity and picturesque beauty that can be invested in a row of trees.

A RED-LETTER DAY.

Stillington Park is full of brightness, beds flaunting vivid colourings and neatly kept lawns tempting folks out of doors these fine days. But it was empty, for it was Stillington's red-letter day, and the Cassidi Hall was filled to over-flowing with the produce grown by the menfolk.

I was late, but Mr. Sherwood and Mr. Williams gave me a warm welcome. I looked at the leeks and the celery and wondered again just how they do it; but this is my third year and I am no nearer the solution of the mystery. The men say hard work and show knowledge, but we all know the cards that matter are kept up their sleeve.

The winning cabbage weighed 20lbs. For a long time I ate a cabbage a day for my dinner, but I would have quaked to tackle a fellow like that. The marrows were "whoppers," but it was the little lad with the satin-smooth skin that got the premier prize.

PRAISE FOR CHILDREN.

Mr. Lonsdale said his children had cut a 20 pounder in the school garden at Kirkleatham. He believed it had been an exceptionally good year for marrows. Mr. Lonsdale was judging free-hand drawings. Dorothy Sherwood, Daisy Pinch, Mildred Atkinson, and Norman Trotter showed unusual talent; the black dog study was most realistic.

I must congratulate Mr. Buchan on the manners of Stillington schoolchildren. Without being shy they show a respect for their elders and propriety that is pleasing.

GOOD FOR THE WOMEN.

The women's section was good, both in quality and quantity; the cake and ginger-bread choice. I understand from the judges that the butter was very even; some of them had been a bit lavish with the salt, and they lost a point or two on that. Mrs. Armstrong, Mrs. Wardale and Mrs. Brown were judging. I was sorry to see Mrs. Armstrong had broken an arm—a bit of bad luck one can do without very nicely in harvest time.

Mrs. Brown had to hurry off home. She has 41 geese which she reared, and lives in fear of a fox raid.

The friendly intercourse with these ladies is an added happiness which goes a long way to make Stillington Show a date to be remembered.

We have a National Allotments Society, with Sir Francis Acland, M.P., as President, which has distributed 10,444 collections of seeds, 415 tons of seed potatoes, 6,900 bags of fertilizer, 6,772 cwts. of lime, and practically 6,000 garden tools to the unemployed in the North-Eastern Area. This has given a tremendous fillip to growing vegetables.

MANY VISITORS.

People had come from far and near to see the best. I saw the schoolmaster from Tursdale, and Mr. Alton from Metal Bridge, lost in admiration at the leek benches. Mr. Simpson, from West Cornforth, and Mr. Taylor, from Mainsforth Colliery, were handling the largest potatoes, six weighing 13 lbs.

Mr. Jack Scorer and Mr. Roberts, from Coxhoe, seemed to spend a long time over the trays of collections of vegetables, which must have been the best ever got together. And these men are so modest about their efforts! Mr. Kendal, the park keeper, had eight firsts and four specials, but Mr. Holborn, Mr. McWilliams and Mr. C. Trotter were hard on his heels. These are young men with extraordinary show knowledge.

GIANT LEEKS.

I saw six men from Ferryhill going from bench to bench, and saw the surprised amazement registered on their faces. The man from Middlesbrough demanded a leek: his pals would not believe without some tangible proof. "But I'll have a 'bus load here to-morrow," he vowed.

I came home in the same 'bus, and was amused at the great pride he displayed in the leek.

A POPULAR RENDEZVOUS.

Bit by bit, as the judging finished, we drifted along to Mrs. Sherwood's, whose house at the moment is a picture, covered with Virginia creeper which has turned a beautiful blood red. On the table was a new kind of pickle, which was so good that I begged the recipe for you.

PEAR PICKLE (SWEET).

Seven lbs. of pears, peel and quarter them, taking away the core, 3½ lbs. loaf sugar, ½ oz. cloves (bruised), and one pint of vinegar. Place the vinegar, cloves and sugar in a pan; when they boil drop the pears in bit by bit so as not to stop the boiling and simmer until tender.

Mrs. Shewood is a clever housewife. She took prizes for bread and plum cake. The latter recipe she also gave to me.

IRISH PLUM LOAF.

Rub ½ lb. lard into 2 lbs. flour, add 1 lb. raisins, 1 lb. currants, 1 lb. brown sugar, ½ lb. lemon peel, 1 teaspoonful cream of tartar. Mix well up together and make up with two eggs, 1 teaspoonful of bi-carbonate soda and 1 pint of sour milk. Cut in slices and butter.

FROM STOKESLEY.

We had Mr. Davis, from Stokesley. On one point he and I are fully agreed, and that is, if we had a prize to give out for the prettiest house and garden it would go to Mr. Robert Garbutt, in Bilsdale, at Ella Bridge. It reminds me of Fairfields, only we pinned our faith to geraniums, Sweet Williams, and dahlias, whereas Mr. Garbutt mixed his colours more freely with the hand and eye of an artist. Mr. Davis feels that the smaller shows should have more open classes, but Mr. Sherwood is unable to do anything, as this show fills the Cassidi Hall to overflowing.

Mr. Weatherill was here also from Stokesley. He's a great tease, and told me that "although I was often in hot water I never got scalded."

"It is just over 50 years since I went to the workhouse," he began.

"That sounds bad," I retorted.

"Well, Peggy, poor folk have poor ways," he declared, with a happy twinkle in his eye. I know that he was a popular master, and his kind heart gave many a sad life happiness.

Mr. Wetherill doesn't exactly believe in the slogan, "Live and let live." He feels "Live and HELP to live" is a far better one. His hobby is bottling fruit, and after a long, successful run, in which he was never beaten, he left off showing—to let someone else have a chance. This, I think, is a sporting attitude, and quite in keeping with his genial slant on life in general.

Mr. Lonsdale is an enthusiastic bee-keeper, and declares there is plenty of good flower honey, but the heather crop is scarce owing to the drought.

THE NORTHUMBRIAN "BURR."

Mr. Sanderson comes from Cowpen, near Blyth, and brings his Northumbrian burr with him. He is a carnation specialist, but very modest about his achievements. Mr. Cleary is a Croxdale man, whose happy smile takes me back to that day when I judged the carnival dress at Sunderland Bridge.

Mr. Williams, from Thorpe Thewles, is saving his voice. He has a Choral Society, which has just begun the winter session. They are practising part-songs and hope to give a concert in early November. Next year they hope to attempt something really ambitious.

A LIVE WIRE.

Mr. Sherwood, the secretary of the show, is a live wire.

I have told you enough to make you realise Stillington Show is a social event. One meets the world and his wife here, and they are people who have done things towards making a name for themselves. Mr. Tingay, the chairman, is a genial leader. The Club members are outstanding for loyalty and unity. The men are clever and industrious. The land was poor when they took it over, and look at what they produce! He is justly very proud of the effort.

A PIONEER.

It was the 18th show. The sad note was the absence of Mr. John Dawson, who, with the Harper family, was the pioneer of this splendid venture, and for 16 years the very able secretary. After the works were disbanded, Mr. Dawson obtained employment near to Scarborough—he had a deal of trouble with his sight, but one was glad to hear that he is doing well.

Grazing in the field outside Mrs. Sherwood's door was the famous "Searchlight," who has left a trail of glory behind him at the various shows. Altogether he has won 199 prizes for scamper, musical ride, potato races, and "flapping." Mr. Young, his owner, is a dairy farmer, and although 21 years old, Searchlight goes in the milk cart every day.

In Stillington there is a strong movement of the G.F.S., run by the Misses Taylor, who consider no effort a trouble to foster happiness among the young people.

UNITY IS STRENGTH.

The villagers are very generous. They have just had a carnival for the Nursing Association, and now are carrying on relays of comic cricket matches and go-as-you please socials for hospital funds. There is also a go-ahead W.I., where the women spend happy nights among interesting demonstrations.

Stillington is a bonny place and all it has come from the endeavours of the people, who believe that unity is strength, and go forward as one, making every venture a success.

BOLTON CAKE.

1lb. flour, ½lb. butter, ½lb. sugar, ½lb. currants, ½lb. sultanas, 2 eggs, 1 gill warmed milk, 1 teaspoonful bicarbonate soda, 1 teaspoonful mixed spice, 2ozs. almonds, 2ozs. peel. Beat the butter, sugar and eggs, add the fruit and flour, melt the soda in the warmed milk, and add last, being careful to mix it well up. Bake in a moderate oven 1½ hours.

DATE AND WALNUT CAKE.

¼lb. butter, ¼lb. castor sugar, 2 eggs, ½lb. flour, ¼lb. dates, ¼lb. shelled walnuts, a little milk, ½ teaspoonful baking powder, ½ teaspoonful bicarbonate soda. Cream the butter, eggs and sugar together, add the rest of the ingredients, putting the flour in last. Dissolve the soda in the milk and mix up well. Bake in a moderate oven 1 hour. Cut in slices and butter.

Report on Stillington Leek Show 1934

This very explicit report tells what an important event the Leek Show was and how it attracted entries from all around the area. It is interesting that the reporter mentioned the horse Searchlight, owned by Walter Young, for it spent many more years grazing the pasture in front of South Avenue and was well known by the villagers.

In 1931 the Women's Institute was formed, and weekly meetings were held with guests invited to speak on many interesting subjects. The ladies of the village would be given hints on household management with an emphasis on economic methods and the preparation of cheap wholesome foods, that was of great value to the younger housewives during this period of enforced shortages.

Football continued to play a major part in the sporting life of the menfolk, and the enthusiasm of some of the women supporters became a talking point well into the 1950s, when referees still dreaded a visit to Stillington. The pitch in those days was adjacent to the beck and, if the women were displeased with the referee's handling of the match he was, so word had it, hit on the head with umbrellas and dispatched into the beck.

Visits to the local towns were rare, but contact with other villages such as Bishopton, Carlton, Thorpe, Old Stillington, Foxton, Shotton, Redmarshall, Great Stainton and Sedgefield was fairly regular, with the footpaths from Stillington to all these villages being in constant use. Sedgefield had been visited by older schoolboys every Shrove Tuesday since 1875, when they would be given a holiday from school to go and partake in the traditional Sedgefield Ball game.

The Stillington menfolk would quite often visit the neighbouring pubs, especially if there was a domino or darts handicap being staged where they could win a bottle of whisky or maybe a chicken. On a fine Sunday evening during the summer months, many families could be seen walking over the fields to these villages to have a drink and a chat before walking home.

The Stillington folk came through these years of depression and the unemployment gloom had just been lifted by the arrival of the Stillite Products factory when, once again, the village and the world were thrown into turmoil by the declaration of the Second World War in 1939. Both men and women of prime ages were taken from the village for the duration and thus, with the blackout and the rationing of food and clothes, a certain amount of gloom descended once again. The food and clothes rationing were not a great problem to the village housewives because they had already survived fifteen years of self imposed rationing because of lack of money, but the absence of loved ones, the blackout and the tensions of war, did have a dampening effect on morale.

At the end of the war in 1945, the village came to life again. Plenty of work was available, not only in the village, but in the local towns that could now be reached by the improved transport services. The improvement in transport and living standards also meant that the village folk, young and old, could now visit the towns, generally Stockton, more frequently and enjoy the varied entertainments available and meet a greater variety of people.

Between the years of 1945 and 1952, when this account of Stillington ends, life within the village was buzzing with lots of social activities and a high degree of community spirit.

A new workingmen's club was formed in 1946, with snooker, billiards, darts, dominoes and cards all part of the entertainment. The club was a member of the local games leagues and, every Friday evening, matches would be held against rival clubs both at home and away, which created an added interest to the indoor games. Self-entertainment was a feature of the club and, when the atmosphere warmed at around 9.30pm on Friday and Saturday evenings, the local lads and lasses would get up on the stage to give a rendering of their favourite songs. Syd Britton, the club secretary for many years, was also a good pianist and he would accompany the singers throughout the evening, with everyone joining in the sing-song before last orders were called at 10.30pm. Dances were held in the club on one or two evenings during the week where members and visitors could enjoy the old-time dancing. This form of entertainment gave way to professional artists coming to the club and, during a spell in the late sixties and early seventies, most of the top stage and television stars performed at the club on Friday evenings under the auspices of the club's entertainment manager.

There was often a dance in the Village Hall on a Friday evening, and these were arranged to commence at 10pm so that the villagers could go to the club or to town for a drink and a dance, and come back to the village hall and dance till 2 'oclock in the morning. These dances were so popular that Stillington, Thorpe, Bishopton and Carlton organised similar events in rotation, so that there was always one venue which one could attend on a Friday evening, even though it often meant a walk of two or three miles home.

Pages of a Typical Programme for the Workingmen's Club during its hey days.

Ces Challis, who was born and bred in Stillington, was a very accomplished pianist, and in 1946, he formed a small group comprising a piano, Hawaiian guitar and drums. He played the piano, Joe Dolan played the Hawaiian guitar and either Bob Kirtley or Danny Dolan played drums, and this trio played at almost all the local dances during this period, and were responsible for many hours of pleasure.

An active youth club was run by Tommy Tingle which all the youngsters, attended, and were introduced to mixed games, visited other clubs, had a regular Thursday night trip to Spennymoor Rink for Old-Time dancing and many other excursions. Tommy also formed a junior football club that played in the Stockton and District Junior League.

The Stillington Parish Players was formed by the Reverend Jasper and, after starting on a low key with Nativity Plays, went on to perform an average of two plays a year in the Lowson Street School, before doing several Gilbert and Sullivan operas with an accompanying orchestra. The fun generated by this sort of organisation comes from the comradeship and friendships that can develop between a great variance of ages during rehearsals, meetings and the general preparation of the stage and lighting for the performances.

The cricket team was in action again reformed by Les Harper with Cyril Butler as captain, and there were three football teams playing under the name of Stillington. They were, Stillington St. Johns, Stillington Workingmen's Club and a younger team, Stillington Church Rovers. The cricket team won many good matches but were not experienced enough to be wholly successful. The football teams, however, all won their respective leagues and various cups with the comradeship and team spirit that the village atmosphere engendered being worth two goals start in any match.

Outdoor games had always played a large part in the social aspect of the village with men and boys alike playing football, cricket and quoits that was very popular with the men, who laid special clay areas in the bottom corner of the cricket field in which to set the hobs.

Some men kept greyhounds, which they would enter into races at the Belle Vue stadium at Stockton and, as well as the normal exercise walks, they would give the dogs training runs over a course they had laid out in one of the fields on the way to Thorpe. The mock 'hare' was pulled round the track by a winch that had been salvaged from several that were in the huge piles of scrap surrounding the North Eastern Iron Refinery.

Sports days were a regular feature in the village calendar with everyone encouraged to enter and take part in the numerous events that were organised. The main events were the races of 100 yards, 200 yards, one mile, a long distance race which included a run over the slag heap, the high jump, the long jump and throwing the cricket ball. The fun events included an egg and spoon race, three-legged race, sack race, obstacle race and a slow bicycle race. Some fine athletes lived in the village, but none greater than Len Jackson, the local sprint specialist who ran against the British champion of the day, MacDonald Bailey, and beat him from a couple of yards start.

Outdoor amusement for the younger boys and girls was usually a seasonal rotation of differing self-motivated activities. These would include playing with bogies, sledging, marbles, conkers, playing with tyres or hoops, cannon, chases, hide and seek, many hours of 'scrounging' over the fields, bird nesting and the collection of various types of bird's eggs. Added to this was the formation of opposing gangs usually 'yon side of the railway versus our side', and having mock fights on and around the slag heap, or setting up a camp among the ruins of the ironworks and lighting a fire on which to cook wild bird's eggs or roast any potatoes that could be obtained. Girls would join some of these activities, especially sledging, but they had their own leisure activities such as skipping, itchy bay and several games with balls at which they were very adept.

During the summer months the young lads would dam the beck in order to form a dub where they could enjoy a swim and although parents were worried about the children catching ringworm from the cattle that drank from the beck, these warnings were ignored and many happy hours were spent in the Foxton and Whitton dubs with a quick run round the field to dry off.

A family named Anderson had moved into Mount Pleasant and Eden, the son, held a film show every Monday evening in a large hut just outside the house. It was sixpence to get in and the seats were anything from old settees to old car seats, but it was great fun and yet another opportunity for the youngsters to meet in a good atmosphere.

During these years both the church and chapel were still commanding healthy congregations and the church still had a choir, although it was now only about a dozen strong. Nellie Daniels, who had been the church organist for many years and had served six or seven different vicars, was the choir-mistress with the main chorister being Mrs Polly Poole, who led the singing with a fine soprano voice.

Special occasions, such as Christmas and New Year, were one great party and on New Year's Eve the village was astir till early morning with people calling at each others' houses to celebrate the New Year with the customary drink, or two, and slice of cake.

Children would try to earn some extra money by carol singing around the streets, and also by asking permission to enter peoples' houses to perform an ancient ritual play which had been carried on by generations of villagers. This entailed a number of children dressing up in appropriate costumes, usually blacking their faces, and acting out the play as follows:

Player one   'I open the door, I enter in, I hope the game will soon begin.
Stir up the fire and make a light for in this house there'll be a fight.
If you don't believe the words I say
Step in King George and lead the way.'

Player two	'In steps King George, King George is my name,
	A sword and pistol by my side I'm bound to win the game.
	The game sir, the game sir.' (The two players have a brief sword fight and player one falls down).
	'See I've killed my father's eldest son.
	Ten pounds for a doctor, nay twenty.'
Player three	'In steps Doctor Brown, I'm the best old doctor in the town'
Player one	'How come your the best doctor in the town?'
Player three	'By my travels.'
Player one	'How far have you travelled?'
Player three	From the bedside to the fireside,
	From Italy, Pitaly, France and Spain and back to dear old England again.
	I can cure humps, mumps and polygrumps.' he bends and gives patient some medicine.
	'Here Jack take a drop of my nick-nack.'

Jack gets up and all join hands and sing.

'Me brother's come to life again, to life again, to life again, me brother's come to life again we'll never fight no more.'

Player four comes in.

'Here comes Elsie Bum, on my back I carry a drum
In my hand a frying pan, I think myself a jolly old man.
A jolly old man I ought to be, three sons all as tall as me,
One tall, two small, I think myself above them all.'

Enter player number five.

'In steps Mickey Funny, I'm the collector of the money,
A hole in my stocking, a hole in my shoe.
If you haven't got silver copper'll do.
If you haven't got copper, God Bless You.'

He goes round the audience collecting the money.

Several groups of children would go round the village performing this little ritual on Christmas Eve and they would vie for the best places to perform. The ones who were allowed in the pub or the club obviously got greater reward than those limited to households.

Crime was so minimal as to be ignored and, the only time there was any thieving was when Culine's fair came to the village and one or two of their lads would steal boxes of cigarettes from the Cooperative Stores. The source of the culprits was so obvious that the local policeman always quickly solved the problem and generally recovered the cigarettes from some hole in the side of the slag heap. This aside, the fair was another attraction that came to the village each year with all the usual swings, roundabouts and side shows for everyone to enjoy. A crawl round the underside of the roundabout ride would prove to be profitable for the village children, as many a shilling or two shilling piece that had dropped from the men's pockets and fallen between the boards could be found in the grass.

Despite all the available contact with the outside world, 58% of all marriages in Stillington were still between two villagers, and the closeness of association and loyalty to each other was very strong among the villagers. In reality, these years 1946–1952, were probably the finest the village had enjoyed with a wonderful and active community life, coupled with a little more affluence and less general hardship.

Things may have improved vastly in a materialistic sense but, regardless of attempts to organise all types of social functions, the community spirit of the village has now been replaced by differing individual priorities.

10

Men who influenced the formation and development of the Village of Stillington

Samuel Bastow

Samuel Bastow must be considered as the man who made the creation of Stillington possible when he purchased the fields known as Moor Closes in 1858–1860. Having bought these fields, he quarried clay from them and set up a small brickmaking plant and then, in 1865, he built two blast furnaces on the site and began producing pig iron.

Bastow's previous business concerns had been in West Hartlepool where he was well established as a the owner of a foundry and a workshop. From 1846 he had manufactured steam engines and later locomotive boilers, railway trucks and cranes.

It was in 1858 when he took his first venture into ironmaking and built the Cliff House ironworks at New Stranton, West Hartlepool, The success of this project decided him to expand by building two blast furnaces on the Moor Closes site. After some further success Bastow found the cost of keeping pace with the rapid development of ironmaking techniques to be overwhelming and in 1867 a severe depression in the trade forced him to abandon these blast furnaces. His brave venture into the industry finally ended in 1869 when he was declared a bankrupt.

Samuel Bastow's only legacy to the Moor Closes site was two outdated blast furnaces and an idle clay quarry but he had provided the embryo around which the village of Stillington was formed and should therefore be remembered as the instigator of circumstances from which the village was developed.

Henry Currer Briggs (1829–1881)

Henry Currer Briggs was born in Halifax into a family who were involved in coal mining, textiles, shipping and banking. His grandfather and two uncles had formed the Halifax Commercial bank, whilst his father was deeply involved in the ownership of several collieries. He was brought up as a strict Unitarian and maintained this belief throughout his life.

In 1854 Henry Currer Briggs married Catherine Shepherd, daughter of Edward Shepherd the governor of Wakefield Gaol and owner of a jute mill at Thornes, Wakefield.

He managed this mill for some time before joining his father's company, Henry Briggs Son and Company Limited as Managing Director in 1865.

In 1868 he succeeded his father as chairman of the company, and his brother Archibald became Managing Director. Output from the pits owned by the company was at this time around 600,000 tons per annum.

Henry Currer Briggs was also involved with Thomson, Shepherd and Briggs, jute spinners of Dundee where he lived until his father died in 1869. After his father's death he moved to Saltburn from where he took an interest in Merrybent Railway, Apedale Lead Mines, Bratsberg Copper Company, Norway and the Samuel Bastow blast furnaces.

In 1870 Henry Currer Briggs and his brother Archibald bought the Moor Closes site that included the blast furnaces, built by Samuel Bastow, and the clay quarry with the brickmaking plant.

Mrs Henry Currer Briggs often visited the Board School at Stillington to inspect the children and the school rooms and sometimes gave the children a lesson.

Henry Currer Briggs
Photographs and some information taken from the book A Merchant, A Banker and the Coal Trade, by Donald Henry Currer Briggs.

The brothers formed a company named the North of England Industrial Iron and Coal Company, with the intention of modifying and expanding the ironworks.

Henry Currer Briggs became its founder Chairman and Managing Director with his brother Archibald appointed as a director.

Henry Currer Briggs was energetic and his far-sighted plans were to be admired for, although not always best advised in the technical facets of ironmaking, he very quickly transformed the Moor Closes site into an area where pig iron could be produced in quantity and at a competitive price. Not only did he develop the company but Briggs was intent on creating a community for his workers and, in consequence, built a lodging house, workmen's houses, shops, a workingmen's club and a hotel. He also encouraged the building of a church and a Mission Hall and allowed one of the houses in South Street to be used as a chapel until a proper chapel was built. In 1874 Henry Currer Briggs was the prime mover in the creation of the United Whitton and Stillington School Board and, under his chairmanship, a school was opened in the Lodging House in 1875, soon to be followed by the building of the Board School in Lowson Street in 1877, which was heavily funded by The North of England Industrial Iron and Coal Company.

In December 1876 Archibald died and Henry Currer Briggs had to once again assume the role of Managing Director and Chairman to Henry Briggs Son and company, so he resigned his position as Managing Director of the North of England Industrial Iron and Coal Company, whilst retaining his position as Chairman of the Board. Thomas Kirk succeeded him as Managing Director and thus relieved him of a very heavy workload.

Archibald Briggs

In 1881, whilst on a business trip to Norway to inspect a silver mine belonging to the Bratsberg Copper Company, Henry Currer Briggs collapsed and died. His achievements however should not be forgotten for, as Chairman and Managing Director of the North of England Industrial Iron and Coal Company, he had transformed two outdated blast furnaces into an industrial concern which had three modern blast furnaces with updated plant and equipment, owned coal mines, owned or held leases on ironstone mines and had created the Village of the Carlton Ironworks. He had been an energetic, hard working business man, who also cared for his workforce and had built good quality houses for their accommodation at all locations where the company were involved and especially at the Village of the Carlton Ironworks.

Henry Currer Briggs should therefore be remembered as the main pioneer and creator of the village that was eventually named Stillington and it is unfortunate that there is no memorial to his name.

Walter Morrison

Walter Morrison was a director of the North of England Industrial Iron and Coal Company from its origin in 1870 and continued as director when the company changed its name to the Carlton Iron Company in 1877. He was appointed Chairman of the Board in succession to Henry Currer Briggs who died in 1881 and held that position until Dorman Long and Company took control of the Carlton Iron Company in 1920.

Born in London on the 21st May 1836, he was the fifth son of James Morrison of the firm Morrison, Dillon and Company. Morrison was heir to a share of great fortune made in business during the Napoleonic Wars and which greatly increased during his lifetime. Educated at Eton and Balliol College, Oxford, where in 1857 he became a formidable oarsman and obtained a first class degree in literae humaniores. The mental and physical vigour he showed here was maintained throughout his long life.

On leaving Oxford in 1858, Morrison did a grand tour which included Egypt, Palestine and the United States. He entered the House of Commons in 1861 as the Liberal member for Plymouth, a seat he held until 1874. He stood unsuccessfully for the City of London in 1880 and then parted from Mr Gladstone over his Irish programme. From 1886 until 1892, and again from 1895 until 1900, he represented his home division of Yorkshire, Skipton, as a liberal unionist. He then retired from politics after a broken career in parliament stretching over nearly forty years. This career was probably not congenial to him, for Morrison was a man with strong convictions and of great independence but not a great orator. His early liberal days were largely centred in the co-operative movement for improving the dwellings of the workingclass but after his break with Gladstone, all his energies were thrown into the fight for Union with Ireland and against the tyranny of the boycott and the plan of campaign.

Mr Walter Morrison
Director of the Carlton Iron Company from 1870 until 1920. Chairman of the Board of Directors from 1891 until 1920.

During his intermittent absorption in politics, Morrison kept a careful stewardship of both his private fortune and his various business interests. In 1874 he joined the board of the Central Argentine Railway in which his family possessed a large stake and became its chairman in 1887, after which he paid a protracted visit to South America which resulted in the absorption of the Buenos Ayres and Rosario line. He was also director of a number of local concerns and travelled constantly between London and Yorkshire in the discharge of his duties, which were undertaken from a keen sense of responsibility rather than any desire to increase his wealth.

His wealth grew, partly because of inheritance from his brother and sister who were childless and died before him, and also from the simplicity of his personal tastes. He was not a miser and consistently, but prudently, gave away large parts of his fortune.

Despite all his business interests he spent a lot of time at Malham Tarn, the wild moorland estate in Craven that had been acquired for him, when he came of age, from the Listers of Gisburn. Here he could indulge his love of walking, of folklore, of a miscellaneous range of literature and of local leadership in many forms. Walter Morrison never married and his notion of company was rather that of an audience than a circle of friends.

He was always something of an aloof and self-centred figure, greatly respected by his neighbours but never popular in the ordinary sense of the word, quite incapable of adapting himself to society but delighted to welcome to Malham a succession of guests among whom, at one time or another, appeared such eminent Victorians as Henry Fawcett, John Ruskin, Charles Darwin, John Stuart Mill, Sir William Harcourt and Charles Kingsley. It was at Malham Cove that Kingsley had his idea for The Water Babies and Walter Morrison was his Squire.

From Malham radiated the princely benefactions for which Morrison will be best remembered, though his dislike of publicity rendered the real extent almost incalculable. He played a considerable part in the development of the northern universities – one single anonymous gift of £10,000 to a new school of agriculture at Leeds was revealed by accident after his death.

For Giggleswick School, where he was chairman of the governors for many years, he built and furnished down to the smallest detail, in celebration of Queen Victoria's diamond jubilee, the remarkable chapel with a dome which was the expression both of his lifelong interest in Oriental architecture and his personal partialities in English history.

It is known that Morrison was the mainstay of Lord Robert's campaign for National Service; that for some years he made an annual contribution of £10,000 to King Edward's Hospital Fund; and that innumerable relief funds owed much to his support during both the South African and European Wars. He was one of the founders of the Palestine Exploration Fund and regarded himself in that connection as the discoverer of Kitchener. By a single gift of £15,000 he made possible the chief Hittite excavations, those of Carchemish, undertaken by the British Museum while the Society (now dissolved) of Biblical Archaeology, owed almost its whole career to his munificence.

Towards the end of his life, Oxford became the special object of Morrison's benefactions and, fired by his experience at Giggleswick, he offered to rebuild the new chapel at Balliol on the lines of the old which he greatly preferred. This offer was rejected, so he then gave £30,000 to the University for the three purposes of: a readership in Egyptology, a professorial pension fund and the study of agriculture. Finally, in 1920, he endowed the Bodleian Library with a single payment of £50,000 and thus took rank among the three chief benefactors in the history of that famous foundation. The honorary degree of DCL which was conferred upon him in the following year was the only public recognition he received, or indeed would have valued. He died at Sidmouth on the 18th December 1921 and was buried at Kirkby Malham.

The foregoing account of Walter Morrison is given in the Dictionary of National Biography and records him a very generous man. This generosity was shown to the Carlton Iron Company on many occasions, during the depressions that were commonplace throughout the iron and coal industries. He invested heavily in the company and on many occasions paid outstanding bills with his own money but Morrison was not just a munificent figurehead, for he attended most of the directors' regular meetings and all the shareholders' meetings. In 1880, he repaid a mortgage of £10,000 when the mortgagee died and his executors wanted repayment; after the miner's strike in 1912 he gave the company a loan of £15,000 to assist it through the difficulties caused by the strike; expended £20,000 to renew the coke ovens in 1895; provided mortgages totalling £175,000 to enable the company to buy Mainsforth Colliery in 1907; bought Manor Farm at Whitton in 1911 and leased it to the company until they could afford to buy it from him. In 1914 when the Carlton Iron Company had to be reconstructed in order to survive, Morrison forfeited a substantial amount of money for the sake of saving the company and to encourage other shareholders to accept a scheme which would prevent the company going into liquidation.

Internal view of the domed area of the chapel that Morrison financed at Giggleswick

House of Commons Library
March 1 1897

Dear Style,,

I have an idea in my head of offering to build the school a chapel with a Dome as an architectural experiment, employing Jackson, the famous Oxford Architect. One would call it the Diamond Jubilee Memorial. Site - the knoll in the Cricket Field. We have very few domes in England and it might give a hint to others.

But I should like to hear any suggestions of yours. A Domed Building on the site should look well. It would need much thinking out as we do not understand Domes. The Round Church at Cambridge gives some hints.

Yours truly,

W. Morrison

Rev. G. Style

Morrison's letter initiating the building of the domed chapel and its beautiful setting above Giggleswick School

Walter Morrison's political outlook always favoured the poor, and there is no doubt that he was instrumental in the building of good quality houses by the Carlton Iron Company for its workers, and the provision of amenities such as the workingmen's club. Two streets in Stillington were named after him – Morrison Street and Morrison Terrace – both of which have now been demolished leaving no memorial to this energetic man, without whose generosity the Carlton Iron Company would not have survived as long as it did. The consequence of an early closure of the ironworks would have meant the abandonment of any further housing and possibly the extinction of the village.

Walter Morrison gave much to the Carlton Iron Company and to the Village of the Carlton Ironworks and it would therefore be fitting if some new memorial to this great and generous man could be arranged within the village.

Thomas Kirk (1835–1908)

Thomas Kirk was one of three brothers whose father founded a family firm of ironworks in 1770 at Chapel en le Frith in Derbyshire. The firm transferred to Workington in 1860 under the name of Kirk Brothers and Company and restarted with the three brothers acquiring a small forge, with two heating furnaces and a steam hammer, from where they manufactured wrought iron. Expansion of the company was rapid and puddling furnaces with forge and rolling mills were installed which enabled the manufacture of wrought iron bars. The whole family was totally immersed in all facets of ironmaking and became well known for their great knowledge and expertise regarding the industry.

In 1872, the directors of the North of England Industrial Iron and Coal Company built at the Village of the Carlton Ironworks a malleable ironworks equipped with a number of Dank's puddling furnaces, which would turn the pig iron produced by the blast furnaces into malleable iron. In anticipation of being able to produce malleable iron successfully, the directors then decided to build two plate mills adjacent to the puddling furnaces, and thereby use the malleable iron to produce ships plates and other engineering components.

After a series of discussions regarding terms, Thomas Kirk was contracted to erect and equip the plate mills and act as consultant and overseer of production for the following seven years. Thus Thomas Kirk became deeply involved in the malleable iron and plate mill section of the North of England Industrial Iron and Coal Company and, in consequence, he removed from Workington to Preston on Tees near Stockton in 1875. He lived a short distance from Eaglescliffe station and on each working day he would walk to the station and catch the train to the Village of the Carlton Ironworks.

Because of his vast knowledge and experience in ironmaking he quickly became a very influential figure in the affairs of the company and, when one of the original founders, Archibald Briggs, resigned his directorship in 1876, Thomas Kirk was elected to replace him on the Board of Directors. Later in the same year, Henry Currer Briggs stepped down as Managing Director of the company, which he and his brother had formed, and although he retained his position as chairman he passed the responsibility of the general running of the company to Thomas Kirk by appointing him Managing Director.

One of the first tasks initiated by Kirk was the changing of the company's name from the cumbersome 'North of England Industrial Iron and Coal Company' to that of the 'Carlton Iron Company', which he said reflected the locality and product of the principal works much better than the old name.

The malleable ironworks were a disaster because the Dank's puddling furnaces completely failed to fulfill their specified function and Thomas Kirk had to spend many months modifying

Mr Thomas Kirk
Managing Director of the Carlton Iron Company from 1876 until 1908

the whole system before finally being able to produce malleable iron in sufficient quantities for use in the plate mills. With a great deal of ingenuity Kirk, had overcome a difficult problem but, by now, the company had lost out in the marketplace and steel was replacing malleable iron as the preferred material in the manufacture of most engineering components. These facts were coincidental with the iron and steel industry undergoing one of its worst depressions, with the consequence that the company's malleable iron organisation, including the plate mills, became redundant and were never to be used in commercial production.

This was a tremendous blow to the Carlton Iron Company, but Thomas Kirk was successful in guiding it through this and many other depressions which overtook this volatile industry. He not only ensured the company's survival but, with the help of Walter Morrison's generosity, he expanded the Company's interests and enabled them to supply their own basic materials by buying or leasing coal mines and ironstone mines. Kirk made another unique move in 1888, when he arranged for the building of forty coke ovens close to the site of the blast furnaces. This was unusual because previously all coke ovens had been built adjacent to a colliery. The building of these ovens at the Village of the Carlton Ironworks proved highly successful, as they not only produced enough coke for the needs of the blast furnaces, but also an excess which could be sold at a fair profit. An added bonus was the by-products which could be extracted during the production of the coke, which again created a profit and the need for even more labour and houses in the village. These forward thinking decisions, and his constant alertness to the modernisation of plant and equipment, helped Thomas Kirk keep the blast furnaces of the Carlton Iron Company at full stretch producing pig iron of good quality at a commercially viable price.

In 1881 the Carlton Ironworks bought the ironworks at Seaton and formed the Seaton Carew Ironworks, with Thomas Kirk appointed Managing Director. The success of the coke ovens at the Village of the Carlton Ironworks led him to build 50 more, with the necessary extraction plant, adjacent to the Seaton Carew Ironworks at a cost of between £60,000 and £100,000.

The previous items are described to exemplify the amount of responsibility carried by Thomas Kirk during his years as Managing Director. He was totally responsible for the efficient and safe running of blast furnaces, coal mines, ironstone mines, coke ovens, housing projects and many other items integrated with the running of an industrial concern.

Thomas Kirk was teetotal and he believed in devotion to duty, honesty in business, hard work, early rising and self discipline. Although he was reputed to drive his managers and workmen hard, it was no harder than he drove himself. He loathed class distinction and snobbishness and was always willing to help the underdog. He could readily assess a man's ability, as was proven when a young traveller called as a representative of an ironmonger and Kirk was so impressed by his business-like manner, that he persuaded him to set up his own business with Kirk providing the required capital. This young man created the firm of Isaac Robson, which flourished as successful ironmongers in Stockton for many years.

Although a regular churchgoer who also insisted that his family attended, he was not fanatical about the subject, and made no restrictive demands on the social life of his children, three girls and seven boys. Tennis was the major sport of the family and their house had a tennis court included in its facilities.

Thomas Kirk refused all attempts to get him to display himself on platforms but was generous in some quarters, for he provided the bulk of the money to build the church at Preston on Tees.

He was appointed as chairman of the Whitton Board School, after the death of Henry Briggs, and carried out this duty with keen enthusiasm until 1904, when the schools in Stillington were taken over by Durham Education Authority.

Thomas Kirk devoted most of his life to the well being of the Carlton Iron Company and, when he died in 1908 at the age of 72, his obituary in the Darlington and Stockton Times summed up his contribution in a discerning manner.

> 'Thomas Kirk exhibited a far sighted and business grasp upon large affairs which has called forth the admiration of those who have understood the strain and stress of the troublesome years following upon the collapse of the famous iron boom in the early seventies. He succeeded to the management of the Carlton Ironworks at a critical time in its financial history and it is entirely due to his calm and steady judgment, and to the confidence which he inspired, that while other similar concerns were struggling and failing on all sides, the Carlton Iron Company kept going, improving its position year by year, always adopting up to date plant and methods until it has long been regarded as standing high in the iron making world. It may be some surprise to the local public only judging Thomas Kirk by his mild, unassuming manner and ways, to know that he has really operated a very large volume of business year by year. He had a wonderful faculty for planning comprehensive schemes for future use and his active brain was never at rest. A man of strong likes and dislikes, a hater of shams, crooked business and insincerity, he was on the other hand the kindliest of men, nothing was too much trouble if he could do a good turn to those who needed it. He had few hobbies.'

If Thomas Kirk had joined the Carlton Iron Company a little earlier, the decision to manufacture malleable iron instead of steel may well have been overturned and, given the great expertise of Thomas Kirk and the wealth and generosity of Walter Morrison, this company would have been one of the major steel producers in the country. Unfortunately the course was plotted before Kirk's arrival, which meant his constant battle would be for the company's survival, a battle he fought with great skill, endurance and success. Kirk Street was named after Thomas Kirk and remains as a fitting memorial to a man, whose contribution to the Carlton Iron Company and the village are inestimable.

Thomas Kirk's Family

Four of Thomas Kirk's sons were recruited into the service of the Carlton Iron Company, and his eldest daughter, Hannah, married William Thomlinson who also gained great influence within the company.

Henry (Harry) was appointed manager of the coke ovens when they were built at the Village of the Carlton Ironworks in 1888 and transferred to Seaton Carew Ironworks to manage the coke ovens there when they were built in 1898.

Thomas jnr. was works manager at the Village of the Carlton Ironworks from around 1894 until 1911.

Thomas lived in the village with his younger brother Harold and was Chairman of Whitton Parish Council from 1895 until c. 1912 when he left the village. He represented the village as a councillor on Stockton Rural District Council from 1898 until 1922.

Harold took over as manager of the coke ovens at the Village of the Carlton Ironworks when his brother Henry moved to Seaton in 1898. He also became one of the founder Directors of the NE Iron Refinery Co. in 1926. He became a Rural District Councillor after Thomas Jnr. resigned in 1922.

Peter was manager of the iron refinery section at the company's Seaton Carew Ironworks. When this section closed down at Seaton and transferred to the Village of the Carlton Ironworks in 1926, under the name of the North Eastern Iron Refinery, he was appointed Managing Director.

Thomas Kirk's daughter, Hannah, married William Thomlinson who was to succeed him as Managing Director of the Seaton Carew Ironworks and, after his death, the whole of the Carlton Ironworks. (See separate section on William Thomlinson for further details).

Peter's son, Geoffrey Peter Kirk, also made a major contribution to the livelihood of the village between 1945 and 1970. He is therefore worthy of some individual recognition within this record. He held many important positions in companies located at Stillington and these included:

Secretary and Director of the North Eastern Iron Refinery. 1945–1959.
Director of Stillington Estates. 1948-59.
Executive Director of Stillite Products. 1946-48.

In 1953 he was the proposer and head of the development workshop at Stillington, where the practical use of high temperature insulation in the aircraft industry was designed and proven. This project was financed by the Chemical and Insulating Company of Darlington who, when the development proved successful, formed the British Refrasil Company in order to manufacture the product on a commercial scale. This company, later to become Darchem Engineering, was highly successful and secured the full and gainful employment of village men and women from 1954 onwards. All this was due to Geoffrey Kirk's ingenious ideas and successful development work and, in consequence, he was appointed Technical

Director of British Refrasil in 1954 until around 1970. In the above capacities he was able to coordinate the efforts and plans of Stillite Products, the North Eastern Iron Refinery, Stillington Estates, the Chemical and Insulating Company and British Refrasil at a time when this was vital to secure the future industrial expansion of Stillington.

Geoffrey Kirk proved himself to be a person of extreme technical ability, an asset which he coupled with foresight, commonsense, patience and tolerance. Despite always holding higher management positions, he was never bumptious and would treat all levels of staff with the same gentlemanly respect. His ability to lead by example and take responsibility without fuss, meant that his workforce was totally loyal to him. He possessed all the qualities that men respect and admire in a leader. Indeed Mr G P Kirk is a man of rare qualities whose energies had been used extensively for the well being of Stillington and its industries. His contribution and, indeed his family's contribution, to the welfare of Stillington cannot be over-emphasised, and even in retirement, retained his love and concern for the village and its people.

Sir William Thomlinson

William Thomlinson was promoted to general manager of the Seaton Carew Ironworks when the Carlton Iron Company took them over in 1881. He was very quickly awarded a directorship and, in 1906, he was appointed Managing Director. When Thomas Kirk died in 1908, Thomlinson took over as Managing Director of the Carlton Iron Company and took full responsibility for all the company's interests.

Thomlinson married Thomas Kirk's daughter, Hannah, in c. 1892, and had four children, all girls. They lived in a house which dominated the green at Seaton Carew, which is now known as the Seaton Hall Hotel. Thomlinson was well known among the ship owners and timber exporters and acquired the title 'Lord of the Foreshore', with people believing that anything found on the beach belonged to him by right.

Thomlinson's marriage to Kirk's daughter was not the reason for his rapid progress within the company for he was a skilled ironmaster in his own right and possessed many other talents which ranked him amongst the most respected business men of the time.

Sir William Thomlinson

During his lifetime he was chairman of the local Conservative Party, although he refused to stand for parliament. He was Deputy Lieutenant for Durham. responsible for raising and training two battalions of the Durham Light Infantry during the 1914–18 war, and attained the rank of colonel even though his interest in the army was slight. He was a brilliant intellect, a technical expert in the processes involved in ironmaking, could speak many foreign languages and was a connoisseur of the arts, especially Chinese pottery.

In 1936 he was knighted for his services to the public.

He carried on the business of the Carlton Iron Company with the same efficiency as Thomas Kirk before him and, in 1914, he took the opportunity to change the product of the furnaces from normal pig iron to ferro manganese, which was more saleable to the steel industry because of the elements it contained. To ensure the supply of manganese, a vital element in the production of ferro manganese, Thomlinson secured a supply from the Gold Coast Amalgamated Mines, with an initial delivery of 6,000 tons and the 'first right' to 49 per cent of that company's Dagwin mine output. The ferro manganese produced from the Carlton Iron Company's three blast furnaces was sold all over the world including America and Canada, where agents were based to enhance the sale and distribution.

When Dorman Long and Company took over the Carlton Iron Company in 1920, the then Colonel Thomlinson negotiated a good deal for the shareholders and was retained as the company's Managing Director. Under his guidance the development of the village continued, the park was constructed and the company bought East Farm at Stillington which gave them more land adjacent to the works.

In 1922, at the age of seventy, Thomlinson decided to retire but Dorman Long and Company were anxious not to lose his great expertise and retained him as a director to act in an advisory capacity. He remained active in retirement being a director of many companies and in 1926, at the height of a nationwide depression, he formed the North Eastern Iron Refinery at the Village of the Carlton Ironworks. He was the major shareholder and chairman of the company and Peter Kirk, one of Thomas Kirk's sons, was appointed Managing Director. Thomlinson was also the first chairman of the newly formed Chemical and Insulating Company at Darlington, a company which in the 1950s was to have a great influence on the industry of Stillington.

Colonel Sir William Thomlinson VDDL died in his 89th year in 1941.

Reverend William Cassidi

All previous persons mentioned in this chapter have been associated with the works around which the village was built, but reference must be made to a man who was completely separate from the industry but understood it sufficiently to foresee the need for the formation of an Ecclesiastical Parish, when the Village of the Carlton Ironworks comprised only twenty houses and a Lodging House.

This man was the Reverend William Cassidi, who at that time was vicar of Grindon Parish.

Cassidi had been successful in promoting the building of a new church in the Parish of Grindon because of the relocation of the population and the disintegration of the church of St. Thomas. In 1848 he laid the foundation stone for the new church named Holy Trinity (later rebuilt as St. James'), and sited at Thorpe Thewles where most of his congregation were now living. In 1862, after numerous letters to the Ecclesiastical Commissioners, he was given permission to have the vicarage relocated from the now badly situated site in Grindon to an area almost immediately opposite the new church.

The Reverend William Cassidi convinced the Ecclesiastical Commissioners of the need for a separate parish that encompassed the growing needs of the Village of the Carlton Iron Works and its immediate area. Consequently it was decided to take portions from the existing parishes of Grindon and Redmarshall and create a new parish named after the existing hamlet of Stillington (now Old Stillington). Cassidi had to contribute £3,000 to the Commissioners in aid of the endowment of the new parish and the maintenance of the minister thereof.

The Parish of Stillington was formalised on May 31st 1872 in the presence of Queen Victoria.

In 1874 the Reverend Cassidi promoted the building of a Mission House in the Village of the Carlton Iron Works and, with the Reverend John Allen Parker, organised the lease of a plot of land from the North of England Industrial Iron and Coal Company on which to build. No doubt Cassidi contributed most of the necessary finance for this building and it was ultimately named the Cassidi Hall.

The Reverend William Cassidi then organised a fund for the building of a church in the village and started it with his own massive contribution of £1108. The foundation stone for the church was laid in 1879, and the building was finalised in 1880, at a cost of £2800. The church was consecrated and dedicated to St. John by the Bishop of Durham in June 1880.

The Reverend Cassidi surely contributed a great deal to the welfare of the village and, although the Cassidi Hall is now demolished, his name was honoured when the 'top' school was renamed The William Cassidi Church of England Primary School in 1985.

Reverend William Cassidi

11

Summary of changes in Stillington since c. 1950

A brief resumé of the most important events that have taken place in the village since 1950 would seem to be appropriate, in order that some understanding of the differences now existing can be appreciated.

New housing development, removal of slag tip and demolition of works and houses

Changes have occurred at regular intervals. As previously mentioned, North Street – the first street to be erected in 1870 – was demolished in 1950, with its residents rehoused in the new council houses of Whitton Grove. The council estate on the south of the railway continued to grow with the construction of Park Crescent and Manor Drive, then later Manor Walk, Mount Pleasant Close, Mount Pleasant Walk and Mount Pleasant Grove. Bungalows and sheltered accommodation for pensioners were among this council development.

Amidst this development, came the gradual demolition of the works and houses on the northern side of the Clarence Railway, among which was the removal of the Blacking Mill and the massive slag heap, that were removed to make way for extensions to Darchem Engineering.

The Blacking Mill represented a financial tragedy for the Carlton Iron Company. The buildings had originally housed two rolling mills and other necessary plant to enable the rolling of plates for shipbuilding. Built at a cost of about £30,000 in 1875 by Thomas Kirk of Workington, the rolling mills became victim to a deep recession within the industry and were never used to produce plates on a commercial basis. The overall loss to the company would have been at least £50,000 when the cost of buildings and equipment were finally analysed.

Demolition of the Blacking Mill took place in 1958 to make way for engineering offices and extra factory space for the fast expanding British Refrasil. A memorable feature of the demolition was the great difficulty experienced by the contractor when trying to excavate the foundations, for they proved to be much tougher, deeper and of greater area than anticipated.

The slag heap, this massive monument to the ironworks through which the village had been created along with the hardship and perspiration it represented, was removed in 1970 and used as hard-core during the construction of the A1(M) road near Bradbury. Some of the area recovered by the removal of the tip was used by Darchem Engineering for the further expansion of their works, with modern fabrication shops and offices erected on the site. British Refrasil changed its name to Darchem Engineering in 1960.

Although it has to be agreed that the removal of these 'eyesores' was a progressive move in the overall evolution of the village, some of the older residents felt an inner sadness at the loss of these and other landmarks. The tip, with its high craggy overhang opposite the Cooperative Stores, projected a strong protective beauty especially in winter when the harsh cascades of solid slag were bedecked with snow giving them the look of some picturesque mountainous peak. The ruins of the old works and the slag tip had served as a wonderful adventure playground for generations of youngsters, who would spend hours making camps and scrounging 'up the tip' and round the site of the old works which, although fraught with obvious dangers, gave endless pleasure without anyone coming to real harm.

Unit Workshops

Stockton Borough Council who had replaced Stockton Rural District Council as the Local Authority responsible for Stillington, also used some of the area to build several Unit Workshops in an attempt to get businessmen to hire them as a manufacturing or service base, and consequently bring more work into the village.

BUILDING DEVELOPMENT WITHIN THE PARK

Women's Institute Hall

In 1953 the Women's Institute, in conjunction with Stillington Estates, built a village hall in the park opposite Railway Cottages, and used many of the bricks recycled from North Street in its construction.

The Women's Institute Hall was to be used as the new village hall but was also fitted with a large modern kitchen that enabled it to double as a canteen for the workers employed on the industrial site. The hall was used to good effect as a work's canteen for several years and then British Refrasil organised their own canteen within the works, which left the hall's canteen with only a few customers and ultimate closure.

The main part of the hall was spacious and had a good stage but, unfortunately, was totally lacking in atmosphere due to the austerity of the inner walls and the structural steelwork being uncovered, revealing the full height of the roofing. In consequence, the hall was little used for social functions, such as dances, whist drives and organised parties, although the Stillington Parish Players did use it to perform a couple of Gilbert and Sullivan operas with great success.

The building met its final demise when the Lowson Street school ceased to function as a school in 1960 and was converted into the village hall, at a cost of

Lowson Street School now the Village Hall

A good view of the building erected in 1877 as the Lowson Street School and now serving as the village hall. The main building has changed little and the teacher's room at the right of the building is still clearly recognisable. The area in front of the building has been landscaped after the demolition of Lowson Street and Morrison Street.

The opening of the Village Hall 1961

The Lowson Street School had been converted to the Village Hall and this was the official opening by G H Metcalfe, the County Director of Education. Standing alongside Mr Metcalfe is Mr G T (Tommy) Tingle, Chairman of the Stillington Village Hall Association.

£1000, thus making the Women's Institute Hall redundant as far as village functions were concerned, and eventually it was used only as a storage area for the works before being demolished to make way for a new Health Centre in 1990.

Doctor's residence and surgery and other dwellings

The Women's Institute Hall was the first building to be erected in the park, but very quickly afterwards, this retreat of peace and tranquility that many villagers had enjoyed over the years, was divided into plots and sold by Stillington Estates for residential building.

Dr MacMahon, who had practiced from 1 South Street, died in 1954 and Dr Rowbotham came to the village as his replacement and immediately built a house and surgery combined in the park adjacent to Messines Lane (the new road) gate.

Around 1956 Mr Tommy Tingle built an integrated home and shop just inside the park perimeter opposite Bell Square, and a little later, four more bungalows and a police house were built on sites adjacent to Redmarshall Street and Kirk Street.

The wooded area of the park (the Plantation) was bought by Mr Norman Argyle, a local entrepreneur who had developed a thriving haulage business in the village. He cleared the majority of trees from the site and landscaped it before building two bungalows, one for himself near the top of the Chapel Bank, and one for his married son, Victor, almost opposite Rosedale in Kirk Street.

Demolition of houses on the north side of the Clarence Railway

The balance of the village population and residential accommodation moved almost totally to the south of the Clarence Railway when over 100 houses were demolished in 1978. These were the terraced rows of Lowson Street and Morrison Street, the shops and Post Office in Morrison Terrace and the school house which, by this time, had been converted into two flats. Within a matter of months the area where a lively, close knit community had lived, was demolished and landscaped, whilst the residents were rehoused in the new council houses. The church, the vicarage, the village hall and the school were now isolated on the northern side of the railway with the only residences remaining being the vicarage, the flat above a garage that had been built opposite Morrison Street, and a bungalow sited beyond the school.

There is no doubt that the residents of the demolished houses were rehoused into better conditions, but the whole balance of the village was destroyed, and some of the houses which were sacrificed in the name of progress, especially the ones built around 1900 such as little Lowson Street, were in better structural condition than houses still remaining in West Street and South Street, where recently a grant of 65% of the cost of improving these houses has been awarded to the owners.

The Stillington Health Centre

Photograph above shows the Health Centre during construction in 1991. The centre was built for Doctors Irvin and Mullins who thought at first that the Women's Institute Hall, built in 1953, could be converted into a Health Centre. On investigation it was found that the hall was not only unsuitable for this purpose but unforseen structural defects would be too costly to rectify. The Woman's Institute Hall was demolished and the new Health Centre was constructed on a site at the north west corner of the park. The top end of Redmarshall Street can be seen behind the framework of the building.

The photograph below shows the completed Health Centre from the same position as the above photo. The winding snake, the emblem of the British Medical Association, appropriately mounted on top of the roof, can just be seen through the centre tree.

If selective demolition and reconstruction had been employed, similar to that carried out at the Clarences (Port and High Clarence), the balance of the village, and maybe some of the community spirit, could have been retained whilst still upgrading the living conditions of the residents. The friendly rivalry of 'yon side' and 'this side' which had been a feature of village life since its inception, had been destroyed 'at a stroke'. Progress is however a continual process and the private houses now being built (1993), on the site of the Morrison Street allotments, may restore some equilibrium to the village.

Health Centre

In 1987, the general practitioners of the day Doctors Irvin and Mullens, who were carrying out their practice from the old surgery in South Street, were intent on creating a health centre for the village. They had originally thought that the redundant Women's Institute Hall could be converted for this purpose, but a closer examination revealed flaws, not only in the idea, but also in the structure of the building, and so the doctors decided to demolish the hall and erect a completely new health centre on the site. This project has been highly successful and all health matters are now organised from these pleasant surroundings in an efficient and friendly manner. The health centre has certainly made a major contribution to the village environment and the welfare of its people. The winding snake, the emblem of the British Medical Association, mounted on the top of the building, gives it instant recognition as a health centre.

Workingmen's Club and the Cassidi Hall

The workingmen's club founded in 1946 proved to be highly successful and, in order to provide greater comfort and more modern amenities to its members, the committee decided to move from the Cassidi Hall in 1968 to purpose-built premises adjacent to the Donkey Bank.

This move made the Cassidi Hall redundant and after being used as a youth club for several years, the decision was taken to demolish it and transform the area upon which it was founded in 1874, into a recreational garden.

The Chapel

Lack of support and the impending cost of essential repairs, forced the trustees to close the chapel in 1972 and then have it demolished. This was a particular tragedy for the Wells' family, four of whom were trustees: John William (father), and his sons Arnold, Cliff and Wilf. For many years they had taken a major role in keeping the chapel functioning, along with their mother and sister Maisie. All had good voices and although Arnold was the appointed organist, all the menfolk could play adequately. Nurse Robinson, the District Nurse, was also a loyal chapel supporter and special mention should be made of Leslie Harper, who ran the Sunday School and Sunshine Corner, and was whole hearted in his efforts to help the children.

The area at the end of South Street where the chapel once stood as a haven of religious and recreational activity is now a rose garden.

The original Cooperative Stores

A happier fate befell the original Cooperative Stores in West Street, that had been built in 1874 and abandoned in 1935 when the Coop moved into the clubhouse in Morrison Terrace. It had stood empty for many years before being revived as a shop by Mrs Mary Tingle around 1950, and then taken over by Mr Keith Wilkinson when the Tingles built their new shop/house in the park.

In 1978 the old shop was given a further lease of life when it was chosen to become the village post office when Joe Parry's shop, which had previously housed the post office, was demolished along with all the other properties in Morrison Terrace. Keith became the postmaster and eventually bought the adjacent 'big' house and linked the two premises with a through door. He sold out in 1990, but after a fairly short period, the new owner could not manage and Keith had to help out.

The post office eventually transferred to the shop in the park, which had changed hands a couple of times since Tommy Tingle's ownership. The first change was to Cyril Butler, who had bought the shop when his newsagent's shop in Morrison Terrace had been demolished and, after about 25 years, Cyril sold out and retired to Whitton.

Station and Rail Services

Rail passenger services to the village from Stockton and Ferryhill ceased in 1952 and, although the station was active in terms of goods and mineral services for a few more years, the shut down of the Durham coal mines and the transference of freight to the roads, gradually forced the closure of Stillington station and, after a fire had created irreparable damage, the station was demolished c. 1965. The goods yard and sidings were also abandoned, which meant yet another area of previous bustling activity where steam engines had constantly shunted freight and mineral trucks, where passengers had congregated on the station platform, where porters busied themselves around the station and goods yard and where the local gang of platelayers could be regularly seen carrying out track repairs, now had this sound of intense activity replaced by a crestfallen silence and desolation.

The four lines of rail track were once again reduced to two, and it would seem the only thing that prevents total closure of this once important line, is the fact that it can be used as an alternative route when the main line from Newcastle to London is being repaired. The one positive action to come from this reorganisation was the construction of a new road bridge to replace the old Carlton Bridge, a move which local councillors had been urging the railway companies to carry out since 1923, because of the inherent dangers of the approaches and narrowness of the old Carlton Bridge.

Railway Cottages and Office Row

Railway Cottages were demolished and replaced with four pensioner's bungalows, whilst Office Row (which had been almost surrounded by the scrap metal of Edward James' scrap yard) was also demolished.

The Glykoline and the Stillite

Glykoline eventually closed in 1960, and the site was taken over by Clarkes, who had earlier taken control of Edward James' scrap company, and the houses of Glykoline Terrace were used by them as office and canteen facilities. This company has expanded and now trades as a successful steel stockist.

The closure of the Stillite in 1965 is described in greater detail in earlier text.

The Village Schools

In 1958, the Infant School in Lowson Street and the Mixed School at the top of the village were amalgamated, and came under the jurisdiction of one headmaster, who at the time had six teachers assisting him. The school was named Stillington County Mixed and Infant School, although initially the infants and mixed classes remained in their own buildings.

In December 1959 the schools were reorganised again, when all children of post-primary age (11 year olds), proceeded to Sedgefield Modern Comprehensive School or Ian Ramsey Comprehensive at Stockton. The Infant's School in Lowson Street closed and all its pupils transferred to the top school that was renamed Stillington County Junior Mixed and Infant School.

Mr Harry Davies took over as headmaster in 1962 and remained until 1975 when Mrs Howard replaced him. Mr Davies also became the village representative on Stockton County Council, a position he held for many years.

In 1985, the school closed at the commencement of the summer holidays and reopened after the holidays with a new name, The William Cassidi Church of England Primary School, and a new governing body linked to the Church of England. The school buildings have been modified and extended several times during the last forty years and now include a nursery.

Obviously many other events have taken place in the forty odd years since 1950, but the above examples serve to illustrate some of the changes that have overtaken the village during that period.

Summary of losses since 1950:

Buildings:
Cassidi Hall, Chapel, Station, Station House, School House, Signal Cabin.
  Engineer's Offices, Station warehouse, Cricket pavilion, the Lowson Street
  School closed and the building now serving as a community centre.
Vicarage sold to private individuals.

Women's Institute Hall built in 1953 at northern corner of park, demolished c. 1987 to make way for Health Centre.

Streets:
North Street, Lowson Street, Morrison Street, Morrison Terrace, Office Row, Railway Cottages, Glykoline Terrace.

Industries:
Blacking Mill, Glykoline, Stillite Products, James' scrap yard, various sand and gravel quarries local to the village.

Other major items:
The slag heap, the original Carlton Bridge and the Park.

Additions include:

Houses and amenities
Extensive council estate including shops, pensioners' bungalows and sheltered accommodation.
Four council bungalows for pensioners on site of Railway Cottages.
Private bungalows and shop in area that was the park.
Private housing estate, St. John Park, built on the north side of Clarence Railway by Shepherd Homes, prices ranged from £57,600 for a three-bedroomed detached to £93,500 for a four-bedroomed detached.
New Health Centre on site of Women's Institute Hall.
New road bridge to replace the old Carlton Bridge.
New workingmen's club.
Natural Gas supply piped into the village around 1993.
Darchem Engineering formed in 1954 as British Refrasil expanded over the industrial site to become the major employer in the village.
Clarkes now operate as a successful steel stockist.
Factory units built to encourage small businesses to the village.
Garage and living accommodation in Morrison Street.
Telephone exchange built in the 'Spring Field' with access from Swann's Lane.
The site of the Carlton Iron Company works has been landscaped where no manufacturing units exist and walks have been created around the whole area. A large pond has formed within the area that is a sanctuary for birds and pond life.

View from Top of Cricket Field c. 1957

Photo opposite: New industry is being developed on part of the site that had previously belonged to the Carlton Iron Company. British Refrasil, later to become Darchem Engineering, have established their South Factory on the little tip adjacent to the railway sidings and are now in the process of building a new fabrication shop. Stillington Estates workshop is the Coseley building directly in front of this new development. The slag heap is shown to good effect with the Cracker Hole on the left where slag was removed by Stillite Products for the manufacture of slag wool. The station is still intact and, although there is no longer a passenger service the freight and mineral business is still going strong as can be seen from the traffic in the sidings. The end house of 'new' West Street can be seen centre right and the base of the old cricket pavilion is shown at the centre bottom of the photograph. The church is in the distance above the tip.

View from top of Little Tip c. 1952

Above: Although not a very clear photograph, this view has been included because it shows several interesting features. In the foreground is the little tip which has had a row of fencing material erected to mark the boundary of British Refrasil just prior to the start of erection of its first factory. Morrison Terrace can be seen running from centre left of the photograph and this housed four shops that were, the Cooperative stores (previously the Workingmen's Club), Parry's general dealers, Butler's newsagents and Post Office and Calverts grocery store. Across the road from Calvert's is the fish shop which at that time was run by Florrie Argyle. A closer look will reveal the top of one of Scurr's buses at its pick up point in Morrison Terrace and at the top right of the picture a goods train on its way from the Durham coalfields to Middlesbrough. The road to Whitton spanned the railway at Whitton Bridge and this can be seen just beyond the locomotive.

View from top of the Slag Heap c. 1956

This view was formed by compounding two photographs taken from the top of the slag heap. In the foreground the early stages of the British Refrasil factory are shown built upon what had been the Little Tip. Behind the factory buildings and running parallel is the Clarence Railway and the sidings which are still busy. Alongside the railway at centre right are Railway Cottages and beyond these Redmarshall Street, West Street and the Royal Hotel. The park, centre left of the picture, is already being used as building land with the doctor's house, built for Dr Rowbotham in 1954, and the Women's Institute Hall, built in 1953, clearly visible. Kirk Street is only just visible above the park trees on the left of the picture.

Remains of Brick Buttress wall at rear of Railway Cottages

This photograph, taken in 1990, shows the end of the buttress wall which was built during the widening of the Clarence Railway in 1884. The end of the wall formed part of a stile which allowed access to the back street of Railway Cottages and was level with the back of the houses giving an example of how close the railway came to them. The cottages have been demolished and replaced, at a further distance from the line, by four pensioner's bungalows that have been numbered as an extension to Redmarshall Street.

SUMMARY OF CHANGES IN STILLNGTON SINCE C.1950

Carlton Bridge 1964

Photographs show work in progress during construction of a new bridge adjacent to the old 'arch'. 1964. The above photograph shows a view of the arch from Morrison Terrace looking south and the photograph below shows a view looking north from the Chapel Bank.

Views from Morrison Terrace showing the removal of the Slag Heap in 1969

Bottom view shows the Darchem workshops at the top of the bank with the special buses waiting to take their employees home.

Wesleyan Chapel immediately prior to its demolition in 1972

The Cassidi Hall

Photograph shows the Cassidi Hall around 1960 when it was used as a Workingmens Club. The outside appearance of the hall has changed little from the original, although the windows have been modernised.

Morrison Terrace

Photograph shows the terrace just prior to its demolition in 1978. The building on the left was used as a Workingmen's Club in 1876 and latterly used as a Cooperative Stores. The other three premises are still being used as shops with the Post Office being housed in Parry's. The postman, Edward Hopps, can be seen in the centre of the picture.

Shunting Locomotive c. 1990

A sad end to the last shunting loco to be used on the site, left as scrap in one of the sidings near the Iron Refinery. Built by Ruston Hornsby in 1949, this four wheel diesel was supplied new to the North Eastern Iron Refinery.

View over the Reservoirs c. 1990
Although a poor photograph, it is included to show the site of the Carlton Company's coke ovens which was where the buildings on the left are now situated. The reservoirs are still remaining after service with the Carlton Iron Company, Stillite Products and latterly Expert Heat Treatment.

Pensioner's Bungalows on site of Railway Cottages 1975.
Another view of the four pensioner's bungalows showing their relationship to the Royal Hotel. The railway abutment can just be seen on the extreme right of the picture.

The opening of the new Pensioner's Bungalows 1975
Photograph shows the first tenants to occupy the bungalows that were built on the site of the old Railway Cottages. Tenants are; Mr Les Simpson and his wife Vera. Mrs Lizzie Fox and daughter Betty. Mrs (Peter) Carr. Mrs Amy Butler was also a first tenant but she is not shown in the photograph.

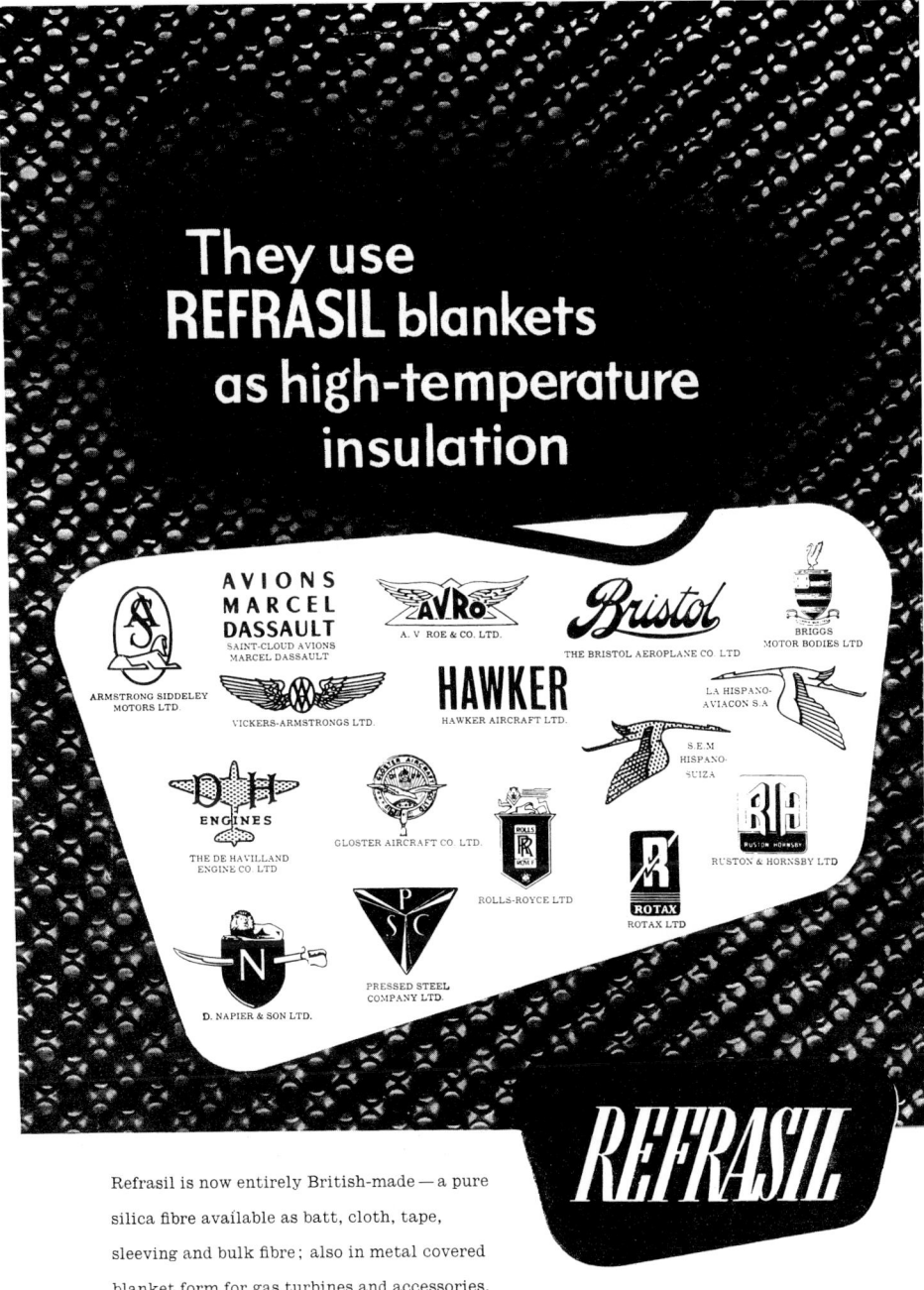

This is the first advertisement which appeared in the magazine, *Aeroplane* on September 2 1955 on behalf of British Refrasil, now Darchem Engineering, depicting the use of their product by most of the major aircraft companies of the time

Ariel view of Darchem Engineering c. 1985
The factory and offices of Darchem Engineering have expanded on to the site of the old slag heap. Relics of the old ironworks still visible are, the engine shed, the reservoirs, the White House, the Engineer's office block and the lodging house. The new Carlton Bridge under the railway is shown bottom left. The railway comprises only two lines and the sidings have been demolished. Clark's works are prominent towards the top of the photograph. The old school yard can just be seen at the bottom of the picture.
Photograph courtesy of Darchem Engineering.

Development of Country Park on the site of the Old Ironworks and Slag Heap 1995
The engine shed built in 1892 is still standing and can be seen just left of centre

Ariel view of top of Village c. 1988

View shows the church, vicarage, school, the school kitchen, hilltop bungalow and the telephone exchange. Further to the right can be seen the school football pitch in what was the Spring Field. Lowson Street and Morrison Street, which were in line with the church, have been demolished leaving the church and school isolated from the main residences of the village, however new houses are now being built on the land shown to the left of the church which had been allotments.

APPENDIX 1
Brief history of the Clarence Railway

The Clarence Railway Company was founded in 1828 by Mr Christopher Tennent in order to provide a shorter, more direct rail route, from the Durham coalfields to the River Tees than that provided by the existing line, built by Darlington and Stockton Railway Company in 1825.

Consequently a line was built and opened in 1833 to run from the existing Darlington and Stockton line at Simpasture junction (near Heighington) to Samphire Batts (now Port Clarence), with a branch line from Harrogate House (between Blakeston lane and Norton) down to the river Tees at North Shore.

The line was named the Clarence Railway because Christopher Tennent had been in the Navy under the command of the Duke of Clarence, the then Lord Admiral of the Fleet, who was to become King William 1V (1830–1837).

Though the Clarence line was 7½ miles shorter than the Darlington and Stockton route, the company never made the expected profit because of heavy restrictions imposed by the Darlington and Stockton Railway Company where the lines joined at the junction near Heighington. This coupled with competition from Hartlepool Docks forced The Clarence Railway Company into a perpetual lease arrangement with Stockton & Hartlepool Railway Company in 1844, and eventual amalgamation.

Steam power could not used on the Clarence Line before 1835 for two reasons:
(a) The Darlington and Stockton Railway Company would not allow the Clarence Railway Company to haul with their own engines from the foot of the Brusselton and Black Boy inclines at Shildon to Simpasture. In September 1837 the Clarence Company made an attempt to take one of their own engines, Sir Robert Peel, from Simpasture to Shildon but they were, 'Denied entrance by Quaker people,' and thereafter Darlington and Stockton Railway Company posted guards to prevent a recurrence.
(b) The Surtees family would not agree to the use of steam through the townships of Mainsforth and Little Chilton that were under their control. This ban was lifted in 1835 and so the Clarence engines began working in 1836.

The Clarence was originally a mineral line using horse drawn trucks with locomotives introduced in 1836 and completely replacing the horses by 1841. Passenger traffic in selected areas began in 1836 – Stockton to Clarence Tavern-and-back twice a day and, in 1838, Coxhoe to Stockton – a journey of 16¼ miles at a cost of 2/6d for inside accommodation and 2s. for outside.

Freight charges were ½ penny/mile/ton for coal, and ⅜ of a penny/mile/ton for other freight. The engine drivers on freight trains were paid 0.1875d/mile/ton for all coal conveyed but from this they had to provide the fireman, coal, oil and lamps, with the company responsible for all repairs to the engine.

In 1837 the booking office at Shildon was the Masons Arms, whilst the station at Sedgefield was the Stag and Dragon public house, with the landlord as station master.

The Clarence was originally a single track with passing places but was soon changed to a two line track. Then, in 1884, two more mineral lines were introduced making it a four line system.

In 1915 the Clarence was electrified between Shildon and Newport, using 1500 DC overhead system, and 10 electric locomotives were especially constructed at Darlington North Road Works for use on the now busy heavy mineral line. However, by 1935, declining traffic and the cost of renewing the overhead equipment led to the abandonment of the electrification.

The 1960s brought a decline in the use of the mineral line from Simpasture to Stillington North, and this part of the line was closed in 1963 and freight from Shildon to Newport reverted back to using the old Darlington and Stockton route of 1825. The two 'new' mineral lines were for a time used to store wagons awaiting repair or those surplus to requirement, until 1965 when the lines were removed.

All passenger services using the Clarence were withdrawn in 1952, thus depriving villages like Stillington of alternative means of reaching the towns of Stockton and Ferryhill.

Sequence of companies formed and amalgamated and some of the rail routes

1821   Darlington and Stockton Company opened Darlington and Stockton line in 1825.

The inaugural Shildon to Newport electrically motivated mineral train leaving Shildon on July 1st 1915.
Courtesy of the K C Appleby collection

1828 The Clarence Railway Company opened Heighington to Port Clarence with branch to Tees (North Shore), in 1833.

1838 Stockton & Hartlepool Railway Company opened Stockton to Hartlepool line in 1839. They also built own dock under the name of Hartlepool West Harbour Dock Company.

1852 The Clarence, the Stockton & Hartlepool, and Hartlepool West Harbour Dock Companies amalgamated to form the West Hartlepool Harbour & Railway Company.

1854 The North Eastern Railway Company was formed by the union of York, Newcastle & Berwick, York & North Midland, and the Leeds Northern

1863 Darlington and Stockton Company amalgamated with North Eastern Railway Company.

1865 West Hartlepool Harbour & Railway Company taken over by North Eastern Railway Co.

1923 North Eastern Railway Company, as a result of further grouping became part of London and North Eastern Railway Company that was one of the four major rail companies prior to nationalisation.
These companies were:
LNER London & North Eastern Railway
LMS   London Midland and Scottish
GWR Great Western Railway
SR   Southern Railway
all of which came under the name of British Rail after nationalisation on January 1st 1948.

Elstob Crossing looking west c. 1950
The road from Great Stainton to Sedgefield crossed the Clarence Railway at this point and the crossing was usually manned by men from Stillington. The two men in the picture are Mr Sid Sayers of Railway Cottages, (an ex platelayer) and Mr Spiking, a blacksmith who had his forge nearby.
Photograph courtesy of the J. W. Armstrong Trust.

Elstob Crossing looking north from the road c.1950
Courtesy Dr C. W. Gibby and Durham Record Office.

The closure of Elstob Crossing c 1965
The new embankment shown is where the road has been modified to by pass the junction.
Photograph courtesy Dr C. W. Gibby and Durham Record Office.

Derelict Redmarshall Station awaiting demolition c.1965
Photograph courtesy Dr C W Gibby and Durham Record Office.

Stillington Station immediately prior to demolition c.1965
Photograph courtesy Dr C W Gibby and Durham Record Office.

Sedgefield Station
Sedgefield Station, unused since the withdrawal of the Stockton to Ferryhill passenger service in 1952, awaits demolition. *Photograph courtesy Dr C W Gibby and Durham Record Office.*

Stillington North Signal Box c.1963
Situated at the junction of the Shildon branch and the Ferryhill line. Usually manned by Stillington men. *Photograph courtesy Dr C W Gibby and Durham Record Office.*

Bishopton Lane Crossing c. 1950
Usually manned by Stillington men.
Photograph courtesy Dr C W Gibby and Durham Record Office.

Stillington Signal Box c. July 1977
View looking west to the site of Stillington station. The station has been demolished and the railway reduced from four to two tracks. The signal box was burnt down in 1993. The railings on the right of the picture are where the steps from the subway emerged for access to the station and, although the subway remains, this access has been closed off. *Photograph courtesy of the K C Appleby collection*

Stillington Signal Box – June 1984
Stillington Station signal box viewed looking east from where the former island platform was sited. The station has been completely demolished, the subway access has been blocked off and the track has been realigned to revert back to a two-line system. This signal box was opened in 1884 as a 32 lever box and extended to accommodate the electrification of the line in 1914. It burned down in January 1995 and was demolished in August 1995. *Photograph courtesy of the K C Appleby collection*

APPENDIX 2

Doctors who practiced in the Village of the Carlton Ironworks/Stillington

1 Dr Thomas Walker Bonnar

The first doctor in the village who practiced from a lean to adjoining his house at 1 Mount Pleasant.

The 1881 census listed him as: unmarried, age 36, born in Scotland.

Came to village in about 1873. Was presented with a certificate of appreciation for his services from the Carlton Iron Works Sick Club for his work since that date but in particular for his devotion to duty during the typhoid epidemic of 1878.

When Parish Councils were inaugurated in January 1895, he was given the task of calling and chairing the first meeting where Whitton Parish Council was formed. When all the councillors had been elected and officials appointed he left the meeting.

After his retirement in 1909, he went to live in Whitton. The certificate mentioned was found in a bag of rubbish thrown into a roadside ditch between Whitton and Stillington.

2 Dr Dunn

Dr Dunn also practiced from 1 Mount Pleasant. First mention found was at a Parish Council meeting in October 1909, with regard to the condition of the path leading from Mount Pleasant to Whitton.

3 Dr John P Cleary

Dr John P Cleary also practiced from 1 Mount Pleasant. He was elected onto the Parish Council in April 1922. He left the district in October 1924.

4 Dr McLister

Dr McLister lived in and practiced from the house at the west end of South Street, which had been extensively modified in 1898 to create a suitable residence for the company secretary of the Carlton Iron Company.

Nominated and elected to the Parish Council in October 1924. Did not stand for re-election in 1925 or 1928 but was elected again in 1929, 1931, 1934 and 1937. He resigned as a Parish Councillor in September 1938. Retired from his practice c.1940.

Copy of the certificate presented to Dr Bonner by the Carlton Iron Works Sick Club for his untiring work during the typhoid epidemic that struck the village in 1878.

5 Dr McMahon

Dr McMahon also practiced and lived in the end house in South Street until c. 1954. In September 1941, he requested that a supply of First Aid items be made available to him from Stockton Rural District Council. This was during World War II and the request was instigated by lack of such equipment when an aircraft crashed in fields local to Whitton and the doctor had to attend three badly burnt airman without an adequate supply of bandages etc.

6 Dr Rowbotham

Dr Rowbotham served the village from 1954 until 1982 and had a house/surgery built in the park on his arrival. His patients thought very highly of Dr Rowbotham for he was a highly professional doctor who was totally dedicated to his work. He was assisted in the last couple of years by Dr Irvin, who took over the practice when Doctor Rowbotham retired and reopened the South Street surgery.

Dr Irvin was joined by Dr Mullins in 1983 and together, in 1991, they organised the building of the Health Centre on the site of the Women's Institute Hall. Doctor Irvin went back to Ireland in 1992 and Dr Reynolds came to assist Dr Mullins, who himself went back to Ireland in 1994.

Dr Reynolds continued the practice and a lady doctor, Dr Dewhirst, came to assist him.

APPENDIX 3

A few examples of
the Carlton Iron Company's
*(renamed from the
North of England Industrial Iron and Coal Company)*
Balance Sheets,
Director's Annual Reports
and
an important letter dated December 1877

NORTH OF ENGLAND INDUSTRIAL IRON AND COAL CO., (LIMITED)   BALANCE SHEET

Showing the receipts and expenditure for eleven months, viz. - from the formation of the company to April 30th 1871

DR.				CR.
	£. s. d	£. s. d		£. s. d.	£. s. d.

CAPITAL, VIZ.
4037 fully paid up shares at £10 each	40,370 0 0		**BY PROPERTY – SOUTH BELMONT MINES, VIZ.**		
5940 ordinary shares at £6 each	35,640 0 0		Original purchase of lease and plant etc	30,000 0 0	
	76,010 0 0		Less – amount paid in advance of workings for Royalty on Ironstone. Transferred to separate account	16,041 8 11	13,958 11 1
Less calls unpaid	1,096 0 0				
	74,914 0 0		**EXPENDITURE., viz**		
Add… Calls paid in advance	188 0 0		Material, new plant and stores	8,095 9 3	
		75,102 0 0	Wages paid	9,694 3 1	
			Railway dues on ironstone	4,023 0 8	
			Proportion of management and office expenses	757 16 10	
			Royalty on Ironstone worked	3,380 2 6	
SALES AND RECEIPTS, viz.			Sundries	6 2 9	
Sales of ironstone South Belmont	18,485 0 0		Gunpowder purchased	825 17 6	
Sundry sales and receipts. do.	298 17 11		Cottage rents, repairs and rates	291 7 7	
Sales of gunpowder. do.	716 6 8				27,074 0 2
Cottage rents received. do	349 19 6				
		19,850 11 0	**PROPERTY – CARLTON IRON WORKS, viz**		
Sundry sales and receipts. Carlton		294 15 1	Original purchase of freehold and plant		13,300 0 0
Interest and discounts		349 19 0	**EXPENDITURE, viz.**		
			Materials, new plant and stores	5,358 19 4	
SUNDRY CREDITORS, viz.			Wages paid	6,027 15 3	
Bills payable	1,686 10 5		Proportion of management and office expenses	757 16 9	
Sundry persons for materials etc	3,066 19 4		Sundries	153 19 4	
		4,753 9 9			22,298 10 8
			Value of office furniture, books, etc.		88 13 8
Balance of purchase money at Carlton Iron Works		11,300 0 0	Preliminary expenses on formation of company		104 4 6
			Interest on prepaid calls and paid up shares		438 9 1
			Bank and commission		56 16 6
			Sundry debtors for Ironstone etc.		4,326 8 9
			Royalty paid in advance. Balance at April 1st		14,021 10 5
			Cash in bank		16,020 14 5
		£111,687 19 4			**£111,687 19 4**

I have examined the books and accounts of the company for the above period and certify that they are correctly made up and that the above is a true and proper statement.

C HOPKINSON, Auditor, 27th May 1871

NORTH OF ENGLAND INDUSTRIAL IRON AND COAL CO., LIMITED

BALANCE SHEET

DR.
APRIL 30th 1872
CR.

LIABILITIES

CAPITAL OF COMPANY £250,000, in 25,000 shares of £10 each

	£. s. d.	£. s. d.
4,260 shares, 1st. issue, £10 paid	426,000 0 0	
5,740 shares, 1st. issue, £8 paid	45,920 0 0	
4,500 shares, 2nd. issue, £2 paid	9,000 0 0	
By advance calls	50 0 0	
		97,000 0 0
Amount owing on security of Carlton property		8,000 0 0
Amount owing on bills payable		4,631 19 9
Amount owing to sundry creditors on open acccounts		8,449 14 7
Amount owing for wages and salaries		1,955 14 8
Amount owing for royalty on ironstone		1,310 19 2
Amount owing for rent of cottages on lease		81 6 0
Gross profit on the year's business transactions	9,190 5 1	
Less;		
Interim dividend paid in January last 1,479 13 9		
Interest on prepaid calls to 31st Oct. last 258 14 0		
	1,738 7 9	
Available for dividend		7,451 17 4
		£129,451 11 6

ASSETS

	£. s. d.
By land, cottages, workshops, ironstone mines, blast furnaces and other works, complete or in progress; as per valuation on April 30th 1872	80,000 3 0
By stocks of materials, pig iron etc on hand at April 30th 1872	5,635 10 6
Royalty on ironstone paid in advance	12,276 4 6
Preliminary Expenses Account	243 17 4
Amount owing by sundry bills	13,797 15 3
Cash and bills on hand and in bank	16,702 0 11
	£129,451 11 6

Examined the above balance sheet and find it correct.

C HOPKINSON, Auditor, 31st May 1872, 13, Barstow Square, Wakefield

NORTH OF ENGLAND INDUSTRIAL IRON AND COAL CO., LIMITED

BALANCE SHEET — APRIL 30th 1873

DR.

LIABILITIES

NOMINAL CAPITAL OF COMPANY $250,000, in 25,000 shares of $10 each

	£. s. d.	£. s. d.	£. s. d.
10,000 shares, 1st issue, $10 each	100,000 0 0		
7,000 shares, 2nd issue, $5 paid	35,000 0 0		
Cash paid by advance calls	4,108 0 0		
		139,108 0 0	
Less calls in arrears		298 0 0	
			138,810 0 0
Amount owing on security of Carlton property			8,000 0 0
Amount owing on bills payable			9,064 5 7
Amount owing to sundry creditors on open acccounts			13,310 13 3
Amount owing for wages and salaries			2,063 2 4
Amount owing for royalty on ironstone			1,529 1 9
Amount owing for rent of cottages on lease			122 10 6
Balance brought from last account		1,496 2 10	
Gross profit on the year's business transactions		14,806 19 5	
		16,303 2 3	
Less;			
Interim dividend paid in January last	4,450 0 0		
Income tax paid in January las	160 8 6		
Interest on prepaid calls to 31st Oct last	232 6 7		
		4,842 15 1	
Available for dividend..........			11,460 7 2
			£184,360 0 7

CR.

ASSETS

	£. s. d.
By land, cottages, workshops, ironstone mines, blast furnaces and other works, complete or in progress; as per valuation on April 30th 1873	131,032 8 10
By stocks of materials, pig iron etc on hand at April 30th 1873	8,861 7 5
Royalty on ironstone paid in advance	10,162 8 2
Cash and bills on hand and in bank	16,637 13 5
Amount owing by sundry debtors	17,666 2 9
	£184,360 0 7

Examined the above balance sheet and find it correct

C HOPKINSON, Auditor, 7th June 1873, 13, Barstow Square, Wakefield

NORTH OF ENGLAND INDUSTRIAL IRON AND COAL CO., LIMITED

BALANCE SHEET

APRIL 30th 1874

DR. | CR.

LIABILITIES

NOMINAL CAPITAL OF COMPANY £250,000, in 25,000 shares of £10 each

	£. s. d.	£. s. d.
10,000 shares, 1st issue, £10 each	100,000 0 0	
8,033 shares, 2nd issue, £9 paid	72,207 0 0	
3147 shares 3rd issue, £2 paid	6294 0 0	
Amount paid to a/c of Workmen's share club	481 11 6	
Cash paid by advance calls.	2,402 17 0	
	181,475 8 6	
Less calls in arrears.	1,500 0 0	179,975 8 6
Amount owing on security of Carlton property		8,000 0 0
Amount owing on bills payable		9,150 0 0
Amount owing to sundry creditors on open accocunts		35,259 6 11
Amount owing for wages and salaries		2,063 2 4
Amount owing for royalty on ironstone		1,693 5 7
Amount owing for rent of cottages on lease		135 12 0
		£252,432 8 1

ASSETS

	£. s. d.	£. s. d.
By Freehold land, houses, workshops, ironstone mines, colliery, coke ovens, blast furnaces, puddling forge, and other works complete or in progress; as per valuation on April 30th 1874		187,959 11 1
By stocks of materials, pig iron etc on hand at April 30th 1874		18,080 13 9
By Royalty on ironstone, coal etc paid in advance		8,682 15 4
Cash and bills on hand and in bank		3,342 19 0
Amount owing by sundry debtors		17,661 3 3
Nett loss on years business	15,922 16 3	
Add; Interest paid on Carlton mortage loan	400 0 0	
Income tax paid	185 1 9	
Interim dividend paid January last	3,500 12 6	
Interest on prepaid calls	123 11 7	
	20,132 2 1	
Less; Balance from last a/c including invested capital and Labour Capital Reserve Funds £3,214 16 7		
Bonuses unclaimed 2 19 10		
Premiums on shares 209 0 0		
	3,426 16 5	
Balance of Profit and Loss a/c carried to next account		16,705 5 8
		£252,432 8 1

Examined the above balance sheet and find it correct

C HOPKINSON, Auditor, 7th June 1874, 13, Barstow Square, Wakefield

BALANCE SHEET
NORTH OF ENGLAND INDUSTRIAL IRON AND COAL CO., LIMITED
APRIL 30th 1875

DR. | **CR.**

LIABILITIES

	£ s d	£ s d
NOMINAL CAPITAL OF COMPANY £300,000, in 25,000 A or ordinary shares of £10 each, and 5,000 B or preference shares of £10 each		
19,176 Ordinary shares fully paid	191,760 0 0	
1,500 Ordinary shares £4 paid	6,000 0 0	
2,220 B preference shares, £2 paid	4,440 0 0	
Cash paid by advance calls	3,298 0 0	
		205,498 0 0
Less calls unpaid		764 14 3
Amount owing on Debentures		204,733 5 9
Amount owing on security of Carlton property		29,200 0 0
Amount owing on bills payable		18,000 0 0
Amount owing to sundry creditors on open accounts		20,777 8 4
Amount owing for wages and salaries		14,833 4 5
Amount owing for royalty on ironstone, coal etc		2,455 7 3
Amount owing for rent of cottages on lease		2,773 9 6
Amount owing to bankers		270 1 2
		7,647 2 6

ASSETS

	£ s d	£ s d
By Freehold land, houses, workshops, ironstone mines, colliery, coke ovens, blast furnaces, puddling forge, and other works complete or in progress; as per valuation on April 30th 1875		213,652 6 0
By advances on incomplete contracts		8,653 16 7
By stocks of materials, pig iron etc on hand at April 30th 1875		17,150 0 0
By Royalty on ironstone, coal etc paid in advance		8,732 11 9
Amount owing by sundry debtors		15,735 11 9
Cash and bills on hand and in bank		589 3 5

PROFIT AND LOSS ACCOUNT. Balance from last year

	£ s d	£ s d	£ s d
Balance from last year			16,705 5 8
Bad and doubtful debts accrued since the company commenced			5,500 0 0
Half year ended October 31st 1874			
Loss on Carlton pig iron		14,365 17 4	
Loss on Carlton Puddled Bars		346 3 9	
Loss on East Howle coal and coke		901 3 10	
Bank interest, commission etc		137 6 5	
		15,750 11 4	
Less; Profit at South Belmont mines	988 9 6		
Profit at Ailesbury mines	1,916 17 4		
Profit at East Howle Brickworks	199 11 8		
Profit on coals purchased	34 3 0		
		3,139 1 6	
Nett Loss on half year's business ending October 31st 1874		12,611 9 10	
Add; Half year's interest on Carlton mortgage		200 0 0	
Half year's interest on Debentures		217 11 4	
Bonus paid to Ailesbury workers		317 14 11	
			13,456 9 10
Total to debit of profit and loss account, October 31st 1874			35,661 15 6
Half year ended April 30th 1875			
Profit at South Belmont Mines		369 14 8	
Profit at Ailesbury Mines		661 8 8	
Profit on East Howle coal and coke		276 6 5	
Profit on East Howle Brickworks		64 14 10	
Total profits		1,372 4 7	
Less; Loss on Carlton pig iron	442 6 8		
Loss on Carlton puddled bars	95 1 7		
Bank interest and commission etc	166 12 6		
		704 0 9	
Nett profit on half year's business to April 30th inc £8 on forfieted shares			676 3 10
			34,985 11 8
Add; Half year's interest on Carlton Mortgage			450 0 0
Half year's interest on Debentures and prepaid calls			739 18 9
Balance of Profit and Loss a/c carried to next Account			36,176 0 5

NORTH OF ENGLAND INDUSTRIAL IRON AND COAL CO., LIMITED

BALANCE SHEET — APRIL 30th 1876

DR.   CR.

LIABILITIES

NOMINAL CAPITAL OF COMPANY £300,000, in 25,000 A or ordinary shares of £10 each, and 5,000 B or preference shares of £10 each,

	£ s d	£ s d
19,474 Ordinary shares fully paid	194,740 0 0	
1,200 Ordinary shares £5 paid	6,000 0 0	
5,000 B preference shares, £8 paid	40,000 0 0	
Cash paid by advance calls	3,522 0 0	
		244,262 0 0
Amount owing on Debentures		31,200 0 0
Amount owing on bills payable		17,681 15 9
Amount owing for wages and salaries		1,757 11 1
Amount owing to bankers		7,389 2 7
Amount owing on security of Carlton property		18,000 0 0
Amount owing to Sundry Creditors on open a/cs		11,795 10 4
Royalties on Ironstore, coal etc		2,367 0 4
Amount owing for rent of cottages, farms etc on lease		115 13 0
		£334,568 13 1

ASSETS

	£ s d	£ s d
By Freehold land, houses, workshops, ironstone mines, colliery, coke ovens, blast furnaces, puddling forge, and other works exclusive of of South Belmont mines		232,882 1 2
By advances on incomplete contracts		19,137 15 7
By stocks of materials, pig iron etc on hand at April 30th 1876		15,208 2 1
Amount owing by sundry debtors		14,533 4 4
Cash and bills on hand and in bank		329 13 11

PROFIT AND LOSS ACCOUNT. Balance from last year

	£ s d	£ s d
Balance from last year		36,176 9 5
Add; Balance of capital and 'shorts' accounts standing against South Belmont mines referred to in last Half Years Report of Directors inclusive of depreciation in value of ironstone in stock on April 30th 1876		15,100 18 5
Amount paid for cancelling Fettling Ore contract made in April 1872		2,501 16 9
		53,779 4 7

Results of business done year ended April 30th 1876

	£ s d	£ s d
Profits on working at Ailesbury mines, East Howle Colliery and Carlton Blast Furnaces	7,459 3 1	
Less; Loss on manufacture of puddled bars	2,708 9 10	
	4,750 13 3	
Deduct interest on loans, prepaid calls and bank advances	3,449 4 8	
Balance to credit of Profit and Loss a/c for year		1,301 8 7
Balance against Profit and Loss a/c carried to next account		52,477 16 0
		£334,568 13 1

Examined the above balance sheet and find it correct

C HOPKINSON, Auditor, 26th June 1876, 13, Barstow Square, Wakefield

The North of England Industrial Iron & Coal Company.
(LIMITED.)

Directors:
HENRY CURRER BRIGGS, ESQ., CHAIRMAN AND MANAGING DIRECTOR, GLENHOW, SALTBURN-BY-THE-SEA.
WALTER MORRISON, ESQ., J.P., MALHAM TARN, YORKSHIRE.
ALFRED HODGETTS, ESQ., ST. BEES, CARNFORTH.
JOHN STEPHENSON M'GOWAN, ESQ., WHITEHAVEN.

Offices:
No. 3, EXCHANGE PLACE, MIDDLESBRO'-ON-TEES.

Secretary:
MR. GEORGE LYNAS.

SIXTH ANNUAL REPORT OF DIRECTORS.

The annexed Balance Sheet exhibits the result of the transactions of the Company during the sixth financial year.

The loss that has almost universally been experienced by those engaged in the Iron and Coal trades in all districts during the last twelve months will doubtless have caused the Shareholders to look forward with anxiety and some apprehension to the Report now issued. The Directors, therefore, feel some gratification in being able to point out that although the balance to the debit of Profit and Loss Account has been increased by the transference from Capital to that Account, of the ultimate deficit arising from the abandonment of South Belmont Mines, (referred to in the last half-yearly Report) the profit on the year's business has not only met the interest on Debentures and loans, but leaves a credit balance of £1,301 8s. 7d.

The Plate Mill at Carlton is so far completed as to be capable of being speedily made available for work when the prospect of the trade justifies a resumption of the manufacture of malleable iron.

The Directors regret that an interruption of work at East Howle Colliery became essential in order to enforce a more economical mode of getting the coal; work has, however, now been resumed under more favourable conditions than hitherto.

The efficient condition of the Works has been fully maintained, whilst several improvements have been carried out, without addition to Capital account, which have contributed to the realization of the comparatively satisfactory result from the year's transactions shewn by the Balance Sheet.

The Directors recommend that at the meeting to be held in accordance with the annexed notice, a half-yearly dividend at the rate of 5 per cent. per annum be declared payable on the capital paid up on the B. Preference Shares to the 31st October last.

Mr. Archibald Briggs being no longer able to attend the meetings of the Board, owing to business engagements abroad and other causes, has resigned his seat, which vacancy the Directors recommend shall be filled up by the election of Mr. Thomas Kirk.

Messrs. Walter Morrison and J. S. McGowan also retire by rotation from the Board, and offer themselves for re-election.

H. C. BRIGGS,
CHAIRMAN.

Middlesbrough,

CARLTON IRON COMPANY, LIMITED

BALANCE SHEET

APRIL 30th 1877

DR.   CR.

LIABILITIES

NOMINAL CAPITAL OF COMPANY $300,000, in 25,000 £ or ordinary shares of £10 each,
and 5,000 B or preference shares of £10 each

		£ s d
20,774 Ordinary shares fully paid	207,740 0 0	
4,998 B preference shares, fully paid	49,980 0 0	257,720 0 0
Amount owing on Security of Carlton Property		8,000 0 0
Amount owing on Debentures		8,400 0 0
Amount owing on bills payable		5,652 6 10
Amount owing for wages and salaries		1,884 6 2
Amount owing to bankers		5,286 11 9
Amount owing to sundry creditors on open a/cs		12,436 19 9
Amount owing for Royalties on Ironstone Coal etc		2,031 6 8
Amount owing for rent of cottages, farms etc on lease		115 13 0
		£353,527 4 2

ASSETS

		£ s d
By Freehold land, houses, workshops, ironstone mines, colliery, coke ovens, blast furnaces, puddling forge, plate mill and other properties		265,232 3 8
By stocks of materials, pig iron etc on hand at April 30th 1877		14,317 7 1
Amount owing by sundry debtors		13,807 19 4
Cash and bills on hand		371 8 8
PROFIT AND LOSS ACCOUNT. Balance from last year		52,477 16 0
Add; Balance of South Belmount Capital Account, land damage award etc not debited in last account		5,541 10 0
Royalty under charged on East Howle Coal and Fire Clay up to April 30th 1876		430 4 0
Dividend paid on B shares August 11th 1976		500 0 0
Amount written off Bad and Doubtful debts a/c		1,500 0 0
		60,449 10 0

Results of business done year ended April 30th 1877

Profits on working at Carlton and Ailesbury mines,	6,457 8 5	
Less: Loss on working at East Howle Colliery and farm	2,411 5 1	
	4,046 3 4	
Deduct interest on loans, prepaid calls and bank advances	3,407 2 9	
Balance to credit of Profit and Loss a/c for year		639 0 7
		59,810 9 5
Deduct for 2 B shares forfeited for non-payment of calls		12 4 0
Balance against Profit and Loss a/c carried to next account		59,798 5 5
		£353,527 4 2

Examined the above balance sheet and find it correct

C HOPKINSON, Auditor, 30th June 1877, 13, Barstow Square, Wakefield

Letter written to shareholders of the Carlton Iron Company Limited

Carlton Iron Company Ltd
December 7th 1877
Middlesbrough

Private and Confidential

Dear Sir,

In view of the present position of the Company and the desirability of fully developing its Works, Colliery and Mines so as to be able to take advantage at the earliest moment of any improvement in Trade, we venture to address you, as one of the larger shareholders of the Company, in amplification of the statements contained in the accompanying Report. The extreme depression from which the Iron Trade of Cleveland is at present suffering arises to a great extent from the substitution of Steel from Iron in the manufacture of rails. At a time when the Company commenced business about 50% of the pig iron consumed in the Malleable Ironworks of the Cleveland district was used in making iron rails. At present time no iron rails, or next to none, are being manufactured in the district and therefore other and more distant markets for pig iron have to be sought out which can only be got at and secured by means of the exceptionally low prices at which Cleveland Iron can be produced and sold.

During the last three years a large number of Public Companies and private firms engaged in the Iron and Coal Trades of the Cleveland district have succumbed to the pressure of the times. Many of these firms and companies originally possessed very large resources, enjoyed special advantages of position and were conducted under the most able and experienced management. We therefore venture to hope that you will consider it a most satisfactory state of things that Carlton Iron Company have thus far successfully weathered the storm, promptly met all the demands on its resources and punctually paid all interest on borrowed capital. This result has not however been obtained without liberal beneficiary assistance from the directors of the company, as it has been impossible all at once to find new outlets for the produce of the Ironworks and Mines and turning it promptly into money without great sacrifices and under risks which have thus far happily been avoided. The time has however now arrived when this temporary and partial help is insufficient and it has become absolutely essential to the prosperity of the company that further capital should be raised, not only to carry the concern smoothly through the remaining period of depression, but to enable directors so to complete and amend the works by taking advantage of the most recent improvements as to be able to produce pig iron of the very best quality attainable from their materials at the lowest possible cost, obtain an outlet for it and for the coal produced at East Howle, maintain the present rate of consumption of Ailesbury Ironstone and find tenants for the empty cottages at Carlton by commencing the manufacture of plates. A large amount of capital has already been expended in putting down the Plate Mill and Puddling Forge plant which is lying idle and unproductive because incomplete, though capable of earning profits for the shareholders if supplemented by the expenditure now proposed.

The directors have done their part, from time to time they have increased their stake and now, including the two lately retired directors, they hold a personal interest of over £100,000 in the shares and debentures, about £18,000 of which has been subscribed during the present long depression of trade. They feel confident however that, as in all similar periods in the past since the Iron Trade assumed its position as one of the leading industries of the country, the existing stagnation will be followed by better times, and it is their opinion that the present is a most fitting opportunity for making the requisite preparations, materials and labour being lower in price, better in quality, and more efficient than for years past. As stated in the accompanying report it is proposed to increase the borrowing powers of the company and the amount which the directors intend to raise is £35,000. This sum will be ample to improve the Carlton Blast Furnace plant, complete the Malleable Works and Plate Mill, ensure the safety of the colliery by renewing the means of ventilation, and provide sufficient working capital. The directors feel such confidence in the future of the company, provided these improvements are effected, that conditionally on the share and debenture holders liberally responding to this appeal by subscribing for the issue of these Mortgage Debentures, which will bear interest at the rate of £6 per cent per annum, payable half yearly, and be redeemable in five or seven years at the option of the subscriber, they are willing to provide what is deficient to any extent not exceeding one half of total required amount.

We trust you will be able to attend the meeting which is arranged to be held at the Queen's Hotel, Leeds in accordance with the notice annexed to the accompanying report, but if you are unable to do so please sign and return the enclosed proxy form to the secretary not later than by Saturday's evening post the 15th December.

H.C.BRIGGS. Chairman
THOS. KIRK. Managing Director

A copy of this letter is shown to illustrate the problems that often faced the directors of the Carlton Iron Company during the years when the iron trade was in deep depression and that even as early as 1877 the future of the company and the village hung in the balance.

The Carlton Iron Company, Limited.

Directors:

HENRY CURRER BRIGGS, Esq., Chairman, Belvedere, Harrogate.
THOMAS KIRK, Esq., Managing Director, West Villas, Stockton-on-Tees.
WALTER MORRISON, Esq., J.P., Malham Tarn, Yorkshire.
ALFRED HODGETTS, Esq., St. Bees, Carnforth.
JOHN STEPHENSON M'GOWAN, Esq., Whitehaven.

Offices:

CARLTON IRONWORKS, near STOCKTON-ON-TEES.

Secretary:

Mr. HENRY HOGGETT, Junr.

HALF-YEARLY REPORT OF DIRECTORS.

It is so well known that the depression in the Iron and Coal Trades has grown more intense from month to month during the past half-year that your Directors need do no more than allude to the fact. They are able, therefore, the more warmly to congratulate their fellow Shareholders, that the Company has so far withstood the stress of the times, and that they can state that an audited Balance Sheet of the Company's present position shews that no bills payable are running, and that after charging to revenue a large sum which has been spent during the past half-year in improving and renovating the Works, a balance of over £1,600 remains as working profit earned during the six months.

Owing to the lessened demand for Pig Iron it has been deemed advisable to work only two Blast Furnaces at Carlton during the half-year. Had it been possible to have kept all three in blast, the Furnaces and Mines, with a larger production, would have been worked with even greater economy.

The outlay referred to above has been principally expended at the Colliery and Mines, and has enabled a much larger quantity of Coal to be wrought at a reduced cost; it will also cheapen to some extent, the expense of working the Ironstone Mines.

The half-yearly meeting of the Shareholders will be held at Carlton Iron Works, on January 15th next, in accordance with the annexed notice, when the Directors will be happy to afford any further information to Shareholders attending the same.

H. C. BRIGGS, Chairman.
THOS. KIRK, Managing Director.
H. HOGGETT, Junr., Secretary.

October 1878.

CARLTON IRON COMPANY, LIMITED

BALANCE SHEET

APRIL 30th 1878

DR.				CR.		
LIABILITIES				**ASSETS**		
NOMINAL CAPITAL OF COMPANY $300,000, in 25,000 A or ordinary shares of £10 each, and 5,000 B or preference shares of £10 each,				By Freehold land, houses, workshops, ironstone mines, colliery, coke ovens, blast furnaces, puddling forge, plate mill and other properties		273,596 2 5
20,774 Ordinary shares fully paid	207,740 0 0			By stocks of materials, pig iron etc on hand at April 30th 1878.		8,386 10 4
4,998 B preference shares, fully paid	49,980 0 0			Amount owing by sundry debtors		8,101 7 1
		257,720 0 0		Cash and bills on hand		410 5 2
Amount owing on Debentures First Issue		40,400 0 0				
Amount owing on Debentures Second Isssue		3,225 0 0		**PROFIT AND LOSS ACCOUNT**: Balance from last year	59,798 5 5	
Amount owing on Security of Carlton Property		18,000 0 0		Add; South Belmount timber damage award etc, not debited in last account	232 1 7	
Amount owing on bills payable		6,946 0 0		Law charges, Director's expenses etc up to April 30th 1877	329 15 1	
Amount owing for wages and salaries		1,715 16 8		Loss on puddled bars, Fettling ores etc. in stock April 30th 1877	554 17 10	
					60,914 19 11	
Amount owing to bankers		12,499 2 2		Less Royalty on coal overcharged in 1876	186 7 3	
					60,728 12 8	
Amount owing to sundry creditors on open a/cs		9,319 9 3		**Results of business done year ended April 30th 1878**		
Amount owing for Royalties on Ironstone Coal etc		3,728 2 4		Profits on working at Carlton and Ailesbury mines,	1,728 9 5	
Amount owing for rent of cottages, farms etc on lease		502 8 6		Less: Loss on working at East Howle Colliery	934 9 5	
				Nett profit on year's business	794 0 0	
				Add interest on loans, prepaid calls and bank advances	59,934 12 8	
				Balance against Profit and Loss a/c carried to next account	3,627 6 2	63,561 18 10
		$354,056 3 10				**$354,056 3 10**

The above Balance Sheet has not been audited for want of time but it may be taken as substantially correct

George Lynas, Secretary

CARLTON IRON COMPANY, LIMITED

BALANCE SHEET — APRIL 30th 1890

DR.

LIABILITIES

NOMINAL CAPITAL OF COMPANY £300,000, in 25,000 A or ordinary shares of £10 each, and 5,000 B or preference shares of £10 each

	£ s d	£ s d
20,774 Ordinary shares fully paid	207,740 0 0	
4,997 B preference shares, fully paid	49,980 0 0	
		257,710 0 0
Amount owing on Debentures First Issue		40,400 0 0
Amount owing on Debentures Second Issue		21,705 0 0
Amount owing on Security of Carlton Property		17,705 0 0
Amount owing for wages and salaries		3,415 7 8
Amount owing to sundry creditors		62,024 2 3
Amount owing for Royalties on Ironstone Coal etc		8,750 15 2
Amount owing for rent of cottages, farms etc on lease		658 5 4
Amount owing on bills payable		4,209 9 2
		£416,577 19 7

CR.

ASSETS

	£ s d	£ s d
By Freehold land, houses, workshops, ironstone mines, colliery, coke ovens, blast furnaces, puddling forge, plate mill and other properties		260,884 1 3
By stocks of materials, pig iron etc on hand at April 30th 1890		59,716 19 3
Amount owing by sundry debtors		39,492 0 6
Cash in hand		158 9 5

PROFIT AND LOSS ACCOUNT

	£ s d	£ s d
Balance from last year's a/c		63,828 0 3

Results of business done year ended April 30th 1890

	£ s d	£ s d
Profits on working at Carlton Blast Furnaces East Howle Colliery and Rosedale Mines	12,930 16 6	
Add interest on Debentures, bank advances, etc	50,897 3 9	
Balance against Profit and Loss a/c carried to next account	5,429 5 5	
		56,326 9 2
		£416,577 19

Examined the above balance sheet and find it correct

C HOPKINSON, Auditor, 20th June 1890, 13, Barstow Square, Wakefield

APPENDIX 4

Report on dilapidation of property in Morrison Terrace

Club House

Club Room	To be papered and ceiling whitewashed. Two escutcheon to door. Sash cords where missing and worn out.
Billiard Room	To be papered and ceiling whitewashed. Sash cords where required. Escutcheon to door. Walls repaired where hat rails and coat hooks are taken away.
Hall & Staircase	To be papered and ceiling whitewashed.
Bagatelle Room	To be papered and ceiling whitewashed. Woodwork to be painted in proper manner. Walls repaired where hat rails and hooks will be removed
Snug	To be papered and ceiling whitewashed. Woodwork repaired and painted.
Kitchen	As per Snug.
Scullery	Walls repaired and coloured. Woodwork repaired and painted.
Yard	Cement repaired. Bricks over drain repaired. Drain replaced. Coal House door repaired.
Stable	Key wanted.
Privy	Door to be repaired.
Cellar	Plaster to be repaired. Cellar 'Flop' down door to be repaired.
No. 1 Side Bedroom	Woodwork to be painted.
No. 2 Back Bedroom	Walls and ceiling coloured. Woodwork painted.
Cloak Room	Key required.
No. 3 Front Bedroom	To be papered. Ceiling whitewashed. Woodwork painted. Sash cords replaced. Cracks in ceiling repaired.
No. 4 Front Bedroom	As No. 3 Bedroom.
No. 5 Front Bedroom	As No. 3 Bedroom.
No. 6 North Bedroom	As No. 3 Bedroom.
Landing	Woodwork painted and ceiling whitewashed.

General:	The whole of this block of property needs painting properly outside. Back door, privy and pantry doors need repairing. All broken and cracked panes throughout the premises want replacing. Wall at back passage wants repairing and cement work doing. Locks to back doors require new ones. Coach house door to be replaced. The outside brickwork to be gone over where necessary and repaired and in some cases painted. Spouts to be repaired and cleaned out. Cast iron downcomers to be repaired where broken. In No. 1 Side Bedroom the wall outside and inside are very damp and wants repairing and making weather tight. Water point for all properties is situated in the Club House yard.
J Bulmer (Draper)	Kitchen to be papered and ceiling whitewashed Workshop to have small panes of glass repaired.
J Dawson (Greengrocer)	Kitchen to be papered and ceiling whitewashed. Woodwork painted. Glass door frame replaced. Sash cords and sash fastener. Window glazed and framed to slaughter house. New lock and key to front door. Doors made for ash pit and coal house missing. Back of buildings, cement repaired where required.
B Stephenson (Grocer)	Kitchen to be papered and whitewashed. Fire range needs resetting. Bedroom to be papered and whitewashed. Outside wall to be properly painted. Shop: Sash cords. New weather boards at door.

Report by William and Douglese, Middlesbrough.

APPENDIX 5

SECTION 1 Brief description of the men who worked on Blast Furnaces and their wages.
SECTION 2 Example of salaries of teachers at Stillington Board School.
SECTION 3 Table of staff wages at the Carlton Iron Company and brief resumé of some of the men involved.

SECTION ONE

Brief description of the men who worked on Blast Furnaces c 1875

The earliest recorded Blast Furnaces in the North of England were at Rievaulx Abbey which commenced working in 1577. Ironstone was found in large quantities in the sea cliffs of the North Yorkshire coastline in 1848, and in the face of Eston Nab in 1850, which led to the highest concentration of Blast Furnaces anywhere in the world being formed on Teesside by 1870.

Cleveland ironstone was always calcinated to improve the quality of the charge and furnaces were worked with a hot blast system using regenerative stoves.

Sixty per cent of the men working the Teesside Blast Furnaces were recruited from the 'green fields of Ireland' although the skilled men generally came from South Wales, where ironmaking had started at an earlier date.

Blast Furnacemen were divided into a number of groups:

1 Gantrymen who worked on the calcinating kilns and coke bunker gantries. They were responsible for handling the railway wagons on the gantry and for loading the kilns with ironstone at the correct rate, along with sufficient coal to ensure combustion at a dull red heat. The coal was normally dropped from the rail wagon on to iron plates then shovelled into the kiln as required. The gantrymen worked under a system of two shifts per day with the kiln left unattended between midnight and 6am. They worked in an atmosphere of sulphurous fumes and dust and had no shelter, except maybe a wooden hut.

2 Scarrers worked at the base of the calcinating kilns and broke down any large fused lumps of calcinated ironstone inside the kiln so that it could be removed from the base. The breaking down would be carried out using long iron bars inserted through special holes called eyes in the side of the kiln.

3 Mine Fillers. These men collected the calcinated ironstone or 'mine' and loaded it into barrows, which held about thirteen hundredweight, with thin rimmed wheels. The skill was in loading the barrows with the red hot 'mine' from different parts of the kiln in rotation so as to ensure an even combustion in the kiln, and in manhandling the barrows .

4 Weighers checked the weight of the barrows as they passed over the weighbridge in front of the weigh cabin and kept records of same.

5 Fillers. The fillers loaded the barrows onto the furnace hoist platform in correct numbers to make up a 'round'. Once a round was loaded, the fillers' responsibility ended and the barrows were hoisted unattended to the top of the blast furnace.

6 Chargers took over the 'round' and arranged the various materials in the bell hoppers of the furnaces. When each 'round' was completed the bell hopper was dropped and the charge slipped into the furnace. At once the whole furnace top was engulfed in smoke, fumes and flame as ignited gases escaped. The bell hopper was then drawn tight against the blast furnace top cylinder and any small leaks sealed with damp coke dust. The hopper was then ready to receive the next 'round' in preparation for the next charge. Chargers had little shelter apart from the iron parapet and, when arranging the charge, they were exposed to all the elements on top of 80 feet towers and, in addition, they were constantly at risk from escaping gas.

7 The Keeper worked at the base of the blast furnace and kept an eagle eye on all aspects of its working. He and his assistant supervised the preparation of the pig beds and carried out the tapping of the furnace about four times each twenty four hours. He also controlled the timing of the slagging.

8 Slaggers or Slagmen were the men who drew off the slag to be teased into slag ladles and drawn away by the shunting engine to be tipped on the nearby slag heap.

9 Enginemen and Boilermen cared for the blowing engines, the hoist engines and the boilers.

10 Craftsmen such as joiners, blacksmiths, fitters and electricians carried out all plant maintenance.

11 Labourers moulded the pig beds, worked as metal carriers and loaded slag trucks. They worked a basic 12 hour shift and were generally paid on a price or tonnage rate.

An average furnace would produce about 30 tons of pig iron per shift.

Average weekly wages in 1874 were;

Keepers	10s 9½d	Assistant Keepers	4s 3½d	Slagmen	6s 7½d
Fillers	5s 4½d	Chargemen	8s 2½d		

All worked twelve hour shifts and each alternating Sunday they worked a twenty-four hour shift to ensure continuity of working during the shift change-over period. This practice survived unchallenged in the Teesside area until 1894. The above information was taken from John Gjers book, *'Ayresome Ironworks.'*

SECTION 2

Examples of teachers' salaries at Stillington Board School

1885 salaries/month

Thos Kirtley, Master at Mixed school	£8.0.0
Miss Knott, Mistress at Infant school	£5.0.0
Mr J Robinson, Asst Teacher, Mixed	£4.11.8
Mr F W Ross, Pupil Teacher Mixed	£1.9.2
Miss J Robinson, Monitor, Infants	£0.4.0
Miss C Lonsdale, Monitor, Infants	£0.4.0
Mrs Roberts, Cleaner of Infants School	£0.14.0
Mrs Pugh, Cleaner of Mixed School	£0.18.0

1892 salaries/month

Thos Kirtley, Master at Mixed	£8.0.0
Miss Knott, Mistress at Infant	£5.0.0
Miss K Jamieson, Asst Mistr. Mixed	£4.0.0
Mr Chas Hart, Asst Master Mixed	£4.6.8
Mrs Roberts, Cleaner of Infants	£0.14.0
Mrs Pugh, Cleaner of Mixed School	£0.18.0

1895 salaries/month

Thos Kirtley, Master at Mixed school	£8.0.0
Miss Smith, Mistress at Infant school	£5.8.4
Mr G D Smith, Asst Master. Mixed	£6.13.4
Miss K Jamieson, Asst Mistress, Mixed	£4.6.8
Mr H W Mills, Asst Teacher, Mixed	£4.3.4
Miss Blenkinsop, Pupil Teacher, Infants	£1.5.0
Three Monitors @ 8s. each	£1.4.0
Mrs Sparks, Cleaner of Infants School	£0.14.0
Mrs Pugh, Cleaner of Mixed School	£0.18.0

1903 salaries/month

Thos Kirtley, Master at Mixed	£8.0.0
Mr G D Smith, Asst Master, Mixed	£7.10.0
Miss S Shearer, Asst Mistress, Mixed	£6.5.0
Miss J Sparke, Pupil Teacher, Mixed	£1.17.6
Miss J Whitewell, 2nd yr, PT Mixed	£1.9.2
Mr F Lonsdale, 1st yr, PT Mixed	£0.8.0
Miss S Iley, Mistress at Infants	£7.8.4
Miss E Hill, Asst Mistress, Infants	£3.15.0
Miss J Hodgson, Prov. Asst Infants	£1.17.6
Miss D Holder, 3rd yr PT Infants	£1.9.2
Miss O Dixon, 1st yr PT Infants	£0.8.0

Mr Kirtley, the Headmaster of the Mixed School was also provided with a free house and free coal, plus one third of the Government Grant giving him an extra £50 to £60 per annum. The remainder of the staff received a portion of the grant on a seniority basis but at a much lower percentage than the Head. eg. the Pupil Teachers would get about £1 per annum. The Infants Head Mistress also received free house and coal.

SECTION THREE

Wages/Month paid to Staff at Carlton Iron Co. and brief resumé of some of the men

Name	April 1895	May 1895	Dec 1898	Dec 1900	Dec 1903	Dec 1905	Dec 1907	Dec 1909	Dec 1911	Dec 1913	Oct 1914
R Barker	11 5 0	*J Wilkinson*		13 0 0	15 3 4	*P Kirk*	16 13 4	16 13 4	16 13 4	16 13 4	16 13 4
T F Fawcett	10 0 0	12 13 4	16 13 4	20 16 8	24 3 4	25 0 0	25 0 0	33 6 8	33 6 8	50 0 0	50 0 0
T Kirk Jnr.	3 0 0	13 0 0	13 0 0	20 16 8	*W Powell*		2 7 8	4 6 8	6 6 8	80 8 4	81 8 4
J S Muncaster	5 14 0	6 5 0		*W Luff*	3 0 0	3 6 8	4 16 8		*Bellag*	6 18 8	6 18 8
R Bell	6 6 8	0 0	8 13 4	10 0 0	10 18 4	10 18 4	11 8 4	13 6 8	4 3 4	15 16 8	15 16 8
T Stephenson	4 10 0	5 4 0	7 0 0	8 13 4	9 11 8	9 11 8	11 8 4	13 6 8	14 3 4	15 16 8	15 16 8
J S Waring	4 10 0	5 4 0	7 0 0	8 13 4	9 11 8	9 11 8	110 8 4	13 6 8	14 3 4	16 13 4	6 13 4
W D Hopper	2 13 4	3 16 8	6 10 0	8 3 4	90 1 8	90 1 8	10 10 0	12 3 4	13 0 0	13 16 8	13 16 8
W Shaw	1 12 6	2 9 2	*H Hunton*		80 6 8	80 6 8	10 10 0	10 10 0		*W Reed* 1 0 1 8	
F Ross	10 16 8	10 16 8	11 18 4	11 18 4	13 0 0	13 0 0	13 0 0	13 0 0	13 0 0	13 0 0	13 0 0
H Kirk	6 5 0	6 5 0		4 0 6 8	8 13 4	13 0 0	13 0 0	19 6 8	20 8 4	22 18 4	22 18 4
C E Duck				3 9 6	5 6 8	6 15 0	6 15 0	7 15 0	9 3 4	9 3 4	
W Thompson				2 12 0	4 6 0	*J H Strickland*	2 12 0	1 4 6	5 0 0	7 1 8	1 1 8
J Peirson				1 14 8	3 8 8	5 1 8	5 10 0	*S Haygarth*	1 14 8	3 6 8	4 0 0
A E Pugh				8 6 8	9 11 8	*N Fawcett*		1 19 0	3 9 4	6 14 0	
E A Loyd				13 0 0	5 3 4	15 3 4	*J W Sherwood*	2 11 4	3 18 0	6 0 0	6 10 0
E Graham				10 16 8	*Tom Fawcett*	1 14 8	3 0 0	4 13 4	6 16 8	8 18 4	9 8 4
F Ross Jun				2 12 0.		*J Paterson*	17 6 8	17 6 8	*A Strickland*		1 14 8
J Blenkinsop					2 11 4	4 3 4	4 11 8	*R Dixon*	2 12 0	4 6 8	4 16 8
H Ross					1 6 0	3 0 0	3 0 0	4 10 0	6 4 2	7 10 10 9 11 8	10 1 8
Bing Dodsworth								1 14 8	3 8 0	4 11 4	6 13 4 7 3 4
E C Powell									1 14 8	3 4 8	5 0 0 2 15 0
B Butterworth									2 13 4		
E Dodsworth									1 6 0	2 11 4	4 6 8 4 6 8
R Butler									3 13 8	5 4 0	6 8 7 16 8
T Sayers									2 11 4	*Left Nov 1912*	
W Lambert									1 16 8		
J G Arnold									10 8 4		
P C Bune	Started July 6th 1911								3 15 0	3 15 0	3 15 0
N Hebron Stewart										2 14 0	
C A Exton										2 10 0	
J H Brotton										1 14 8	2 8 0
R Sergeant										1 16 10	2 6 10
C Trotter	Started end of 1912									4 0 0	4 10 0
Hy Alton										1 14 8	2 8 0
John Stewart										13 0 0	13 0 0
Totals	77 18 2	72 13 10	113 6 4	148 5	145 13	123 8	168 10	219 5	253	298 14	308 16
Christmas Bonus				13 10	14 5	14 5.	none	16 15	27 5	33	35 10

APPENDIX FIVE

In December 1911 W Powell and J H Strickland worked on Rosedale Schedules and got an extra 6/3d and 3/9d at the rate of 6d/hour.

In December 1909, W D Hopper was paid £3 extra for stocktaking on Sundays. Last salary paid to T Kirk Junior was on April 1901.

On October 1st 1914 B Dodsworth (18th Hussars), and C Trotter joined the colours.

On October 15th 1914 E C Powell joined the colours.

On October 16th 1914 R Dixon and E Dodsworth left for war (18th Hussars at Tidworth).

The following gives some outline details of some of the men shown in the table Details of some of the staff noted in salary table.

R Butler signed for Middlesbrough as a professional footballer in 1912.

J H Brotton a salaried worker at the Carlton Iron Company who started late 1912 and lodged with Chris Trotter and his family at 11 Redmarshall Street. They both started work at the ironworks at the same time, which would indicate they came to the village together. From the salaries received, it would seem that Trotter was the eldest and Brotton only a youngster.

Harry Alton appears in the salary book at the same time as above on the same salary as Brotton, at a level which suggests they were starting as boys. Alton's father was the village policeman and lived in 10 Redmarshall Street. Harry married a nurse, Jennie Robinson, who lodged at Mrs Wells' (Maisie's mother). After they were married they lived in 57 West Street.

T F Fawcett lived at the end of South Street. He was promoted to the post of company secretary at the Carlton Iron Company, taking over from Henry Hoggetts who lived in Mount Pleasant (two original houses converted into one large house). Hoggetts had been the company secretary from 1879 until some time in the late 1890s. Fawcett's house at the end of South Street was extensively modified for him in 1898 being doubled in size and given a large front garden. They had two daughters and three sons, Tom, Norman, Doris, Oswald and Mildred, who were a familiar sight playing tennis on the front lawn. Mildred, a pretty girl with bronze curly hair died when she was 14 years old, Tom eventually started a coal business and Oswald became a farmer. Norman played football for Stillington but was unfortunately killed in the 1914–18 war. When T F Fawcett retired through ill health at the end of December 1921 he received full salary until the end of May, after which he received a further five months salary at the rate of £1,000 per year.

R A F Bell appears in the list throughout the whole period covered, ie. 1985–1914. He was given one of the houses in Mount Pleasant, but he was not in Mount Pleasant 1888–89 tax schedules. He appears in the parish council records as a councillor from 1904 till 1921 and its chairman from 1916.

Thomas Stephenson worked all through the period covered at a similar salary as that of J S Waring. Thomas was Anthony Stephenson's son. Anthony was one of the first tenants to occupy a house in Mount Pleasant, worked as an engineer at the Carlton Iron Company and had twelve children. Thomas married Elizabeth Nesom, farmer's daughter from Whitton and eventually lived in No 3 Mount Pleasant. At least one of his family lived there until around the 1970s. He was a parish councillor from 1907 until 1928 and was appointed Clerk to the Council in 1934, a position held until he died in 1955.

J S Waring also worked through the period shown and remained in the employ of Dorman Long and Company until around 1945 to manage their affairs in the village after the Carlton Iron Company works closed. He collected the rents and generally organised things relating to the company's property. Originally he lived in South Street but moved to a house especially built for a managerial person of the works at the end of Kirk Street, so although he started as a clerk, he must have achieved some promotion to be allocated this house. The house was named Rosedale, after the ironstone mining area where the company had mined iron ore. He and his wife had two daughters, Sybil and Anne.

Francis Ross lived in No 2 Mount Pleasant and was working as a draughtsman at the Carlton Iron Company during the years listed.

Mr P C Bune came to the village in 1911 to take over the duties of Works Manager at the Carlton Iron Company in place of Mr Thomas Kirk junior who had resigned. He lived in Mount Pleasant. Bune came from Kettering and was known as a strict disciplinarian at the works, who kept an equally watchful eye on events in the village. He was a parish councillor from 1916 until 1922, and from 1925, until he left the village in March 1930.

*Frank Sherwood s*tarted at the Carlton Iron Company in 1909. Lost wife suddenly when she died on Christmas Day leaving him with a daughter aged 14 to look after. Lived in South Avenue.

W D Hopper lived in South Street and had two daughters. Margaret, one of the daughters, went to Stockton to live, the other daughter sat at the same desk as Violet Bell (author's mother) at school. The son, Cyril, who married and went to pit country, was suspected of setting fire to the Glykoline factory. W D Hopper was a parish councillor from 1916 to 1922 and from 1928 until 1934.

E C Powell lodged at Cissie Blenkinsop's in Glykoline Terrace. Can be seen on early football photographs as a committee member of the football club.

Walter Powell lodged at Cissie Blenkinsop's. Maggie Lavell, Peter Carr's sister courted him very strongly but he would not change his religion so the courtship was broken off. Walter was also involved in the football club and acted as Hon Secretary for many years.

S Haygarth also lodged at Cissie Blenkinsop's, who would only take staff personnel as boarder.

A E Pugh lived in accommodation above the workingmen's club in Morrison Terrace.

Thomas Kirk Jnr. (1870–1928) started at the Carlton Iron Company after leaving school and was appointed as work's manager when he was about 25 years old. He continued in this position until he resigned in 1911. He was involved with Whitton Parish Council from the date of its inception in January 1895, and was its chairman and treasurer from 1896 until 1913, when he left the parish and returned to Eaglescliffe for a brief period before buying a house near Norton Green, named Oak Lea, where he had tennis lawns laid and invited tournaments to be played there. Thomas was a very good tennis player and although he had many lady admirers he remained a bachelor. He had lived with his brother Harold in the Village of the Carlton Iron Works until they moved back home and shortly afterwards bought the house in Norton where they lived until they died, Thomas in 1928 and Harold in 1940.

Thomas represented Whitton Parish Council on Stockton Rural District Council from 1898 until 1922.

Harold Kirk, (1879–1940) took over as manager of the coke ovens when his brother Henry moved to take over the management of the coke ovens at Seaton Carew in 1898. He remained with the company until the takeover by Dorman Long and Company in 1920, when he resigned. He continued to remain well occupied and was a director for several small businesses including the North Eastern Iron Refinery. He was also a County Councillor on Stockton Rural District Council, Chairman of the Stockton Hospital's Board and President of Norton Cricket Club. Both Harold and Thomas were buried in St Mary's Churchyard at Norton.

Henry Kirk, (1868–1908) is not mentioned on the salary list, but he was the coke ovens' manager at the Village of the Carlton Ironworks, until being transferred to take charge of the newly built coke ovens at Seaton Carew in 1898.

Peter Kirk (1874–1959) Manager of the Iron Refining Section of the Seaton Carew Ironworks until that business was transferred to the Village of the Carlton Ironworks in 1926 to become the North Eastern Iron Refinery. This transfer was largely the work of his brother-in-law, William Thomlinson, who was chairman of the company with Peter Kirk given the responsibility of running the refinery as its Managing Director, with his brother Harold as one of the directors. When Thomlinson died in 1941, Peter Kirk took over as chairman and J K Smithson, a metallurgist who had come from the Seaton works, took over as Managing Director.

APPENDIX 6

The Royal Hotel

The Royal Hotel was built for the North of England Industrial Iron and Coal Company Ltd. in 1876 by a builder named Stephenson.

It was built as a residential hotel, for which purpose it was used until the decline of the ironworks.

It was leased to Mr John Redshaw in January 1877 for a period of fourteen years at a fixed annual rent of £52. Although Redshaw went bankrupt in 1878, the lease was taken over by a brewery agent until 1880 when, after paying the amount owed on the original lease, Mr Hodgetts, a director of the ironworks, took control of the lease. John Redshaw however remained as manager of the hotel.

December 1893. The Royal Hotel was leased by the ironworks, now named the Carlton Iron Company to Mr James Denny Ingram for the clear yearly rental of £100 per annum plus 5 per cent of the valuation of the fixtures in and around the hotel belonging to the Carlton Iron Company.

February 1895. The hotel was leased to William Robert Wardle under the same terms as above.

October 1928. Dorman Long and Company Ltd, who had taken over the Carlton Iron Company and consequently the Royal Hotel, leased it to John Smith's Tadcaster Brewery Company Ltd. This lease was agreed on a five year term at an annual rent of £120. The Royal Hotel had by this time been reduced to usage as a 'fully licensed public house'.

The property remained on lease to John Smith's until 1944 when they bought it from Dorman Long through the Bradford Property Trust for £6,000.

The Royal Hotel remained with John Smith's until May 1991 when Vaux took it over as part of a bigger deal in which they did not actually want possession of the Royal but John Smith's insisted that if Vaux wanted the more attractive Public Houses they had to take the Royal as part of the agreement.

List of landlords since 1928 and approximate dates of tenancy

James Argyle	October 1928
Henry (Happy Harry) Adam	May 1941
Walter Young	March 1944
Mrs Mary Tingle	May 1945. Now a freehold tenancy.

SAVIOUR OF THE PALACE

A HERO pilot saw the engine of his fighter plane raised from the ground – 64 years after he used it to save Buckingham Palace.

Ray Holmes, 89, watched as archaeologists dug up the Hurricane he used to ram a German bomber which was heading for the palace on September 15, 1940.

He sent the plane crashing into London's Victoria station. Ray parachuted to safety and his Hurricane buried itself in Buckingham Palace Road. He said as the engine was raised at the weekend: "It's such a mess."

HERO: Pilot Ray at dig

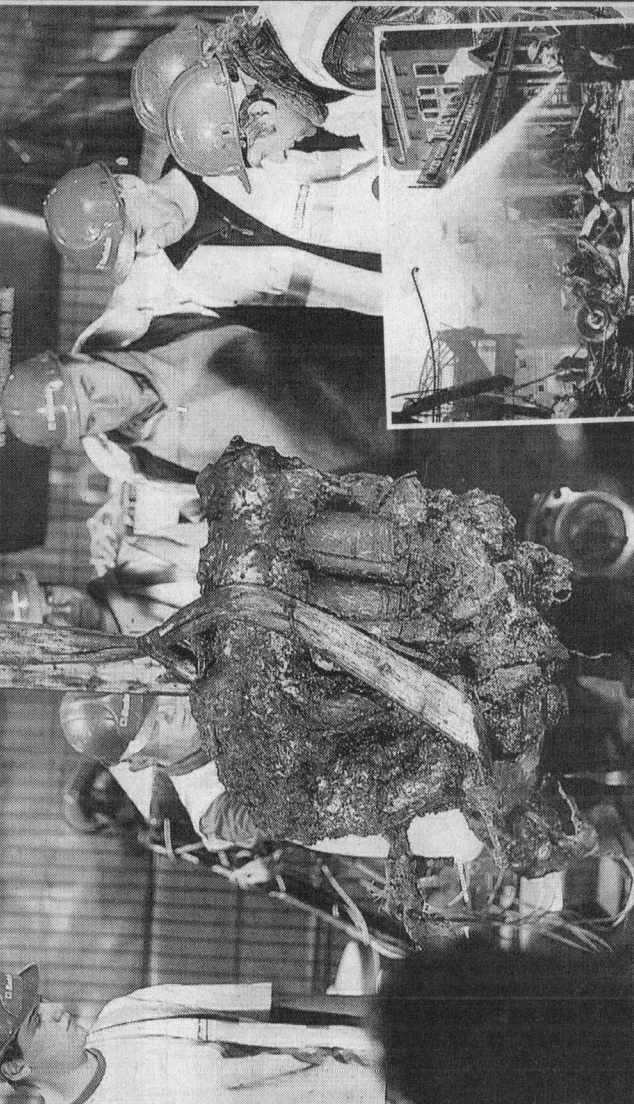

AIRBORNE: Hurricane's engine. Right, the bomber after crash

COLLECT THIS HISTORIC INVASION ISSUE

92p A LITRE

Saudi attack sparks huge fuel rise fears

By BOB ROBERTS and GARY JONES

EXCLUSIVE

FUEL prices will rise 20 per cent

most important crude oil producer
Twenty-two people died at the

Mr Theodore	May 1955
Cyril Argyle	October 1957
Adam Hird	April 1964
Joe Innes	1965
Stan Westwood	1967
George Connor	1970
Judith M Turner	December 1991

During the period May 1945 until May 1955, it was generally thought Walter Young was running the Royal with the help of a lady friend. Although not known by the name Mary it can only be assumed that her name was Mary Tingle and that the tenancy was held in her name.

APPENDIX 7

Scavenging Contracts

'Scavenging' meant the removal of contents from all the ash pits and privies in and around the Village of the Carlton Ironworks and the carting of said contents to an agreed disposal point. The contract was tendered for and agreed on a yearly basis.

The following persons were chosen by the Guardians of the Poor of the Stockton Union acting as the rural sanitary authority and latterly Stockton Rural District Council to carry out the 'scavenging' of the village of the Carlton Ironworks.

Year	Name	Cost p.a.	Year	Name	Cost p.a.
1874	Robert Arton	£1 10s 0d	1907	Carlton Iron Co.	£46 0s 0d
1875	Abraham Hugh	£4 0s 0d	1908	Carlton Iron Co.	£46 0s 0d
1876	Abraham Hugh	£4 0s 0d	1909	Carlton Iron Co.	£46 0s 0d
1877	Abraham Hugh	£4 0s 0d	1910	Carlton Iron Co.	£46 0s 0d
1878	Abraham Hugh	£4 0s 0d	1911	Carlton Iron Co.	£46 0s 0d
1879	Daniel Parson	£4 0s 0d	1912	Carlton Iron Co.	£46 0s 0d
1880	Daniel Parson	£4 0s 0d	1913	Carlton Iron Co.	£70 0s 0d
1881	Daniel Parson	£4 0s 0d	1914	Carlton Iron Co.	£70 0s 0d
1882	Wm. Jacob Dunn	£4 0s 0d	1915	Carlton Iron Co.	£70 0s 0d
1883	Wm. Jacob Dunn	£4 0s 0d	1916	Carlton Iron Co.	£70 0s 0d
1884	Wm. Jacob Dunn	£4 0s 0d	1917	Carlton Iron Co.	£80 0s 0d
1885	Wm. Jacob Dunn	£4. 0s 0d	1918	Carlton Iron Co.	£100 0s 0d
1886	Wm. Jacob Dunn	£4 0s 0d	1919	Carlton Iron Co.	£110 0s 0d
1887	Wm. John Hunter	£5 0s 0d	1920	George McWilliams	£340 0s 0d
1888	Wm. John Hunter	£5 0s 0d	1921	C J Bell	£234 0s 0d
1889	Wm. John Hunter	£6 0s 0d	1922	C J Bell	£234 0s 0d
1890	Wm. John Hunter	£6 0s 0d	1923	Ernest Gibson	£180 0s 0d
1891	Carlton Iron Co.	£45 0s 0d	1924	Geo. McWilliams was paid	
1892	Carlton Iron Co.	£45 0s 0d	1925	£3 16s a month as part of a team,	
1893	Carlton Iron Co.	£45 0s 0d	1926	and £10 a month for scavenging.	
1894	Carlton Iron Co.	£26 0s 0d	1927	Fred McWilliams	£130 0s 0d
1895	Carlton Iron Co.	£26 0s 0d	1928	Fred McWilliams	£130 0s 0d
1896	Carlton Iron Co.	£26 0s 0d	1929	Fred McWilliams	£130 0s 0d

1897	Carlton Iron Co.	£26 0s 0d		1930	Fred McWilliams.	£90 0s 0d
1898	Carlton Iron Co.	£30 0s 0d		1931	Fred McWilliams	£90 0s 0d
1899	Carlton Iron Co.	£36 0s 0d		1932	Mr T Wheldon	£84 0s 0d
1900	Carlton Iron Co.	£36 0s 0d		1933	Mr T Wheldon	£80 0s 0d
1901	Carlton Iron Co.	£36 0s 0d		1934	Mr T Wheldon	£80 0s 0d
1902	Carlton Iron Co.	£46 0s 0d		1935	Mr T Wheldon	£80 0s 0d
1903	Carlton Iron Co.	£46 0s 0d		1936	Mr T Wheldon	£80 0s 0d
1904	Carlton Iron Co.	£46 0s 0d		1937	Mr T Wheldon	£75 0s 0d
1905	Carlton Iron Co.	£46 0s 0d				
1906	Carlton Iron Co.	£46 0s 0d				

Conversion of Ash Privies to Water Closets took place at approximately the following dates although some individual premises were converted earlier.

Mount Pleasant – 1913.

North Street, Morrison Street, Big Lowson Street and Morrison Terrace – 1919, Office Row, Old West Street and South Street – 1934.

It was reported that all properties under the jurisdiction of Stockton Rural District Council were converted by 1936. The chapel privy was converted in 1936 and Railway Cottages were finally converted in 1954.

All houses built after 1913 had to be fitted with water closets.

APPENDIX 8

St John's Church – Stillington

Founder of Parish of Stillington in 1872 – William Cassidi

	Names of Vicar	*Dates*
1	John Allen Parker	1872–1875
2	Thomas Varley	1875–1891
3	Firth Newsome	1891–1918
4	Reginald Victor Bury	1918–1924

The Reverend Reginald Victor Bury was found lying dead at the bottom of the vicarage stairs. It was believed he had had a seizure whilst going upstairs. He was educated at the University of Yale, USA, and had served at Belfast, Dublin, London and Holy Trinity, Stockton before coming to Stillington.

5	Evan Morris Young	1924–1927
6	John Charles Douglas	1927–1939
7	Charles John Lockyer	1939–1948
8	Ronald Claude Dudley Jasper	1948–1955
9	Alex Moore Smith	1955–1963
10	John Derek Hodgson	1964–1966
11	John M Davey	1967–1969
12	Oswald W Weare	1970–1977
13	Leonard Constantine	1978–1982

The vicarage was built adjacent to the church in 1884 and, from that date, the vicars shown above lived there. In 1982 the vicarage was sold into private ownership and the parishes of Stillington and Grindon were joined to Redmarshall, Bishopton and Great Stainton with the Reverend Timothy Ollier becoming the priest in charge and living at Redmarshall. When he left to go to Gainford in 1988 these parishes were, after a period without any incumbent, served by two vicars. The Reverend P. S. Atkinson administered Bishopton, Redmarshall and Great Stainton and the Reverend Malcolm Goodall serving Stillington and Grindon. A new vicarage was built at Thorpe to house the Reverend Goodall, whilst the Reverend Atkinson resided at the vicarage in Redmarshall.

APPENDIX EIGHT

Financing the building of St. John's Church

After the formation of Stillington Parish in 1872 the founder, William Cassidi, started a building fund in order to finance the building of a church for the new parish. Below is shown a list of the major contributors to this fund, with Cassidi himself heading the list with a contribution of £1108.

Balance Sheet of the Building Fund of St. John's Church, Stillington, 1873–1883

Subscriptions	£. s. d.
The Rev William Cassidi, Vicar of Grindon	1108 0 0
The Right Rev Bishop Baring	500 0 0
The Warden and Fellows of Merton College, Oxford	250 0 0
Incorporated Church Building Society	150 0 0
Diocesan Church Building Society	100 0 0
The Marquess of Londonderry	100 0 0
The Barrington Fund	70 0 0
The Marchioness of Londonderry	50 0 0
Lord Boyne	50 0 0
The Governors of Sherburn Hospital	50 0 0
The Rev. Thomas Varley	50 0 0
Collected by the late Rev.J A Parker from Mrs Atkinson	38 0 0
Lord Castlereagh	25 0 0
Collected at consecration and opening services	24 7 8
Walter Morrison Esq	20 0 0
The Rev.George Brown, Redmarshall	10 0 0
The Rev.J.Cartwright, Durham	10 0 0
Anthony Wilkinson Esq, Sheraton	10 0 0
Proceeds of Public Concert, June 23rd 1879	9 10 1
Offerings at laying of Memorial Stone	7 14 6
Monthly Offertories in Mission Hall 1876–1880	18 7 10
Dividends and Profit on sale of £500 NER Stock	86 14 1
Interest of money in bank	18 12 8

There were many more subscriptions ranging from £5 to 12s.6d. giving a total of £2,822

Expenditure	£. s. d.
Messrs. Boyd and Harewood, Contractors	2217 14 10
Messrs. Alexander and Henman, Architects	149 3 0
Boundary wall to enclose church	62 3 10½
Bell with fittings complete	42 5 0
Cost of site. 1 1/2 acres. Nominal sum of	50 0 0

Legal expenses	34 8 6
Levelling, Road making and planting churchyard with trees	36 12 3
Vestry furniture and hassocks for church	35 3 4
Messrs. Jones and Willis for lamps and fittings	35 7 10
Communion Plate. Silver	32 8 0
Consecration fees. Church and burying ground	22 12 0
Heating apparatus	11 15 8
Gates and gateposts. Complete	35 2 11
Draining of churchyard. 6ft.deep	14 17 6
Printing and Bill Posting	5 7 0
Advertising	1 18 3
Forms of consecration	1 10 0
Railway carriage of various boxes and parcels	1 19 0
Plan of churchyard	18 0
Coal	12 9

Total £2,822 0 2 1/2

APPENDIX 9

Origin of the name Stillington

The name of Stillington has been derived from the original name of Styfel(a)'S Ingtun.

Styfel was the name of a person, and ingtun was the word originally used to describe a farm.

Over the years the name became distorted and the following sequence shows how the name periodically changed to become Stillington.

Original name. Styfel(a)'S Ingtun.

In the Domesday Book of 1086 the name had become Stivelinctun

In 1176 the Pipe Roll Society described the name as Stivelinton

In 1242 the Pipe Roll Society changed the name to Stivil(l)ington

The Yorkshire Lay Society retained this name in 1301.

In 1280 and 1286 The Registers of the Archbishops of York, or the Ebor et Passim, Testamentom Eboracensia, quoted the name as, Sti-, Styvelington.

In 1351 the Callender of Entries of the Papal Register stated the name as Stillyngton.

This name was retained in W Baildon's Monastic Notes of 1442.

Since that date the final derivation has taken place resulting in the present place name of **Stillington**.

APPENDIX 10

Local Entrepreneurs

During the years immediately following the war, several young village men decided to escape from the normal tradition of working for a major employer by starting their own businesses. All of these local entrepreneurs were highly successful in the businesses they had chosen to follow and are to be much admired for the energy, skill and resilience they applied in attaining this success. Some brief details of them are given in the following text.

Some of Norman Argyle's early fleet of wagons

Norman Argyle When Norman was demobbed from the army he vowed that he would make a living working for himself, and had no intention of being employed by anyone else. He commenced by modernising his mother's fish shop and helping to manage it whilst also taking on the role of the local Turf Accountant. The opportunity arose for him to purchase a lorry at a very reasonable price and he used this to obtain various haulage contracts around the village. The success of these contracts led him to expand and, within a few years, he had developed into a major haulage company with a fleet of modern wagons and some earth-moving equipment. He acquired long-term contracts with the North Eastern Iron Refinery but also had a great deal of other work throughout the country and would deliver anything anywhere. He always operated from his base in Stillington and remained highly

Typical advert for Alan Argyle's betting shop

successful until he retired when he passed the business on to his sons Victor and Graham. Norman had previously transferred the Turf Accountant business to his cousin **Alan Argyle** who, when off-course betting became legal in 1960, moved into a betting shop that he ran with success until he retired.

George Pipe worked as an inspector for the Wilkinson Bus Company that ran a bus service between the Trimdons and Stockton. Meanwhile **Jack Scurr** was still managing the bus service from Stillington to Stockton but he was ready to retire and, around 1948 George teamed up with Mr Reg Thompson from Sedgefield to take over Scurr's Bus Company. George and Reg continued to provide the service from Stillington to Stockton but also organised tours throughout Britain and Europe. They became a nationally known company with a fine fleet of buses, including executive class for their European excursions. George and Reg continued in this business with great success until they they were ready for retirement and sold out to Trimdon Motor Services.

Pat Carroll who had married local girl Stella Smith and played football for Stillington St John's, worked as a driver for a local company involved in the transportation of sand and gravel. Pat decided that if the person who owned this company could make money from this business, so could he. Consequently he bought himself a wagon, started hauling sand and gravel and became so successful that he had to expand his capability. Gradually he became probably the biggest sand and gravel haulier in the district, and built up an impressive fleet of modern wagons

Part of Pat Carroll's fleet of wagons at his Stockton depot.

and other equipment. Unlike Norman Argyle, who would transport almost anything and kept his base at Stillington, Pat concentrated most of his business on the transportation of sand and gravel and eventually moved his depot to Stockton, from where he continued with infinite success until he retired. One of Pat's last contracts was the supply of all the sand, gravel and hardcore for Middlesbrough Football Club's new stadium and pitch at the Riverside

Reg Moore Reg's father, Dick, was a jobbing builder who worked locally and when Reg was demobbed from the army after the war, he and a friend named Cartwright, joined together to form a small building contractors named Moore & Cartwright. The company became highly successful, and Moore and Cartwright was soon the major building contractor in the area, building many council and private housing estates as well as landscaping the golf course at Billingham. When Reg retired from Moore and Cartwright, he formed a small company of his own and built an executive estate on the outskirts of Wolviston and also extended the new workingmen's club at Stillington. From a small beginning, Reg reached the pinnacle of success in the building trade with success coming so quickly he was still living in a council house in Stillington when he became the owner of a Rolls Royce car that he had to park outside the house.

Jackie Atkinson returned home after the war and started work with Edward James, who had established a scrap metal company at Stillington. Jack's flair for the profession soon led him to start up on his own at a site in Boathouse Lane Stockton (*site of the Stockton Darlington railway terminus*), that he

A scrap loco being unloaded at Jack's scrap yard.

transformed into a very successful scrap metal business. As well as being a shrewd 'scrap metal' merchant, Jack became known as the highest authority in assessing the value of large industrial electrical equipment such as motors, turbines and generators. The scrap value of such equipment could be tens of thousands of pounds with the removal from their site being very costly and highly specialised. Major companies would employ Jack to dispose of their generating systems, because of his skill in assessing the value of the redundant equipment and his expert ability to remove them. For his part, Jack would make his money by selling the copper for recycling. Jack also became well known in the pony trotting circles and owned several championship 'trotting' horses.

Pictures of one of Jack's trotting horses and some of the trophies he had won

APPENDIX 11
Summary of local government development

Well into the 19th century those areas which were not Boroughs were governed by a Parish Vestry. The origin of the vestry was the calling together of parishioners to discuss church business and it was basically an ecclesiastical organisation.

The 1601 Poor Law made the Overseers of the Poor, appointed by the Vestry, responsible for the Local Poor Law administration. Later acts made the Vestry itself responsible.

Vestry's, working in partnership with Justices of the Peace, became outmoded and overworked as parishes grew in size, so some became an Open Vestry which meant most ratepayers could attend the meetings. There was no procedure for a small body to be elected to administer, and consequently mobs and cliques took over, and the weaker residents were totally ignored and exploited.

The alternative to the Open Vestry was the Closed Vestry which generally comprised the larger land owners and occupiers of the area. They were self-perpetuating bodies who were under no control or audit and were thus able to administer in any way they desired, which ultimately led to a great deal of unfairness and corruption within the parish.

Neither the Open or Closed vestry was a satisfactory means of governing the parish.

The Vestry's Act of 1818 sought to control the Open Vestry and qualified the voting rights of the parishioners. These were assessed as follows:

If you possessed £150 or over you were allowed 6 votes, going down pro rata to 1 vote for under £50. This gave greater domination to the wealthy in the hope of weakening the power of the bullies.

The Poor Relief Act 1819 enabled the Open Vestry to appoint a representative vestry. Those elected however had to be substantial householders or occupiers, which still gave the power to the wealthy.

In 1844 the Poor Law Amendment Act made 6 votes permissible to persons possessing £250, with those with £50 allowed 1 vote (This would not have a great effect on the representation of the poor).

Vestry's Act 1831 A minor breakthrough for democracy. It provided for the election of a Select Vestry and introduced the provision for a Secret Ballot if this was requested by 5 ratepayers.

All parishioners who had paid rates for one year could cast 1 vote for each vacancy.

It should be noted that the owners of rented properties usually paid the rates themselves and thereby the voting rights of the majority was still very limited.

Local Elections Act 1845 This act extended the Franchise (Right to Vote) in Local Government elections to all those registered for Parliamentary elections.

The Guardians of the Poor of the Stockton Union

The Guardians of the Poor of the Stockton Union was formed to oversee the general governing of the district around Stockton, similar to a vestry but covering a whole district. Membership of the Guardians comprised local dignitaries such as landowners, wealthy farmers, doctors, vicars and solicitors. There was a hard-core of men representing Stockton, supplemented by at least one member from each of the Parochial Committees in the area which included Whitton, Redmarshall, Carlton, Thorpe and Wolviston.

The Parochial Committee representing Whitton was: Clark Nesom, J Hunton (also a member of the Carlton Parochial Committee), J Blenkinsop, J Thompson, J Brownless, R Foster and D Parsons, all of whom were farmers from in and around Whitton with no representative from the Village of the Carlton Ironworks.

Clark Nesom and J Hunton were both active and influential members of the Guardians being elected to serve on several committees.

In 1872 the Guardians also began acting as the Rural Sanitary Authority of the Stockton Union and from this juncture, they took on the responsibility of trying to ensure that all buildings in their district were fit for habitation and that adequate drains and sewers were installed. They employed an Inspector of Nuisances who would scour the district for any nuisance and report back to the Rural Sanitary Authority who had the power to order the nuisance to be abated. They employed a Medical Officer of Health to oversee all health hazards within the district and advise on action to be taken during epidemics

They also formed a planning committee, comprised of all the Guardians, to whom all plans for new buildings or extensions had to be submitted for adherence to local by-laws and the Guardians approval.

The formation of this new authority meant that the directors of the Ironworks now had to submit the plans of any new houses they were to build in the Village of the Carlton Ironworks to the Rural Sanitary Authority of the Stockton Union, and be prepared for the inspection of their houses by the Inspector of Nuisances and abide by his decisions on drainage and sanitation. The inhabitants of the Village of the Carlton Ironworks were generally unaffected by these new regulations, because their lives were controlled wholly by the managers and directors of the Ironworks, who not only provided them with work but also owned and allotted the houses in which they lived.

Taking into consideration the conditions of the period, the Company treated their work force and their families in a fair and reasonable manner, providing them with decent houses to live in and supplying all necessary amenities as quickly as possible, including shops, a workingmen's club, a hotel and schools.

The above situation prevailed until the government passed the Local Government Act of 1894, which brought a greater chance of democracy to the less wealthy inhabitants of the parishes and towns throughout the country. This was achieved by replacing organisations such as the Guardians with Borough and Rural District Councils, and the Parochial Committees with Parish Councils, and ordering that all Local Government should be the subject of elections.

The following text details how the Local Government Act of 1894 affected the district around Stockton, and brought local government to the people living in the Village of the Carlton Ironworks.

During the enforcement of the Local Government Act of 1894 the following instruction was received by the Board of Guardians from Durham County Council who were acting on behalf of the government.

1894 – July   COUNTY COUNCIL ORDERS No 11
THE STOCKTON UNION COUNTY PALATINE OF DURHAM
LOCAL GOVERNMENT ACT 1894

At a meeting of the Local Government Committee of the County Council of Durham, (to which committee all the powers under the above act have been duly delegated), held at Shire Hall, Durham on Thursday 28th June 1894. Present from the Stockton Union was J Horsley who was in the chair.

It was ordered as follows: Whereas the Poor Law Union of Stockton is wholly situate within the administrative County of Durham and comprises parishes and townships named in the schedule hitherto.

And Whereas the Board of Guardians for the said Union have applied to the County Council to provide for the simultaneous retirement of the whole Board of Guardians the County Council consider it expedient that such provision should be made.

Now therefore in pursuance of the powers given by the Local Government Act 1894 it is hereby ordered as follows:

1   There shall be Sixteen guardians elected for the Parish or Township of Stockton in the said Union.
2   The number of Rural District Councillors for each of the parishes or townships mentioned in the schedule hereunder written shall be the number set opposite the name of that parish or township.
3   The Rural District and other Guardians to be elected in pursuance of this order shall retire together on the 15th of April 1898 and in every third year thereafter.

4   The number of Parish Councillors to be elected for each of the parishes or townships mentioned in the schedule shall be the number set opposite the name of that parish or township.
5   This order shall come into operation on the appointed day as defined by section 84 of the said act but for all purposes connected with the preparation of lists of electors the completion of the register of electors and first elections it shall come into operation from the date hereof.

Name of Parish	No. of Guardians	No. of Rural District Councillors	No. of Parish Councillors
Aislaby		1	none
Billingham		3	11
Carlton		1	none
Cowpen Bewley		2	9
Eaglescliffe		1	7
Elton		1	none
Hartburn East		1	7
Longnewton		1	None
Newsham		1	none
Newton Bewley		1	none
Norton		3	11
Preston On Tees		1	none
Redmarshall		1	none
Stockton	16	none	none
Thorpe And Grindon		1	7
Whitton		1	9
Wolviston		1	7

And in pursuance of the aforementioned powers it is hereby further ordered that the seal of the council be affixed to this order

John Horsley Chairman

Sealed pursuant of above order Ralph Swiney Clerk of the Durham County Council 1894 December 12th

The aforementioned instruction led to the final meeting of the Rural Sanitary Authority held in the Board Room, Nelson Terrace, Stockton on Tees.

Present were: W J Parkin, Chairman W C Fidler, J Knowle, F W Smith, A Liverseed, J W Page, A Dobson, M Fowler, R C Denton, R Noddings, R Gregg.

It also resulted in the name of the authority being changed to the Stockton Rural District Council, which was elected on the 17th December 1894 and came into office 28th December 1894.

All parishes under the new authority held 'elections' for Parish Councillors and the appropriate number of County Councillors were also chosen to serve on the Rural District Council. (As per schedule).

Officers elected were J W Page Chairman, W T Parkin Vice Chairman.

Meetings were to take place at the Board Room on alternate Wednesdays at 10 30 am.

Note: An analysis of the names attending the meetings highlights the fact that all of the persons involved with the Sanitary Authority were now members of Stockton Rural District Council.

1894 Results of elections for Rural District Councillors affecting local parishes

Parish	Name of Candidates	Abode	No. of votes cast	Name of person elected
Whitton	Clark Nesom (only candidate)	Whitton	None	Clark Nesom
Carlton	William Hunton (only candidate)	Greystones, Carlton	None	William Hunton
Redmarshall	Thomas Bell (only candidate)	Redmarshall	None	Thomas Bell

Votes were recorded in the larger parishes such as Billingham and Norton where there was more candidates than places scheduled.

1898 April – Elections for Stockton Rural District Councillors from local parishes

Parish	Candidates	Address	Elected
Carlton	William Knowles Hunton (only candidate)	Greystones, Carlton	W K Hunton
Redmarshall	Thomas Bell (only candidate)	Oxbridge	Thos Bell
Whitton	Thomas Kirk jnr 79 votes	Mount Pleasant Village of the Carlton Ironworks	Thomas Kirk jnr
	Clark Nesom 57 votes	Whitton	

Clark Nesom lost his place on the Rural District Council after many years as a member of the Guardians and a councillor for the last three years.

Local Elections Act 1918 This act established a common Franchise for County Councils, Boroughs, Parishes and Urban District Councils.

Men   Six months occupancy of premises or land within the area.

Women As for men, or else the wife of a man qualified to vote, if she was over 30.

Representation of the Peoples Act 1928.
Women over 21 were allowed to vote at Local Elections.
Note: Results of 1894 Parish Council elections are given in text for that year.

MUNICIPAL CORPORATIONS

Municipal Corporations Act 1835

The reform of Local Government representation in Boroughs was long overdue and the New Franchise conditions laid down in this act were generally those of the 1832 act. The Franchise was extended to each male person over 21 who occupied, as owner or tenant, any house or place of business; if he had occupied the premises for 2½ years; had paid rates; or had lived within seven miles of the Borough for the previous six months.

Those qualified for election were:
(a) In towns, divided into 4 or more wards, owning estate or property worth £1000, or occupying land assessed at £30 or more per annum.
(b) Elsewhere, possessing estate or property worth £500 or occupying land assessed at £15 or more

Voting was by signed voting papers. A tenant paying his rates via a landlord was not necessarily given the right to vote. Usually he had to apply for his name to be substituted for that of his landlord to obtain the vote.

The voting rights of a tenant in this situation was the subject of a protracted legal debate.

The Small Tenements Rating Act 1850 rated owners rather than occupiers of property at less than £6 per annum.

The Representation of Peoples Act 1867 reversed this, making voting for the tenant easier but collection of rates harder, and the Assessed Rates Act of 1869 restored the 1850 position although updating the Rateable Value qualification.

SCHOOL BOARDS

The Education Act 1870 allowed for the election of School Boards.
All ratepayers had one vote each for each vacancy and could use all votes on one candidate.

APPENDIX 12

Photographs of Groups and Events relating to the Village of Stillington between c. 1900 and 1960

Group of second generation villagers c. 1912

Second-generation villagers from the Village of the Carlton Ironworks. They would have cycled from home to Seaton to enjoy a Sunday afternoon by the sea.

Those known (*Standing*): William Plant; Violet Butcher (m. Albert Pinch); Lizzie ?; Bob Robinson (these two married); Boxer Hardy. (*Sitting*): Mattie Plant; Florrie Hardy; Lizzie Plant (Maureen Fox's grandmother); Lizzie Whitewell (m. Geo.Stephenson); (*On grass*): Harold Britton; Harry Argyle (m. Florrie Hardy); Jack Harper; Arthur Butler.

The musical Brittons

Some of the Britton family when they lived at 11 Lowson Street. They were all musical and later formed a band with other villagers, which travelled the area playing at dances and other functions.

(*Standing*): Teddy b. 1867; Arthur b. 1879; Thomas b.1870; William b. 1877; (*Sitting*): Ernest b. 1886; Frederick b. 1884.

The funeral of 'Indi' Allan

'Indi' Allan was a professional speedway rider who was killed on the track at Manchester in 1931. Photograph shows the cortege preparing to leave his parent's home at 16 West Street. The family wreath was in the shape of a motor cycle.

Mr Edwin and Mrs Mary Butler outside their home c. 1915
Cyril Butler's grandparents, who lived at 14 West Street for many years, raised twelve children and often looked after two lodgers in unison. One of their sons, Stanley (Cyril's father), ran the Post Office for many years.

Sports Day organised by the Boy Scouts 1913
The women of the Village of the Carlton Ironworks took advantage of the Fancy Dress Parade to enhance their Vote for Women campaign.

Stillington Band 1916

Those known (*Standing*): Harry Harper (m. Ethel Horner); Walter Britton (Arthur's son); Lou Dixon; Billy Britton, jnr; Tom Harper; Bob Carlton; (*Sitting*): Teddy Britton (Billy's son); Joe Parry (drowned in Billingham beck); Walter Harper; Arthur Britton, Leader; Harold Britton (Arthur's son); Billy Dixon (Lou's son); Billy Harper (m. Doris Walkington); Arthur Britton, jnr.

The band was renowned throughout the district for their musical ability and smart presentation. Photograph loaned by Mrs Henderson who lived at Spennymoor but was an avid follower of the band when they played at dances.

Stillington St John's Choir c 1921

(*Back row*): • Harry Dixon; Jack Cole; Joe Carter; Francis Flint; Arthur Johnson; (*Middle row*): Billy Fenwick; • Rene Stephenson; Dot Hindley; • • Ella Callender; Anne Waring; Olive Dixon; Sybil Waring; Tom Swales; • Chandler; Harold Britton; (*Sitting*): May Moore; Eva Moore; Anne Taylor; Rev. Bury; Jessie Chandler; • Taylor; Rene Stephenson; Doris Stephenson; (*Squatting*): • • Syd Britton; Arthur Britton; • Roy Ross.

• *not known*

Stillington St John's Choir c 1926
(*Rear*): Les Stibbart; Norman Young; Joe Carter; Francis Flint; Billy Fenwick; Tom Swales; (*3rd row*): Arthur Stewart; Ella Callender; Amy Dawson; John G Dawson; Doris Newcomb; Rene Stephenson; Margaret Taylor; Mr Corner; (*2nd row*): Doris Stephenson; Anne Egerton; Loui Hodgson; Ella Cook; Evan Morris Young; Freda Body; Lily Hindley; Sybil Waring; Nellie Daniels; (*front*): George Beadle; Walter Beadle; Jimmy Hudson; Les Harper; Hoofa Argyle; Ali Hodgson; Tom Pinch; Albert Oskins; Ernie Clayton.

Sunday School teachers c. 1928
(*Rear*): Billy Fenwick; (*Middle*): Roy Ross; Eva Oskins; Freda Boddy; (*Front*): May Dawson; John G Dawson; Nellie Daniels.

Nellie Daniels
Organist and choir mistress at St John's Church, Stillington. (Organist throughout the tenure of seven vicars).

(*L–R*): Mary Wills; Dolly Snowball; Gladys Wrigby; Gladys Wright; Betty Stephenson; Eva Snowball; Nellie Daniels. (*Sitting behind*): Geo. Pipe; Gin Deacon.

John G Dawson (chorister)
St John's Stillington, 1888–1934;
Muggleswick Church, 1934–1937;
St John's Castleside, 1937–1954;
All Saints Ferriby, 1954–1958.

Mr Chandler c. 1922
Chorister at St John's and also the first village park keeper. The photograph was probably taken in the early years of the park's development.

Stillington Ladies Cricket Team c. 1928

Rene Stephenson; Mary Stephenson; Hilda Argyle; Maisie Wells; Eva Snowball; Alice Nevison; Maude Hunt; Amy Dawson; Laly Wills; Rene Plant and Cecelia Ivam

GROUPS AND EVENTS RELATING TO THE VILLAGE OF STILLINGTON

Stillington choir on day's outing c. 1927
(*Rear*): Dot Swales; Joe Carter; Sybil Waring; Roy Ross; Georgina Dawson; Annie Fenny; Thomas Swales; (*Front*): Amy Dawson; Arthur Newcombe; Ethel Wheatley; Nellie Daniels; Leslie Stibbart.

Stillington Choir 1943
Photograph taken on vicarage lawn – note the criss-crossed tape on vicarage windows.
(*Rear*): Audrey Collins; Mary Bell?; Rev. Lockyer; Mrs Poole; Audrey Smithson; (*4th row*) Doris Gilbert; Minnie Milton; Sybil Horner; (*3rd row*) Doreen Scott; Dot and Joyce Featherstone; Jenny Butler; Mary Hodgson; (*2nd row*) Hilda Kennedy; Norma Bell; ? Mould; (*Front*) Dave Kennedy; Bob Tingle; Harry Harper; Ron Ayther; Bert Wyeth.

Stillington Choir outing to Saltburn c. 1939
(*Rear*): Betty Minto; Gladys Warner; Mrs Lockey; Alice Tuffs; Laura Harper; Nellie Daniels; Polly Poole; (*Middle*): Vera Wells; Margaret Johnson; Margery Whitewell; Margaret Carr; (*Front*): Beatrice Wells; Stan, Doris and Kenneth Johnstone; Gilbert Poole; John Lockey; Harry Wells; Freddy Bell; Audrey Collins.

Day Trip to Redcar c. 1932
Probably the 'once a year trip' organised by the Sunday School when most of the village would catch the special train to Redcar for their day at the seaside.

(*Rear*): Alec Swales; Mrs Townsend; John Swales; Reg Cole; (*3rd row*): Maud Swales; Lizzie Breckon; Susan Hart; Elsie Horner; (*Sitting, 3rd row*): Gran Swales; Amy Butler *nee* Cole; Mrs Cole; Sally Waites *nee* Harper: (*Front*): Betty Townsend; Tom Swales; Sybil Horner; Doris Horner; Dot Heignley *nee* Swales.

GROUPS AND EVENTS RELATING TO THE VILLAGE OF STILLINGTON

The smart set. Redcar c. 1932
(*Rear*): Mrs Lil Swales (Alec's wife); Elsie Horner *nee* Cole; (*Front*): Mrs Townsend; Doris Horner *nee* Cole.

H.M. King George V's Silver Jubilee celebrations. 1935
The Silver Jubilee celebrations included a Sports Day and these villagers dressed up as a King and Queen plus entourage, and went to Redmarshall to catch the train back to Stillington, where they were met by a reception committee and taken around the village on Freddie McWilliams' horse and cart, decorated for the occasion. The tour of the village ended at the Cricket Field, where the sports were held, and the 'king' would open proceedings by cutting the tape fastened across the gate of the field. Caravans and the roundabout belonging to Culine's Fair can be seen in the Cricket Field. The photograph was taken as the 'King and Queen' walked from the station.
King – Jim Swales; Queen – Jimmy McWilliams; Frank Sherwood; Court Jester – unknown.

Fancy dress competitors

Mrs Johnson (Bob Johnson's mother); Greta Johnson *nee* Lonsdale; Annie Scott *nee* Jackson; Cissy Argyle.

Another function for the 'King and Queen' to attend

Jim Swales and Jim McWilliams in action again during a village celebration. All villagers joined in wholeheartedly at sports days and other events to ensure a good time was had by all.

Bert Swales c. 1936

Bert, shown in his Ba-zoo-ka band uniform, lived in the village all his life and took an active part in all events. The Ba-zoo-ka band was in attendance at all local events and functions. The photograph was taken at the bottom of big Lowson Street where Bert lived. The little school is centre picture with a shed in front of the school wall.

The Ba-zoo-ka band c. 1936

This band comprised mainly unemployed villagers, who organised themselves to go around the district and play for charity. The photograph was taken outside the Smith's Arms at Carlton and the banner denotes the charity of the day, which would appear to be a hospital. The leader was Mr O'Donnell, who would march at the head of the band as they paraded through local villages.

(Rear): Bob Watts; Victor Gent; Billy Dixon; (3rd row): Hugh Gaffney; Jim Swales; Bert Swales; Joe O'Donnell; unknown; Stewart Donaghy; Bob Stephenson; Nelson Lonsdale; Arthur Hardy; *(2nd row)*: Alec Swales; Nellie Cook; Wally Allen; Billy Gaffney; Billy Lonsdale; George Jackson; Arthur Jacques; Norman Fletcher; Joe O'Donnell; Harrison Wills; Fred Swales; *(Front)*: Mr O'Donnell; Gwen Stephenson; Mary Collaine; Olive Goodman; Vera Watts; Mary Wills; Ethel Wills; Lizzie O'Donnell; Edwin Hopps; unknown lady; Charlie Williams, with collection box.

Stillington Women's Institute – participants in play c. 1935

(*Rear*): Lily Butler, Harry Butler's wife; Marion Lawson, m. Jack Bell; Elsie Cole; Mrs Lynn *nee* Rowley; Violet Pinch *nee* Butcher; Mrs Milton, mother of Reg, Hilda and Minnie; Kate Allison; Mrs Smith, Bobby Smith's wife; Ethel Horner, m. Tom Harper; Kate Wheighell; Mrs Douglas, vicar's wife; (*3rd row*): Rye Warner *nee* Stewart, Billy's mother; Polly Hunt/Poole *nee* Cowans; Maude Allison m. Trotter; Mrs Lawson; Mrs Beadle, mother of George & Walter; Amy Cole, m. Stan Butler; Mrs Swales, Alec's mother; Jessie Egerton; Mrs Gilbert, wife of Albert Gilbert; Mrs Plant, mother of Lizzie who married Mr Fox; (*2nd row*): Hannah Kennedy; Lizzie Butler, Arthur's wife; Sarah Hart *nee* Egerton; Mrs Chandler, Sonny Hindley's aunt; Mrs Townsend, Charlie's wife; Doris Cole, m. 'Snack' Horner; Nellie Cook, Frank & Doreen's mother; Mrs Donaghy, mother of Stuart, George, Charlotte & Les; Mary Harper *nee* Barr; (front): Mary Butler, Lizzie's daughter; Doris Pipe, m. Tom Scurr; Charlotte Donaghy, m. George Dilks; Stella Smith, Bobby Smith's daughter, m. Paddy Carroll.

Freddy Bell (*left*) and Bob Robinson with one of Mr Robinson's cart horses, near Whitton Farm in 1926.

Below
Village wedding photograph 1936
This photograph typified the weddings which took place in Stillington in the 1930s when the majority of men were unemployed and could not afford a big expensive wedding or a honeymoon. A reception would probably be arranged in the Cassidi Hall, where friends would prepare tea and sandwiches for the guests. A dance in the evening may also be arranged, that the whole village was welcome to attend.

This particular wedding is of John Harrison Wills of 10 Lowson Street and Maud Hunt of 16 Lowson Street, who are the couple on the right of picture. The bride's mother Polly Poole (remarried), is on extreme left, the bridesmaid is Mary Wills, the groom's sister. Other in the photograph include Lal Wills, behind the bride, Mrs Harper the bride's auntie and Gilbert Poole, the bride's stepfather.

Village wedding custom
During the wedding ceremony villagers would tie the church gates together with string, and the wedding party had to throw money to the children waiting at the gate, before being allowed to leave the churchyard.

Pensioners' Outing June 1939
Pensioners assembled at the Stores' Corner ready to board Scurr's buses for their annual day trip, probably to the seaside. The slag tip on the right dominates the background, with the little tip on the left, the Blacking Mill just visible in the centre above the little tip. Not all the pensioners have been identified, but they include:

(*Back row*): Mr Fordham – flat cap; Jack Lund – right of lamp post; Jack Whitelaw – bowler hat; Mr Snowball – flat whitecap; 2 unknown; Mr Beadle – between buses wearing trilby; Jack Glass – half facial view, wearing trilby; Lil Swales – peeping over top; Mrs Trotter; (*middle row*): Mrs Fletcher – left of lamppost; Mrs Allan, Wally's mother, – right of lamppost; Les Harper – flat cap almost hidden; Mrs Peakman; Mr Goodman – trilby & moustache; Mr Colbeck – pipe & flat cap; Mrs Milton; Elsie Cole; (*front*): Mr & Mrs Allison; Mr & Mrs Clayton, Tommy's grandparents; Mrs Hudson – with bag; Loui Hodson; Mrs Prest; unknown; Mr & Mrs Johnson – flat cap & beard; Mr Phillips – bowler hat, Mrs Newcombe; Mr Bean; Mrs Barr – holding straw bag; Mrs Stockdale; Ketula Britton; Mr Henderson – cap and moustache; Doris Cole; Mrs Beadle.

Old Folks Christmas Party held in the Function Room of the Royal Hotel c 1938
(*Rear*): Unknown; Mr Donaghy; Mrs Lonsdale; Mrs Pannet; unknown; Mr Pannet; Mr Stewart; 'Ice' Wills; Mr Gent; Mrs Peacock; Jack Glass; George Lowes; Jack Berry; Mrs Stibbard; (*5th row*): unknown; Mrs Moore; Mrs Plant; Mrs Britton; unknown; Bob Bell; (*4th row*): unknown; Mr Snowball; Mr Tingay; Billy Waites; Geo. H Wills; Ada Berry; Mrs Prest: Mrs Hardy; Mrs Goodman; Mrs Fletcher; Mrs Bell; unknown; Sally Waites; Gran Swales; (*3rd row*): Mrs Lowes; Mrs Hodgson; Mrs Gilchrist; Mrs Cole; (*2nd row*): Mrs Hudson; Mrs Alice Wills; Mrs Stockdale; Mr Butcher; Mr O'Donnell; (*front*): Jack Lund; Mrs Wills; unknown; Larry Oskins; Joe Henderson; Jos. Lonsdale (senior).

Villagers' day out at the seaside c. 1938
Mothers enjoying a drink, while the children have a donkey ride. The adults are Mrs Smith, Ketruna Britton and Mrs Butler.

Group of ladies enjoying a weekend in Blackpool c. 1938
Organised trips to Blackpool were a regular feature of village life in the 1950s, but this was unusual in the late 1930s, when Stillington was in the grip of almost total unemployment and poverty. These ladies must have contributed weekly towards the necessary funding to enable them to make the trip and enjoy a weekend of freedom from the usual household chores.

(*l.to r.*) Ethel Prest; Gran Prest – mother of Mary & Ethel; Mary Garrity *nee* Prest; Annie Scott *nee* Jackson; Hilda Prest, m. John Prest.

Stillington and Fishburn Schoolboys – a week's holiday at Newbiggin on Sea c. 1938
(*Rear*): Mr Summers, teacher; 6 unknown; Billy Barr; Freddy Bell; (3rd row): Tom Britton; 7 unknown; Ron Freeman; Jimmy Whitwell; Bert Clayton; (*2nd row*): 2 unknown; Alan Argyle; 2 unknown; Ronnie Norman; Jimmy Pannett; unknown; Thomas Redfern; John Scott; (*front*): Stan Johnstone; Harry Wells; 2 unknown.

Jack Smith c. 1940
Jack Smith (better known as Bobby Smith) was the local policeman at Stillington from 1925 to 1945. Photograph taken outside his house in New West Street.

Photograph taken c. 1946 shows Jack Smith's son, Ossie, with Walter Featherstone, just inside the Cricket Field, with New West Street houses in the background.

Women's Institute outing c. 1946
(Rear):Bus driver; unknown; Mrs Trotter; Mrs Carr; *(3rd row)*: Mrs Durham; Nellie Cooke; Mrs Smith; Mrs Mortimer; Mrs Beadle; *(2nd row)*: Mrs Herol; Mrs Dilks; Elsie Cole; Sally Waites; Mrs Lavelle; Mrs Townsend; *(front)*: Charlotte Donaghy; Doris Horner; Nan Hethrington.

Village girls enjoying a frolic in the hayfield near Chapel Bank c. 1946
Dorothy Sherwood; Stella Smith; Bessie Stewart; Mary Stewart; Bessie Bell in foreground.

Same girls in a more subdued mood
Bessie Bell; Mary Stewart; Bessie Stewart; Stella Smith; Dorothy Sherwood.

Pensioners enjoying a day's outing c. 1946

Joe Henderson; Billy Waites; Harrison (Ice) Wills (Hilda Kennedy's grandad); George H Wills (Eva Jacques' granddad); Bob Scott; Jack Goldie.

Reg Moore and Stella Smith in the park at Stillington. 1946

This photograph was taken just after the war, before both Reg and Stella became highly successful in business. Reg, with his army pal Cartwright, formed the building company, Moore & Cartwright, and became major contractors in the area, building many council and private houses, as well as creating Billingham Golf course. Stella married Pat Caroll and assisted him in creating one of the most successful haulage companies in the district, ending up with a large fleet of lorries.

Village lads in the park on a Sunday afternoon 1946

As football was not allowed on a Sunday and 'best' clothes had to be worn, rougher activities had to be abandoned and time was spent in the park. This group of lads are pictured on the seat near the entrance to the new road. (*From left*): George Longbottom; Terry Wells; Brian Simpson; John Hodgson; Dick Cutler; Wally Billington's father-in-law; Don Tuffs.

Stillington Women's British Legion c. 1946
(*Rear*): Lil Mortimer, sec.; Mrs Marshall; Rose Savage; Mrs Beadle; (*middle*): Mrs Savage; Liza Poxon; Mrs Wood; Mrs Gilchrist; Mrs Fox; Charlotte Dilks; Mrs Gaffney; (*front*): Mrs Wilkinson; Gran Swales; Flossie Wills; Sally Waites; Nan Hethrington; Mrs Watts.

Group of Lowson Street residents c. 1946
Photograph taken in the Lowson Street school yard with the slag heap as the back-drop. (*Rear*): John Swales; Joyce Durham; Eva Wilkinson; Len Jackson; Vera Simpson; unknown; Mrs Ali Hodgson with Jennifer; (*middle row*); Mary Millan; Miss Blair; Lil Jackson; Polly Poole; Rene Donaghy; Mrs Jack Bell; (*front*): Doris Gudgeon; Gladys Littler; Mary Hardy; Maude Swales; Doreen Swales with Peter.

Women's Institute outing c. 1946

(Rear): Mrs Glass; Linda Bell; Mrs Townsend; *(3rd row)*: Nan Ethrington; Mrs Poole; Elsie Horner; Kitty Pipe; Mrs Butler; Mrs Mortimer; Mrs Carr; Mrs Trotter; *(2nd row)*: Mrs Wilkinson; Mrs Robinson; Charlotte Donaghy; Mrs Savage; Lil Swales; Mrs Wood; Mrs Clayton; Gran Swales; Mrs Gaffney; Greta Johnson; *(front)* Mrs Dilks; Mrs Freeman; Sally Waites; Doris Horner; Mrs Artley; Mrs Jacques; Mrs Beadle; Lizzie Butler.

A small group of Stillite workers c. 1946
(*Rear*): Edna Harper; Jessie Parnaby; Dot Featherstone; Dot Turner; Betty Wales; (*middle*): Brenda Ferguson; Eva Trotter; Marian Davies; Muriel Henderson; Pam Whitewell; Elsie Jacques; (*front*): Irene Storey.

Village children on the big roller in the cricket field. 1947
The photograph shows the end of New West Street. The big roller was made at the Ironworks around 1925 when the men of the village were given permission by Dorman Long to create a cricket pitch in what had been a field ridged with an ancient agricultural drainage system.

(*Rear*): George Longbottom; Brian Simpson; Cliff Artley; Jimmy Clayton; Jean Lennon; (*3rd row*): Lena Lonsdale; Mabel Moore; Wilf Berry; Rita Argyle; Betty Wales; (*2nd row*): Don Tuffs; Mr Walker; Olive Hodgson; Nancy Jobling; (front): Billy Fletcher; Gladys Farley; Jean Cutler. (Keith Britton is peeping round the left of the roller.

Stillington Pensioners' day out c. 1946

Pensioners assembled on the steps of Isa Parry's shop in Morrison Terrace before boarding their special bus for their day's outing. On the extreme right of the picture Cyril Butler is on the steps of his father's newsagent shop. *(Rear)*: Mr Pannett; Mr Anderson; Cyril Butler; *(4th row)*: Mrs Prest; Mrs Hardy; Mrs Britton; Matt Taylor; Lizzie Wills; Bill Waites; Mrs Wood; Mrs Herrol; *(3rd row)*: George Lowes; Mrs Plant; Mrs Wyeth; Mr Arksey; Mrs Weighell; Mrs Beadle; Nan Trotter; *(2nd row)*: Lil Jackson; Mrs S Smith; Mrs Stephenson; Polly Bell; Mrs Pinch; Gran Swales; Lil Mortimer; *(1st row)*: Billy Wells; Alec Stewart; Jack Glass and wife; Mrs Lowes; Mrs Wells; Mrs Glass; Phoebe Hodgson; Sally Waites; Mrs Peacock; Mrs Horner; Mrs Gaffney; (front): Mrs Hart.

Pensioners outing c. 1947

Photograph taken in Morrison Terrace with the tip on the left hand side. The driver of the bus appears to be John Whitehead, with Lily Jackson sitting in the front seat and Rene Donaghy at the fourth window from the front. The building sporting the sign of the Cooperative Stores was built by the Ironworks as a Workingmens Club in 1876, and the lamp post alongside is one of 12 cast iron posts erected by Dorman Long, 1912.

(Rear): Harry Stokell; George Beadle; Mr Tingay; Prince Tingle; Eva Wilkinson; *(3rd row)*: Doris Horner *nee* Cole; Lil Swales; Alec Stewart; Jack Lund; Nan Trotter; Mrs Beadle; Joe Henderson; Mr Oskins; Bob Scott; Jack Rose; Billy Waites; Jack Glass; Mrs Marshall; George Lowes; Mrs Harper; *(2nd row)*: Harrison (Ice) Wills; Bill Nevison; Billy Wells; Billy Stewart; Mr Pannet; Gran Swales; Mrs Hodgson; unknown; Sally Waites; Mrs Stephenson; Mrs Stibbart; Mrs Plant; Mrs Wyeth; Mrs Waring; Mrs Milton; Mrs Hardy; Kitty Pipe; *(front)*: Ketula Britton; Mrs Lowes; Mrs Goodman; Mrs Bob Bell; Mrs Prest; Mrs Peacock.

Stillington Pensioners' outing c. 1948

Photograph gives a good view of the Cooperative Stores. The store manager, Mr Bill Trotter, is standing on the steps of the entrance to the store. Scurr's bus is waiting to take the pensioners on their outing with the driver, John Whitehead, somewhere in the picture. The slag heap provides the backdrop and it can be seen from this picture how it dominated the north side of the village.

(*Pensioners from rear*): Bill Waites; Mr Collins; Lizzie Fox; Bill Trotter; Prit Hodgson; Isa Parry; Mrs Warner; Mr Snowball; Lizzie Wills; Emily Breckon; Lil Swales; Mary Millan; Mr Thurston; George Lowes; Mrs Glass; Jack Glass; John Whitehead; Nan Trotter; Mrs Taylor; Kitty Pipe; Doris Gudgeon; Polly Poole; Mrs Waring; Mr Pannett; Nellie Daniels; Polly Bell; Mrs Stephenson; Mrs Goodman; Mrs Lonsdale; Mrs Jobling; Mrs Townsend; Mrs Prest; Gran Swales; Mrs Featherstone; *Front Row* Mrs Carr; Mrs Peacock; Sally Waites; Mrs Stockell; Mr Butcher; Mrs Hart; Mrs Lowes; Alice and George Wills.

GROUPS AND EVENTS RELATING TO THE VILLAGE OF STILLINGTON

Lunch during a Women's Institute Outing c. 1948

(*From rear L to R*): Mrs Weighell; unknown; Mrs Dilks; Charlotte Dilks; Gran Swales; Mrs Beadle; Sally Waites; Rene Donaghy; Mrs Marshall; Mrs Gaffney; Flossie Wills; Doris Bell; Mrs Artley; Mrs Freeman; *Front Table*: Bert Swales, driver; Kitty Pipe; Nan Trotter; Mrs Snowball; Mrs Smith; Mrs Townsend; Mrs Littler; Lizzie Butler; Amy Butler; Elsie Horner; Lil Mortimer; Greta Johnson; Mrs Peacock; Mrs Glass; Mrs Wilkinson; Mrs Durham.

Women's Institute outing c. 1949

(*From rear*): Mrs Butler; Mrs Jobling; Nan Trotter; Lil Swales; Mrs Stibbard; 3 unknown; Mrs Harry Stokell; (*2nd row*): Mrs Peekman; Mrs W Young; Mrs Durham; Isa Parry; Mrs Britton; Mrs Prest; Mrs Tingay; Gran Swales; Mrs Smith; Mrs J Glass; (*front*): Mary Tingle; Sally Waites; Reg Thompson, driver; Doris Horner; Elsie Horner; Mrs Pipe; Mrs Townsend.

Women's Institute outing c. 1949

(*From rear*): Mrs Townsend; Gladys Littler; Nan Trotter; Lil Mortimer; Vera Simpson; Mrs Smith; Mrs Whitewell; unknown; Ethel Smithson; Mrs Dilks; Mrs Beadle; (*second row*) Mrs Savage; Lil Swales; Polly Poole; Mrs Carr; Lizzie Fox; Mrs Wood; Lily Jackson; Flossy Wills; unknown; Mrs Gilchrist; Gran Swales; Nan Hethrington; (*front*): Charlotte Dilks; Ada Hardy; unknown; Sally Waites; Mrs Gaffney; Olga Gaffney.

Pensioners' day trip c. 1950

(From rear, known pensioners included l to r): Mr Pannett; George Lowes; Nan Trotter; Bill Trotter; Mr Tingay; Jack Glass; Geo H Wills; Bill Nevison; Mrs Peacock; Mrs Lowes; Joe Henderson; Prince Tingle; Mrs Waring; Mrs Thurston; Mr Thurston; Mrs Hudson; Mrs Britton; Alec Stewart; Albert Hoskins; Neil O'Donnell; Ice Wills; Mr Snowball; Mrs Gaffney; Mrs Gilchrist; Mrs Jack Glass; Mrs Glass; Mrs Stephenson; Mrs Stockell; Jack Lund; Bill Waites; George Beadle; Mrs Peekman; Mrs Goodman; Gran Swales; Mrs Prest; Mrs Hardy; Mrs Hart; Mrs Stibbard; Polly Poole; *(front row)* Kitty Pipe; Charlotte Donaghy; Mrs Artley; Mrs Beadle; Sally Waites; Mrs Collins; Alice Wills; Mrs Harper; Mrs Featherstone; Polly Bell; Bob Bell.

Male pensioners ready for a day out c 1950
(*Rear*): Bob Scott; Jack Rose; Jack Glass; Mr Donaghy; Ernie Arksey; (*front*): Mr O'Donnell; Bill Nevison; Mr Lonsdale, Jos's brother; Mr Arksey; Mr Ash Goodman; Bill Waites. Mrs Swales and Mrs Cole are in Scurr's bus looking out.

The assembly point, Redcar c. 1950
When an organised trip from the village arrived at the seaside an assembly point would be chosen on the beach, and deck chairs and windbreaks would be placed in a circle to identify the position. During the day members of the party would come and go from this point, either to have a swim or walk around the town, but they were assured that their belongings would be safe because there was always someone at the assembly point.

Amy Hopps *nee* Poxon; Mrs Wood; Mrs Harper, Les's mother; Mrs Goodman; Olive Wells, *nee* Goodman; Ivy Laverick, *nee* Gent; Ethel Hopps, *nee* Wills.

Traditional annual event – the Leek Show 1945
Photograph taken outside the Cassidi Hall. Les Simpson; Mr Snowball; George Lowes; Harry Stokell; Jackson Wilson; Norman Trotter; Ali Hodgson; Walter Young; (*front*): Bob Robinson; Kit Trotter; Jim Swales.

Traditional annual event – the Leek Show 1954
Photograph taken outside W.I. Hall. Fred Hodgson (senior); Robert Wilson; Fred Hodgson; Jackson Wilson; Walter Featherstone; Jack Glass; Alf Kendall; Kit Trotter; Harry Stokell; (*front*): Billy Oskins; Lenny Wilks; Cyril Butler; Bert Swales; Les Harper; Peter Swales.

Sunday School trip c. 1946
(*l.to r*): Mrs Barratt; Mrs Sayers; Mrs Storey; Vera Wells; Mrs Harper; Margaret Barratt; (*front*): Elizabeth Barratt; Judy Storey; John Storey.

Sunday excursion to Redcar c. 1956
On summer Sunday afternoons, if the weather was hot and sunny, Lily Jackson would ask her friends and neighbours if they would like a trip to the seaside. If there was sufficient interest, she would locate one of Scurr's drivers and a bus would be immediately arranged to do the trip. No planning or great organisation was necessary – just good weather and sufficient people who fancied a few hours by the sea. (*Rear*): Peter and Pat Swales; Mrs Drury; John Gudgeon; Eddie Drury; (*middle*): Ruth Breckon; Ivy Gent; Lil Jackson; Don Tuffs; Sally Waites; Mary Millan; (*front*): Elizabeth Millan.

Contentment at home c. 1945
Some of the Garrity family and friends relax on their doorstep at No. 5 Railway Cottages. This was a sight familiar throughout the village, especially during the summer months. With everyone in the village knowing each other there was always someone stopping for a few minutes friendly chat, which was a good way of keeping in touch and preventing loneliness. (*Rear*): Ivan Freeman and Martin Garrity; (m*iddle*): Mrs Mary Garrity; son Peter and daughter Mary; (*front*): Richard Hutton, neighbours' child.

Pensioners' outing via Scurr's bus c. 1952. Slag heap in background

Pensioners include (*from rear*): Lil Wills; Rene Donaghy; Kitty Pipe; Stan Johnson, bus driver; Gilbert Poole; Mr Pannett; Vera Simpson; Eva Wilkinson; Maude Wills; Frank Breckor; Mr Tingay; Nan Trotter; Ice Wills; Mr Arksey; Mrs Beadle; Bob Scott; Mr Beadle; Mrs Prest; Harry Stokell; Elsie Horner; Prit Hodgson; Gran Swales; Mr Anderson; Mr Nevison; Joe Henderson; Mrs Stokell; Alec Stewart; Jack Scurr; George Lowes; Mrs Townsend; (*front row*) Mrs Peacock; Mrs Weighell; Sally Waites; Mrs Hudson; Matt Taylor; Mrs Wyeth; Mrs Poole; Mr & Mrs Wells; Mrs Stibbard; Mrs Colbeck; Mrs Hodgson; Mrs Lowes; Mrs Stephenson; Mrs Plant; Lizzie Wills; Mrs Waring; Mrs Artley; Mrs Alice Wills, in wheelchair; Mrs Hardy; Mrs Glass.

Stillington Parish Players 1951–Baa baa Black Sheep

The Parish Players were formed in 1949 and basically the same group performed a couple of plays a year and Nativity plays at Christmas until 1952 when they expanded and started doing Gilbert and Sullivan operas. Reverend Jasper went on to become the Dean of York. Betty Orwin was employed as nurse for the village Doctor. (*Back row*): Vicar's father or in-law; Lofthouse from Sedgfield; Ken Maguire; (*middle*): Kitty Pipe; Wally Billington; Arthur Taylor; Mary Wills; Don Tuffs; George Jobling; George Longbottom; Tommy Tingle; Rev. Jasper; (*front*): Sheila Artley; Monica Artley; Betty Stephenson; Betty Orwin; Judy Storey; Lally Wills.

Stillington Parish Players 1950
Don Tuffs and Ken McGuire in a scene from *Tobias and the Angel*.

Stillington Parish Players 1951
Kitty Pipe; Mrs Storey; Tommy Tingle; George Jobling.

Stillington Parish Players 1954–Trial by Jury
(*Rear*): Ann Masterman; Mary Millan *nee* Wills; Betty Orwin; Betty Lupton *nee* Stephenson; Mrs Billington; Mrs McWilliams; (*front*): Nancy Jobling; Vera Simpson; Lal Wills; Charlotte Dilks *nee* Donaghy; Maisie Hindley (Wells); Olive Wells (Goodman); Jean Anderson.

Stillington Parish Players 1954–Chorus line for a Gilbert and Sullivan opera
Dorothy Simpson; Monica Artley; Nancy Jobling; Greta Johnson; Vera Simpson; Linda Donaghy; Lily Donaghy; Mrs Calvert; Gladys Wells; Maisie Wells; Jenny Anderson; Mrs Sammy; Mrs McWilliams; Betty Stephenson; Olive Goodman; Judy Storey.

GROUPS AND EVENTS RELATING TO THE VILLAGE OF STILLINGTON

Stillington Parish Players 1954—Some of the cast of Trial by Jury

(*Rear*): Mr Anderson; Bob Tingle: Arnold Wells; Cliff Wells; Wilf Wells; John Hodgson; Jack Blackett; John Storey; Mr Calvert; (*3rd row*): Jeffrey Lupton; Mrs Calvert; Judy Storey; Wally Billington; Maisie Wells; Rev A Smith; Mrs Sammy; Mrs Billington; Betty Lupton; Gordon Calvert; (*2nd row*): Aggie Britton; Greta Johnson; Gladys Farley; Vera Simpson; Mary Millan; Liz Barrett; (*front*): Olive Wells; Monica Artley; Dorothy Simpson; Valerie Britton; Audrey Wells.

Typical scenes as pensioners assemble for their annual trip. Villagers came to the departure point in Morrison Terrace to wave them off and wish them well for a good day. Two of Scurr's buses were hired for this trip, which would have been around 1950.

Group of Stillington housewives c. 1948
(*Rear*): Doris Smithson; Vera Simpson; Mrs Masterman; Jean Dilks; (*front*): Prim Hopps; Mrs Sammy; Mrs F Bell; Doreen Swales; Lal Wills.

Day at the seaside c. 1950
(*Rear*): Queenie Peakman; Doreen Swales; (*middle*): Ali Peakman; Bob Kirtley; Hetty Kirtley; Jim Swales; Lil Swales; (*front*): Gillian and Geoff Peakman; Peter and Pat Swales.

The girls enjoy a paddle in the sea
Vera Simpson; Dorothy Simpson; Isa Parry; Lal Wills; Doris Gudgeon *nee* Wills; Mary Millan *nee* Wills; Doreen Swales; Lil Swales; Mrs Stevens.

Teddy Britton; Jim Swales; Karl Millward; Bert Swales; Philip Egerton; Len Jackson; Maude Charlson; Peter Swales.

Villagers' weekend at Blackpool c. 1954

(*Rear*): Stan Butler; Martin Garrity; Len Jackson; John Lockey; George Dilks; Len Oliver; Wally Allan; Whitfield; Maurice Butler; Ely Hardy; Sandy Pounder; Dave Percival; (*middle*) Mr Savage; Mrs Savage; Rose Stevens; Doreen Swales; Rene Donaghy; Jenny Tinkler; Lily Jackson; Jim Swales; (*front*): Emily Oliver; Sally Waites; Lucy Drury.

Blackpool Trips–Late 1940s and early 1950s

These trips were generally organised by Wally Allen whose sister had a boarding house in Blackpool where the villagers used to stay for their weekend trip.

included–Peter Lavelle, Wally's sister, Lol Carlton, John Whitehead, Ted Smithson, Ely Hardy, Martin Garrity, Rob Carlton, Karl Millward, Les Smith, Phil Egerton, John Hodgson, (*second row*) Geo Dilks, Dennis Littler, John Bremner, Mick Gaffney, Len Jackson, Geo Longbottom, Peter Swales, Ted & Barry Drury, (*third row*) Brian Wills, John Featherstone, Frank Hodgson, (*sitting*) Wally Allan, Lily Jackson, Polly Poole, Hilda Walker, Prit Hodgson, Sally Waites, Mary Millan, Jean Smith, Rene & Charlotte Donaghy, (*front*) Mr Walker and Billy Drury.

included–Brian Wills, Mr Walker, George Dilks, Wilf Wilkinson, Tommy Hardy, George Longbottom, Phil Egerton, Lenny Warner, Dennis Littler, Ted Drury, Barry Hodgson, Dave Kennedy, Neil Parker, Len Jackson, Lil Jackson, Jack Lockey, Judy Storey, Dora Farley, Lena Lonsdale, Mabel Moore, Mrs Drury, Wally Allan & sister, (*sitting*) Sally Waites, Charlotte Donaghy, Maude Wills, Hilda Walker, Bena Hodgson and Rene Donaghy.

WEEKEND TRIP TO BLACKPOOL

The lads having a drink before going to the dance
Lenny Warner, George Jobling, Phil Egerton, Alan Farley, Donald Harding, John Lockey

Ladies having their morning walk along the pier
Milly Atkinson; Charlotte Dilks, *nee Donaghy*; Rene Donaghy, n*ee Plant*; Emily Oliver, *nee Breckton*; Lilian Hopps, *nee Marshall.*

Stillington Workingmen's Club 1947
Alec Swales; Reg Milton; Pat Carroll; George Dilks; Tom Lonsdale; Stewart Donaghy; Bobby Bell;
Ted Drury; Harry Harper;
(*kneeling*) Ces Challis; Ronnie Farley; Cyril Butler; Lenny Johnson; Kenny Johnstone
Winners of the Stockton and District League

Stillington Workingmen's Club 1951
Don Tuffs; Mick Gaffney; Trevor McMann; Tommy Clayton; Bob Errington; George Dilks
Bill Cowley; Tommy Henderson; Tom Swales; Ernie Dilks; Alan Farley; Teddy Crowe
Winners of the Stockton and District League (Div. B)

CORONATION OF ELIZABETH II–JUNE 1953

View of Morrison Terrace and Lowson Street from the little tip, all is quiet awaiting the Coronation celebrations later in the day.

Crowds starting to gather for the crowning of the Coronation Queen.

Coronation Street Party 1953
A group of Stillington ladies celebrating the 'Coronation' in Whitton Grove. The coronation mugs which were given to the children as a memento of the occasion are in the box on the table.

Ada Savaage; Mrs Tommy Glass; Mrs Reg Moore; Mary Millan; Dolly Bean; Joyce Jaques; Mrs Bean; Edith Sharp; Dot Bean; Mary Tingle; Hilda O'Donnell; Elsie Bean; Aileen Argyle, *nee Garrity*; Joan Johnson, *nee Farley*; Alice Cell.

The Cornonation Queen is crowned on the steps of Parry's shop in Morrison Terrace. A big crowd in attendance despite the poor weather.

Doris Wells, centre, Stillington and Whitton Coronation Festivity Queen
Maids of Honour are Jane Wells (*left*) and Joan Simpson These girls were chosen from 26 entrants at one of the Festival Dances, Coronation of Elizabeth II, 1953,

Festival Queen and Maids of Honour–1953
As part of the 'Coronation' celebrations, a Festival Queen and two Maids of Honour were chosen. They are pictured in attendance at the sports day which was one of the many functions organised for the occassion. The weather was obviously unkind as most people are pictured wearing raincoats and hats. Jim Swales is prominent in the background.
centre
Festival Queen, Doris Wells; Maids of Honour, Joan Simpson (*left*) and Jane Wells

Retirement presentation c. 1950
A group of Stillite employees attending the retirement of Mrs Greener, a long time secretary at the works. A few village people are in attendance. Those pictured include Albert Hardy; Jim Swales; Wally Billington; Alf Hogg; Walter Fowler; Blanche Smithson; Jane Wells; Dot Featherstone; Eva Mortimer; Miss Greener; Mr B Robinson; Mr Sidebottom; Albert Gilbert; Margaret Hodgson; Mrs Greener; Margaret Barrett.

Helpers at the wedding of Mary Hodgson–1956
At the request of the bride's mother, neighbours and friends would help in the preparation and serving at the reception. This group of helpers are photographed in the kitchen of the Womens Institute Hall. Elsie Horner, *nee Cole*; Doris Horner, *nee Cole*; Lil Swales; Alf Hogg, *m. Hilda Hodgson*; Della Trotter, nee Kennedy; Mrs Tissy Johnstone; Audrey Wells; Olive Wells, *nee Goodman*; Mrs Gilbert.

Miss Blair's Retirement–1958

Miss Elizabeth Blair had been the headmistress at the Infant School for 30 years. These photographs show scenes from her retirement presentation which took place in the school yard with the slag heap as the backdrop. Names of adults present are shown.

Mrs Drury; Mrs Bean; Ruth Pearson, Mrs Farley; Mrs Lonsdfale; Joyce Farley, *nee Lonsdale*

Ada Savage; Miss Blair; Eva Pernie; Mrs Swales; Mrs Wyeth; Doreen Cook

Mrs Sheila Sayers makes a speech before Miss Blair receives her retirement presents from the children

Miss Blair receives her presents from the children

Miss Blair saying farewell to the children
Eva Pernie; Mrs Swales; Mrs Savage; Mrs Wyeth; Mrs Argyle; Mrs Doublet; Loui Smithson; Lal Wills; Joan Drury; Connie Lennon; Violet Savage.

British Refrasil Work's visit c. 1956
Work's visits were a regular feature of the early days of British Refrasil. This visit to an airfield would have been arranged so that interested workers could see the application of some of their products, within the aircraft. *Those shown include:* Wally Thompson; George Warner; Bert Swales; Air Force guide; Roy Rogers; Lol Thomas; Bob Norman; Bill McGregor; Ainsley Clarke; Tommy Garrity; Bert Sammy; Harry Robinson; Colin Chapman; Roy Arnold; Jimmy Chisholm.

British Refrasil Social Club Dance

A few of the ladies enjoying the annual Social Club dance: Maude Wills; Mrs Garrity; Doreen Swales; Maureen Haylett; Emma Collins. In the background on the right, are Billy Oskins, (*sitting*) and John Lythe (*leaning over*).

The Stillington Adventurers Drama Club

A scene from Have You Anything To Declare which was presented in the Stockton Youth Drama Festival at Norton. Among those pictured are: Dennis Littler; Maureen Fox; Bobby Hardy; Dorothy Simpson; Ann Masterman; Charlie Parker; Betty Charlton; Dennis Bean; Brian Wills; (*sitting*) Marjorie Johnson; Cliff Artley; Brenda Smithson and Bessie Bell.

Visit of Queen Elizabeth II and the Duke of Edinburgh to Teeside in 1956

The picture shows children of the Stillington schools waiting along the route to be taken by the Queen. They are accompanied by Lynda Bell; Miss Blair; Sheila Sayers and Doreen Cook.

Stillington School Fancy Dress Competition c. 1956

The Original Dominoes c. 1959

The Dominoes were a group, formed by Brian Wills and John Snowball. The group are pictured playing at a dance in the Queen Hotel, Stockton. The group later reorganised, with only Brian and John surviving to become one of the best groups in the north of England.

Don Tuffs, *base guitar*; Brian Wills, *lead guitar*; Colin Chapman, *piano;* John Snowball, *drums;* Derek Waggett, *rythm guitar.*

Don, Brian and John lived in Stillington, Colin came from Middlesborough and Peter came from Sedgefield.

The Dominoes
Lol Storey; Gloria Knowles;
Denis Houghton; Peter Renolds; Ken Potts; Brian Wills
John Snowball (*drums*) Tony Storey (*lead guitar*), and Bill Johnson (*bass*) have just been replaced by the final grouping shown above.

Village Outing c. 1960

Those shown include: Arnie Scott; Edwin Hopps; Bell jnr; Frank Breckton; George Dilks; Dick Berry; (*second row*) Bill Tinkler; Bob Glass; Jack Rose; Jack Cottey; Kath Gaffney; Len Oliver; Jim & Alice Bell; Edna Glass; Mrs Bob Glass; Mr Hardy; Bill Gilchrist; Charlotte Donaghy; Margaret Scott; (*front*) Emily Oliver; Mrs Rose; Mrs Cotty; Ruth Breckton; Lily Hopps; Mrs Gaffney and Emma Gilchrist.

Visit from the MP for Belper, George Brown, May 22 1965

The deputy Prime Minister to Harold Wilson, Mr George Brown MP, visited Darchem Engineering to undertake a tour of the works and open a new section. He arrived by helicopter which landed on the cricket field. The photograph shows him about to leave surrounded by villagers who include: Marjorie Dunning; Myra Ferguson; Mary Millan; Linda Bell; Maude Wills; Flossie Wills; Vera Simpson; Pam Whitewell; Ada Hardy, Mum Wilks, Jean Wilks; Joyce Jacques and Jenny Tinker.